GENESIS UNVEILED
THE LOST WISDOM OF OUR
FORGOTTEN ANCESTORS

The Author

IAN LAWTON was born in 1959. Formerly an IT consultant and chartered accountant, he turned his back on the commercial world in his mid-thirties to become a full-time writer-researcher on ancient civilizations. His first book, *Giza: The Truth* (Virgin Books, 1999) co-authored with Chris Ogilvie-Herald, sold over 20,000 copies and gained widespread acclaim. He has a growing reputation for thorough scholarship and an innovative approach to revisionist history, and has lectured about his work extensively in both the UK and US. He currently lives on the South Coast of Britain.

GENESIS UNVEILED

THE LOST WISDOM OF OUR FORGOTTEN ANCESTORS

Ian Lawton

To the perceptive eye the depth of their degeneration was clear enough, but to those whose judgment of true happiness is defective they seemed, in their pursuit of unbridled ambition and power, to be at the height of their fame and fortune.

From Plato's *Critias*, on the fall of the divine Atlanteans

CONTENTS

LIST OF PLATES

LIST OF FIGURES

ACKNOWLEDGMENTS

This book has not been the easiest to write, mainly because of the huge range of topics I have had to cover to ensure everything is placed in its proper context. The assistance of a number of friends and colleagues, each with his or her own particular specialist skills, has therefore significantly improved its quality.

Marcus Williamson, whose ability to proofread an enormous amount of material in no time at all is quite astounding, made a huge contribution, in particular by pinpointing arguments that required further clarification. Robin Crookshank Hilton acted as an invaluable sounding board for my ideas in the earliest planning phases. Greg Taylor, the founder of the excellent Daily Grail website, has not only repeatedly drawn attention to my work but also provided further vital feedback on the manuscript. And my former coauthor Chris Ogilvie-Herald never tired of forwarding snippets of important breaking news that I was often too busy to keep pace with.

I also received vital assistance in specialist areas where my orthodox knowledge was relatively weak. Michael Brass expended considerable time and effort reviewing the evolution and archaeology chapters. Colin Reader did likewise with the geology chapter, while Paul Heinrich's input to the latter was also significant. Crichton Miller's discovery of the true purpose of the Celtic cross as a prehistoric navigational instrument, and suggestions concerning the maritime survivors of a worldwide catastrophe around 11,500 years ago, acted as a major addition to my own ideas. The whole esoteric field was another in which I had to cover a lot of ground in a short time, and the assistance of Clive Prince, Lynn Picknett, Adrian Gilbert, David Elkington, Michael Carmichael, Nigel Skinner-Simpson and Nigel Foster made the task considerably easier. And my discussions with Andrew Collins concerning the Watchers in particular were stimulating, as were my more general discussions of this work with Nigel Blair, Edmund Marriage, Simon Cox and Mark Foster.

I extend my heartfelt thanks to all of the above, many of whom are also close friends. I would also like to thank Garret Fagan for acting as a vital buttress of orthodox scholarship for me to test myself against in certain areas; Flavio Barbiero for taking the time and trouble to provide me with translations of certain Italian manuscripts; all the people and organisations who allowed me to reproduce their photographs, especially Danielle Stordeur for forwarding the excellent material on Jerf el-Ahmar; and all the staff at the British Library, whose efficiency and helpfulness are second to none. Thanks also to Souvenir Press for their kind permission to quote from Joseph Campbell's *The Masks of God*.

On the publishing front my former UK and US agents, Simon Trewin and Elizabeth Joyce, both worked tirelessly to bring this work to the attention of publishers, unfortunately without success. But after several years of intense frustration the publishers of my previous work, Virgin, recognised its value, for which I am eternally grateful. In particular my editor, Kerri Sharp, has been a tower of strength and support in finally getting it to press, while copy editor Ian Allen and cover designer Mark Swan both played vital roles.

There are several personal friends without whose help this work would probably not have seen the light of day for several years yet. Nick Woolven bailed me out of extreme financial problems on a number of occasions, while Stewart Barnard and Andrea Shaw did likewise and were also extremely lenient with the bar tab at the Olde Whyte Harte pub in Hamble – and for me, to get out of the house and have a beer or two and a chat late in the evening after a whole day chained to my writing desk is not just a luxury but a survival necessity! To all of them I give my sincere thanks for their friendship and patience.

Finally, one person in particular made sure I stuck with this not-inconsiderable task – especially during the drafting of the first manuscript in 2001, and in the dark days that followed while I attempted to find a publisher – and that is my former partner Debbie Thornton. Although we are no longer together, her tireless and unselfish support and love allowed me to focus on the job at hand without distractions. I am eternally grateful to her, and to her son Dameion, for their patience. And last, but by no means least, I must thank Willy our cat; although he is now no longer with us, his tenacity in trying to get some attention by walking up and down on my keyboard produced some of the finest writing in this book.

Ian Lawton
Hamble, England
April 2003

Anyone wanting to keep up with the latest news on the contents of this or any of my other books, or to make contact to provide further information or ask questions, should visit my GENESIS website at <www.ianlawton.com>.

AUTHOR'S NOTE

On a number of occasions in this work I take issue with the theories of fellow revisionist authors and researchers. I do not do this to belittle their work, or to aggrandise my own. Nor do I do it to strengthen my own arguments, which do not require such bolstering and stand on their own merits. I would hope that in all cases it is clear my criticisms are of well-established theories that either overlap with, or are diametrically opposed to, my own – and as a result it is important that I document my areas of disagreement. Given that in the past there has been an almost complete failure of leading members of the revisionist camp to be prepared to criticise each other's work constructively, it may take a little time for people to become accustomed to and accept such an approach. However, in my view it is essential to the advancement of the revisionist movement's general cause – which must surely be to move together towards a better understanding of the enigmas of our past, and to share this research in an honest and responsible way with the general public.

Wherever possible I use the most up-to-date and readily available English translations of ancient texts as prepared by orthodox scholars. None of the quoted translations is my own interpretation. Biblical references are taken from the Authorised King James Bible unless otherwise stated.

The textual extracts I present are often quite lengthy. It is my view, however, that information is often lost or misrepresented when such passages are paraphrased, and that it is time the ordinary reader was given a more accurate view of the style and content of these texts without necessarily having to trace the original.

Where extracts from other works have been quoted, any comments inserted for clarification have been placed in square brackets. Similarly, italics in these quotes are used for my own emphasis unless otherwise stated.

References to the work of other authors in the endnotes are abbreviated, with full details provided in the bibliography.

Internet information and addresses are correct at the time of writing; I cannot accept any responsibility for changes or updates made thereafter.

DEFINITION OF CULTURE

Because the word *culture* can be used in many different contexts, and my specific meaning in particular instances is of vital importance to the arguments I will be developing, I should provide some outline definitions. I propose that we split cultural development into four stages:

- Stage 1, which I will call *primitive culture*, includes language, co-operation and a degree of ritualistic behaviour, and is typified by early hunter-gatherer and planter cultures.
- Stage 2, *culture proper,* includes artistic expression in carvings and paintings, sometimes of high complexity, as well as in music, and is typified by the Cro-Magnon culture of southern Europe.
- Stage 3, *advanced culture,* includes the development of permanent settlements with buildings constructed, if not from stone, then at least from wood or mud-brick; ocean navigation; and scientific skills in astronomy, mathematics and medicine. It is typified by the city-states of ancient Mesopotamia – although I do not *necessarily* include writing in this stage.
- Stage 4, *technologically advanced culture,* includes the use of sources of power for lighting and heating, and of powered vehicles for terrestrial, aerial and even space travel, as typified by our modern society.

I will also refer to *spiritually advanced cultures* that may be identified with any of these other stages, but in particular with Stage 3 in the context of our 'forgotten race'.

INTRODUCTION

In the predominantly Christianised Western world, we are all familiar with the book of Genesis from the Old Testament: how God created the world in six days, and rested on the seventh; how he created the first man, Adam, and then his companion Eve; how Adam's descendants acted as patriarchs, overseeing human affairs up to the time of the great flood, which God sent to destroy humankind; and how Noah was spared in the ark and went on to father the new human race.

Over the last 150 years, spurred on by Darwin and the breakthroughs of scientists in all fields who have followed in his footsteps, we have increasingly been told to reject all of this as myth, a simple story constructed to bolster a religious outlook in simple people. Any Christian fundamentalist who still insists the world was created in 4004 BC receives, quite rightly, extremely short shrift. Nevertheless, in recent years the fact that a catastrophe tradition persists on a global scale, and is backed up by considerable geological evidence, has received widespread publicity and acceptance.[1] And it is now more or less accepted that many of the postflood biblical traditions are based more on fact than fiction.

However, for many years I have been fascinated by the possibility that the sparse and enigmatic record of a *preflood* civilisation in the early chapters of Genesis might also contain some elements of truth. My first surprise came when I investigated the older Mesopotamian texts on which many of the biblical traditions were based. A number of intriguing themes emerged, including some detailed accounts not only of the flood but also of life *before* it. Although my close examination of these original source texts led me to reject certain authors' interpretations that human-kind was genetically created by visitors from another planet, I nevertheless felt there was something in this mass of material that deserved further investigation; that it was wrong to write off the whole lot as superstitious fiction. Ultimately I decided to unearth as many of the ancient texts and native traditions from around the world as I could, to find out what the rest of our ancestors had to say about the prehistory of humankind on earth.

It soon became clear that the people who compiled these texts and traditions were anything but intellectual dwarfs trying to concoct a simplistic philosophical framework with which to make sense of the world around them, as some would have us believe. It became equally clear, however, that those who attempt to take everything within them as literal truth are also misguided. One of the most respected scholars of mythology, Joseph Campbell, reflects this view in his four-volume masterwork *The Masks of God*, published between 1959 and 1968:

> It must be conceded, as a basic principle of our natural history of the gods and heroes, that whenever a myth has been taken literally its sense has been perverted; but also, reciprocally, that whenever it has been dismissed as a mere priestly fraud or sign of inferior intelligence, truth has slipped out the other door.[2]

To a degree Campbell developed the work of his equally eminent predecessor Carl Gustav Jung, who prefaced the English version of his *Psychology and Alchemy*, first published in 1953, with the following overview:

> Some thirty-five years ago I noticed to my amazement that European and American men and women coming to me for psychological advice were producing in their dreams and fantasies symbols similar to, and often identical with, the symbols found in the mystery religions of antiquity, in mythology, folklore, fairytales, and the apparently meaningless formulations of such esoteric cults as alchemy . . . From long and careful comparison and analysis of these products of the unconscious I was led to postulate a 'collective unconscious', a source of energy and insight in the depth of the human psyche which has operated in and through man from the earliest periods of which we have records.[3]

In my view there is little doubt that Jung's symbols, or archetypes, are the key to unlocking the hidden or esoteric meaning of much of the body of myth from around the world that our ancestors have left as their legacy. This is one of the main reasons why the most sacred texts and traditions of all ancient cultures can appear so enigmatic and obscure to the uninitiated: because to a large extent the archetypes, whether in picture or textual form, are not designed to speak to the logical left brain, but rather to the intuitive right brain that is the link to both the personal and the collective unconscious. Nowhere is this more clearly demonstrated than in the written texts of the ancient Egyptians that were recorded using hieroglyphs, pictographic symbols that often had multiple and subtly different meanings appreciated only by those fully initiated into their mystery. These were often accompanied by symbolic drawings of their gods, usually represented as part-animal, part-human beings, who in turn represented various *neters* or divine principles that could vary according to the context.[4]

It is also true that the most important texts and traditions of our ancient cultures tended to be handed down orally, even after they had been recorded in writing. This is why we often find important philosophical concepts embedded into a story format: so they could be more easily memorised and, indeed, would be entertaining to relate. This allowed them to survive over centuries or millennia, even if the real understanding of their symbolic message was lost on most of the audience. In addition, of course, couching such traditions in symbolism and archetype was particularly useful when, as has happened throughout history, esoteric sects were trying to maintain them under threat of heresy charges from the dominant religious orthodoxy.

We must also recognise that many of the messages found in the ancient texts and traditions are explainable in political and sociological terms – for example, acting to reinforce the rule of the prevailing political and religious hierarchy. Moreover, many of the versions that have survived have clearly been edited with similar motives in mind, making it much harder to see through the fog and establish the nature of the original message, if any indeed existed.

The foregoing analysis is fine as a general summary of the modern approach to mythology. But are there any grey areas where it would be right to debate whether at least a part of a particular text or tradition is more than just symbolism and myth? Might it have some basis in fact that, albeit perhaps in only the broadest of senses, can act as a pointer to real historical events? My research has led me to believe these grey areas do exist, particularly with respect to the passages I encountered repeatedly that appear to describe a veiled history of humankind – one only hinted at in Genesis. Above all, various ancient cultures right across the globe preserve a tradition of a forgotten antediluvian race that was originally highly spiritual but degenerated until it was wiped out by a major catastrophe. These traditions are far more widespread than is normally recognised – and most revisionist authors have, in my view, failed to appreciate the essentially spiritual message they contain. Meanwhile, orthodox scholars' attempts to explain them away as mere psychological, sociological, political or religious constructs strike me in this case as unconvincing.

Of course, I appreciate that the orthodoxy is conditioned by the prevailing archaeological, and to some extent philosophical, paradigm. I would argue, however, that these paradigms are increasingly proving to be unduly restrictive, and that we should reappraise these traditions to see if we can unveil the history of our forgotten race from the many common and consistent elements, while still operating within the basic principle of appreciating the role played by symbolism and archetypes.

Meanwhile, I do not intend for this work to rely solely on my reinterpretation of ancient texts and traditions. In support, firstly I propose to turn to archaeology and use the mounting body of artefactual and cultural evidence – only a small part of which is still regarded by the orthodoxy as 'anomalous' – that increasingly suggests modern humans have been around in highly cultured form, although not necessarily with the levels of advanced technology proposed by some commentators, for somewhat longer than has hitherto been accepted. As to what I mean by 'somewhat longer', as we will see I have good reason to suggest this is only of the order of tens of thousands of years, rather than millions. Thus, unlike some other commentators, I do not believe we have to fundamentally question the theory of evolution – although as we will see we might find that a slight philosophical tweak to that theory is appropriate. Secondly, I will bring in the geological evidence that in the relatively recent past the earth was rocked by a major catastrophe that *would* have wiped out virtually all traces of advanced culture other than those few that, arguably, still remain.

With these and other additions from the realms of science and philosophy, the various pieces of the puzzle start to fit together. It is my contention that our ancestors all over the world have left us textual clues about our hidden past stretching into antediluvian antiquity, if only we look for them in the right places.

I would not wish to conceal the fact that some of the material in this book has been presented before. Ever since the Western scientific orthodoxy wrested power from the church a few centuries ago, a succession of mavericks has stepped into the breach to ensure those who believe the rationalism of science does not have *all* the answers have plenty of material with which to back up their view. This long tradition of questioning is undoubtedly a healthy one – even if some of the revisionist views put forward have been little short of criminal in their lack of attention to scholarship. The number of researchers and writers involved in this revisionist quest has proliferated dramatically in recent decades, and a great many of them have touched on subjects included in this work. It would be invidious to select just a few for special mention, while to list them all would take a book in itself. Suffice to say, although I have significant areas of disagreement with many of them, it is their groundwork, and that of their predecessors, which has inspired new researchers like me to take up the challenge.

So what am I bringing to the debate that has not already been covered? I believe my approach is fundamentally different from that of most of my colleagues and predecessors. For a start, many of them have, either explicitly or implicitly, shown a serious lack of respect for the specialists in a number of orthodox disciplines – which I think belittles their arguments. Although there are exceptions in any walk of life, by and large these scholars have not achieved what they have by being narrow-minded imbeciles. There must be a new 'middle way' that questions aspects of the orthodoxy that deserve re-evaluation without blatant disrespect – and one that does not gloss over or remain ignorant of orthodox arguments, but instead faces them head on.

In particular, when postulating a 'forgotten', 'lost', or 'hidden' former race of humans on earth, many revisionist authors have demonstrated a disturbing lack of understanding of orthodox arguments in three main areas. The first is human evolution, where certain of them provide supposed evidence of great antiquity for modern man without placing it in any philosophically or scientifically logical context, while others propose that extraterrestrial intervention is the only answer to supposed enigmas they have perhaps not fully investigated. The second is the roles of context and symbolism in myth, where certain of them make unduly literal translations of specific texts with no regard for the context of similar themes in other cultures. The third is the dating of monuments from our earliest civilisations in the postdiluvian – or in my terms 'modern' – epoch, where certain of them appear to disregard the significant body of contextual evidence archaeologists have painstakingly amassed; and nowhere more so than in their attempts to ascribe a far earlier date to the Giza Pyramids and Sphinx, a subject covered in detail in my previous book *Giza: The Truth*, coauthored with Chris Ogilvie-Herald.

On the other hand, some revisionist historians take a different tack and, even if they accept the orthodox view of human evolution and of the dating of ancient monuments, suggest the level of technology displayed by these early civilisations could not possibly have 'developed overnight', some even arguing that highly advanced technology must have been handed down by survivors from the legendary Atlantis or even introduced by extraterrestrials. However, in my view they fail to properly appreciate just how much can be achieved by a civilisation with superb organisation and focus, but not necessarily high levels of technology in the modern sense of the word. Moreover, if we look at how far modern Western civilisation has developed in only a handful of centuries, this argument just does not ring true, because there *is* a development period in the archaeological record of these ancient civilisations that they tend to ignore.

My approach here is fundamentally different because, rather than using the argument that the supposedly advanced technology of our earliest civilisations in the modern epoch *implies* that previous civilisations must have existed, I would argue there is prima facie textual and to some extent archaeological evidence of humankind's extensive cultural prehistory – although in my view it does *not* suggest these earlier cultures were technologically advanced in the modern sense of the word. They might have constructed settlements of considerable size, but not necessarily with huge structures or advanced techniques, or even durable materials. They might have developed a high state of civilisation, but one based primarily on group co-operation, and on knowledge development and education. And, what is more, they might have continued like this for millennia before becoming slaves to the great god of material progress.

Above all, instead of extrapolating the *technical* knowledge of our postdiluvian ancestors back to their antediluvian forebears, I believe we should concentrate on extrapolating their *spiritual* knowledge back. Although many other commentators have touched on the esoteric wisdom displayed by our earliest civilisations in the modern epoch, for the most part they have not been able to put this into any overall philosophical context; even more importantly, they seem to have overlooked the fact that this more than anything else may be the key to unveiling the hidden messages of the ancient texts and traditions regarding our forgotten antediluvian race. It is their original *spiritual* advancement in a 'golden age', their subsequent debasement through concentration on the material world and forgetting their spiritual roots, and their consequent destruction, that shines through loud and clear.

Moreover, once the texts are properly decoded by the removal of distortions, they tell us that the original spiritual worldview of the golden age was totally consistent with that maintained by the most enlightened Eastern and Western esoteric sects of the modern epoch. In my view the reason for this consistency is that there exists a universal spiritual wisdom that transcends all barriers of space and time. Not only that, but the valiant and ongoing attempts by modern theoretical physicists and cosmologists to uncover the true nature of the physical, and indeed not-so-physical, universe are increasingly confirming the universal truths that various of our pre- and postdiluvian forebears took for granted – even if from a somewhat less technological perspective. A proper appreciation of the legacy left by them, and a reappraisal of their entire worldview, is long overdue.

Finally, despite the fact that fundamentally I am an evolutionist, I do believe that at a certain point in humankind's history there was a sudden impetus to its evolution that cannot, or at least should not, be analysed in purely scientific terms. For a proper evaluation, as we will see, we will have to turn to the realms of philosophy, and listen to what the ancient texts have to tell us about the onset of the golden age. Then, perhaps for the first time, we will be able to develop a framework in which a spiritual worldview forms a logical corollary to a scientific, evolutionary approach, rather than remaining essentially irreconcilable and illogical. And this is perhaps where a revisionist author such as myself can really contribute something, by insisting we look at the big picture and not be afraid to cross disciplines in our search for an all-encompassing paradigm that merges science, history and philosophy into a coherent whole.

In Part 1 I will examine the orthodox approach to supposed mythology, and the evidence to support a spiritual worldview, before exploring what the ancient texts and traditions have to say about, in turn, the debasement and destruction of our forgotten race, the introduction of civilisation by various sages, the golden age, potential multiple world ages, and the creation of humankind. In Part 2 I will turn to the potential corroborative evidence from archaeology and geology; I will also reappraise the work of certain celebrated modern-day 'seers', along with the body of material on Atlantis, other lost continents, and supposed advanced technology, to establish how well it stands up to scrutiny and whether or not any of it provides useful support for my arguments. Finally, in Part 3 I will return to the ancient texts and traditions and their descriptions of the origins and nature of the universe, evaluating the extent to which the universal truths they reveal are consistent not only with the worldview of the most enlightened Eastern and Western esoteric sects, but also with that emerging from modern theoretical physics.

One final preliminary comment is essential. By its very nature this work is far more speculative than my previous endeavours. Although I cannot prove that my reinterpretation of the antediluvian aspects of the texts and traditions is correct, I can guarantee it has been researched and compiled with as much regard to scholarship and integrity as I can personally muster. Moreover, it is my strong belief that the conclusions I draw just may take us closer to the truth of these traditions than we have ever been before.

As a result, I believe our hidden history, and the wisdom of the ancient universal truths, have profound implications for our understanding of our place in the world, and of our future as well as our past. Above all, they warn us of the dangers of repeating past mistakes by forsaking our spiritual roots and allowing material preoccupations to predominate. Placed in this context, they can act as a wake-up call for us all.

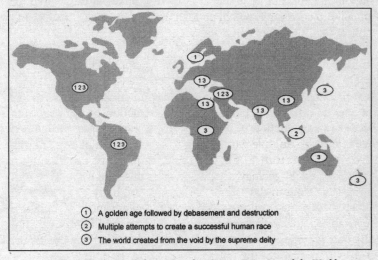

① A golden age followed by debasement and destruction
② Multiple attempts to create a successful human race
③ The world created from the void by the supreme deity

Figure 1: The Common Themes Found in Ancient Texts Around the World

PART ONE
REVELATIONS

1. MYTHS IN THE MAKING

We face a formidable task in attempting to identify genuine historical pointers in the body of ancient texts and traditions from around the world that are broadly categorised as 'mythical' by the established orthodoxy. Across the whole spectrum of mythical analysis, from the learned opinions of specialist scholars to those of the more crackpot revisionist theorists, if we read between the lines we come to realise that *everyone* is heavily influenced by their own largely subjective judgments regarding what is possible as history and what is not.

As I indicated in my introduction, I am convinced there *are* some aspects of the ancient texts and traditions – particularly those dealing with the time before the catastrophe they all report – that are not only worthy of reappraisal in terms of possible historicity, but are also of the utmost importance. I feel justified in proposing this reappraisal precisely because I do not agree with what I regard as the unduly restrictive paradigm under which the orthodox consensus has been developed, which has been conditioned by everything from the archaeological to the scientific, religious and philosophical perspectives of its main developers and proponents.

Many revisionist authors have uttered similar sentiments before. However, unfortunately many of them have also proved to have a somewhat inadequate understanding of the body of orthodox interpretation they seek to overthrow. I hope to ensure that my own work does not incorporate this deficiency, and accordingly I will attempt to lay out the foundation of the orthodox position before I put forward my alternatives. I want to present both sides in order that intelligent people can make up their own minds as to the validity, or otherwise, of my propositions.

I shall begin by considering the backbone of the consensus attitude toward mythology that now prevails.

A BRIEF HISTORY OF MYTHOLOGY

A variety of definitions of *myth* have been attempted, and they have varying degrees of usefulness. In most cases they attempt to make distinctions between historical or canonical records on the one hand, and myths, legends, and folklore on the other. Of course, most historical attempts to differentiate between history and myth in this broad sense have been conditioned by the prevailing religion of each culture. Consequently, and as a broad generalisation, the Christian West has tended to regard the Bible as canonical history and all other ancient texts as, almost by definition, myth. This doctrinaire attitude has been progressively relaxed in recent times, but we are all only too well aware how destructive the force of conflicting dogmas can be, even in the twenty-first century.

Meanwhile, myths in their own right are normally held to deal with important philosophical concepts such as the origins of the world and of humankind, and to involve gods or supernatural beings. Legends, by contrast, tend to involve human heroes, usually on great quests of one sort or another, while folk tales are pretty much dismissed as localised superstitions of minimal significance. Even these broad categorisations suffer from myriad weaknesses – for example, many legends contain important motifs also found in myths, so to exclude them from this study where relevant would be a nonsense. In any case, I tend to prefer the terms *texts* and *traditions*: they do not have the pejorative connotations of terms such as *myths* and *legends*.

Leaving any spurious attempts at categorisation behind, and accepting a broad definition of the term, let us look at the history of what has been referred to as the 'science of myth'.[1] A number of important contributions are worth noting, starting in 1856 with that of the man regarded as the founder of the discipline of comparative mythology, Max Müller, who proposed in his *Essays on Comparative Mythology* that all myth was an attempt to explain natural phenomena. This was closely followed by the work of Daniel G Brinton, who brought in the burgeoning study of the New World as well as the Old; of Adolf Bastion, who attempted to introduce psychological factors into the study of 'constants' in mythology; and of Edward Burnett Tylor, who used similar methods to analyse animistic motifs. In the late nineteenth century Bronislaw Malinowski kept the psychological theme to the fore in his study of various surviving native cultures, while in 1890 Sir James George Frazer published the first two volumes of what would eventually become his twelve-volume *The Golden Bough*, a landmark work that introduced the importance of the cyclical nature of life as an underlying mythical motif.

In 1889 Leo Frobenius presented a counterargument to the psychological school, positing that a primitive cultural continuum once existed around the equator, with the similarities in myth resulting more from transoceanic diffusion than from parallel development. However, while his theories have not been entirely discarded, and indeed should be regarded as an important adjunct to psychological analyses, the focus in the twentieth century remained on the latter. This began with Freud and his emphasis on sexual and relational tensions in the make-up of myth, and continued with his collaborator-turned-opponent Jung, whose concept of archetypes I briefly discussed in my introduction.

Overlapping with Jung, three of the giants of modern mythology took the arguments forward in the 1950s and subsequent decades. I have already mentioned Joseph Campbell, whose four-volume masterwork *The Masks of God* represents the apogee of general studies of the subject, containing an incredible breadth and depth of knowledge of myth from all over the world and all ages – combined with detailed and erudite commentary. Mircea Eliade has also made a huge contribution to the study of comparative religion and mythology in a number of books, including *Myth and Reality*, *The Sacred and the Profane*, *Shamanism*, and *Patterns in Comparative Religion*. Likewise Claude Levi-Strauss, who has especially attempted to analyse the contradictions and opposites so often found in myth, in books such as *Myth and Meaning* and *The Way of the Masks*.

THE DEVELOPMENT OF MYTH

Any summary of the orthodox approach to the analysis of myth should use Campbell's *Masks* as its primary reference; as I have already indicated, its breadth and depth of analysis are unrivalled, and although certain aspects have been questioned by some of his successors, it remains the definitive study of worldwide mythology.

At the very root is the suggestion that myths in their purest form evolved primarily because of certain psychological features of the human race.[2] Campbell begins by discussing the differences between 'innate' stimuli built into all humans, and those that are 'impressed' by cultural influences. This can be understood if we look, for example, at the three basic stages of human growth.

At the beginning we have the psychological trauma of birth, of switching from the safety and warmth of the womb to the unpredictability of life outside it. Those who place emphasis on the purely psychological factors suggest this innate experience, common to all humans, may underlie the recurrent theme of the search for nirvana, which in this context is really only a desire to return to the womb. Then, in the period of childhood, individual desires – for sustenance, warmth, and affection – predominate, and most are seen as being satisfied by the mother, perhaps leading to the massive importance attached to the mother figure in myth. As we move into adulthood, we find the childhood dominance of self-oriented behaviour has to be re-engineered into a sense of social responsibility – especially in more primitive cultures where the group has to work together just to survive. There is little doubt that a great deal of early myth sprang up to assist this process, because it is the 'sacred lore' into which young adults are initiated even in modern tribal cultures that helps prevent them from disintegrating. Of course, the stimuli here are culturally impressed, and will to some extent vary from one group to another. Finally, with the onset of old age we find ourselves orienting once again toward the individual, universal and innate in our contemplation of death – and Campbell is not alone in emphasising that the human species is the only one that has developed sufficiently to become aware of the inevitability of our own death. It is clear this stimulus, perhaps above any other, lies at the very heart of myth, leading to the themes of life after death, and of reincarnation and rebirth, which so predominate in one form or another.

However, this by no means represents the full story. As humans evolved, especially in recognising a sense of self, they became increasingly interested in their surroundings. Interested, that is, not only in understanding how they were going to affect them from the practical point of view – of food, shelter, and survival in the face of changes in weather and climate – but also, increasingly, in their underlying philosophy from a more abstract perspective. For the first time, our ancestors started to ask the fundamental questions about how the earth, sun, moon, plants, animals, and indeed humankind itself, originated. They tended toward supernatural explanations involving supernatural beings. Of course, many scholars who emphasise the psychological basis of myth tend to leave it at that, without questioning whether some part of this supposedly primitive philosophy actually derives from innate stimuli – which themselves derive from a universal consciousness, as Jung suggested, and therefore may have serious philosophical significance. However, this is an argument I must leave to one side for now.

In any case, the aspect of their surroundings that most impressed itself on early humans was the extent to which all nature is cyclical. They noticed the cycles of the sun and moon, of the seasons, of plant life – all of which implied a continuous cycle of birth, growth, death and rebirth. They also recognised the impact the cycles of the moon had, for example, on female menstruation and on the tides. And they became intrigued by the opposing forces that so often dominate myth: of night versus day, dark versus light, fear versus happiness, male versus female, life versus death and so on. These are the underlying factors that led to the sun and moon in particular playing such a decisive and enduring role in myth. Moreover, it was this impetus that led to the more detailed study of the night sky, and of the stars and planets, and this in turn would lead eventually to the body of myth in all advanced cultures that saw the earth as a mirror of what was happening in the skies: the all-pervasive theme of 'as above, so below'.

Of course, the foregoing is necessarily an extremely brief survey of the major psychological and philosophical stimuli that underpin much of mythology – sufficient, I hope, to provide a backdrop I can develop when examining specific cases in the chapters that follow. To complete this backdrop, however, we should consider – once again in highly summarised form – the orthodox view of the major mythological movements that developed in our earliest recorded history.

In the earliest stages of humankind's development of mythology, so this view goes, two major cultural variants developed.[3] On the one hand, the primitive planter cultures of the equatorial zone depended primarily on protoagriculture; even if they were not sowing seeds, they were at least harvesting the crops produced by nature, and their communities were relatively settled. The emphasis of worship was on Mother Earth as a provider, and as a result these cultures were typically matriarchal. The serpent was the dominant animal symbol, with its ability to periodically shed its skin being representative of death, rebirth and renewal.

On the other hand, the hunter-gatherer cultures of the less temperate zones, especially to the north, were typically more patriarchal given their dependence on their menfolk to hunt and kill game. The dominant animal symbol was the bull. In the glacial ages, when tundra prevailed and the prey was largely nonmigratory, these cultures tended to be more settled, and the gatherer aspect meant the mother goddess was also revered. Later, however, as the climate warmed and the prey changed to more migratory species, the return to a more primitive nomadic existence meant the emphasis was once again on the hunter and the bull.

According to the orthodoxy, the combination of these two cultural influences dominated until civilisation proper emerged in Sumer in the latter half of the fifth millennium BC. The new hieratic city-states, with their newly created hierarchies of kings, priests, merchants and peasants, required an entirely new form of control – needed, indeed, to create 'order out of chaos', another fundamental theme of myth. This is how Campbell describes the huge impact this had on the development of mythology:

> The new inspiration of civilised life was based, first, on the discovery, through long and meticulous, carefully checked and re-checked observations, that there were, besides the sun and moon, five other visible or barely visible heavenly spheres (to wit, Mercury, Venus, Mars, Jupiter, and Saturn) which moved in established courses, according to established laws, along the ways followed by the sun and moon, among the fixed stars; and then, second, on the almost insane, playful, yet potentially terrible notion that the laws governing the movements of the seven heavenly spheres should in some mystical way be the same as those governing the life and thought of men on earth. The whole city, not simply the temple area, was now conceived as an imitation on earth of the cosmic order, a sociological 'middle cosmos', or mesocosm, established by priestcraft between the macrocosm of the universe and the microcosm of the individual, making visible the one essential form of all. The king was the centre, as a human representative of the power made celestially manifest either in the sun or in the moon, according to the focus of the local cult; the walled city was organised

architecturally in the design of a quartered circle (like the circles designed on the ceramic ware of the period just preceding), centred around the pivotal sanctum of the palace or ziggurat (as the ceramic designs around the cross, rosette, or swastika); and there was a mathematically structured calendar to regulate the seasons of the city's life according to the passages of the sun and moon among the stars – as well as a highly developed system of liturgical arts, including music, the art rendering audible to human ears the world-ordering harmony of the celestial spheres.[4]

As for the effect this had on the symbolism of these new civilisations:

The impression one gets from these is of a considerable hodge-podge of differing mythologies being coordinated, synthesised, and syncretised by the new professional priesthoods. And how could the situation have been otherwise, when it was the serpent of the jungle and the bull of the steppes that were being brought together? They were soon to become melted and fused – recompounded – in such weird chimeric creatures as the bull-horned serpents, fish-tailed bulls, and lion-headed eagles that from now on would constitute the typical apparitions of an extremely sophisticated new world of myth.[5]

THE FUNCTION OF MYTH

To complete our necessarily brief introduction to the orthodox view of mythology, let us finally see what Campbell has to say about the function of myth, and the closely associated activity that puts it into practice – ritual:

Functioning as [an innate] 'way', mythology and ritual conduce to a transformation of the individual, disengaging him from his local, historical conditions and leading him toward some kind of ineffable experience. Functioning as an [impressed] 'ethnic idea', on the other hand, the image binds the individual to his family's system of historically

conditioned sentiments, activities, and beliefs, as a
functioning member of a sociological organism. This
antinomy is fundamental to our subject, and every failure to
recognise it leads not only to unnecessary argument, but also
to a misunderstanding – one way or the other – of the force of
the mythological symbol itself, which is, precisely, to render
an experience of the ineffable through the local and concrete,
and thus, paradoxically, to amplify the force and appeal of the
forms even while carrying the mind beyond them. The
distinctive challenge of mythology lies in its power to effect
this dual end; and not to recognise this fact is to miss the
whole point and mystery of our science.[6]

From this we can see Campbell, although he describes the
astronomical developments of myth in the hieratic city-states as
'almost insane' and 'playful', takes some other aspects of myth
extremely seriously on a religious or philosophical plane. And so
should we all. The problem lies in the subjective judgments we
each make as individuals in deciding which bits to take seriously,
and which to largely ignore.

CONCLUSION

Mythology is fickle. Every single ancient text or tradition handed
down to us from every part of the world has had a multitude of
influences brought to bear on its composition. These include
psychological, cultural, political, religious and philosophical influences, as well as the potentially historiographical ones with which
we are most concerned. One of the simplest and most poignant
examples of editing for political and religious purposes, which came
as a great surprise to me when I learned of it many years ago, is that
there are two separate Hebrew words translated as 'God' in English
translations of the Old Testament: one is Yahweh, a singular proper
name; the other is Elohim, a plural collective term. These two words,
broadly speaking, derive from two separate sources known as the
Yahwist and the Elohist texts. In any sensible translation the latter
word would have to be rendered as gods – plural. This, of course,
would tend to contradict the entrenched monotheism of Christianity; so the simple removal of the s at the end is one of the finest
examples of expedient editing of older texts that we have.

Moreover, it is sometimes difficult to distinguish between the different influences in any given text. We will find, for example, that the traditions of the indigenous tribes across the globe contain much that is obviously conditioned by local sociological factors, along with much that is quite clearly allegorical. Does this mean it will be impossible or pointless to attempt to discern any historiographical material they may contain? Not necessarily, but we must tread extremely carefully in attempting to find it.

Another general factor we will have to consider is the way in which traditions that were originally firmly founded in historical fact can be distorted by the passage of time and by geographic diffusion. Campbell himself uses the term *regressed mythology*, and discusses an example of this by tracing certain distorted aspects of the tenth-century *Tales of the Arabian Nights* right back to the now-proven custom of ritual regicide that prevailed in many early cultures:

> So, from what we now know, it can be said with perfect assurance that in the earliest period of the hieratic city state the king and his court were ritually immolated at the expiration of a span of years determined by the relationship of the planets in the heavens to the moon; and that our legend of Kash is, therefore, certainly an echo from that very deep well of the past, romantically reflected in a late story-teller's art.[7]

Such a statement does, of course, support my case for a historical re-evaluation of certain aspects of supposed mythology. However, before we become too complacent, let us look at the other side of the coin – here is Campbell discussing the 'great traditional books' of history:

> The world is full, also, of great traditional books tracing the history of man (but focused narrowly on the local group) from the age of mythological beginnings, through periods of increasing plausibility, to a time almost within memory, when the chronicles begin to carry the record, with a show of rational factuality, to the present. Furthermore, just as all primitive mythologies serve to validate the customs, systems of sentiments, and political aims of their respective local

groups, so do these great traditional books. On the surface they may appear to have been composed as conscientious history. In depth they reveal themselves to have been conceived as myths: poetic readings of the mystery of life from a certain interested point of view. But to read a poem as a chronicle of fact is – to say the least – to miss the point. To say a little more, it is to prove oneself a dolt. And to add to this, the men who put these books together were not dolts but knew precisely what they were doing – as the evidence of their manner of work reveals at every turn.[8]

Strong words, and mainly ones with which I concur – but I disagree with the emphasis. Such records may not represent strict and detailed chronicles of historical fact. Still, it is quite clear they may carry a germ of underlying factuality in certain aspects. And it is the possibility that such a germ resides in the passages describing a civilised race existing before the catastrophe that we will examine in this part of the work. But, before we do, there is one other set of preliminary foundations I need to establish – those of the spiritual worldview on which my entire analysis is based.

2. A SPIRITUAL WORLDVIEW

In my introduction I made no secret of the fact that my main objective in this work is a reappraisal of the traditions of an antediluvian race along *spiritual* lines. In fact to clarify this somewhat, I already subscribed to a spiritual worldview when I began my research many years ago, but only after some considerable time did I realise that it might well hold the key to unlocking their secrets properly. Prior to that I had been looking for more rationalistic, prosaic and, to some extent, symbolic interpretations, as do many of my colleagues. Now, clearly I feel no need to justify my own personal beliefs per se. But if I am to justify my spiritual reinterpretations of the traditions, then equally clearly I *am* duty bound to explain the basis of the spiritual worldview I hold, and indeed to attempt to support it with whatever evidence I feel is appropriate.

KARMA AND REINCARNATION

My worldview is based around the fundamental and mutually dependent principles of karma and reincarnation. And before I explain them more fully, we should remember that as much as they are clearly at odds with Christianity, Judaism and Islam, which allow for a single incarnation followed by an afterlife only, the majority of the world's population – mainly in the East through Hinduism and Buddhism but also in many other places – *do* accept these principles. But, like many other like-minded individuals, I am not a devotee of any particular religion or philosophy that can be given a specific name. I prefer, as we will see throughout this work, to think in terms of what I call 'universal truths'.

However much personal experience is the ultimate key to spiritual development, I believe there are ways of attempting to provide a rational and philosophically logical justification for this spiritual worldview in addition to the scientific angle that we will explore in detail in Part 3. But before I can demonstrate them I must properly describe the main tenets of this worldview as I, and countless others down the ages, see them:

- The soul is separate from the incarnate or physical body; it is ethereal and eternal, and lives on after physical death.
- The soul reincarnates repeatedly in different physical bodies at different times.
- The aim of all souls is to advance from one incarnation to the next – even though our normal consciousness retains no detailed recollection of previous lives and lessons learned – because our souls assimilate their experiences after each physical death, at which point decisions are made about the next incarnation.
- As a result, different levels of souls or spiritual entities exist in various stages of advancement or development.
- The aim of all souls is to reach a level of karmic advancement whereby as humans we escape from the 'earthly karmic round' and reincarnate, if at all, only by choice.
- Karma is the principle of cause and effect that underlies all these processes and more; in the very broadest of terms, 'positive' or 'progressive' actions and attitudes are rewarded by more opportunities for advancement, while 'negative' or 'regressive' actions and attitudes attract repeated bad experiences until the soul wakes up to these consequences and attempts to break out of the cycle of negative karma.

Anyone familiar with the teachings of the predominantly Eastern religions will recognise much if not all of this worldview, albeit that as we will shortly see these contain some important specifics with which I fundamentally disagree.

But to backtrack for a moment, the position of the rational atheist is that there is no separate soul or afterlife at all, and this is clearly a logically valid proposition – though I hope to show that it not only has significant philosophical defects, but is also unable to explain an abundance of highly persuasive if not conclusive evidence to the contrary from a variety of sources. But what of those predominantly Western religions that accept the notion of the separate soul, but believe we only incarnate once and then live ever after either in heaven or hell? It is surely inconceivable that we would only 'get one go'? What could we possibly expect to achieve and learn in one human lifetime? How scary would it be for the ultimate judgment of the spiritual worth or otherwise of our soul to be based on just one minuscule period of a few decades, when set against the backdrop of the timelessness of the universe itself? Just as we will see later that it makes no philosophical sense to think the universe as a whole started at one particular point in time and will ultimately end at another, instead of being involved in an endless series of lengthy cycles of emergence and reabsorption, it makes no sense whatsoever that our souls should incarnate at one point in time and then disincarnate at another on the point of physical death, with no return. The principle of karmic advancement in a variety of physical bodies on the dense plane of manifestation that earth represents surely makes far more sense?

Before we move on, it must also be allowed that there are a few minority religions, sects or native traditions throughout the world that accept reincarnation without the accompanying principle of karma. But to me none of these offer a valid philosophical framework as an alternative to the idea that the only reason we reincarnate is with the express aim of long-term karmic advancement.

EVIDENCE

A huge variety of supposed evidence has been collated to support elements of this worldview, but if we are to be at all practical we must be extremely discriminatory in how we analyse it. For example, considerable efforts have been made to document anecdotal evidence of an afterlife in general, particularly in terms of people who claim to have had 'near-death experiences' when seriously ill, but have then survived to tell the tale. These usually involve some variation on seeing a 'brilliant white light at the end of a tunnel' and an overwhelming sense of love and wellbeing, and possibly a sense of meeting up with other souls in some way linked to their own.[1] I find this evidence perfectly plausible, despite the fact that some scientists claim to have replicated at least some of these effects by stimulating particular parts of the brain in experiments, because in my worldview it should be possible to transcend the physical realm when in incarnate life anyway – indeed this is surely what neophytes have always attempted to do.

However such anecdotal evidence is ultimately highly subjective, and while it should not be dismissed out of hand it is hardly the stuff to make sceptics even look twice. If we now turn to attempts to prove the reality not just of the survival of the soul, but of *past* lives as well, we must turn to undoubtedly one of the pioneers in this field, Ian Stevenson, a professor of psychiatry at the University of Virginia. He has published a variety of books and papers on the subject of reincarnation, the best introduction being his 1987 work *Children Who Remember Past Lives*.[2] Although Stevenson has, unsurprisingly, attracted some criticism from the obvious scientific quarters, it is quite clear he approaches his work with about as much scientific professionalism as it is possible to muster in such an area of study, which makes a refreshing contrast to the plethora of other material that has been published on the subject. Moreover, not only does he avoid overtly placing his work in the context of any declared religion or philosophy – clearly a sensible approach for a researcher attempting to maintain a high degree of scientific rigour – but he also insists that what he presents is not *definitive* evidence, preferring instead the use of the more cautious phrase 'cases *suggestive* of reincarnation'.

He briefly discusses cases in which apparent experiences of past lives during *déjà vu* sensations, vivid and lucid dreams, drug-induced hallucinatory trips and meditation can be argued to provide some evidence for reincarnation, but can equally well be disqualified by other explanations, especially our human ability to fashion a subconscious fiction out of a jumble of pieces of information gleaned via normal conscious processes. His attitude to past-life readings by supposed clairvoyants is similarly balanced and reserved, especially in that he rightly acknowledges the unavoidable fact that many charlatans operate in this arena.

He devotes a little more space to hypnotic regression techniques which purport to take the subject back not only into childhood but beyond and into past lives, noting that in these cases not only is the subject particularly prone to suggestion, but that also they will be actively trying to please the hypnotist and again drawing on any information stored in their brain to concoct a past life in which the experiences can *seem* very real. His point is proved by a number of examples that show clear historical anachronisms, and also by experiments in which subjects were finally asked about their sources while under hypnosis and revealed them to be historical books or similar. On the other hand, with appropriate balance he does accept that a small number of well-documented and re-searched cases of regression do appear to point towards genuine recall of a past life. Some involve detailed facts that are so obscure it would have been virtually impossible for the subject to have gleaned them from normal sources – unless they were a historical specialist perpetrating an elaborate hoax, which seems unlikely in these cases and given that they were supposedly under hypnosis anyway. Others involve the subjects fluently speaking foreign languages they insist they have never learned in this life.[3]

But there is only one area of research on which Stevenson places any real reliance, and that is the testimony of young children from various parts of the world who have had regular recall of a previous life, sometimes with astonishingly verifiable results. Of course, a believer such as myself would support this approach by arguing that young children are temporally closer to their most recent past life, and moreover that their innate and intuitive recollection facilities have been less culturally suppressed than those of an adult – which is arguably why most people experience *déjà vu* and lucid repetitive dreams far more in childhood than in later life. More importantly for the sceptic, not only do these cases *not* involve any of the mechanisms discussed above, they also take advantage of the fact that young children have had less time to assimilate historical details by normal means, so the process of crosschecking possible normal sources can be far more comprehensive and reliable. So it is these cases that Stevenson has actively pursued across the globe since 1962.

CHILDHOOD RECALL

To provide a scientific framework for his research Stevenson applies a number of criteria, regarding cases as 'solved' if the subject's recollection indubitably points to the life of a clearly identifiable and now deceased individual, and as 'unsolved' if not. And he splits the types of memories into three categories: 'imaged' or effectively factual, that is regarding dates, people and places; 'behavioural', that is traits displayed by the subject that have no origin in their current incarnation but a clear origin in a past one; and 'subliminal cognitive', whereby the subject automatically displays a complex skill such as speaking a language or playing an instrument that they could not have learned in their current life.[4]

CASES

Stevenson summarises a selection of twelve typical cases in *Children Who Remember Past Lives*.⁵ I do not intend to outline them here, because I would necessarily have to summarise them even more, and it is in the detail that his research gains its credibility – indeed he is at pains to point out that any serious student should consult his more detailed papers on each case. However, I should note that he deliberately includes a few weaker and unsolved cases to demonstrate his methods and his laudable attempts at scientific impartiality.

They are selected from a total of some two thousand Stevenson has on file, more than fifty per cent of which he has investigated personally while the remainder have been documented by his team of associates. They come from all parts of the world, especially India, Sri Lanka, Burma, Thailand, Lebanon, Syria, Turkey, West Africa and the northwestern tribal regions of North America. He has also investigated cases in other parts of North America and in Europe, although these appear to occur less frequently, and he surmises that *one* of the reasons for this geographical disparity, although by no means the only one, is that the people of the former regions have a widespread and ingrained belief in reincarnation, unlike the latter. Consequently the children in potential cases in the West are more likely to be misunderstood, ignored or deliberately silenced.

That having been said, Stevenson makes it clear his cases can hardly be regarded as fully representative of a world population of billions of people. Many factors affect a bias, including the relatively haphazard way in which reports of cases come to him, and the decisions he has made in selecting the regions he has taken the time and trouble to visit. Nevertheless, he is right to suggest that a number of similar characteristics of typical cases can be determined, and it is on these I would like to concentrate.⁶

COMMON CHARACTERISTICS

First, the mother of a child subject often reports that during pregnancy she had an 'announcing dream' in which a deceased person proclaimed their intention to reincarnate as her child. Sometimes this announcement is more symbolic than literal, and of course in many cases such dreams are only remembered if the deceased is someone known to the mother. Clearly the reaction of any cynic would be that if this happens the mother is bound to influence the child once it is born, but I can only emphasise that, while individual aspects of individual cases can be dismissed or even ridiculed, when taken in their totality the picture is very different.

Second, birthmarks on child subjects often correspond to injuries sustained by the deceased person, which is how I will refer to the personality of their previous incarnation. Clearly these correspondences can only be determined in solved cases, but he has made sure that where possible – in some thirty cases – he has consulted autopsy or other medical records of the deceased to confirm details provided by their family.

Third, most subjects start to talk about their previous life at some time between the ages of two and five, with the average being about three, which is hardly surprising given that this is more or less when we expect a child to start talking with any degree of lucidity. This suggests the memories are with them more or less from birth. Meanwhile, the vast majority stop talking about their previous life between the ages of five and eight, although here there is more variety based on the extent to which they are encouraged or discouraged in so doing by their families, and on the degree of forcefulness with which their memories impinge on them. Nevertheless, this shows that cases need to be investigated early in the child's life if they are to have real merit.

Fourth, the subjects' imaged memories almost always relate to the later years of the deceased person's life, and particularly to their mode of death, especially if this was violent, sudden and unexpected, or occurred at an early age. Now this in itself is interesting, because it appears there is a far greater incidence of these types of death in the cases than exists in the general population, suggesting this factor itself plays a significant part in making memories of a past life more prevalent. The other common trait at work here is if the deceased in some way felt they had unfinished or ongoing business. This all suggests that memories of past lives work in exactly the same way as normal incarnate memories, inasmuch as they fade over time, and is backed up by the fact that hardly any of the subjects remember more than one previous life.[7] Moreover, the fact that the interval between lives in the cases studied is normally less than three years, with in some cases hardly any interval at all, seems to indicate that those that most easily remember a past life are also those that were in the most hurry to come back again.

Fifth, subjects often express a desire to visit the place and family of their previous life, if these are identifiable. This is where the plot becomes more complex, because as soon as such communication takes place there is a far greater chance of supposed memories being influenced or obtained by perfectly normal means. For this reason Stevenson places relatively small reliance on statements made after such contact has been made, although in a number of cases it does provide further highly compelling evidence, such as when recognitions are made completely spontaneously, without prompting, and without the accompanying adults having any knowledge of the place or person recognised so that these are only subsequently verified. Recall of private nicknames of people known by the deceased, or of private events in their lives known only by themselves and perhaps one other person, all add to the authenticity of many cases. Moreover, the idea that large portions of the previous 'personality' have survived with a clear sense of ongoing purpose, and that the subject is not just picking up telepathic communications, is enhanced by the attitudes adopted by many of them to the people known to them in their past life. They show friendship or animosity in exactly the measure that would have been expected of the deceased.

Sixth and finally, subjects often display behavioural traits that are completely out of character for their present incarnation, but entirely in keeping with their previous one. These include phobias, such as of guns or knives or water, that are often related to the supposed manner of their previous death and displayed even before the subject starts to speak about their past-life memories; a fondness for certain types of food, or even in some cases tobacco or alcohol, that are completely alien to their current environment; interests, aptitudes and skills, such as in engineering or music or business to which they have had no exposure in their current incarnation; and, perhaps most compelling of all, in a significant number of cases a total rejection of their current gender on the basis that they still identify with the opposite gender of their previous incarnation. Stevenson surmises that if a number of consecutive previous incarnations had been in the opposite gender this trait would be especially pronounced, even if the subject had no memories of these past lives. This is one of the finest examples of how behavioural traits that vex modern psychologists and geneticists in the 'nature versus nurture' debate might be better explained by a belief in reincarnation.[8]

ALTERNATIVE EXPLANATIONS

Stevenson examines a number of alternatives to reincarnation as an explanation for the cases he has studied.[9] First, he accepts that in a very few cases fraud has been proved, and also that in just a few more it may have occurred but not been picked up. Second, he assents that gross self-deception is another valid explanation in a few cases, especially those tending to involve suggestions of the reincarnation of a famous or prominent person. Third, he accepts that there may be a few cases in which the information in the subject's memory *was* obtained in an entirely normal way by transmission from someone who was acquainted with the deceased, but this transmission has been entirely overlooked and forgotten. Fourth, he gives some weight to the possibility of significant parental exaggeration of sparse early comments made by the subject, so while this is neither deliberate fraud nor self-deception as such, it could lead to a case appearing to be far stronger than it really is.

Stevenson's arguments against these alternative explanations are detailed, but we can make a few general observations that to some extent apply to them all. First, his research methods have been deliberately designed to reveal any of these alternatives, and while some might have slipped through the net they could be no more than a handful.[10] Second, none of them can properly account for the genuine and unusual behavioural traits and phobias displayed by a great many subjects. Third, there is far less motive for fraud, self-deception or exaggeration than might normally be assumed. While there is no doubt that in some cases the subject or their family gain a degree of attention and notoriety from their experience, in many others the subjects place themselves in an extremely awkward position in relation to the rest of their family, for example because of their unusual behavioural traits. Moreover, the family of the subject often face rejection in favour of the family of the deceased, or at least rivalry for the child's affection. For their part, the family of the deceased sometimes suspect the motives of the subject and their family, especially if they are wealthier, or are fearful of revelations about them that they would prefer remained private.

Stevenson also considers the possibility that somehow past-life memories are passed on genetically through the offspring of the deceased, but it is clear that in most cases the interval between the death of the previous personality and the birth of the reincarnated subject is far too short for this to be possible, quite apart from the fact that in many cases the possibility of their being even in any distant blood relationship is virtually zero. Accordingly, he finally turns to the paranormal alternatives.

The first of these is extrasensory perception, or telepathy, whereby the memories might be assumed to come from communication either with the soul of the deceased or with a more universal memory or consciousness. But the subjects are hardly ever reported to have any particular gifts in this regard, other than that they have past-life memories. The second is possession of the subject by the soul of the deceased, but this cannot explain why they nearly always tend to lose their memory of the other life at an early stage. And while the latter option can perhaps be regarded as explaining the unusual behavioural traits shown by so many subjects, which the former probably cannot, it undoubtedly cannot account for the widespread phenomena of correlative birthmarks.

Stevenson sums up his position with great reserve, as follows:

> I may have a duty here to say what interpretation of the cases I myself favour. I have no preferred interpretation for all the cases, and I do not think that any single one of them offers compelling evidence of reincarnation. Yet I can say that I think reincarnation is, for some cases, the best interpretation. I am not claiming that it is the only possible interpretation for these cases, just that it seems the best one among all those that I have mentioned . . .
>
> After you have read my detailed case reports, I do not think you will say that there is *no* evidence for reincarnation, although you may certainly say that you find what we have unconvincing. If you reach that point, I think it fair to ask

you: 'What evidence, if you had it, *would* convince you of reincarnation?'[11]

This is a valid question that even the most ardent sceptic would do well to consider carefully.

LIFE BETWEEN LIVES

I am broadly in agreement with Stevenson's cautious attitude to the use of hypnotic regression techniques to elicit details of past lives. It is quite clear to me that, as unfortunate as it is that human nature has to be this way, there are many charlatans operating in this field who tend to discredit the whole area of research. But there is at least one regressor whose work seems to me to provide an invaluable contribution to our understanding of a spiritual world-view, and that is Michael Newton. A qualified counsellor and hypnotherapist, he lives in northern California and has been regressing patients for over ten years. Although initially he rejected the idea, one particular case in which the origin of a patient's persistent ailment could not be traced to their current life left him with no option but to regress them into their previous life, after which appropriate techniques led to an effective cure. After that he had increasing requests from patients to do the same. So we can see that his initial motive was not to uncover details of patient's past lives per se, but to examine them to find the origins of current ailments when these could not be traced to their current life. This approach shows an integrity of intent that is clearly devoid of motives for showmanship.

However, it is not the details of the past lives of his patients that Newton concentrates on, as interesting as they may be in their own right. What he gradually discovered was that certain patients were consistently talking about the time *between* lives, that is the time after the previous death and before the current birth, in the ethereal or spiritual realms. He realised this was an area that had received little previous attention, and the combination of his own intellectual curiosity and the consistency of what he was hearing in initial reports of the after-death experience led him to probe further. Clearly the potential dangers of regressing subjects into the gaps between their lives, and into their existence in the ethereal realms, are even greater than those for more normal regressions, and he swiftly came to understand the key words and other techniques he needed to use in these special situations to keep his subjects safe and well.

Newton first published his work on these cases in 1994 in *Journey of Souls*, and I can only say that, for me at least, his revelations are quite astonishing. The format of the book takes us through the various stages between death and rebirth, and much of it uses transcripts from various cases as the main narrative. The first thing that struck me was the incredible consistency of the reports, to such an extent that in some instances as the transcripts move from one stage to another in the ethereal realms the reader would be forgiven for thinking Newton is continuing with the same subject's case study, when in fact he has moved on to another subject. The other important point is that he directly takes on the criticism of Stevenson and others about regression techniques, in particular with respect to the idea that subjects are highly influenced by the regressor, by emphasising that in many cases subjects argue with him or even laugh at his ignorance when he appears to misinterpret what they are saying; and this assertion is repeatedly borne out by the transcripts of the cases he presents.[12]

So let us now look at the subjects' descriptions of the various stages of their travel through the ethereal realms between incarnations. I will often present the material as if it were undisputed fact rather than information gleaned via what many might still regard as an unreliable method, but I hope it will be appreciated that this is only to avoid the clumsy repetition of qualifying phrases such as *apparently*, and so on.

THE TRANSITION FROM THE PHYSICAL TO THE ETHEREAL REALMS

We commence with the experience of death and the departure of the soul from the physical body.[13] We find there is complete consistency between the initial stage of this experience and that of the near-death experience we mentioned earlier, with the sense of hovering over the physical body and of a brilliant white light. An additional common feature of the genuine death experience is that the subject often feels a strong urge to communicate with friends or loved ones that are with their physical body at the time of death, in order to let them know they are all right and 'not really dead', but this communication is rarely successful in the early stages because their friends' and families' grief tends to block it out. This desire to comfort those close to them can result in the subject being highly reluctant to 'leave the scene', and this is strengthened if death was sudden or unexpected and they have had little chance to come to terms with having to leave their physical body behind and move on.

Nevertheless, we find almost all subjects soon do come to terms with their plight, and feel a great sense of freedom and release. They also feel a 'pulling sensation' guiding them towards the 'tunnel' that we know is also a common feature of near-death experiences. They enter the tunnel either almost immediately, or perhaps only after several days have elapsed – for example, once they have seen themselves buried and been able to send at least a general feeling of love and wellbeing to those they have left behind – although it is clear the sense of time is totally different in the ethereal realms, and what might seem like several days to us may seem like just a few minutes to a discarnate soul. In fact, the cases reveal that the subjects' souls are in various stages of karmic advancement, just as we would expect, and that the more advanced they are the less their desire to hang around in the 'astral plane' of the physical world before departing properly.

Once the subjects are in the tunnel, they all perceive the bright light at the end into which they emerge without apparent delay. Their descriptions of the world they enter vary somewhat although, while most are immediately aware that it does not obey normal three-dimensional laws, they also describe it as being in some senses divided into different 'layers', which is again what we might expect if we allow for the idea that there are multiple 'planes' or dimensions of existence in the ethereal realms themselves. The less advanced souls also report initially seeing great crystalline castles, or rivers and meadows and rainbows, and it would appear these are 'visions of heaven' that are particular to each subject and which they are 'allowed to perceive' to make them feel more at home and relaxed.

At this point most subjects become aware that one or more other souls are coming to greet them, and here we must make a clear distinction between their 'soul mates' and their specific 'spirit guide' or 'guardian angel' that is relatively advanced and always looks out for them over time immemorial. Less-advanced souls tend to be met by other soul mates first, who they will recognise because they tend to take on a human-type form, either from the waist up or perhaps just as a face, again to make the subject feel more at home and render the transition less painful. However, even these souls seem to appreciate that they are all really just 'balls of intense energy' shining especially brightly against an already bright background. As to the human form taken, they report that in this welcoming situation the souls take on the form they 'feel' the subject will be most comforted by, although again even these subjects also realise immediately exactly what other incarnations the other souls have had with them. Having said that, one of the refreshingly comical aspects of these communications, which in my view only adds to their likely authenticity, is that some less-advanced souls apparently show a high degree of vanity in choosing what physical form to take on – even to the extent of choosing one they have never actually had on earth – without realising that the other more-advanced souls can 'see through them' immediately and are laughing at them in a good-natured way.

The subjects also report that most communication in the ethereal realms is by telepathy, although especially private communications are effected by 'touch which passes between the two souls as electrical sound impulses'. When pressed on what she meant when she said she was 'hugging' one of her closest soul mates, one subject described it as 'two masses of bright light whirling around each other'.

There are exceptions to these patterns. It appears that especially if the subject has died suddenly and is not ready for the transition, their spirit guide will be the first to greet them to take the brunt of their frustrations; and even when they are not the first point of contact, they are usually around keeping an eye on things. On the other hand, more-advanced souls are met by no one straight away, and one subject revealed he could not wait to get away from the physical realms and move as quickly as possible to his appointed level in the ethereal realms.

In this connection he described his mode of travel as like being on a 'homing beacon of sound and light' that was part of his own individual 'tonal pattern or frequency'. This fits in entirely with the idea that harmonics and energy vibrations lie at the core of all realms, as we will examine further in Part 3, and even less-advanced souls describe hearing 'musical vibrations' straight after death that become more harmonious as they enter the ethereal realms.

The other major exceptions are two types of soul that do not enter these realms in the normal way after death. The first are what we on earth would term 'ghosts', who are usually immature souls that are so affected by a sudden death or so focused on unfinished business in the earthly realm that they simply refuse to go with their spirit guide and, in not really accepting they are dead, continue to hang around earth's astral plane. They also tend to stick to the geographical location of their death, and because of their confusion and frustration they can make a nuisance of themselves to incarnate humans. However, these cases are relatively rare, and above all such souls are not in any sense evil or demonic, so that sooner or later they will go back with their spirit guide, even if sometimes only after assistance by the earthly process of exorcism from their place of residence.

The other type of soul is more of a concern, because they have committed serious crimes against others in their incarnate life. The consensus of the subjects appears to be that there is no such thing as an inherently evil soul, and nor is there a hell into which such souls are cast for eternity, but that after death – because they succumbed deeply to the most negative and base of incarnate human influences – they are taken to a separate part of the ethereal realms away from their normal level or group, where they undergo a period of seclusion and reorientation, of varying length, before rejoining the normal process. Subjects also appear to confirm that no matter how much an individual soul may repeat the same mistakes, it is never 'destroyed' because energy cannot be destroyed, but it may well be 'remodelled'.

PAST-LIFE REVIEWS AND SOUL GROUPS
Newton's subjects universally report that after their initial meetings with either their spirit guide or various soul mates, or both, they are 'propelled' to a place where they receive a healing 'shower' of positive light energy that washes away all the negative emotional influences of physical incarnation as a human, allowing them to 'become whole again'.

At this point they are taken to another place in which their initial life review, or in Newton's terms *orientation*, takes place with their spirit guide. In the case of less-advanced souls, again this place will take on a familiar physical appearance of a room or other location in which they felt particularly comfortable. In line with what we learned before about seriously disruptive souls, this process is not one of punishment, and nor is the guide in any sense strict or unkind, acting more as a benevolent counsellor. But at the same time everything is laid bare, there are no secrets, and any harshness appears to come from the subject themselves being forced to analyse both the positive and negative aspects of the life they have just led, including especially any important things they did not achieve but had intended to.

So, while for the most part these initial reviews appear to be fairly good-natured, and the subject is then able to move on to other stages without undue worry, the guide is persistent in pushing them to take responsibility for, and fully understand, their actions. Moreover, some subjects undoubtedly feel apprehension, and this is not only because of the abruptness with which realisation of the totality of their past lives comes back into clear focus. One in particular, who had committed suicide in her life just completed, already realised as she approached her initial review that she had 'blown it' and would have to reincarnate to do it all over again, wasting a lot of time. Committing suicide in this way is not, according to the subjects, a cardinal sin, but is simply regarded as a failure to take on the allotted problems properly this time round – while committing suicide to escape severe pain or bodily infirmity is regarded as perfectly acceptable in the ethereal realms.

After this initial review, the subjects report being transferred to a 'staging area' that might be thought of as a huge railway station, in which many incoming souls are in transit to their proper destination in the ethereal realms. Less-advanced souls are escorted by their guide, while the more advanced are again propelled by unseen forces. Many report that while they leave this staging area they travel along corridors that bulge in places with 'soul groups' who belong and work together in the spirit world, and they are themselves in transit to their own soul group. These groups, which Newton refers to as 'primary', usually contain between three and twenty-five souls, with the numbers increasing with the degree of advancement. All members of the group are the most intimate soul mates, and will have known each other from the start of their existence and lived together in various different incarnations and relationships to each other many times. So the subjects normally realise they are now 'going home', and in looking forward to the rapture of seeing those really closest to them again describe themselves as 'like salmon swimming upstream to the place of their birth to spawn'.

On arrival, the less-advanced souls once again report seeing their home in familiar earthly terms, as a favoured house or school or temple from a particular incarnation. They are greeted by the other members of the group and, interestingly, even those members still in incarnation on earth are present in a more dormant way, appearing as lower-energy light emissions. This suggests that such souls leave a portion of their energy make-up back in the ethereal realms at all times, and the idea that souls can 'split' to some extent is reinforced when we find from some subjects that any of them can split themselves and lead two, and in rare cases three, concurrent lives on earth. This is reported as not easy or normal, but it is a method chosen sometimes to speed up development. More-advanced souls even report that the word *split* is misleading, because each part 'remains whole'.

Not long after their arrival home most subjects receive another life review, this time with a 'council of elders', which appears to be similar to the initial review but slightly more formal and in-depth. After this they rejoin their group, and it is in this setting that most of their time in the ethereal realms is spent. Contrary to the image of the afterlife presented in many popular accounts, subjects report that, although they do spend some time just hanging out in what they describe as 'recreational areas', they do not just sit around in a blissful state all the time. Instead, they are pretty constantly engaged in discussion of their former lives, of the lessons they have learned and the good and bad choices they have made, and of the things they have not yet properly learned or mastered, with the other members of their group. This is consistently described as an educational setting, and the members of a primary group can be regarded as a particular class who have a similar level of experience – and, except at the higher levels of advancement, similar character traits such as being extrovert or introverted. Such traits are therefore considered as an inherent orientation of the soul itself, and not just qualities manifested only when in human form.

These classes also have a teacher inasmuch as the group all share the same spirit guide, and because much of the learning process is by good-natured criticism between peers the teacher will be present less often the more advanced the group. In fact some will have two guides, a junior one who will themselves still be under 'teacher-training', and a more senior one that appears less often and looks after far more groups. In the course of time all souls have the chance to become teachers and guides although, just as in the physical world, some show more aptitude and progress faster than others. As for the souls outside the group, Newton's subjects report that there are 'secondary' groupings of at least a thousand souls, and that apart from the most advanced souls subjects rarely have contact with any other soul outside of this group at all, although they may have sporadic dealings with souls in other primary groups within it.

In all incarnations our closest friends and relatives will tend to come from our primary group, while others who are important to us in some way will tend to come from our secondary grouping. The exception is parents, who often tend not to be from the same primary group, and this is merely because primary group members tend to try to incarnate together at the same time, with their human life spans approximately coinciding with each other, which is obviously impossible across successive generations. Nevertheless, it is clear that the idea of a soul group explains the immediate chemistry all of us sometimes experience on meeting someone new for the first time.

Although all souls are androgynous, and can and do take either gender in incarnation in order to gain a balance of experience, the subjects report that most of them do tend to favour one sex over another and to express themselves in that gender even when in the ethereal realms. It appears that the gender orientation in the soul groups can either be mixed or predominantly same sex.

When we come to levels of advancement, it would seem that there is a fairly consistent set of classifications that are to some extent in accordance with the 'hierarchies of angels' reported in many ancient traditions, as we will see in later chapters. This level is most obviously recognised by the colour and depth of energy the soul radiates, which is reminiscent of the idea that humans have a coloured 'aura', although as far as I can tell the colours do not correspond closely. In the ethereal realms the 'beginner' souls have a bright white radiance, which becomes increasingly off-white and then yellow before reaching bright gold as they progress through the 'intermediate' stages, while 'advanced' souls display a light-blue radiance that gradually deepens in colour to a dark bluish-purple for the most advanced.

As we might expect given the principle of karmic advancement, the subjects report that the more advanced the soul becomes, the less it needs to incarnate and the less it is tied to its original group. The eventual aim of all souls is confirmed as being to achieve sufficient perfection that they no longer have to reincarnate on earth, and are ultimately 'reunited with the source'. As for the pace of advancement, completely novice souls appear to require about five incarnations before they join a soul group proper as a 'beginner', and they may incarnate many times over a lengthy earth time span before advancing to intermediate status; for example, by regressing one subject right back to their earliest incarnation Newton found they had taken more than 30,000 years to reach this stage, although in another exceptional case a subject had achieved this in only a few thousand years. Accordingly, he estimates from the totality of his case files that approximately three-quarters of the current human population are only in the early stages of soul development, albeit that this is perhaps to be expected given the rapidity with which humankind is proliferating. Interestingly, he finds that more-advanced souls do not necessarily display psychic abilities when in incarnation.

Subjects also report that they are expected to spend some time in the 'place of projection', where they deliberately make contact with incarnate souls to provide energy or other assistance. This is in contrast to the constant activities of guides, who keep a regular eye on their group members while they are on earth, and can contact or be contacted by them any time they choose. Less senior guides may even be in incarnation at the same time as their group on occasion.

CHOOSING THE NEXT LIFE AND RETURNING INTO INCARNATION

The amount of time spent in the ethereal realms appears to vary depending on the level of advancement and other less well-defined factors, although again we must remember that notions of time are not the same as on earth. Nevertheless, most souls reach a point where they either decide themselves or are 'made aware' that it is time for them to go back, and although it appears that subjects may show a degree of resistance to leaving the security and comfort of their real home for the trials and tribulations of earthly incarnation, they all agree sooner or later and forceful coercion is never required.

The first stage of this process may involve the subject having another meeting with their guide and elders, or at the very least telepathically notifying the elders of their decision to reincarnate, of the lessons they would particularly like to learn, and of the potential geographic setting for their next life. This latter seems to come first, although subjects report that affiliations to particular countries or races are rare and, if they do exist, relatively short-lived. In exceptional circumstances, such as a sudden death, they might choose to come back in the same location as their last life, and even to the same family, but this is consistent with what we learned from Stevenson's research.[14] In any case, the elders then set up a session in the 'place of life selection', which is described as like a giant movie theatre with screens all around. Here the subject is able to review the various options available to them in terms of the human beings that will be incarnate with more or less the right sort of family and professional circumstances, at about the right time, in each location. So effectively this place is one where time is fast-forwarded for the subject, who can even control the movie telepathically as if it were a video playback, fast-forwarding where necessary and even pausing the scene to enter it temporarily and gain direct experience of that particular incarnation.

Now this raises interesting questions, and might initially suggest that once we have made our life choice everything else is predetermined. However, nothing could be further from the truth, and in fact what the subjects appear to see are merely snippets of various important *probabilities* in the future lives of their potential incarnations, so that even these are not totally predetermined. Much is left out, and there are many alternatives along the way, so that some subjects describe the process as like being given a road map and a rough point of departure and destination, but many possible alternative routes. Admittedly where serious injuries or disabilities or even untimely death are probably involved, these will usually be seen in advance, and this may sound strange until we remember that such supposedly negative facets of a human life may be deliberately chosen to help us learn important lessons. At the very least such adverse circumstances seem to accelerate the soul's learning curve.

The overall emphasis of subjects' descriptions of both this process and of incarnate life in general is that it is one involving personal responsibility for karmic choice in a climate of free will. The idea is to experience incarnate life in as many and varied circumstances and bodies as possible in order to gain full karmic balance. Moreover, a consistent theme is that when in one incarnation we are the precipitator of a major event such as a deliberate separation from our partner or a close family member, or worse still their deliberate injury or murder, sooner or later we will have an incarnation in which we are on the receiving end of similar treatment, and often at the hands of the very same soul. As an example, one subject reports that another soul of his acquaintance had 'hurt a girl terribly', and that after a period of reorientation he immediately *requested* to be incarnated in the form of a person who would themselves be hurt in similar fashion. As disturbing as this might seem initially, the principle is clearly that we obtain so much clarity in the ethereal realms that we *ourselves* deliberately choose lives that will at some point involve similar suffering to that which we have inflicted on others in the past – not as a penance, or as part of any process of vindictive divine retribution, but merely in order that we fully experience both sides of the coin and arrive at a position of karmic balance. The saying 'what goes around, comes around' would appear to be true not only within one incarnation, but also across many.

Of course, while we are learning our own lessons we are also playing a part in the lessons learned by others around us. An extreme example of this is reported to be that souls may unselfishly choose to have a 'filler life' of extremely short duration, such as when a child dies at birth or soon afterwards, where the lessons are not for the soul incarnating in the child at all, but rather for those of, normally, its parents. So another part of the life selection process involves subjects making decisions with other members of their soul group. This is the one stage of events in the ethereal realms that is not completely explained by Newton or his subjects because on the face of it, even if they all decide to incarnate more or less at the same time, each member of the group should be able to make their own completely independent decision about who they come back as and where; but in fact we find there is clear deliberation about coming back as people who will be part of each other's lives to a greater or lesser degree. We can only assume therefore that the elders program the life choices each member sees in the place of life selection to have certain probable or possible interactions already built in.

However this process works, the outcome is that a whole host of souls finally meet in the 'place of recognition' immediately prior to their rebirth. Those present will not only be other members of the primary soul group, but also others from the broader secondary group, and perhaps even some from outside this who will potentially interact with the given subject on a lesser but still potentially important level. The overriding principle is that all of these souls plan to impact on each other's lives to a greater or lesser extent in a complex web of partially predefined interactions, which combine to best allow the potential fulfilment of a number of mutual life goals for each of the participants. Moreover, it is not the length of the potential interaction that defines the strength of the bond between the two souls, but the importance of the potential impact.

The nature of this 'revision' programme is that a number of 'prompters' provide details to each group of important triggers they should remember once they are incarnate in the next life. An essential part of the karmic process is that our memories are progressively wiped clean of knowledge of former lives and understanding of the ethereal realms in the years after birth, which ties in well with Stevenson's research, and Newton's subjects report that this amnesia is crucial in order that we do not allow preconceptions from these memories to limit our potential for action and choice in the next life. However, the recognition triggers are left with us to prompt us at certain points in our lives that this is something crucial to our life plan. This feeling may just come through as a strong intuition in incarnate life, and they are usually small and otherwise insignificant details about other people we will meet along the way. In the most important way these triggers might provide for us meeting our intended partner, but in other cases they will signal a meeting with an apparent stranger that has some other important role, such as providing a change of career or a stimulus to move to another geographical area or country. Subjects report that clearly we can miss these signs, as no doubt many of us do, and that there may even be contingency plans to provide us with another chance for important interactions; but at the end of the day if we completely miss any given sign, life goes on but in a different direction from that originally planned, and we may fail to learn our chosen lessons as effectively as we had hoped.

After the recognition class, subjects are finally ready for rebirth into their chosen human body, and this process appears to be very similar to that experienced at death inasmuch as they describe travelling quickly down a dark tunnel. However there is little delay this time, and they suddenly find themselves in the womb. Apparently the process of assimilation with the human mind of the unborn child takes some time, and must be carefully handled. As to the timing of the incarnation, subjects report entering the child's body either only a few months into pregnancy or, in exceptional cases, leaving it to the last minute just before birth, although it seems this is not an ideal approach. Nevertheless, subjects report that they can 'absent' themselves from their host while still in the womb, and indeed for some years after birth, usually up until the time when the child goes to school and becomes more constantly active. They report that they stay in the astral plane of earth to be nearby in case of emergency, but one even describes these early years as the one time they can 'goof off' and just have fun with other souls without too much responsibility. However, they also report that a soul is never trapped in the body as such, and that it can leave even the body of an adult when they are sleeping or in deep meditation, or in more trying circumstances even when they are under anaesthetic or in coma.

CORROBORATION

I recommend that anyone should read the detailed transcripts in Newton's book. By contrast with regressions that concentrate on past lives only, the details of life in the ethereal realms provided by the 29 different subjects whose cases are discussed is incredibly consistent – and although he does not mention the total number of regressions of this type he has performed, it would appear from his commentary that these are only a small subset of a much larger number of similarly consistent cases. The transcripts themselves reveal just how remote is the possibility that all this information has either been concocted from the imaginations of the subjects themselves, or that Newton has fabricated the whole thing by leading his subjects on. He admits that he does do this deliberately on a few selected occasions in order to elicit particularly specific information, but this is rare, and in general the regularity with which they correct, scold or laugh at his lack of knowledge or perception is in my view more than sufficient to counteract any accusations of widespread subjective control on his part.

As for corroboration, a few of Stevenson's child subjects report conscious memories of their time in the ethereal realms, and the scant details are not inconsistent with those provided above.[15] However, I might conjecture that the lack of detail in and infrequency of these conscious memories is in part due to the general amnesia that seems to affect recall of the ethereal realms more than of past lives, even in children, and also to the fact that in these somewhat unusual cases the normal processes of amnesia seem to be disrupted – which may of itself be indicative of relatively immature or at least disturbed souls.

Far greater corroboration is, however, provided by Joel Whitton, a Toronto-based pioneer in life between lives regression who started work in this area in the mid-1970s. A qualified psychiatrist and hypnotherapist, he did initially specialise in past-life regression but, like Newton after him, stumbled on the existence of an 'interlife' by accident when he asked one of his subjects an imprecise question. He too became so engrossed in this aspect of regression that he decided to specialise in it, and the reports of his subjects in his 1986 compilation *Life Between Life* show great consistency with Newton's. Moreover, Newton does not make any mention of Whitton's earlier work, so if these two came to their research entirely separately this can only increase the extent of independent corroboration.

LOGISTICS

The final element of a spiritual worldview that is often raised is that of logistics. In particular, what is the source of souls when we have such a rapidly expanding human population on the planet? One way in which one could imagine such an increase being accommodated is by the principle that less-advanced souls that have incarnated previously as various types of animal could be promoted up the ranks, and not only is this idea part of most Eastern philosophies but it is also one that I have myself tended to favour in the past.

However, Newton's subjects seem unanimous that this is not how the logistics of soul progression work. They strongly assert that there are different types of soul, which seem to be created as required for the various broad categories such as plants, insects, reptiles and so on, and also of course for humans.[16] Consequently they report that population demands are not a major factor in decisions about the regularity with which we reincarnate, even though his statistics seem to indicate that the average gap between lives has reduced from hundreds or even thousands of years in the Middle and Upper Palaeolithic periods to just a few decades by the time of the twentieth century.[17]

This assertion has a number of major implications. First, it indicates that karmic development is not achieved by progressively incarnating in various plant and animal bodies before achieving human status, despite this being a fundamental tenet of Hindu and Buddhist thinking. The only rider to this is that it is possible the energy of the less-advanced souls of animals is actually used in the 'creation' of human souls, although Newton's subjects do not say as much and this is only a conjecture of my own, but even then from the sparse details they do provide it appears this process would not allow for the survival of the individual identity of the soul involved, so previous karmic experience would not be retained.[18] Second, and perhaps more important, it is clear from this – and indeed the subjects report explicitly – that human souls do *not* regress into animal forms as a punishment for regressive karma, as Hindus and Buddhists suggest.[19] Moreover, we have seen that the assertion of these religions that human physical disabilities represent punishments for wrongdoing in previous lives is similarly much too formulaic and simplistic, inasmuch as the subjects report that we deliberately choose these conditions of life for far more varied and complex reasons.[20] Indeed they may sometimes be seen as positively beneficial from the perspective of rapid karmic advancement, allowing a soul to learn clearly important lessons far faster than they otherwise might.[21] I can only reiterate that I am aware some of this may still be extremely sensitive for a number of people, even if less so than the conventional Eastern stance, but I can only hope that on proper reflection the idea we deliberately choose the circumstances of our lives both good and bad – and that no circumstances, however dire, are brought about as a direct punishment, or by arbitrary chance, or by divine whim – can be seen as immensely empowering and liberating.

Before we leave the issue of logistics there is one further major revelation from Newton's subjects that is perhaps startling at first sight, although it makes perfect sense when one considers it: and that is that there are myriads of souls that incarnate in other sometimes equally advanced life forms on other planets. After all, we are all aware of the overwhelming statistical likelihood that there exist planets orbiting other suns that would make perfectly suitable homes for other life forms; and it is surely philosophically inconceivable they would not have souls too. Moreover, the subjects report that human souls often gain their early karmic experience in such life forms, albeit ones of slightly lesser complexity than humans, although they normally remain attached to the realm of earth once they have been allocated to it. Many of the subjects discuss such incarnations on other planets, and they also consistently express the view that incarnation on earth in human form is one of the most testing of experiences, due to the complexity of the human condition especially in the modern world.[22]

CONCLUSION

I hope I have gone some way towards proving that my support for a spiritual worldview is based far more on practical evidence and philosophical logic than on 'blind faith' and a 'need to believe' – however frightening that possibility may be to the army of cynics, rationalists and atheists who dominate intellectual culture in the West, and love to belittle those who do not share their view.

Moreover, when we expand this worldview to include rather more complex and esoteric concepts in Part 3, we will find that further solid, objective, a priori reasons for supporting it come from the world of modern theoretical science.

I would recommend that anyone who remains sceptical of this worldview should go to the source and read Stevenson's and Newton's detailed case studies. And if scepticism remains even after that, I would pose a similar challenging question to that put by Stevenson above: 'What other phenomena do you think *could* explain so many children having memories of past lives they could not have gained in any normal way, and also so many adults having such vivid, consistent and detailed recall of their time in the ethereal realms?'

With that, we will now turn our attention to the ancient texts and traditions, and see how well a spiritual worldview serves our ability to interpret them properly. And what better place to start than with the biblical Genesis itself.

3. DEBASEMENT AND DESTRUCTION

The book of Genesis is the first book of the Torah, or Pentateuch, which itself constitutes the first five books of the biblical Old Testament and is traditionally attributed to the patriarch Moses himself. Scholars still cannot be sure of the identity of the authors of the books now handed down to us, but we do have access to several early Hebrew and Aramaic forerunners that were in circulation in the first half of the first millennium BC. These were compiled into the form with which we are all familiar some time around the turn of the third century BC.[1]

I indicated at the outset that I want to concentrate on the early chapters in Genesis that deal with the period between the creation of humankind and its destruction in the flood. The former event is now regarded as entirely fanciful, while the latter is seen by many as the point at which the text turns from myth to reality – and although some commentators suggest that the biblical and Mesopotamian flood traditions were likely to have been describing a merely localised and relatively recent event, in my view this argument is largely nullified by the similar catastrophe traditions that exist all over the world.[2] So what are we to make of the biblical account of what happened in between – the account that suggests humans lived in relatively civilised circumstances for a long time *before* the flood?

THE ANTEDILUVIAN PATRIARCHS

Ten antediluvian patriarchs are listed in the fifth chapter of Genesis. They are Adam, Seth, Enos, Cainan, Mahalaleel, Jared, Enoch, Methuselah, Lamech, and Noah; and they are given life spans of anywhere from 365 to 969 years. Even though these are clearly unrealistic, I was at first persuaded by the arguments of those revisionist authors who suggest that this list offers proof positive of a precatastrophe civilisation – especially given that it is similar to a number of older lists from ancient Mesopotamia, Egypt and China in particular. I even undertook a detailed analysis of the contents of all these so-called 'king lists' from the original sources, which was to form an early chapter of this work, because this information is rarely properly recorded.[3]

However, my research revealed the full scale of the problems with these lists, not least of which are the political and religious motives that may well have lain behind their compilation. As I was reminded by Garrett Fagan, a professor of ancient history at Penn State University:

> In every instance, to my knowledge, the lists start out with the gods. The lists then function to show (a) the antiquity of the regime or culture that composed them and (b) that regime or culture's direct connection with the gods. It is much harder to challenge a divinely ordained system than an admittedly human one.[4]

In my view this is certainly a plausible explanation as to why the antediluvian sections of the lists *may* have been fabricated, and accordingly I decided they do not provide *firm* evidence of a precatastrophe civilisation. But this is not the only textual evidence. There is much, much more, as we will shortly find out.

THE NEPHILIM REAPPRAISED

The first place we find such evidence is in the celebrated and rather more intriguing account of life before the flood in the very next chapter of Genesis:

> 1. And it came to pass, when men began to multiply on the face of the earth, and daughters were born unto them,
> 2. That the sons of God saw the daughters of men that they were fair; and they took them wives of all which they chose.
> 3. And the Lord said, My spirit shall not always strive with man, for that he also is flesh: yet his days shall be an hundred and twenty years.[5]
> 4. There were giants in the earth in those days; and also after that, when the sons of God came in unto the daughters of men, and they bare children to them, the same became mighty men which were of old, men of renown.
> 5. And God saw that the wickedness of man was great in the earth, and that every imagination of the thoughts of his heart was only evil continually.

6. And it repented the Lord that he had made man on the earth, and it grieved him at his heart.

7. And the Lord said, I will destroy man whom I have created from the face of the earth; both man, and beast, and the creeping thing, and the fowls of the air; for it repenteth me that I have made them.

8. But Noah found grace in the eyes of the Lord.

Who were these 'sons of God', and their 'giant' offspring? Are they mere fictional creations of an earlier age? Or was there really a race of culturally advanced humans who lived in a remote time before a great catastrophe wiped them out?

The Hebrew word for these biblical giants is *Nephilim*, while their progenitors, the 'sons of God', are normally referred to as the Watchers because of the way they are described in the celebrated *Book of Enoch*. We will examine this text in detail shortly, because it holds many clues to their identities. However, perhaps more than any other biblical characters apart from Jesus himself, these enigmatic figures have fired the imagination of a whole host of theologians, artists and poets down through the ages – as well as, more recently, a host of revisionist historians. And before I launch my own attempt to find out who they were and what they signified, I must identify why, in my view, other attempts have failed to do them justice.

It would be impossible in the space available, and in any case somewhat tedious and unedifying, to catalogue the entirety of the theories about the Watchers and the Nephilim. What I can do, however, is identify the main schools of thought and their main proponents.

Ignoring the theological explanations for the moment, there are really two that have sprung up in the modern era. The first, and probably most widely publicised, is the 'Ancient Astronaut' school. Although a number of lesser-known writers had gone down this road in the preceding decades, it was Erich von Däniken who really captured the public's imagination in 1969 when *Chariots of the Gods* was published for the first time in English. It perfectly reflected the anti-Establishment spirit of the age, and became an overnight and huge success. He did not specifically mention the Nephilim, but he certainly examined some of the relevant Enochian and Mesopotamian literature, provocatively asking, 'Does not this seriously pose the question whether the human race is not an act of deliberate "breeding" by unknown beings from outer space?'[6] I said in my introduction that I owe a great debt to various of my predecessors in the revisionist movement, and nowhere is this more true than in the case of von Däniken, whose books I read eagerly as a young teenager. I only found out much later that when his work was put under the spotlight it was revealed to be riddled with holes. A fine example was his suggestion that one part of the infamous Nazca lines in Peru, an enigma he admittedly did much to put on the map, were 'reminiscent of the aircraft parking bays of a modern airport' – when any serious student of the lines has always known full well that most of them, including the pictorial example he was describing, form huge drawings of various animals, birds and insects. Admittedly these can only really be appreciated from the air, and they do remain something of an enigma, but aircraft runways they are not. Meanwhile other questions – for instance, 'Why should ancient gods be associated with the stars?' – only served to indicate that his understanding of myth and symbolism was not everything it might be.[7]

After a few rather less impressive sequels, von Däniken disappeared amid typical allegations of a conspiracy to silence him. However, the public imagination had been fired. Into the fray stepped Zecharia Sitchin, who rocketed to fame in 1976 with *The Twelfth Planet*, then followed it up with a number of sequels to form his *Earth Chronicles* series. He *was* intrigued by the Nephilim specifically, and proposed that they were a race of high-longevity beings, originating from a now-unknown planet in our solar system with a highly eccentric orbit, that came to earth and genetically engineered the human race – the latter aspect giving rise to that special breed within the Ancient Astronaut school known as 'Interventionism', while also having clear echoes of von Däniken that Sitchin does not appear to acknowledge.[8]

Sitchin, too, attracted a huge, worldwide army of fanatical supporters who regard him as nothing less than a guru, and I must admit it was his work that to a large extent reignited my own interest in revisionist theories when I decided to forsake my commercial career and pursue my own research full time in the mid-1990s. I can only reiterate that both he and von Däniken should be commended for exciting the interest of a great many people – myself included – in ancient texts, monuments, artwork and artefacts of which we would perhaps otherwise have remained largely ignorant. Nevertheless, I would be in dereliction of my own duty to the future of the revisionist movement if I failed to point out that Sitchin's scholarship has proved no more reliable than von Däniken's, to such an extent that his translations and interpretations of many texts – especially those of ancient Mesopotamia – can arguably only be viewed as entertaining fiction. There is much evidence to suggest that they reveal a fundamental lack of knowledge not only of basic Sumerian and Akkadian grammar and linguistics, but also, once again, of mythological symbolism.[9] Unfortunately, this has not stopped others following Sitchin's lead and using his work to develop further ill-founded theories. The process continues to this day, with authors who should know better still referencing his work without checking it.[10]

In my view the result has been that a large proportion of the substantial worldwide readership of these revisionist 'classics' has been presented with a false understanding of our prehistory. I should emphasise that, while I do not regard the Ancient Astronaut or even Interventionist hypotheses as inherently implausible, I do believe the evidence used to develop them has been misinterpreted and distorted, and these are issues to which we will return in Part 2. In any case, arguably none of this would matter much were it not for the fact that these theories tend to suggest that humankind is under the control of an extraterrestrial master race rather than masters of our *own* fate. Indeed, supporters of these hypotheses have often taken offence at my relatively outspoken attacks thereon, but in my view this is a matter of the utmost importance, and such a pervasive influence is not easily dislodged. Furthermore, any body of work that is at least in part based on such an unscholarly approach has provided an easy target for the Establishment, and helped to blacken the name of revisionist historical research in general. Nevertheless, it is my fervent hope that one of the outcomes from the present work will be to help set the record straight, and to establish that there *is* scope for constructive reappraisal of certain aspects of the ancient texts.

One author who has done more than most to restore a decent standard of scholarship to the revisionist movement is Andrew

Collins, and his excellent 1996 study *From the Ashes of Angels* is the prime source for the other main school of thought concerning the Watchers and Nephilim. In short, he suggests that these were flesh-and-blood beings, not of extraterrestrial origin, but remnants of a more advanced culture that migrated from Egypt around 9000 BC and introduced civilisation to areas of Anatolia and Kurdistan, from where it spread in due course throughout Mesopotamia. Collins develops a highly convincing argument, but in my view there are a number of problems with it.

The first is that, although his thorough analysis of the development of civilisation in the Near East cannot be faulted, his suggestion that the cause was the migration of an Egyptian 'elder culture' is founded on what, in my view, is a mistaken analysis of the age of the Great Sphinx of Giza and its associated temples. While this monument may indeed be older than the current orthodoxy suggests, in my view it is not of the antiquity originally suggested by Collins.[11] Of course, in making this assumption he was only working from the theories of fellow researchers John Anthony West, Graham Hancock and Robert Bauval, all of whom are prime movers in that section of the revisionist movement that postulates the existence of prior civilisations of great antiquity, primarily from the same evidence of supposedly advanced technology first brought to our attention by the Ancient Astronaut and Interventionist schools – coupled with attempts to redate monuments such as the Sphinx to a much earlier time. However, these affiliates of the 'Redating' school differ in that they do not postulate an extraterrestrial origin for this prior civilisation. As I have noted, I believe that to a large extent these researchers are coming at the problem from the wrong angle; in my view an emphasis on technology and redating is not the answer. We will examine these issues in more detail in Part 2, but for the time being we should note that this approach has not, so far, produced the incontrovertible evidence that would prove once and for all that there once existed a civilisation of great antiquity and high technological advancement on earth.

In any case, Collins is not exactly a fully paid-up member of this school, and tends to pay careful attention to what the texts themselves reveal – an approach that in general I clearly support – so his views on the Watchers and Nephilim are well worth exploring, even if I do not necessarily agree with his 'out of Egypt' hypothesis. He argues that these people were of different physical appearance, taller than the indigenous Near Easterners who encountered them, with elongated heads, emasculated white faces, narrow slitlike eyes and long white hair – although exactly where this racial type is supposed to have originated is never made clear, and it is certainly not indigenous to Egypt or the Near East. He further suggests that they were primarily a shamanic people that identified with the vulture, serpent and goat and wore long robes made of feathers; and that the cause of their supposed fall and subsequent demonisation was that certain of their number left their isolated enclave in the Kurdish mountains to live among the indigenous people of the surrounding plains, where they took wives and taught the more advanced aspects of their culture. This included not only the usual subjects of astronomy, metalworking and so on, but also more esoteric wisdom such as the use of a 'wonder drug' that could prolong life.

Even if we ignore this last somewhat Sitchinesque interpretation of the texts, another flaw in this argument seems to be the logic behind the demonisation of those who left the enclave. Although those who apparently remained in splendid isolation in the mountains might have had cause to disapprove of their secrets being taught to the locals, it was not them but instead these very indigenous peoples who would have developed the mythology surrounding the incomers. Furthermore, even if originally their sporadic trading appearances brought a degree of terror at their strange features, appearance and size, their eventual cultural gifts to the locals, and the apparently complete intermingling and acceptance that would have been necessary for their continued presence over several millennia, would surely have ensured that any mythology connected with them was positive rather than negative. Moreover, Collins' attempts to associate them with vampirism go completely against the grain of their necessary assimilation into the indigenous culture.

Perhaps a rather more important issue is that, in order to develop a logical chronology, Collins attempts to overcome the problem of the texts clearly stating that the Watchers and Nephilim lived *before* the flood by postulating *two* floods: a devastating one at the end of the last ice age circa 9000 BC that caused the migration out of Egypt, although it remains unclear why such a migration was necessary; and another localised one circa 5000 BC, which is the one Noah survived, albeit Collins does have the courage to admit there is no evidence for a single Mesopotamian flood of any ferocity at this time.[12]

Still, even if we allow this escape route, perhaps the most serious problem with Collins' argument seems to me to be the clear existence, in these Near Eastern traditions and in all the others from around the world, of the theme of the *debasement* of a forgotten race that resulted in its destruction. Although he briefly discusses the catastrophe traditions that exist in other parts of the world, and links them to the end of the last ice age, he does not properly acknowledge this associated theme of debasement which, to me, lies at the heart of a proper understanding of the Watchers and Nephilim.

Of course it is possible there are two sets of traditions regarding the Watchers and Nephilim in the Near Eastern texts – one a more recent theme of postcatastrophe survivors from elsewhere who did dominate life in the area for several millennia, the other a more original theme of precatastrophe debasement – and that the two have become jumbled together. If this is the case, then our two approaches are not incompatible. Be that as it may, and as much as I admire Collins' work and approach, I believe we have to look farther beneath the surface to appreciate the true original message of these texts.

A TALE OF TWO CITIES

One clue to what is going on in Genesis 6 lies in a less frequently discussed preceding passage. The first two chapters describe God's creation of the world, of all animals, and of Adam and Eve, while the third deals with the latter's 'first fall', having tasted the forbidden fruit in Eden, and their expulsion from it. The early part of the fourth chapter commences with the birth of their first two sons, Cain the shepherd and Abel the farmer, and describes how the former slew the latter in a jealous rage, for which he was rejected by God and banished to the 'land of Nod', east of Eden. And now we get to the heart of the matter, because the remainder of the chapter is devoted to a genealogy of *Cain's* descendants, who, although their life spans are not given, are named as Enoch,

Irad, Mehujael, Methusael, Lamech, and his sons Jabal, Jubal, and Tubalcain – although it is quite clear that *this* Enoch and Lamech are not the same as the celebrated patriarchs descended from Seth as listed in Genesis 5. Furthermore, we are told briefly that Cain built a city, which he named after his son Enoch, and that Lamech, like his forefather, was guilty of murder.[13]

So here we have another line of preflood ancestors, appearing to have coexisted with the line descending from Adam via his last son, Seth, who we might regard as a replacement for the murdered Abel. Moreover, it is clear that Cain's line was damned as evil and murderous, while Seth's was regarded as God-fearing and righteous. In fact, the first-century historian Flavius Josephus, in his *Ancient History of the Jews*, provides more useful details.[14] He describes how Cain 'built a city named Nod', and 'only aimed to procure every thing that was for his own bodily pleasure', becoming 'a great leader of men into wicked courses'. Even more intriguingly, we find that:

He also introduced a change in that way of simplicity wherein men had lived before; and was the author of measures and weights. And whereas they lived innocently and generously while they knew nothing of such arts, he changed the world in to cunning craftiness.

The venerated Saint Augustine's fourth-century biblical commentary, *The City of God*, provides a further useful insight into the sparse Genesis narrative:

When the human race, in the exercise of this freedom of will, increased and advanced, there arose a mixture and confusion of the two cities by their participation in a common iniquity. And this calamity, as well as the first, was occasioned by woman, though not in the same way; for these women were not themselves betrayed, neither did they persuade the men to sin, but having belonged to the earthly city and society of the earthly, they had been of corrupt manners from the first, and were loved for their bodily beauty by the sons of God, or the citizens of the other city which sojourns in this world.[15]

The explanation for God's wrath and his decision to destroy humankind in Genesis 6 is therefore shown to have arisen because what was originally a 'godly' and simple race, here represented by Seth's descendants, appears to have been gradually perverted and swallowed up by a far more materialistic and decadent race, the descendants of Cain. Can we shed any more light on the underlying causes and significance of this 'second fall'? And on why the early Christian Church decided to massively edit and condense the more comprehensive Judaic material that so obviously must have existed at the time?

FORGOTTEN SPIRITUAL ROOTS

To answer these questions, we must examine the *Book of Enoch*, which, as I have already suggested, contains far fuller details of the passage in Genesis 6. Attributed to the enigmatic preflood patriarch, it is impossible for us to say with any certainty when this book was originally compiled. It is thoroughly proven that a version of it was regarded as part of the genuine divine revelation of early Judaism.[16] However, just as with the discovery of the Dead Sea Scrolls of the curious Essene community in various caves at Qumran in 1947, its clearly messianic content – which apparently predated the birth of Jesus – rendered it something of an embarrassment to the founders of the Christian Church.[17]

Moreover, there were perhaps even stronger reasons for the *Book of Enoch* to be omitted from the Old Testament. Saint Augustine reported that it was of 'great antiquity', and went on to suggest that this 'brought it under suspicion' because it was 'impossible to ascertain whether these were Enoch's genuine writings'.[18] Moreover, there are those who suggest that, despite the obvious Judaic distortions in the version we now have, it is indeed of great antiquity; so great that it contains information originally recorded before the flood, and therefore represents one of the best surviving records of preflood history, at least in the public domain. We might also note that the figure of Enoch exerted a huge influence on the development of Masonic tradition. We will return to all of these issues later.

In any case, by the fourth century, instead of being given canonical status by the Christian church, this book was rejected as part of the Apocrypha – and it is a supreme irony that this

Greek-derived word actually means 'something that is *hidden*'. What we also know is that, as a result of this deliberate prejudice, the text remained largely unknown in the West for more than fifteen hundred years. Then three manuscripts were discovered in Ethiopia in 1773 by James Bruce who, along with his more famous ancestor Robert, was a leading Scottish Freemason, and had almost certainly gone looking for it quite deliberately. Even then, however, the main public copy lay forgotten in the Bodleian Library in Oxford until 1821, when Archbishop Richard Laurence translated it into English for the first time, at which point this long-hidden text immediately caused a sensation.

So what are the explosive secrets within the text that have generated so much controversy? Because it is so important, and because I am ever wary of the distortions that can arise when extracts are paraphrased, I will take the liberty of reproducing the most relevant verses in full. Let us start with the seventh chapter:

1. It happened after the sons of men had multiplied in those days, that daughters were born to them, elegant and beautiful.
2. And when the angels, the sons of heaven, beheld them, they became enamoured of them, saying to each other, Come, let us select for ourselves wives from the progeny of men, and let us beget children.
3. Then their leader Samyaza said to them; I fear that you may perhaps be indisposed to the performance of this enterprise;
4. And that I alone shall suffer for so grievous a crime.
5. But they answered him and said; We all swear;
6. And bind ourselves by mutual execrations, that we will not change our intention, but execute our projected undertaking.
7. Then they swore all together, and all bound themselves by mutual execrations. Their whole number was two hundred, who descended upon Ardis, which is the top of mount Armon.
8. That mountain therefore was called Armon, because they had sworn upon it, and bound themselves by mutual execrations.
9. These are the names of their chiefs: Samyaza, who was their leader, Urakabarameel, Akibeel, Tamiel, Ramuel, Danel, Azkeel, Saraknyal, Asael, Armers, Batraal, Anane, Zavebe,

Samsaveel, Ertael, Turel, Yomyael, Arazyal. These were the prefects of the two hundred angels, and the remainder were all with them.

10. Then they took wives, each choosing for himself; whom they began to approach, and with whom they cohabited; teaching them sorcery, incantations, and the dividing of roots and trees.

11. And the women conceiving brought forth giants,

12. Whose stature was each three hundred cubits. These devoured all which the labour of men produced; until it became impossible to feed them;

13. When they turned themselves against men, in order to devour them;

14. And began to injure birds, beasts, reptiles, and fishes, to eat their flesh one after another, and to drink their blood.

15. Then the earth reproved the unrighteous.[19]

And the following chapter continues the theme:

1. Moreover Azazyel taught men to make swords, knives, shields, breastplates, the fabrication of mirrors, and the workmanship of bracelets and ornaments, the use of paint, the beautifying of the eyebrows, the use of stones of every valuable and select kind, and of all sorts of dyes, so that the world became altered.

2. Impiety increased; fornication multiplied; and they transgressed and corrupted all their ways.

3. Amazarak taught all the sorcerers, and dividers of roots:

4. Armers taught the solution of sorcery;

5. Barkayal taught the observers of the stars;

6. Akibeel taught signs;

7. Tamiel taught astronomy;

8. And Asaradel taught the motion of the moon.

9. And men, being destroyed, cried out; and their voice reached to heaven.[20]

There are sufficient similarities between this and the parallel biblical passage in Genesis 6 that there can be little doubt they share a common origin, except this time those who err are described as 'angels' or 'sons of heaven' rather than 'sons of God'. Theological commentators down the ages have interpreted both versions to mean that the angels, who were normally incorporeal beings, took some sort of temporary physical form in order to consort with the daughters of men. This idea is in some senses an attempt at the spiritual solution that, as I indicated in my introduction, I believe is appropriate. It is somewhat impractically 'religious', however, and not philosophically logical. By contrast, the flesh-and-blood human being approach is also close to the truth, but in my view ignores the fundamental spirituality of the message. After much careful study, it has become clear to me that there is an interpretation of these Judaeo-Christian passages that properly recognises the spiritual message without the need to resort to philosophically illogical concepts and phenomena.

Perhaps the most obvious and practical clue to this enigma lies in the meaning of the original Hebrew word used for these angels. On the one hand it can be translated as 'those who watch', and this correlates with the word used in the Greek versions of these texts that is now translated as 'Watchers'. It is, of course, this translation on which most other commentators have concentrated. However, as Collins himself points out – although it is an idea that he does not develop – the other translation of the word is 'those who are awake'.[21] As soon as I saw this it put me on the alert, because it is clear to me that this seems to imply some sort of special *awareness* on the part of the angels.

So, looking at these extracts in the light of the spiritual worldview I elucidated in the previous chapter, I believe we have a number of separate themes that have been somewhat distorted, condensed and interwoven. If my analysis initially appears a little confusing, I can only ask that I am indulged for a while because it will be considerably clarified and strengthened in the remainder of this and subsequent chapters dealing with the similar traditions from other parts of the globe. On the one hand, we have in the final verses of Enoch 7 and the opening ones of Enoch 8 a clear echo of the debasement theme we have already encountered in the biblical commentaries, which this time not only includes rampant materialism but also excessive fornication and impiety of all kinds. There are other confusing elements in these verses, but we will return to them shortly.

On the other hand, we have in the earlier verses of chapter seven a fuller description of the biblical passages concerning the angels deciding to take 'wives from among the progeny of men'. And it appears from the Enochian version that there was some consternation among the angels *themselves* about this approach. In fact, we find more details in another version of the *Book of Enoch* found in Slavonic Russia.[22] It seems to suggest that there were two or even three groups of 'fallen angels', and that they 'fell' at different times and suffered different fates.[23] Although myriad interpretations have been placed on these passages, I propose that they only make any sense at all if we bring a spiritual worldview into play.

We have already seen that under this worldview at least all animate things have a soul of sorts, with the human soul being more advanced than that of any other animal, whatever our current and past shortcomings. And yet, I accept that we evolved from our ape cousins. So it would appear logical that, as part of the genus *Homo*, we must somehow have acted as a receptacle for progressively more advanced souls as we evolved. So what if, at some point in our evolution, the human species appeared ready to receive at least some incarnating souls with a hitherto unmatched degree of karmic advancement? Souls that were waiting in the ethereal wings for that time to arrive? Souls that could be readily described as of more 'angelic' quality, and with a special 'awareness'? Moreover, what if they were unsure about the timing of their incarnations? What if they could not be sure that if they incarnated in human form too early they might not suffer some form of 'karmic damage'?

All this may sound a little far-fetched at first sight, but in fact it does make a high degree of logical sense, and such an interpretation is backed up significantly by other non-Judaic traditions, as we will see in a later chapter. Viewed in this light, this aspect of the 'fallen angel' theme should not be regarded as negative at all, except inasmuch as there may have been a degree of disagreement as to the timing of their 'fall' into incarnation. In fact, the combination of the mass incarnation of *relatively* advanced 'human' souls accompanied by selective incarnations of *seriously* advanced 'angelic' souls would surely have had just about the most explosive impact on human cultural evolution that it has ever received. And the later verses of the Enochian extracts above are indeed interspersed with descriptions of the angels educating others in the fields of technology, astronomy, astrology, divination, and magical practices generally, albeit that they are here confused with the subsequent debasement of the 'real' fall. But the positive theme of 'divine beings' that teach the 'arts of civilisation' and reveal various other 'secret' knowledge to humankind is widespread in other traditions that we will consider in more detail in the next chapter.

Meanwhile, although the Judaic texts themselves are not explicit on this issue, we have seen clues in Josephus' commentaries, for example, that this education process appears to have initially produced a 'golden race' with a high degree of spiritual awareness – and we will encounter far more evidence to support this notion in a later chapter. It is precisely this that allows me to assert that our antediluvian ancestors eventual debasement, or genuine 'fall', not only involved an excessive focus on the material world, which would be of no great consequence if there were nothing else of importance, but a simultaneous loss of the spiritual worldview with which they had originally been imbued – indeed to such an extent that only a few remembered, appreciated and honoured the real truth about their spiritual roots, and about the whole nature and philosophy of existence. And, moreover, it allows me to assert that as a race we have previously faced exactly the same crisis of spirituality against materiality that we face now at the beginning of the twenty-first century.

But did this process really bring about the destruction of our forgotten race? And could the same fate befall us again?

KARMIC CATASTROPHE

In the tenth chapter of the Ethiopian version of the *Book of Enoch* the flood tradition emerges for the first time.[24] It starts with God instructing an angel to visit 'the son of Lamech' – that is, Noah – to warn him of the deluge that is about to occur.[25] However, displaying a clear combination of at least two original sources, it then goes on to explain how the fallen angels and their offspring are to be slaughtered one way or another. It is clear that in this latter section no universal obliteration is intended – indeed, the text explicitly states that 'all the sons of men shall not perish' – and there is certainly no mention of a deluge.[26]

This confusion is in fact found throughout the text. In a much later chapter Enoch himself has a vision of the earth sinking into a great abyss, and as a result begs God 'that a posterity may be left to me on earth, and that the whole human race may not perish'.[27] This is clearly Enoch speaking, and, while the word *abyss* is used, there is no direct mention of a flood. Is this somehow a distorted echo of an earlier destruction separate from the more celebrated flood? This prospect is perhaps increased when, in another chapter, we find Enoch reporting the following:

6. For I know, that oppression will exist and prevail on earth; that on earth great punishment shall in the end take place; and that there shall be a consummation of all iniquity, which shall be cut off from its root, and every fabric raised by it shall pass away. Iniquity, however, shall again be renewed, and consummated on earth. Every act of crime, and every act of oppression and impiety, shall be a second time embraced. 7. When therefore iniquity, sin, blasphemy, tyranny, and every evil work, shall increase, and when transgression, impiety, and uncleanness also shall increase, then upon them all shall great punishment be inflicted from heaven.[28]

If this were Enoch speaking in his own time – whenever that might have been – he could be 'foreseeing' one destruction in the near future and another farther away.[29] Perhaps his second predicted destruction is one that is yet to be visited on humankind? Still, we should not become too carried away with the possibility of multiple destructions, because the various Enochian manuscripts contain so many variations of themes and contradictions, proving that they are clearly composite creations from other earlier sources, that to be unduly pedantic in interpretation is a mistake. This confusion is compounded by the fact that the tenses are often confused, and that we are often skipping between prophetic visions and historical events. There are also suggestions that Enoch may actually represent a *generic* name for a multitude of different seers, in which case not all references may be to the same person.

Nevertheless, there is one other revealing aspect of the Ethiopian text, and that is the phenomenon of the flood catastrophe itself. Our first clue is that, after one brief description of the flood, God repents and swears that he will never act in the same way again – at which point he says that he will 'place a sign in the heavens' as a token of his covenant, a theme that is possibly repeated in more veiled terms in Genesis itself.[30] Can this mean that in some way the sky was altered after the flood? Another chapter contains a most intriguing description of how Noah saw that 'the earth became inclined, and that destruction approached', and then that 'the earth laboured, and was violently shaken', and of how God reports that 'respecting the moons have they [humankind] inquired, and they have known that the earth will perish'.[31] Are these descriptions of some sort of catastrophic axial tilt of the earth that would cause all heavenly bodies to shift in the sky? And if, for example, this were caused by the impact of an extraterrestrial body, would it be possible that humankind had some sort of advance warning?

This is not all. Even more enigmatic descriptions are provided in another chapter: 'In the days of sinners the years shall be shortened . . . the rain shall be restrained, and heaven shall stand still . . . the moon shall change its laws, and not be seen at its proper period . . . many chiefs among the stars of authority shall err, perverting their ways and works . . . all the classes of the stars shall be shut up against sinners.'[32]

This is persuasive stuff, and we will return to the potential nature of the catastrophes that may have affected our planet in the past in Part 2. But for the moment, we should concentrate on the implications of these passages. On the face of it, if we can prove that the catastrophe described in traditions throughout the globe was the result of a natural phenomenon, the idea that it was divinely inspired seems preposterous. But perhaps it is not that simple? What if we accept, as surely we should if we hold with the spiritual worldview I have already outlined, that karma operates not only on an individual level but also on a more universal level – of, for example, the human race as a whole? Surely we could then assume that the widespread debasement of our forgotten race would have had a karmic effect on them as a whole? And if we can, then I would argue that – however natural the agent – it was the laws of universal karma that dictated they should perish en masse, as a race, forcing the rebuilding and re-emergence of a new race that could either learn the lessons from the mistakes of the past, or choose to repeat them.

Now this argument is central to my main concern in this work – the concern that universal karma could once again play a hand, given the complete loss of spirituality and obsession with all things material that we as the human race have once again allowed to develop. If there were strong arguments that the previous catastrophe was *not* karmically driven, then my suggestion that it has implications for the present would be invalidated. So, despite the fact that my argument is, I trust, philosophically logical if one accepts the spiritual precepts on which it is based, are there any such counterarguments? I can think of several, and I will deal with each in turn.

The first possibility is that such worldwide catastrophes have repeatedly ravaged the earth, even if only the most recent one affected the modern human race. We will discover in Part 2 that there is good evidence to suggest this is indeed the case. Does that mean they have all been karmically driven? I cannot properly answer that, except to say that to a large extent my worldview suggests that pretty much all events – whether on an individual or more universal scale – happen for a karmic reason, even if we do not always understand the dynamics at the time. Who knows, perhaps the powers that be did not want another planet dominated by a predominantly lizard species such as the dinosaurs?

The second possibility is that not only have such catastrophes occurred repeatedly during the life of our planet, but that they occur at regular intervals. Were this to be the case, it would be hard to argue that they were karmically driven, especially because – and this is a crucial point that is often misunderstood – karma involves choice and *not* predestiny. But, as we will see when we examine these issues in more detail later, in my view there is no scientific or philosophical reason to believe that *worldwide* catastrophes occur on earth with *cyclical* regularity.

The final possibility – which will undoubtedly occur to anyone of a more rationalist persuasion who struggles to accept a spiritual worldview at all – is that even if the most recent catastrophe did occur, and did wipe out the bulk of the human population, the simplistic reaction of the survivors would be to assume that their forebears had done something wrong for the 'gods' to want to inflict such serious punishment. This would indeed be a plausible suggestion were it not for the more general context of the worldwide traditions. As we will shortly see, many of the descriptions of the golden race *before* the catastrophe, handed down by survivors long *after* the catastrophe, are so clearly full of spiritual insight that this explanation, which relies on them being rather stupid, makes no sense either. This view is supported by the impressively esoteric descriptions of the origins of the world that are included in many of the same traditions, as we will see in Part 3. And we will also see in a later chapter that, for example, the eminent Greek philosopher Plato fully supported a spiritual interpretation of the catastrophe; are we to suppose that a man of his intellect would unquestioningly adopt such a simplistic approach?

Overall then, I maintain there is still good reason to suggest that the last worldwide catastrophe was a karmically driven event – provided, of course, one accepts a spiritual worldview in the first place. And, the *Book of Enoch* having provided so much food for thought, let us now go in search of other texts that support the theme of the debasement and destruction of a forgotten race.

GNOSTIC REVELATIONS

Staying with the Near East, significant support for our interpretation of the biblical and Enochian texts is provided in the Gnostic literature. The Gnostics were a separate sect that had their roots in both Judaism and Christianity, but had broken away to plough a lone furrow, much like the Essenes. The largest source of their traditions is a cache of scrolls found buried in a jar in Nag Hammadi, Upper Egypt, in 1945, in circumstances somewhat reminiscent of the discovery of the Dead Sea Scrolls. It is comprised of 52 tractates, some of which are duplicates, all in Coptic script – Egyptian written in the Greek alphabet – but clearly translations from Greek originals, and the texts as we have them date to the middle of the fourth century.[33]

We will examine the general nature of these texts in more detail in Part 3, but the most crucial passage for our current purposes is from the *Apocryphon of John*, which describes the behaviour of the fallen angels thus:

> They brought gold and silver and a gift and copper and iron and metal and all kinds of things. And they steered the people who had followed them into great troubles, by leading them astray with many deceptions. They became old without having enjoyment. They died, not having found truth and without

knowing the God of truth. And thus the whole creation became enslaved forever, from the foundation of the world until now. And they took women and begot children out of the darkness according to the likeness of their spirit. And they closed their hearts, and they hardened themselves through the hardness of the counterfeit spirit until now.[34]

We can see that this time there is no mention of giants being created, and the message of debasement through materialism and of generations cut off from any knowledge of their spiritual roots comes across loud and clear. However, the distorted notion that somehow angels themselves were responsible for the fall into debasement remains, and I can only re-emphasise that in my view, to the extent they were involved, it was only as the angelic souls whose initial fall into incarnation allowed the education of other newly incarnating human souls to create the golden race. That this race that eventually became debased should be described as angels themselves strikes me as misleading, although we can perhaps understand how their long-lasting reputation for being originally highly spiritual might have led to such a confusion. And, of course, what makes matters more confusing is that once again the Gnostic traditions omit the entire golden race aspect.

By way of addition, this text also explicitly states that the account of the flood in Genesis is wrong, and that there were multiple survivors:

It is not as Moses said, 'They hid themselves in an ark', but they hid themselves in a place, not only Noah but also many other people from the immovable race.[35]

We can see from this, however, that rather than the following of a spiritual path being a matter of personal choice for each individual, the Judaic concept of a chosen or 'immovable' race pitted against an evil one until the day of reckoning, both maintained by heredity, remains fundamental in Gnostic literature.[36] And we all know how destructive such a view can be.

THE NOISE OF HUMANKIND

The most obvious place to continue our quest is ancient Mesopotamia, originally located between the Tigris and Euphrates rivers in what is now modern-day Iraq. The Sumerian civilisation first developed here in the latter half of the fifth millennium BC, more than a thousand years before the dynastic era commenced in ancient Egypt at the beginning of the third millennium BC, and it revolved around city-states with advanced religious, political and legal systems. The Sumerians dominated the region for several millennia, but increasing political upheaval meant their power was eventually usurped, first by the Akkadians in about 2300 BC, and more conclusively by the Assyrians, who established their capital at Babylon in about 1750 BC.

From around the middle of the nineteenth century the diligent efforts of numerous explorers and archaeologists – Paul Emil Botta, Sir Austen Henry Layard, Stephen Langdon and Sir Leonard Woolley notable among them – led to the unearthing of the ruins of Mesopotamian cities such as Eridu, Nippur, Lagash, Uruk, Shuruppak, Ashur, Ur, Babylon and Nineveh. Not only did these excavations confirm that a number of biblical sites previously thought to be fictitious were real, but they also unearthed a plethora of clay tablets inscribed with a variety of scripts.

With incredible dedication, scholars including Sir Henry Rawlinson, Edward Hincks and Julius Oppert set about deciphering the various Mesopotamian scripts that, broadly speaking, commenced with Sumerian pictographics and progressed to Sumerian and finally Akkadian cuneiform, named after its distinctive wedge-shaped characters. Ultimately a multitude of fragmented tablets were diligently reassembled, producing translations of a huge variety of texts. These encompass not only the fascinating literary texts that are normally divided into the 'myths' of the gods and 'legends' of the epic heroes, but also more historical or administrative texts, such as votive inscriptions detailing a ruler's major achievements, law codes, court decisions and royal letters.[37] Moreover, for the first time scholars uncovered texts that were clearly the precursors to many biblical traditions.

The numerous literary works contain a plethora of gods, referred to collectively as the Anunnaki or sometimes Igigi. The chief members of the original Sumerian pantheon were An (Anu in Akkadian texts), residing in heaven; Enlil (Ellil), the chief god of the earth often portrayed, especially in later texts, as somewhat harsh on humankind, and also associated with air; Enki (Ea), who is usually represented as the god who brought civilisation to humankind, and associated with water; Ninhursag (Ninmah), the Mother Earth goddess; Inanna (Ishtar), the goddess of love; Nanna (Sin), the moon god; Utu (Shamash), the sun god; Ninurta (Ningirsu), the war god; Ishkur (Adad), the storm god; and Nergal (Erra), the plague god and ruler of the underworld, and his consort Ereshkigal. Remember, however, that as in many other ancient cultures these names changed over time, and in later Akkadian texts in particular we often find localised gods elevated to the main pantheon in certain areas. A case in point is the relatively late emergence of the pre-eminent Babylonian god Marduk.[38]

As for the nature of the Mesopotamian texts, as a broad generalisation they tend to emphasise the warriorlike nature of the patriarchal society that developed them, and are full of descriptions of ferocious battles involving gods and heroes. But this is not to say they do not have their more subtle side as well.

For our current purposes there are three main texts that include the flood tradition. The most detailed is the Akkadian *Atrahasis*, the oldest version of which is thought to date to circa 1700 BC, and is named after the text's flood hero. It contains themes repeated throughout Mesopotamian literature, and is composed of three tablets. The first describes how the gods rebelled against their excessive workload in digging and maintaining the irrigation canals that were so fundamental to the area; how they asked that humans be created to assist them; and how their request was granted. This all takes place in a clearly mythical epoch that has little relevance to the current inquiry, although I will return to it in a later chapter. The second tablet goes on to describe how the new creations proliferate, but Enlil protests that 'the noise of humankind has become too much', so he sends first a plague of sickness, then a drought – towards the end of which the people are so hungry they resort to cannibalism – and then, when neither appears to work, he decides to destroy humankind in its entirety with a flood. The third tablet, meanwhile, describes how Enki warns Atrahasis of the impending flood and how to survive it; the flood itself; and finally the argument and subsequent *rapprochement* between Enlil and Enki when the former finds out that Atrahasis and his family have survived.[39]

It is really only the second tablet that interests us here, but even then there is no real useful information about life before the flood.

Meanwhile, the message we find repeatedly in these texts – that the reason for the flood was that humankind made too much *noise* – is confusing to say the least. I can only assume that in some sense it is consistent with the theme that humankind was becoming more degenerate. Indeed, a clue may lie in Enki telling the people 'not to revere their gods' in response to the plague and drought, which could be a distortion of the fact that in an earlier tradition this was exactly why divine retribution was felt to be justified. However, I am clearly straying into conjecture here.

Another text that contains a description of the flood is the *Eridu Genesis*, and although the earliest version we have is thought to date to only around 1600 BC, it is written in Sumerian script and is therefore likely to be of earlier provenance. We find that although the surviving text is far more fragmented and as a result shorter than *Atrahasis*, its tone is quite similar, with the hero here being called Ziusudra.[40] Again, however, there is little of interest that survives about why the flood was sent or about life before it – other than a brief description of the building of the early cities of Eridu, Bad-Tibira, Larak, Sippar, and Shuruppak, as if they had been constructed *before* the flood. This suggests either that this aspect of the account is fictitious, or that the flood described was only a local and relatively recent event that has been confused with a more widespread, earlier event.

The other main text to mention the flood in any detail is the Akkadian *Epic of Gilgamesh*, although it is known that this lengthy text is to some extent a composite of a number of Sumerian originals. The flood story is recounted to Gilgamesh by its main survivor – this time called Utnapishtim – in the first part of the eleventh tablet, and again, although it is broadly similar to the other accounts, it contains little relevant information concerning the time before the flood.[41]

So far, apart from a clear flood tradition and a vague possibility that it was caused by the degeneration of a forgotten race, the more celebrated Mesopotamian texts have added little to our body of evidence. But important additional information is contained in one of the lesser-known texts, entitled *Erra and Ishum*. Although this dates only to around the eighth century BC, it is likely to be based on far older traditions. The version we have appears to be mainly politically inspired, reflecting the instability of the time. It mostly consists of a series of rhetorical, warmongering speeches by Erra, the god of the underworld and of plagues, and his rival, the chief Babylonian deity Marduk, interspersed with placatory comments by the lesser-known deity Ishum.

Here we find clear echoes of *Atrahasis* in that once again plagues and a flood are sent against humans, but this time there is a far greater emphasis on them not revering their gods. The events are somewhat jumbled, but we find that: 'The people abandoned justice and took to atrocities. They deserted righteousness and planned wickedness.'[42] Moreover, Erra asserts that 'I shall make their words wicked, and they will forget their god, will speak great insolence to their goddess', and that 'the belt of god and man is loosened and cannot be retied'.[43] These passages provide far more support for my theme of debasement and destruction.

Also intriguing are the clear echoes of the Judaeo-Christian fallen angels in those aspects of the text that deal with seven 'divine sages' sent by Enki to teach the 'arts of civilisation' to humankind before the flood.[44] These sages were always depicted as 'fish-men', a point that has deep esoteric significance – remember that Jesus himself is described as a 'fisher of men' and is often symbolised by the sign of a fish in esoteric literature. Moreover, this symbology of part-fish, part-human 'bringers of enlightenment' is found all over the ancient world. These are all themes that I will explore in more detail in later chapters, but to return to *Erra and Ishum* we find that after the flood the sages angered Enki – although here his place is usurped by Marduk – and that as a result they were banished back to the 'Apsu' from which they originally came.[45] Although the idea of banishment – for what, we are not told – is a negative one, in general even in this relatively late text the sages are described in a positive light. Indeed, their place of banishment is described as 'a domain of sweet, fresh water beneath the earth', and it is the same as that of their origin.[46] Clearly it is in no sense the fiery hell of Christian tradition. Surely this suggests that the late Mesopotamian texts started the process of confusion that the later Judaeo-Christian traditions thoroughly completed – that of merging the two originally separate themes of initial education and subsequent debasement, and of crediting the same set of 'angels' with doing both at the same time.

If we now turn once again to the more prosaic phenomenon of the flood catastrophe itself, there are several more interesting passages in this text. In one, perhaps a more accurate description of who remained after it is provided in the suggestion that, instead of just one survivor and his family, Erra 'left a remnant'.[47] In another passage Marduk – who this time is usurping the original role of the god Enlil – recalls sending the flood against humankind:

> A long time ago, when I was angry and rose up from my dwelling and arranged for the Flood, I rose up from my dwelling, and the control of heaven and earth was undone. The very heavens I made to tremble, the positions of the stars of heaven changed, and I did not return them to their places.[48]

Once again, does this short extract represent an accurate description of a shift in the earth's axis, the memory of which somehow managed to survive the ravages of time?

THE VEDIC ASURAS

Let us now turn our attention to India, because we find in its earliest texts an intriguingly similar theme of some sort of debasement of the gods. According to the orthodox view, an extremely high level of civilisation emerged in northwest India quite suddenly in the middle of the third millennium BC. The two most celebrated sites of this high Indus culture are at Harappa, on the River Ravi in the Punjab, and at Mohenjo-daro, on the Indus in Sind. Even Joseph Campbell, hardly a member of the revisionist school, remarks that 'no one has yet quite explained their sudden appearance'.[49]

Although they had developed a script that appears, for example, on their stamp seals, it has yet to be deciphered, and we have no real written texts from this period. We do know from the cultural remains, however, that while they exhibit a degree of Western influence from Mesopotamia, they also exhibit clear strains of an indigenous culture that is assumed to have already developed in India by this time – perhaps in the east in the Ganges delta and Bengal areas, or perhaps in the Dravidian south. This indigenous culture appears to have been more spiritually advanced than any other of the time, perhaps even including that of the Egyptians whose Old Kingdom dynasties were by this time in full flower. This is no more clearly demonstrated than in the meditative Yogic poses found for the first time in this era again on, for example, various stamp seals.[50]

These two cities seem to have remained largely unchanged for something like a thousand years, until they were overcome and destroyed by the incursion of largely nomadic Aryan or Indo-European warriors from the West, who had by now mastered the art of horsemanship and developed the wheeled chariot and sword. According to the orthodoxy, this marks the start of the so-called Vedic Age, circa 1500 BC, which represents something of an enigma. This is the era of the first written Sanskrit records of India, by far the most important of which for our purposes are the *Vedas*. Campbell and other Western scholars, presumably allowing their arguments to be dominated by the essentially negative and regressive influence of the invaders, have suggested that the Vedic religion was largely exoteric, and that the indigenous traits were not re-established until some five hundred years later in the Brahmanic Age.[51]

Many commentators would disagree with this view, however, and would argue that the *Vedas* represent the earliest written embodiment of a largely indigenous and esoteric Eastern philosophy that had probably been passed down verbally for many millennia beforehand. In fact, in their excellent 1995 study *In Search of the Cradle of Civilisation*, Georg Feuerstein, Subhash Kak and David Frawley go as far as to suggest that the Vedic Age should be properly dated to 3000 BC or even earlier, and that the 'Aryan invasion' never happened, while they further emphasise the wisdom and philosophy of the *Vedas*.[52]

Whether or not we agree with the entirety of these suggestions, in a similar vein we find that Ganga Prasad, in his 1927 work entitled *The Fountainhead of Religion*, argues it was the *Vedas* that influenced the development of all the other major religions that came after, and that as yet we can trace no precursor for them:

We have seen that the principles of Mahommedanism and Christianity are derived from Judaism, those of Christianity being partly traceable also to Buddhism, that the doctrines of Judaism can be deduced from Zoroastrianism, and further that both Zoroastrianism and Buddhism are directly traceable to the Vedic religion. Can we similarly trace the teachings of the

Vedas to any other religion? No; for history does not know of any older or prior religion.[53]

This is not intended to be a definitive study of comparative religion, and the whole question of the interplays between the three most ancient known civilisations of India, Egypt and Mesopotamia is infinitely complex. Nevertheless, the point seems to be well made that we find in the *Vedas* a level of philosophical advancement that cannot have derived from either of the other two, and that is either indigenous or, more controversially, perhaps represents the legacy of a prior, more universal wisdom. We will return to this latter possibility in Part 3.

In any case, to concentrate on the texts themselves, a good indication that we should take them seriously is that the Sanskrit word *veda* itself means 'knowledge' or 'wisdom', and it is here that we first encounter the Brahman priests who held such enormous influence. There are four main Vedic texts: the *Rig Veda*, *Yajur Veda*, *Sama Veda*, and *Atharva Veda*. As with most Indian literature, they are extremely lengthy, to the point that any common English translation provides only excerpts – although that did not stop the Brahmans from memorising them word for word, as their forebears would have done when there were no written records. Later on, various commentaries known as the *Brahmanas* were developed to help to explain their contents.

So much for the background. We find in the *Vedas* that the major gods such as Indra, Varuna, Agni, Savitri, Rudra and Shiva are all originally described as Asuras, and that this term translates as 'breather or giver of life', or alternatively 'spiritual, signifying the divine, in opposition to human nature'.[54] The tradition of the Asuras is more complex than this, however, because we find scholars united in suggesting that in later texts the term came to be associated also with demons or devas, the enemies of the true gods.[55] This must surely be seen as related to the fallen angel motif we have already encountered. However, can we shed any light on what caused this fall in Vedic tradition? I found that Prasad's commentaries on the Asuras are highly illuminating:

In later Sanskrit the word has come to be used in a bad sense being a synonym of Rakshasa, an evil being. The idea then is 'one who takes pleasure in, or enjoys, his present life disregarding the next or future life; *one who only cares for his body and not for the spirit.*'[56]

Of course, the suggestion appears to be that the Asuras' context changes according to the *age of the texts* in which they appear, and not that the change describes genuine events in remote antiquity. Still, it seems likely that this is an oversimplification. For example, in one hymn of the most celebrated *Rig Veda* itself, entitled 'Indra Lures Agni from Vrtra', the position of the various gods in relation to the Asuras, and the nature of the Asuras themselves, is already unclear.[57] It even seems to be attempting to describe the conflict between two sets of gods, in which the 'good' set 'has the sacrifice' and has 'regained the power of kingship', while the 'bad' set have 'lost their magic powers'. It also makes a brief reference to Varuna 'letting the waters flow', which could be indicative of an original destruction theme related to these events.

Although it would take a braver man than me to attempt too literal an interpretation of this enigmatic hymn, and although there is sparse mention of any major catastrophe per se in the *Vedas*, I do believe there is a hidden message in the traditions of the Asuras that, even if it has been somewhat confused by the passage of time, does perhaps provide a degree of support for my main theme of debasement and destruction. Furthermore, we also find far more support for the idea of an original golden race in other Indian traditions that we will consider in a later chapter.

CONCLUSION

The Near and Far Eastern texts of varying antiquity that we have considered in this chapter are not the easiest to decipher, but I have started with them because they are clearly some of the best known. If this were the only evidence I could produce to support my overall theme of a forgotten race that became debased by forgetting its spiritual roots and concentrating on material pleasures, to such an extent that the forces of universal karma dictated its destruction, it would probably be fair to say that I have an interesting but hardly conclusive case. But in fact we will find that it is echoed often with far more clarity in a mass of other texts from around the world that we have yet to examine.

4. THE ARTS OF CIVILISATION

In the last chapter I noted that the *Book of Enoch* describes the Watchers or angels educating other humans in the fields of technology, astronomy, astrology, divination and various other magical practices – and that the idea of civilisation being introduced to humankind is another widespread theme that is interwoven with that of debasement only in the distorted Judaeo-Christian traditions. This theme is often bound up with the idea of *secret* or even esoteric knowledge being transmitted, and there are various Enochian passages that emphasise this aspect. For example, 'they [humankind] know every secret of the angels, every oppress-ive and secret power of the devils, and every power of those who commit sorcery'.[1] If we ignore the distorted negative tone, this is an intriguing addition to the theme.

The Watcher account is a typical example of what I call 'knowledge transfer' traditions, and it is with these that we will commence.

KNOWLEDGE TRANSFER
In the last chapter I briefly referred to the Mesopotamian tradition of Enki sending the 'seven sages' to teach the arts of civilisation to humankind, and of these being associated with fish. This theme is not fully developed in any of the original Mesopotamian source texts that have so far been discovered, but survives mainly through the writings of Berossus, a Babylonian historian-priest of the third century BC. Although his original *Babyloniaca* has not survived, much of it has been preserved for us in the commentaries of subsequent historians such as Alexander Polyhistor, Abydenus, and Apollodorus. Polyhistor's account opens by informing us of the records that Berossus had said existed in his time:

> He mentions that there were written accounts preserved at Babylon *with the greatest care*, comprehending a term of fifteen myriads [ten thousands] of years [that is, 150,000]. These writings contained a history of the heavens and the sea; of the

birth of humankind; also of those who had sovereign rule; and of the actions achieved by them.[2]

This tends to confirm the suspicion that also arises from many other sources that at one time there were far more written records of what we now call 'prehistory', which if they ever emerged would require us to drop the prefix.

He then goes on to describe how the sages' leader Oannes – referred to in the original Mesopotamian sources as Adapa – 'emerged from the Erythraean sea', how he was part man, part fish, how 'his voice too was articulate and human', and how 'a representation of him is preserved even to this day'. This latter is true, at least to the extent that depictions of a man wearing fish scales as a headdress have been discovered in multiple Mesopotamian and Babylonian reliefs. Moreover, the lesser-known historian Helladius reports that 'some accounts say that . . . he was actually a man, but only seemed a fish because he was clothed in the skin of a sea creature.'[3] All this tends to confirm that the sages were not monstrous amphibious creatures, nor for that matter extraterrestrials as some would have us believe, but real humans, and that the fish motif is purely symbolic of wisdom and education. Remember also that Enki himself is associated primarily with both water and wisdom.[4]

Moving on, we then reach the description of what Oannes actually did:

This Being in the day-time used to converse with men; but took no food at that season; and he gave them an insight into letters and sciences, and every kind of art. He taught them to construct houses, to found temples, to compile laws, and explained to them the principles of geometrical knowledge. He made them distinguish the seeds of the earth, and shewed them how to collect fruits; in short, he instructed them in every thing which could tend to soften manners and humanise humankind. From that time, so universal were his instructions, nothing has been added material by way of improvement.

Although this does not seem to portray much in the way of esoteric or spiritual education, we can see that it has none of the negative tone of the Judaeo-Christian accounts. We do not know what Berossus' source was for this particular information, but it must have been old enough to have avoided the admittedly lesser late-Mesopotamian distortions that we encountered previously in *Erra and Ishum*. Moreover, Polyhistor then goes on to report that 'after this there appeared other animals like Oannes, of which Berossus promises to give an account when he comes to the history of the kings'. Were there indeed a number of these sages, and did they perhaps assist their peers over a prolonged period?

Although none of the Mesopotamian texts that we now have completely mirrors Berossus' account, certain of them do reveal important details that considerably predate the Babylonian tradition. The introduction to the short and incomplete Akkadian text in which Adapa takes the title role, which dates to around 1500 BC, reveals the following about him:

> Ea made broad understanding perfect in him, to disclose the design of the land. To him he gave wisdom, but did not give eternal life. At that time, in those years, he was a sage, son of Eridu. Ea created him as a protecting spirit among humankind. A sage – nobody rejects his word – clever, extra-wise, he was one of the Anunnaki . . .[5]

This description of Adapa as 'extra-wise' is in fact the same as the epithet given to the flood heroes Atrahasis, Utnapishtim and Ziusudra, while they all have the additional epithet 'far-distant'.[6] As for the other six sages, unsurprisingly we find elsewhere that they are all described in similar terms to Adapa, as 'the holy carp, who are perfect in lofty wisdom like Ea their lord'.[7] It is surely not going too far to suggest that these descriptions were, at least originally, intended to convey a high degree of spiritual and esoteric insight?

There exists an even older, Sumerian text entitled *Inanna and Enki: The Transfer of the Arts of Civilisation from Eridu to Erech*. The title itself is revealing, although we should appreciate that the text has an obvious political message in that it attempts to justify the ascendancy of Inanna's ancient city of Erech over that of Enki in Eridu. Nor does it contain any details of who bestowed these gifts on humankind in the first place. Nevertheless, it does include a detailed description of more than one hundred of these so-called arts – an approximate translation of the Sumerian word *me* – although, as Mesopotamian scholar Samuel Noah Kramer points out in his 1963 work *The Sumerians*, 'only some sixty-odd are at present intelligible, and some of these are only bare words which, because of lack of context, give but a hint of their real significance.'[8] As well as more mundane arts such as those of the metalworker, smith, leatherworker, builder and basket weaver, the list includes words and phrases that have been translated as godship, kingship, truth, ascent from and descent into the netherworld, various unidentified priestly offices, law, art, music, scribeship, wisdom, attention, judgment and decision. As we can see, it may be that this list, if it were properly understood, would prove to contain some intriguigingly esoteric concepts that were taught to humans at some point in what appears from the overall context to be our *antediluvian* past, as suggested by the traditions of Adapa–Oannes.

However, before we leave the Mesopotamians, I must point out that their spiritual understanding appears to have been fairly limited from the outset, inasmuch as they obviously did believe in an afterlife but – given their obsession with gaining immortality as witnessed in the later tablets of the *Epic of Gilgamesh* and indeed in *Adapa* itself – felt that the gaining of heaven was by no means guaranteed. As we will see in Part 3, the ancient Egyptians felt the same. One might argue that both were concerned with immortal life in heaven rather than on earth, and that this equates to the aim of release from the earthly karmic round that is fundamental to any spiritual worldview, but it is far from proven that either of these ancient civilisations even had a general belief in reincarnation. So it is arguable that both had already moved far away from the spiritual understanding that in my view would have existed before they came to the fore, and which remains largely preserved in, for example, the Indian *Vedas*.

In any case, these accounts of knowledge transfer are by no means restricted to Mesopotamia. For example, Chinese tradition reports that the Yellow Emperor, Huang Ti:

... taught the arts of divination and mathematics, composed the calendar, invented musical instruments of bamboo, taught the use of money, boats and carriages, and the arts of work in clay, metal, and wood. He established the rituals of address to *shang ti*, built the first temple and the first palace, studied and taught the properties of healing herbs.[9]

There are other similar accounts from all round the world, for example in the Mexican Toltec tradition of Quetzalcoatl.[10] They all tend to corroborate the idea that humans had knowledge *transferred* to them by certain more advanced counterparts at some point in the remote past. Moreover, some suggest that this process may have occurred *repeatedly*, for reasons we will shortly examine.

KNOWLEDGE PRESERVATION

It is not entirely irrelevant to the current study for us to note that, by way of contrast, we also find many accounts of knowledge being *preserved* for the future by our ancient forebears, and sometimes the two types of tradition tend to overlap and become confused. As an example, a number of flood accounts contain this idea. In Berossus' Babylonian version, the hero Xisuthros is asked by the deity to 'commit to writing a history of the beginning, procedure, and final conclusion of all things, down to the present term'.[11] And this is substantiated by Josephus, to whose commentary I referred in the last chapter, when he describes how the descendants of Adam's favoured son Seth took precautions before the onset of the flood:

> And that their inventions might not be lost before they were sufficiently known, upon Adam's prediction that the world was to be destroyed at one time by the force of fire, and at another time by the violence and quantity of water, they made two pillars; the one of brick, the other of stone: they inscribed their discoveries on them both, that in case the pillar of brick should be destroyed by the flood, the pillar of stone might remain, and exhibit those discoveries to humankind; and also inform them that there was another pillar of brick erected by them. This remains in the land of Siriad to this day.[12]

It seems pretty clear from this that some of the early Judaic material must have contained this tradition, on the one hand because it would have been assimilated from the Babylonian sources that Berossus used, and on the other because Josephus was clearly writing specifically about Judaic traditions that were consistent with, but more detailed than, those found in the Old Testament. It is interesting to note that Josephus admits that, before writing his account, he deliberately spent time at Qumran in the company of the Essenes – the authors of the Dead Sea Scrolls, whom most scholars accept had a somewhat different and probably more esoteric take on the Judaic and other material available to them than that of the founders of the Christian church.[13] Moreover, we find that the Gnostic literature contains many texts that extol Seth as the father of the bloodline of the 'immovable race'; one in particular, entitled *The Three Steles of Seth*, is clearly based on the same theme, although unfortunately the contents are not particularly revealing.[14] Accordingly, we cannot help but wonder exactly why the church fathers decided to omit this aspect of the flood story from Genesis.

Intriguingly, it is not contained in the Ethiopian version of the *Book of Enoch* either – although it is implicit that the information recorded 'by Enoch' has come directly from God, and constitutes its own 'preserved revelation'. However, the Slavonic version does make it perfectly clear that Enoch was instructed to record everything that the archangels showed and taught him during his visionary trip to the 'seven abodes of heaven':

> And now, my children, I know all things from the lips of the Lord; for my eyes have seen from the beginning to the end. I know all things and *have written all things in the books* . . .[15]

The list of the 'things' that follows includes mainly details of astronomy, of calendars, and of the seasons. Nevertheless, there is a strong suspicion that some Enochian literature may have contained far more 'secret' knowledge, because the Masonic traditions that have built up around Enoch are numerous and well known, as suggested by Manley P Hall in his oft-quoted 1928 work *The Secret Teachings Of All Ages*:

> He [Enoch] also constructed an underground temple consisting of nine vaults, one beneath the other, placing in the deepest vault a triangular tablet of gold bearing upon it the absolute and ineffable Name of Deity. According to some

accounts, Enoch made two golden deltas. The larger he placed
upon the white cubical altar in the lowest vault and the
smaller he gave to into the keeping of his son, Methusaleh,
who did the actual construction work of the brick chambers
according to the pattern revealed to his father by the Most
High. . . . According to Freemasonic symbolism, Enoch,
fearing that all knowledge of the sacred Mysteries would be
lost at the time of the Deluge, erected the two columns
mentioned in the quotation [that is, of Josephus]. Upon the
metal column in appropriate allegorical symbols he engraved
the secret teaching and upon the marble column placed an
inscription stating that a short distance away a priceless
treasure would be discovered in a subterranean vault. After
having thus successfully completed his labours, Enoch was
translated from the brow of Mount Moriah. In time the
location of the secret vaults was lost, but after the lapse of ages
there came another builder – an initiate after the order of
Enoch – and he [presumably King Solomon], while laying the
foundations for another great temple to the Great Architect of
the Universe, discovered the long-lost vaults and the secrets
contained within.[16]

We also find that these accounts have many parallels in later
traditions. The Arab accounts preserved, for example, by the
ninth-century Arab writer Abd al Hokm describe an antediluvian
king named Saurid who supposedly built the three pyramids of
Giza before the flood to secrete and preserve knowledge of the
'profound sciences . . . of astrology, arithmetic, geometry and
physics', and also 'the commentaries of each priest . . . concerning
what was done in his time, and what is, and what shall be, from
the beginning of time, to the end of it . . .'[17] In my previous book
Giza: The Truth I discussed the extent to which this account
contains clear distortions – for example, with respect to the fact
that the pyramids were clearly built only circa 2500 BC. But does it
also contain any grains of underlying fact?

And what about the many other accounts from Egyptian, Greek,
Roman, Arab and Hermetic sources that suggest that some sort of
secret knowledge of the remote past was preserved in Egypt in
particular? I have similarly discussed these accounts at great length

in *Giza: The Truth*, so I do not propose to go into them in any detail again now.[18] However, for example, we find the suggestion in the *Hermetica*, a set of texts that we will examine in far more detail in Part 3, that Hermes – the Greek equivalent of the Egyptian Thoth and, arguably, of the Judaic Enoch – inscribed 'knowledge of all' on certain tablets.[19] These various accounts led eventually to the now celebrated suggestions that a 'Hall of Records' awaits discovery somewhere in Egypt, and perhaps also elsewhere.

One final tradition that appears to unite the various strands is contained in the so-called *Edfu Documents*. These are inscribed on the walls of a Late-Period Ptolemaic temple located midway between Luxor and Aswan in Upper Egypt, dated to the last half of the first millennium BC. The only information on these texts comes from the descriptions provided by E A E Reymond, former professor of Egyptology at the University of Manchester, in *The Mythical Origin of the Egyptian Temple*, first published in 1969:

> The introduction of the first Edfu cosmogonical record
> discloses the tradition that the contents of these records were
> the *words of the Sages*. We are told that this sacred book was
> believed to be a *Copy of writings which Thoth made according to
> the words of the Sages of Mehweret* [original italics].[20]

Not only does this represent a somewhat earlier and arguably more authentic reference to the tradition that Thoth preserved various records, but it also appears to have parallels with the Mesopotamian knowledge transfer tradition of the seven sages.

If any of these knowledge preservation traditions were to prove correct, it would certainly indicate that an antediluvian race of high culture existed. The suggestion is that at some point in the past some of the records were lost, and some were destroyed by religious fundamentalists – but some may, just may, have been secreted away. This does raise intriguing possibilities that have provided massive incentives to a variety of researchers and explorers who have devoted their lives to attempting to locate such records, and perhaps even caches of artefacts developed using lost technology. However, I have to say that my own intuition is that the bulk of at least the Egypt-based traditions, and in particular those related to the Hall of Records, are built up from the sort of rumour and exaggeration that has always been associated with the pyramids. Certainly the more extravagant claims are unlikely ever to be substantiated.

This is not to say, though, that we may not find veiled clues to a lost history and wisdom in those texts that still exist in the public domain around the world, which is exactly what the present work attempts to unveil. Nor is it to say that there may not be caches of ancient documents that have been secreted away in other locations around the world – perhaps the two most discussed contenders being some hidden vault in the Vatican, and some secret hideaway in a remote area of Tibet – and we will return to these issues later.

However, leaving the possibility of proper historical records of a highly cultured antediluvian race aside, I should provide a brief further qualification concerning concepts like the Hall of Records and the in-many-ways similar Holy Grail. It should come as no surprise by now that my overriding feeling is that, if these concepts in particular have any real significance, it is that they are veiled references to a wisdom that can be accessed by each and every one of us, because it is inherent in the make-up of our souls. Moreover, it is my belief that the veiled secrets and esoteric philosophies of the various texts and traditions that form the basis of the present work are the key to unlocking this inner and universal wisdom, as we will see. Above all, its primarily internal rather than external nature is what makes it *wisdom*, and not just knowledge that can be uncovered in some secret cache or found on a bookshelf.

CONCLUSION

Let me now attempt to place these traditions into the context of my main themes. The knowledge preservation traditions are relatively simple, and it could be argued that they provide at least a degree of general support for the idea that a relatively cultured antediluvian race did exist.

The knowledge transfer traditions are more complex, particularly inasmuch as they may relate to vastly different periods in our history. Essentially there are two possibilities. On the one hand, many of these appear once again to have an *antediluvian* context, and therefore provide support for my argument from the last chapter that at some point in human history a number of angelic souls incarnated deliberately to introduce 'civilisation' once the time was right. Of course, this would not have been a one-off process, but more likely a gradual one that was repeated over a lengthy period. Crucial to this however, in my view, is the idea that one of the first issues they would have concentrated on would have been the teaching of a spiritual worldview to their human-souled fellows, so that it became as entrenched into the fabric of human culture on earth as it is by definition in the more ethereal realms.

On the other hand, to the extent that there may be some confusion in these traditions concerning events that may also have occurred *after* the catastrophe, I will attempt to construct a relatively pragmatic scenario. There is good reason to believe that the most culturally advanced – even if by this time largely debased – elements of our antediluvian race would have lived in coastal areas, because it is likely that their whole system of trade relied on ocean navigation. There is similarly good reason to believe that these would have been the areas worst affected by the catastrophe. Consequently, most pockets of survivors would have perhaps been inland farmers who led a more basic existence. But perhaps a very few people from the more culturally advanced settlements did survive, for example because they were at sea in the deep ocean when disaster struck, or because they were in a less affected part of the globe. These are all issues that we will examine more fully in Part 2. The point is that, although *any* survivors would probably have had a hard time for at least several generations, when at some point the latter came into contact with the former, would they not perhaps have been seen as 'educating gods' of some sort, or at least have made an enormous and permanent impact on the 'receiving' culture, and as a result have become highly prominent in its traditions?

This is, of course, a detailed speculation based on the 'cargo cult' theory that many revisionist historians have promoted for decades, and I do not doubt that it has a role to play in the interpretation of these knowledge transfer traditions. Still, I do not believe that the story ends there, because I also have little doubt that, under the circumstances, universal karma is likely to have dictated that various angelic souls needed to incarnate once again after the catastrophe to assist the rebuilding and re-education process, and, in particular, to reintroduce the spiritual worldview that had been lost. So we can see that these traditions are likely to have been describing a variety of different interactions at different times.

5. THE GOLDEN AGE

I have now built up a reasonably comprehensive picture of a forgotten race of humans that became debased and was largely destroyed by some sort of worldwide catastrophe. I have also suggested that they must have originally been highly 'aware' people who fully appreciated both their own true spirituality and that of the world around them, and that it was the loss of this spiritual awareness and concentration on material pleasures and gain that led to their downfall – as part of a universal karmic process. But I have also indicated that the traditions we have so far studied tend to omit or only hint at any description of what life was like *before* the process of degeneration commenced. So it is to those that fill in this gap with their widespread references to an antediluvian 'golden age' that we should now turn.

In fact there are a few gaps we can fill in even from the Judaeo-Christian traditions, in that we are all aware that the biblical Eden was regarded as a 'paradise' from which Adam and Eve were expelled after their fall. Although the details in Genesis are sparse and fairly prosaic, and although there is little doubt in my view that the suggestion that some kind of 'first fall' happened right at the outset of humankind's existence on earth is a gross distortion – something we will consider further in a later chapter – I think it is reasonable to suggest that the Eden story is at heart still a thinly veiled reference to a golden age in the distant past. Furthermore, we have already noted Josephus' description of how 'evil' Cain altered the 'simple and innocent lives that men lived before', and he provides more details when he discusses the nature of 'good' Seth's descendants:

> All these proved to be of good dispositions. They inhabited the same country without dissensions, and in a happy condition, without any misfortunes falling upon them, till they died. They were the inventors of that peculiar sort of wisdom which is concerned with the heavenly bodies, and their order.[1]

Meanwhile, in the Slavonic manuscript of the *Book of Enoch* we find the following description of the conditions that God originally provided for Adam in Eden:

> I made for him the heavens open that he should perceive the angels singing the song of triumph. And there was light without any darkness continually in paradise.[2]

I would argue that this 'continual light', which clearly should not be taken literally, is most likely a veiled reference to the idea that Eden was filled with 'spiritual light'. Therefore, even in the often-distorted Judaic traditions, we can perceive the message that our antediluvian ancestors originally lived in a 'paradisal' spiritual state. Moreover, it would appear that some managed to retain that state for longer than others.

As we saw previously, the Mesopotamian texts are also not exactly forthcoming on this issue, but one passage at least gives us some reason to assume that the Judaic traditions were once again informed by these far earlier predecessors. The Sumerian text known as *Enki and Ninhursag* has been dubbed 'A Sumerian Paradise Myth', and the version we now have was composed primarily to entertain visiting merchants from Dilmun, identified usually and certainly here with the island of Bahrain. However, it was clearly composed from at least two separate original traditions, both of which appear to have been ruthlessly culled judging from the contextual jumps that remain. Nevertheless, the opening stanzas undoubtedly reflect a description of a paradisal state that may originally have been much longer and more detailed, and not associated with Dilmun at all. It is described as a 'pure' and 'virginal' land, where there was no disease.[3]

THE FIRST OCCASION

Apart from brief references to their king lists and to the *Edfu Documents* in previous chapters, we have so far not considered the wealth of ancient Egyptian literature that has been bequeathed to us. This comprises literally thousands of inscriptions inside burial chambers, on sarcophagi, on temple walls and on stone steles, as well as on clay tablets and later papyri. The subject is rendered more complex because, although early Sumerian pictographic script is difficult to interpret, Egyptian hieroglyphs are arguably even more so – despite the popular fascination with them and the massive amount of time devoted to their study in the last century and a half.[4] Later texts that use the simpler demotic script may not present such a problem, but the farther back we go, the less scholars can be certain that they have really appreciated the nuances and idiosyncrasies that the hieroglyphs are attempting to convey. Indeed, as I intimated in my introduction, we can be pretty certain that the only people who would ever have properly understood them would have been the most highly initiated ancient Egyptian priests of the time, which is why my earlier comments about their apparent lack of a rounded spiritual worldview were slightly guarded.

This is not to say that scholars have not made commendable attempts to provide translations for us, although most of us can still only guess at the significance of some of the enigmas they seem to contain, even with the experts' commentaries to assist us. We have already learned that we require a significant appreciation of symbolism to properly interpret most of the ancient texts and traditions from around the world, but this is nowhere more the case than in Egypt.

There are a number of main 'books' that were clearly of great importance, including the *Book of What is in the Duat*, the *Book of Gates*, the *Book of the Dead*, and the *Pyramid Texts* and *Coffin Texts*.[5] Some of these date back at least to the end of the Fifth Dynasty, circa 2350 BC. However, there are many other lesser-known texts that commentators reference; and to make matters worse, these commentators often describe various ancient Egyptian traditions without explicitly identifying the relevant source texts.

In any case, the main books describe a number of deities that we will meet at various times as we progress through this work. The ancient Egyptian pantheon of the Ennead is normally thought of as comprising nine gods: Ptah, also known as Amon and Atum, the creator god; Shu, the air god, and his spouse Tefnut, the goddess of water or moisture; Geb, the earth god, and his spouse Nut, the sky goddess; Osiris, the god of the underworld, and his spouse Isis; and finally Seth and his spouse Nepthys. Other important deities include Ra or Re, the sun god; Horus, the son of Osiris and Isis; Thoth, the god of wisdom; and Ma'at, the goddess of truth and justice.

As for the concept of a golden age, we find that most scholars do not emphasise this as an aspect of ancient Egyptian tradition. However, a former professor of Egyptology at the University of Birmingham, R T Rundle Clark, did so in 1959 – and it is his work more than any other that is referenced by a number of revisionist authors, especially Robert Bauval and Adrian Gilbert in their best-selling 1995 work *The Orion Mystery*, and Bauval and Graham Hancock in the follow-up work *Keeper of Genesis*, which both rely heavily on Rundle Clark's description of *tep zepi*, or the 'first time':

The basic principles of life, nature and society were determined by the gods long ago, before the establishment of kingship. This epoch – *'Tep Zepi'* – 'the First Time' – stretched from the first stirring of the High God in the Primeval Waters to the settling of Horus upon the throne and the redemption of Osiris. All proper myths relate events or manifestations of this epoch.

Anything whose existence or authority had to be justified or explained must be referred to the 'First Time'. This was true for natural phenomena, rituals, royal insignia, the plans of temples, magical or medical formulae, the hieroglyphic system of writing, the calendar – the whole paraphernalia of the civilisation. . . .

All that was good or efficacious was established on the principles laid down in the 'First Time' – which was, therefore, a golden age of absolute perfection – 'before rage or clamour or strife or uproar had come about'. No death, disease or disaster occurred in this blissful epoch, known variously as 'the time of Re', 'the time of Osiris', or the 'time of Horus'.

The Golden Age was disturbed. The entry of evil was generally thought to have happened when the eye of the High God grew angry seeing that it had been supplanted by another in its absence. The partial restoration of this Golden Age – *hetep* – is the chief theme of the ritual. Hence the emphasis on the constraint of evil forces and the defeat of the powers of chaos. After the triumph of the Osiris cult the chief disturber of cosmic harmony was Seth.[6]

I find it somewhat strange that this is the only real reference to an Egyptian golden age tradition that I have been able to locate. It is certainly the main and only substantial reference used by Bauval, Gilbert and Hancock, while the main reference works on Egyptian mythology and the main texts listed above do not contain any such clear tradition or reference. It is also worthy of note that this description of the 'first time' is almost identical to the concept of the original 'dream time', which is the fundamental basis of the shamanic traditions of indigenous peoples in Australasia and elsewhere – particularly with respect to the suggestion that everything has to be 'referred back' to it. I will return to this concept in Part 3, but for the moment I must question whether Rundle Clark may not have attributed a tradition to the ancient Egyptians that is found rather more elsewhere, without a sound basis from the texts for so doing.

The only other source that lends some credence to this concept of the 'first time' is the *Edfu Documents*. Once again, these texts have been referenced extensively by various revisionist authors, and as we have seen the only source is E A E Reymond's work. She describes the main texts found there, including a number of apparently cosmogonical records, the first of which is entitled *Sanctified God Who Came into Being at the First Occasion*. These appear to represent severely edited extracts from original works perhaps of extreme antiquity – albeit that no other copies of them have survived – that were not specifically associated with Edfu, and were entitled the *Specification of the Mounds of the Early Primaeval Age* and the *Sacred Book of the Early Primaeval Age*.[7]

These titles suggest a similar overall idea to that expressed by Rundle Clark. Still, it is important to realise that – however much various revisionist authors have attempted to extrapolate this sparse basic information – Reymond's commentary on these texts is not specific about the 'first occasion', and nowhere do either she or the texts themselves indicate that this was in any sense a true golden age, with, for example, the absence of illness and corruption that Rundle Clark suggests. It is merely described as a time when the earliest 'gods' inhabited the earth.

Nevertheless, we can still infer that some form of the concept of a golden age persisted in ancient Egypt, even if the specifics of the 'first time' may have been somewhat overemphasised. For example, we see at the end of Rundle Clark's comments the suggestion that at some point evil interceded to disrupt the previous harmony, and that the 'High God' was angered. This time it is confirmed, indeed expanded upon, by mainstream Egyptology, which includes the celebrated tradition that as Ra, the sun god, aged, humankind began to plot against him, to the point that he decided to send his 'divine eye' to destroy them.[8]

This certainly appears to corroborate the debasement and destruction theme, and we might allow ourselves the conjecture that the brief references to 'evil' and to 'plotting against Ra' in the commentators' summaries are, once again, indicative of a forgotten race forsaking the spiritual or 'golden' path that it had previously trodden.

THE DAYS OF DASA-RATHA

We saw in an earlier chapter how Brahmanism emerged to take over from the Vedic Age in India around the start of the first millennium BC. Meanwhile Buddhism – based on the teachings of Gautama Buddha, who lived in the middle of this millennium and was arguably the first of the archetypal 'world saviours' – first emerged in northern India sometime in the latter half of the first millennium BC. The two main strands that developed were the broad-based Mahayana school and the more orthodox Hinayana school, and their teachings were recorded for the first time in writing several centuries later – the former in a number of sutras, of which the most important is the *Avatamsaka Sutra*, and the latter in the *Pali Canon*. But while Buddhism then spread to the Orient in the early centuries of the first millennium, in northern India Hinduism developed out of a resurgent Brahmanism, until the relentless eastern spread of Islam took over in the twelfth century.

The two main Sanskrit 'epics' of Indian literature are the Hindu *Mahabharata* and *Ramayana*. The former is described by Joseph Campbell as the 'chief mythological document of the Indian golden age . . . much of the material of which is indefinitely old, perhaps ante 400 BC, but of which the final style and tone are rather of c. AD 400 and thereafter.'[9] Both epics are extremely lengthy and full of references appropriate to our current theme. The following example is taken from a translation of extracts from the *Ramayana* undertaken by Romesh C Dutt at the beginning of the twentieth century – it is a lengthy passage from the first book entitled 'The Bridal of Sita', but to paraphrase or edit it would be to miss out on the beautiful poetry of Dutt's translation:

Rich in royal worth and valour, rich in holy Vedic lore,
Dasa-ratha ruled his empire in the happy days of yore,
Loved of men in fair Ayodhya, sprung of ancient Solar Race,
Royal *rishi* in his duty, saintly *rishi* in his grace,
Great as Indra in his prowess, bounteous as Kuvera kind,
Dauntless deeds subdued his foemen, lofty faith subdued his
    mind!
Like the ancient monarch Manu, father of the human race,
Dasa-ratha ruled his people with a father's loving grace,
Truth and Justice swayed each action and each baser motive
    quelled,
People's Love and Monarch's Duty every thought and deed
    impelled,
And his town like Indra's city – tower and dome and turret
    brave –
Rose in proud and peerless beauty on Sarayu's limpid wave!
Peaceful lived the righteous people, rich in wealth in merit
    high,
Envy dwelt not in their bosoms and their accents shaped no
    lie,
Fathers with their happy households owned their cattle, corn,
    and gold,
Galling penury and famine in Ayodhya had no hold,
Neighbours lived in mutual kindness helpful with their ample
    wealth,
None who begged the wasted refuse, none who lived by fraud
    and stealth!
And they wore the gem and earring, wreath and fragrant
    sandal paste,
And their arms were decked with bracelets, and their necks
    with *nishkas* graced,
Cheat and braggart and deceiver lived not in the ancient town,
Proud despiser of the lowly wore not insults in their frown,
Poorer fed not on the richer, hireling friend upon the great,
None with low and lying accents did upon the proud man wait!

Men to plighted vows were faithful, faithful was each loving
    wife,
Impure thought and wandering fancy stained not holy
    wedded life,
Robed in gold and graceful garments, fair in form and fair in
    face,
Winsome were Ayodhya's daughters, rich in wit and woman's
    grace!
Twice-born men were free from passion, lust of gold and
    impure greed,
Faithful to their Rites and Scriptures, truthful in their word
    and deed,
Altar blazed in every mansion, from each home was bounty
    given,
Stooped no man to fulsome falsehood, questioned none the
    will of Heaven.
Kshatras bowed to holy Brahmans, Vaisyas to the Kshatras
    bowed,
Toiling Sudras lived by labour, of their honest duty proud,
To the Gods and to the Fathers, to each guest in virtue
    trained,
Rites were done with true devotion as by holy writ ordained.
Pure each caste in due observance, stainless was each ancient
    rite,
And the nation thrived and prospered by its old and
    matchless might,
And each man in truth abiding lived a long and peaceful life,
With his sons and with his grandsons, with his loved and
    honoured wife.
Thus was ruled the ancient city by her monarch true and
    bold,
As the earth was ruled by Manu in the misty days of old . . .[10]

Although this passage does not deal with the original golden age
itself – which is presumably the time when 'the earth was ruled by
Manu in the misty days of old' – it is nevertheless clearly
attempting to describe a period of rule in which it was supposedly
re-created. And although it contains only sparse spiritual references
– such as to 'twice-born' men, which we will discuss in Part 3 –

we will find plenty of these in the broader Indian material that we will consider in the next chapter.

THE AGE OF PERFECT VIRTUE

As with Egypt, apart from the king lists that I briefly mentioned in an earlier chapter, we have not yet considered the important Chinese texts and traditions. The first 'formalised' religion to emerge in China was Confucianism, around the middle of the first millennium BC. Its main texts include the *Shu King* or 'Book of History', which commences with the 'Canon of Yeo' who ruled circa 2300 BC; the *Shih King*; the *Hsiao King*; the *Yi King*, the basis for the I Ching system of divination; and the *Li Ki*. Its emergence was accompanied by a purge of earlier literature and traditions that culminated in the 'burning of the books' by the emperor Shih Huang Ti in 213 BC, at about the same time that the Great Wall was constructed. From this time on the rulers of the Han dynasty set about reinventing their early traditions, and a whole series of experts has found it extremely difficult to piece back together the original traditions of the earliest historical dynasties, those of Shang and Chou. Taoism emerged shortly after Confucianism, and its main texts including the *Tao Teh King* and the *Writings of Kwang Tze*. As we saw, Buddhism did not come to China until some time in the first half of the first millennium.

Translations of and commentaries on all of these main texts are available in a monumental forty-volume compilation entitled *The Sacred Books of the East*, compiled in the late nineteenth century by Max Müller – in particular in the subset entitled *The Sacred Books of China* prepared by leading Orientalist James Legge.[11] His translation of the Taoist *Writings of Kwang Tze* contains a number of excellent descriptions of the nature of man in the 'Age of Perfect Virtue':

> In the age of perfect virtue they attached no value to wisdom, nor employed men of ability. Superiors were (but) as the higher branches of a tree; and the people were like the deer of the wild. They were upright and correct, without knowing that to be so was Righteousness; they loved one another, without knowing that to do so was Benevolence; they were honest and loyal-hearted, without knowing that it was

Loyalty; they fulfilled their engagements, without knowing that to do so was Good Faith; in their simple movements they employed the services of one another, without thinking that they were conferring or receiving a gift. Therefore their actions left no trace, and there was no record of their affairs.[12]

And again:

> . . . in the age of perfect virtue, men lived in common with birds and beasts, and were on terms of equality with all creatures, as forming one family; – how could they know among themselves the distinctions of superior men and small men? Equally without knowledge, they did not leave (the path of) their natural virtue; equally free from desires, they were in the state of pure simplicity. In that state of pure simplicity, the nature of the people was what it ought to be.[13]

To add to this picture we have extracts from another Taoist text, this time translated by Evan Morgan of the University of Wales in his *Essays from Huai Nan Tzu*. One essay, entitled 'Beginning and Reality', contains the following description:

> The ancients lodged within the realm of the Tao; desire was controlled and passion mastered; and, in consequence, the spirit did not wander into the extraneous. They derived repose from the calm of creation: they were not disturbed by the baneful effects of comets and the tail of the Great Bear. Though noxious, they refused to be disturbed by their appearances.
>
>   During this period, the people were in a state of Arcadian simplicity; they ate and rambled about: they smacked their stomachs and rejoiced. All together enjoyed the blessings of heaven and ate of the fruits of the earth. They did not wrangle in mutual recriminations, nor dispute over rights and wrongs. Peace and plenty existed. This may be called the Ideal Rule. . . .
>
>   The perfect man of ancient time stood in the very root and centre of being, the foundations of Heaven and Earth themselves, and wandered at will, unhasting and free, in this

central seat of being. He cherished and diffused virtue, he enkindled the spirit of harmony of existence and thus enabled creation to come to full maturity.[14]

A lengthy passage in another essay, 'Natural Law', further reinforces the point:

The rule of the T'ai Ch'ing was in accord with Heaven, and beneficial to creation. Nature was constant, the spirit simple and centred. The mind had no appetites: it was quiescent: it was active, not stagnant. Mental activities were consistent with the Tao, and outward activities were in agreement with right. The activities of the mind worked artistically; action was correct with benefit to things. Words were prised and in accord with reason. Actions were simple and direct, in accordance with nature. The mind was contented and without cunning. Actions were simple and without ostentation. So there was no recourse to horoscopy and divination of the eight signs and the tortoise. There was no thought of where to begin and how to end. Action took place when it was demanded. Principles were embodied: the spirit of Yin and Yang were envisaged. All was in conformity with the four seasons. All was bright and clear as the sun and moon: man was a fit mate of the Creator. Hence Heaven overshadowed them with grace, and Earth sustained them with life. The four seasons did not lose their order, nor did the wind and rain fall with violence. The sun and moon were limpid and lucent, shining in their brightness, and the five planets moved in their orbits without error.
During these periods the primal fluid was surpassingly glowing (in men of the period) and transmitted its brilliancy.[15]

Once again, we have highly eloquent descriptions of a golden race whose mode of being can now *only* be properly interpreted in spiritual terms – with the new assertion that their mode of being was the only one that accords with the 'plan of creation' that, in my view, was triggered by the incarnation of the first angelic and human souls. However, the latter essay also continues by providing a description of the decadence that resulted when the way of Tao was eventually forsaken:

When we arrive at the decadent age, we find that men dug into the mountains for precious stones. They wrought metal and jade into cunning vessels and broke open oysters in search of pearls: they melted brass and iron; the whole of nature withered under the exploitation. They ripped open the pregnant and slew the young, untimely (in order to get skins and furs). The Chilin, as a result, did not visit the land. They broke down nests and despoiled birds that had not lain, so that the phoenix no longer hovered around. They drilled wood for fire: they piled up timber to make verandas and balustrades: they burnt forests to drive out game and drained the waters for fish. In spite of this, the furniture at the service of the people was not enough for their use, whilst the luxuries of the rulers were abundant. Thus, the world of life partially failed and things miscarried so that the larger half of creation failed of fruition.

The classes made mounds and built on high grounds: they fertilised their land and sowed their corn: they dug the land for wells, to drink from, and opened up irrigation channels, for their enrichment. They laid foundations for their cities, so that they were munitioned. Captured wild beasts were domesticated: thus, there was grievous rupture of the Yin and Yang, and the succession of the four seasons failed. Thunder-bolts wrought havoc, and hailstones fell with violence. Noxious miasma and untimely hoarfrosts fell unceasingly, resulting in atrophy and the failure of nature to bear abundantly. Luxuriant grass and thick brushwood were cut down in order to get land. They cut down the jungle in order to grow ears of corn. The plants and trees that died before germination, flowering and bearing fruit, were innumerable.

Does all this sound familiar? I would suggest that the message of the fall of our forgotten race, reaching across the millennia, mirrors and highlights the materialism and debasement that are progressively threatening the survival of our own modern race.

THE RACE OF GOLD

It is well known that some of the most celebrated writers of classical Greece provided details of a golden age. For example, one of their earliest historians, Hesiod, records the following in *Works and Days*, compiled in the middle of the eighth century BC:

> The race of men that the immortals who dwell on Olympus
> made first of all was of gold. They were in the time of Kronos,
> when he was king in heaven; and they lived like gods, with
> carefree heart, remote from toil and misery. Wretched old age
> did not affect them either, but with hands and feet ever
> unchanged they enjoyed themselves in feasting, beyond all
> ills, and they died as if overcome by sleep. All good things
> were theirs, and the grain-giving soil bore its fruits of its own
> accord in unstinted plenty, while they at their leisure
> harvested their fields in contentment amid abundance. Since
> the earth covered up that race, they have been divine spirits
> by great Zeus' design, good spirits on the face of the earth,
> watchers over mortal men, bestowers of wealth: such is the
> kingly honour that they received.[16]

This theme remained unscathed in Greek literature for nearly a thousand years, with Ovid repeating it in *Metamorphosis* at the start of the first century:

> Golden was that first age which unconstrained,
> With heart and soul, obedient to no law,
> Gave honour to good faith and righteousness.
> No punishment they knew, no fear; they read
> No penalties engraved on plates of bronze;
> No suppliant throng with dread beheld their judge;
> No judges had they then, but lived secure.
> No pine had yet, on its high mountain felled,
> Descended to the sea to find strange lands afar;
> Men knew no shores except their own.
> No battlements their cities yet embraced,
> No trumpets straight, no horns of sinuous brass,
> No sword, no helmet then – no need of arms;
> The world untroubled lived in leisured ease.[17]

Clearly the original spiritual message has been somewhat left behind in these Greek accounts. Nevertheless, Hesiod's description of how the golden race went on to become 'divine spirits' and 'watchers over mortal men' perhaps represents a distorted remnant of it.

Similarly, Snorri Sturluson's *Edda* is one of the earliest surviving compilations of Scandinavian tradition, and dates to the beginning of the thirteenth century. Although it is extremely difficult to follow in detail, the first part – 'The Deluding of Gylfi' – contains a clear reference to a golden age, describing how their chief god Odin set up his temple in Asgard, and everything within it was made of gold. He also 'saw over the whole world and what everyone was doing, and he understood everything he saw'.[18] This latter is undoubtedly a surviving reference to the 'awareness' that we encounter in other traditions from around the world, but, even more than with the Greek accounts, it is about the only vestige of a spiritual message that remains by this late period.[19]

THE DIVINE ATLANTEANS

I have suggested that in the main the classical Greek writers managed to erode the original spiritual message of the golden age from their accounts. There are a few extremely important exceptions, however, primary among them the great philosopher Plato. Most people are aware that his *Timaeus* and *Critias* dialogues, written towards the end of his life in the middle of the fourth century BC, contain a detailed description of the location and layout of Atlantis – a subject to which we will return in Part 2. However, it is much less well known that at the very end of *Critias*, which in fact stops in mid-sentence and is unfinished – apparently because he suddenly decided to abandon it and commence his last work, the *Laws* – Plato provides a detailed description of the nature of the Atlantean people. And what an eye-opener it is:

> For many generations, so long as the divine element in their nature survived, they obeyed the laws and loved the divine to which they were akin. They retained a certain greatness of mind, and treated the vagaries of fortune and one another with wisdom and forbearance, as they reckoned that qualities of character were far more important than their present prosperity. So they bore the burden of their wealth and possessions lightly, and did not let their high standard of

living intoxicate them or make them lose their self-control, but saw soberly and clearly that all these things flourish only on a soil of common goodwill and individual character, and if pursued too eagerly and overvalued destroy themselves and morality with them. So long as these principles and their divine nature remained unimpaired the prosperity which we have described continued to grow.

But when the divine element in them became weakened by frequent admixture with mortal stock, and their human traits became predominant, they ceased to be able to carry their prosperity with moderation. To the perceptive eye the depth of their degeneration was clear enough, but to those whose judgement of true happiness is defective they seemed, in their pursuit of unbridled ambition and power, to be at the height of their fame and fortune. And the god of gods, Zeus, who reigns by law, and whose eye can see such things, when he perceived the wretched state of this admirable stock decided to punish them and reduce them to order by discipline.

He accordingly summoned all the gods to his own most glorious abode, which stands at the centre of the universe and looks out over the whole realm of change, and when they had assembled addressed them as follows . . .[20]

Whatever we may think of the Atlantis myth itself, how can we ask for a clearer elucidation of my theme of a highly spiritual antediluvian race that became debased? It has often been suggested that Plato himself spent a number of years in the company of Egyptian priests, becoming an initiate into their sacred mysteries, and that his writings were a coded 'story' version of what he learned – coded because, like other initiates, he was not allowed to reveal the full extent of his knowledge to the common people. Whether or not this is the case, I would argue that in this final passage we have an extremely clear and lucid account of what happened to the forgotten race that inhabited this planet, coded only to the extent that the other more prosaic details of the Atlantis tradition may represent something of a fiction.

Just look at what he has given us. The idea that the original inhabitants had a 'divine element' and 'loved the divine to which they were akin' is surely indicative of their spiritual awareness.

Admittedly the idea that this was diluted by 'admixture with mortal stock' represents, in my schema at least, the kind of unphilosophical distortion that we find so often in the Judaeo-Christian traditions. Nevertheless, the remainder of the account provides an all-too-familiar tale of debasement and materialism.

CONCLUSION

We have now come full circle in our review of the golden age traditions around the world. Well, not quite full circle, because we find a similar theme in many Native American traditions, but I will save those for the next chapter. Nevertheless, we have already seen that the majority of the ancient texts, especially the older and less distorted ones, seem to emphasise that this was a time in which humankind was possessed of a high degree of awareness and adopted a predominantly spiritual approach to life.

6. ROUND AND ROUND WE GO

We must now turn our attention to the somewhat more controversial theme, found in a number of parts of the world, of multiple world aeons. We have already seen a few brief references to the possibility of more than one destruction. We will now find that they exist in a number of other cultures, and can be primarily split into two categories – although these sometimes overlap. On the one hand, we have the 'world *ages*' traditions that are most obviously found in ancient Greece, Scandinavia and the Americas, and these tend to be relatively unstructured. On the other, we have the 'world *cycle*' traditions found primarily in the East that are based on regulated long-term cycles.

We will examine each category in turn, and then consider how they fit into the themes already developed.

OF SILVER, BRONZE AND IRON

Returning to Hesiod's account from the last chapter, it is well known that, after describing a golden age, he records four further races of humankind that succeeded it. As usual, we should look at the extract in full to obtain a proper perspective:

> A second race after that, much inferior, the dwellers on Olympus made of silver. It resembled the golden one neither in body nor in disposition. For a hundred years a boy would stay in the care of his mother, playing childishly at home; but after reaching adolescence and the appointed span of youthful manhood, they lived but a little time, and in suffering, because of their witlessness. For they could not restrain themselves from crimes against each other, and they would not serve the immortals or sacrifice on the sacred altars of the blessed ones, as is laid down for men in their various homelands. They were put away by Zeus son of Kronos, angry because they did not offer honour to the blessed gods who occupy Olympus. Since the earth covered up this race in its turn, they have been called the mortal blessed below, second in rank, but still they too have honour.

Then Zeus the father made yet a third race of men, of bronze, not like the silver in anything. Out of ash-trees he made them, a terrible and fierce race, occupied with the woeful works of Ares and with acts of violence, no eaters of corn, their stern hearts being of adamant; unshapen hulks, with great strength and indescribable arms growing from their shoulders above their stalwart bodies. They had bronze armour, bronze houses, and with bronze they laboured, as dark iron was not available. They were laid low by their own hands, and they went to chill Hades' house of decay leaving no names: mighty though they were, dark death got them, and they left the bright sunlight.

After the earth covered up this race too, Zeus son of Kronos made yet a fourth one upon the rich-pastured earth, a more righteous and noble one, the godly race of the heroes who are called demigods, our predecessors on the boundless earth. And as for them, ugly war and fearful fighting destroyed them, some below seven-gated Thebes, the Cadmean country, as they battled for Oedipus' flocks, and others it led in ships over the great abyss of the sea to Troy on account of lovely-haired Helen. There some of them were engulfed by the consummation of death, but to some Zeus the father, son of Kronos, granted a life and home apart from men, and settled them at the ends of the earth. These dwell with carefree heart in the Isles of the Blessed Ones, beside deep-swirling Oceanus: fortunate Heroes, for whom the grain-giving soil bears its honey-sweet fruits thrice a year.

Would that I were not then among the fifth men, but either dead earlier or born later! For now it is a race of iron; and they will never cease from toil and misery by day or night, in constant distress, and the gods will give them harsh troubles. Nevertheless, even they shall have good mixed with ill. Yet Zeus will destroy this race of men also, when at birth they turn out grey at the temples. Nor will father be like children nor children to father, nor guest to host or comrade to comrade, nor will a brother be friendly as in former times. Soon they will cease to respect their ageing parents, and will rail at them with harsh words, the ruffians, in ignorance of the gods' punishment; nor are they likely to repay their ageing

parents for their nurture. Fist-law men; one will sack
another's town, and there will be no thanks for the man who
abides by his oath or for the righteous or worthy man, but
instead they will honour the miscreant and the criminal. Law
and decency will be in fists. The villain will do his better
down by telling crooked tales, and will swear his oath upon it.
Men in their misery will everywhere be dogged by the evil
commotions of that Envy who exults in misfortune with a face
full of hate. Then verily off to Olympus from the wide-pathed
earth, veiling their fair faces with white robes, Decency and
Moral Disapproval will go to loin the family of the immortals,
abandoning humankind; those grim woes will remain for
mortal men, and there will be no help against evil.[1]

This is a heady concoction, and one that, like most of the other
world age traditions we will encounter, is not easy to interpret. We
can see that the silver race is to some extent credited with the lengthy
life spans that we encountered in the main biblical list of antediluvian
patriarchs, and which is a common feature of many traditions. Their
successors, the bronze race, appear to reflect the fixation with a race
of giants that, as we also saw earlier, came to infect the Judaic
traditions of the offspring of the fallen angels, the Nephilim. After
these apparently regressive races, we have a somewhat more
progressive shift to the 'demigods' who were 'more righteous and
noble', and yet still manage to perish through 'ugly war and fearful
fighting'. Finally we come to the iron race, apparently our own,
which appears destined to be as debased as any of its predecessors.

What are we to make of this? In my view, not a great deal.
Although this is a relatively early text, it appears heavily infected
by distortions that we know have little basis in reality. The silver
race does clearly exhibit the spiritual debasement that we have
already encountered on numerous occasions, but apart from that I
think Hesiod's account provides little credible support for the idea
that multiple races of humans have existed on earth, each in turn
destroyed. In fact the clear theme that these races were 'created'
makes this account comparable in some respects with the multiple-
creation-of-man traditions, especially from the Americas, which we
will consider in a later chapter. However in these, by stark contrast,
the last-created race is the most perfect.

Ovid's much later account contains a number of major differences.[2] The silver and bronze races are dealt with swiftly, and do not differ substantially from Hesiod. The demigods are then omitted, which leaves a clear path for the even more regressive iron race that is no longer our own, as in Hesiod, but whose members are this time actually destroyed for their debased behaviour. As a result there is another race thereafter, unnamed but presumably our own, which is unfortunately just as bad. Although it could be argued that if we omit the silver race from this account it is consistent with my main themes in that we have a golden age followed by a regression that ends in the destruction of the iron race, with our own modern race then repeating the same mistakes, it can also be argued that there is so much confusion in these classical Greek traditions of multiple ages of man that we should place little credence on them.[3]

SOLON'S SOJOURN

Just as we saw in the previous chapter, Plato takes a somewhat different tack from the other Greek traditions. We should now clarify the structure of the Timaeus and Critias dialogues, which remain his key works for our purposes, because it is somewhat confusing and often poorly explained. Although each is – unusually for Plato – primarily a monologue by the two title characters, the former commences in his more usual style with a dialogue between these two, Socrates and Hermocrates. In this opening dialogue it is Critias who describes a world age tradition told to him by his grandfather, also called Critias, who in turn received it from Solon – who, perhaps with esoteric echoes, is described as 'the wisest of the seven wise men'. As we all know, Solon had visited the Egyptian priests at Sais on the Nile delta, and the following dialogue is, once again, well worth reproducing in some detail:

And a very old priest said to him, 'Oh Solon, Solon, you Greeks are all children, and there's no such thing as an old Greek.'

'What do you mean by that?' inquired Solon.

'You are all young in mind', came the reply: 'you have no belief rooted in old tradition and no knowledge hoary with

age. And the reason is this. There have been and will be many
different calamities to destroy humankind, the greatest of
them by fire and water, lesser ones by countless other means.
Your own story of how Phaethon, child of the sun, harnessed
his father's chariot, but was unable to guide it along his
father's course and so burnt up things on the earth and was
himself destroyed by a thunderbolt, is a mythical version of
the truth that there is at long intervals a variation in the course
of the heavenly bodies and a consequent widespread
destruction by fire of things on the earth.'[4]

Plato is clearly suggesting that multiple catastrophes have
plagued the earth, and that these occur at cyclic intervals related
to variations 'in the course of the heavenly bodies'. I do not believe
that he is here referring to the phenomenon of precession – caused
by the axis around which the earth rotates having a wobble akin
to that of a spinning top, which makes the stars appear to move in
the sky over prolonged periods – because I am aware of no
mechanism by which this 25,920-year cycle might produce regular
catastrophes. On the other hand, despite his use of the term 'long
intervals' it does not seem likely that he is referring to the 'world
cycle' traditions that we will consider later in this chapter, which
stretch to millions or even billions of years. The only other
possibility is that Plato and possibly our ancestors in even more
remote epochs were aware of being plagued at regular intervals by
the passage of a particular comet or of a significant amount of space
debris – but even if this were the case it is likely that such a
phenomenon would fall a long way short of producing a major
worldwide catastrophe each and every time.

In any case, this is followed by an interesting passage in which
the Egyptian priest describes how they have managed to preserve
far more ancient records than the Greeks:

'On such occasions those who live in the mountains or in high
and dry places suffer more than those living by rivers or by
the sea; as for us, the Nile, our own regular saviour, is freed to
preserve us in this emergency. When on the other hand the
gods purge the earth with a deluge, the herdsmen and
shepherds in the mountains escape, but those living in the

cities in your part of the world are swept into the sea by the rivers; here water never falls on the land from above either then or at any other time, but rises up naturally from below. This is the reason why our traditions here are the oldest preserved; though it is true that in all places where excessive cold or heat does not prevent it human beings are always to be found in larger or smaller numbers. But in our temples we have preserved from earliest times a written record of any great or splendid achievement or notable event which has come to our ears whether it occurred in your part of the world or here or anywhere else; whereas with you and others, writing and the other necessities of civilisation have only just been developed when the periodic scourge of the deluge descends, and spares none but the unlettered and uncultured, so that you have to begin again like children in complete ignorance of what happened in our part of the world or in yours in early times. So these genealogies of your own people which you were just recounting are little more than children's stories. You remember only one deluge, though there have been many, and you do not know that the finest and best race of men that ever existed lived in your country; you and your fellow citizens are descended from the few survivors that remained, but you know nothing about it because so many succeeding generations left no record in writing. For before the greatest of all destructions by water, Solon, the city that is now Athens was pre-eminent in war and conspicuously the best governed in every way, its achievements and constitution being the finest of any in the world of which we have heard tell.'

Apart from Plato's clear political message of the pre-eminence of the earliest Athenian civilisation at the end of this passage, the supposedly multiple catastrophes here do not necessarily seem to be worldwide or even cyclical. Moreover, the early part shows some interesting parallels to my own prior suggestions regarding what might happen to the survivors after a major catastrophe. These ideas are echoed further in a later reprise in *Critias*:

Their names have been preserved but what they did has been forgotten because of the destruction of their successors and

the long lapse of time. For as we said before, the survivors of
the destruction were an unlettered mountain race who had
just heard the names of the rulers of the land but knew little
of their achievements. They were glad enough to give their
names to their own children, but they knew nothing of the
virtues and institutions of their predecessors, except for a few
hazy reports; for many generations they and their children
were short of bare necessities, and their minds and thoughts
were occupied with providing for them, to the neglect of their
earlier history and tradition. For an interest in the past and
historical research came only when communities had leisure
and when men were already provided with the necessities of
life. This is how the names but not the achievements of these
early generations came to be preserved.[5]

Returning to *Timaeus*, Plato continues from where we left off by
providing a clue as to when the 'greatest of all destructions by
water' actually occurred:

Solon was astonished at what he heard and eagerly begged the
priests to describe to him in detail the doings of these citizens
of the past. 'I will gladly do so, Solon', replied the priest, 'both
for your sake and your city's, but chiefly in gratitude to the
Goddess to whom it has fallen to bring up and educate both
your country and ours – yours first, when she took over your
seed from Earth and Hephaestus, ours a thousand years later.
The age of our institutions is given in our sacred records as
eight thousand years, and the citizens whose laws and whose
finest achievement I will now briefly describe to you therefore
lived nine thousand years ago; we will go through their
history in detail later on at leisure, when we can consult the
records.'

Of course many commentators have seized on this and –
assuming that if Solon really did visit Egypt it would have been
circa 500 BC – suggested that the flood must have occurred some
time before 9500 BC. Can we take this at all literally? It is difficult
to say. There is no clear psychological or symbolic interpretation
of these numbers, and even if many of the specifics of the Atlantis

and early Athenian traditions were fabricated by Plato, this does not mean that the general theme of a debased race being destroyed by flood, perhaps around 9500 BC, can have no basis in fact. We will have to reserve judgment until we examine the geological evidence in Part 2.

As for Plato's general theme of multiple catastrophes, we can see that there is good reason to question it if he meant that they were cyclically based. But if not, he does seem to suggest that only one was a truly *worldwide* event involving flooding that affected the whole of humankind.

DEPARTURE FROM TAO

We saw in the last chapter that the Chinese Taoists had a flourishing tradition of a golden age that was terminated by debasement. We find hints that this too is mixed in with a tradition of world ages. For example, Donald Mackenzie suggests the following in *Myths of China and Japan*:

> Here we touch on the doctrine of the World's Ages. Like the Indians of the Brahmanic period, the Chinese Taoists believed that the first age was a perfect one, and that humankind gradually deteriorated.[6]

This is to some extent substantiated by a brief passage from the *Tao Teh King*:

> In the highest antiquity, the people did not know that there were rulers. In the next age they loved and praised them. In the next they feared them; in the next they despised them.[7]

This brief original account does not suggest that there were multiple *catastrophes* as such, perhaps making it more believable, and it can arguably be seen to support the proposition that there was a gradual increase in debasement over a prolonged period.

THE FOUR WORLDS

The most abundant sources for the world ages theme are the traditions of the various Native American cultures, every one of which appears to have some sort of variant of it. However, they also contain my key theme of a golden age followed by progressive debasement and eventual destruction.

The finest example of the North American genre is found in the traditions of the Hopi of northern Arizona, who regard themselves as the first inhabitants of America. Although never written down in antiquity, these traditions were handed down orally from generation to generation for centuries and kept a closely guarded secret from the outside world. That is, until the elders took the brave step of allowing them to be recorded properly for the first time in 1963 by Frank Waters, who had since childhood cultivated close ties with various native cultures. Working from the information provided by thirty elders, and especially Oswald White Bear Fredericks, his *Book of the Hopi* has gained deserved and widespread acclaim. Its contents in general demonstrate the huge erudition and spirituality of these people, and anyone who reads it and still maintains that indigenous natives around the world are backward or primitive, and that modern technological progress makes the rest of us superior, is in my humble opinion a hopelessly lost cause.

The Hopi commence by describing the creation of the earth by the god Sotuknang, acting under instructions from the all-powerful creator, Taiowa, and then of the first humans by the creator goddess Spider Woman – to both of which themes we will return. They then proceed to describe how the human race multiplied and spread out over the earth during the first 'world', Topkela:

> The First People knew no sickness. Not until evil entered the world did persons get sick in the body or head . . . they understood themselves . . . were pure and happy . . . they felt as one and understood one another without talking.[8]

This is, of course, yet another revelation of the 'awareness' of our earliest ancestors, this time including the concept of telepathy. However, this golden age did not last:

> . . . gradually there were those who forgot the commands of Sotuknang and the Spider Woman to respect their Creator. More and more they used the vibratory centres of their bodies solely for earthly purposes, forgetting that their primary

purpose was to carry out the plan of Creation. . . . It was then that animals drew away from people. . . . In the same way, people began to divide and draw away from one another – those of different races and languages, then those who remembered the plan of Creation and those who did not.

We can see that this account is even more explicit in its confirmation that the debasement was based on a loss of spiritual roots that departed from the 'plan of creation'. In any case, as the situation worsened, Sotuknang decided to destroy the first race by fire and volcano, but not before he had selected an untainted group to survive and father a new race. These were secreted under the earth with the 'Ant People'. Then Sotuknang created the second world, Tokpa, 'changing its form completely, putting land where the water was and water where the land had been'. When the second race first emerged they 'multiplied rapidly, spreading . . . even to the other side of the world'. But 'this did not matter, for they were so close together in spirit they could see and talk to each other from the centre on top of their head.' Ultimately, however, they once again fell into wicked ways:

More and more they traded for things they didn't need, and the more goods they got, the more they wanted . . . they forgot to sing joyful praises to the Creator and soon began to sing praises for the goods they bartered and stored. Before long it happened as it had to happen. The people began to quarrel and fight, and then wars between villages began.

We can see that this second debasement clearly emphasises the dominance of materialism. So again Sotuknang was forced to destroy the world, except for a chosen few survivors hidden under the ground. This time the Hopi's description of the destruction seems to suggest a monumental shift of the earth's axis:

. . . the world, with no one to control it, teetered off balance, spun around crazily, then rolled over twice. Mountains plunged into seas with a great splash, seas and lakes sloshed over the land; and as the world spun through cold and lifeless space it froze into solid ice.

For many years the earth lay frozen and dormant, and the survivors remained underground. Finally, Sotuknang created the third world, Kuskurza, and after they emerged, the third race 'multiplied in such numbers and advanced so rapidly that they created big cities, countries, a whole civilisation'. However, we can guess what happened next:

> More and more of them became wholly occupied with their own earthly plans. Some of them, of course, retained the wisdom granted them upon their Emergence. With this wisdom they understood that the farther they proceeded on the Road of Life and the more they developed, the harder it was. That was why their world was destroyed every so often to give them a fresh start . . . some of them made a *patuwvota* (shield made of hide) and with their creative power made it fly through the air. On this many of the people flew to a big city, attacked it, and returned so fast no one knew where they came from. Soon the people of many cities and countries were making *patuwvotas* and flying on them to attack one another. So corruption and war came to the Third World as it had to the others.

Once again Sotuknang called for destruction, this time by flood, although a select group were yet again to be saved, this time by being sealed inside hollow reeds:

> . . . he loosed the waters upon the earth. Waves higher than mountains rolled in upon the land. Continents broke asunder and sank beneath the seas. And still the rains fell, the waves rolled in.

When the survivors emerged into the fourth world, Tuwaqachi, all they could see was water. Having crossed a number of seas and islands, heading eastward, they arrived at the land in which Sotuknang wanted them to settle. At this point he instructed them to look west and south, at the way they had come, and then he made all the islands disappear:

> 'I have washed away even the footprints of your Emergence: the stepping-stones which I left for you. Down on the bottom

of the seas lie all the proud cities, the flying *patuwvotas*, and the worldly treasures corrupted with evil, and those people who found no time to sing praises to the Creator from the tops of their hills. But the day will come, if you preserve the memory and the meaning of your Emergence, when these stepping-stones will emerge again to prove the truth you speak. . . . What you choose will determine if this time you can carry out the plan of Creation on it or whether it must in time be destroyed too. Now you will separate and go different ways to claim all the earth for the Creator. Each group of you will follow your own star until it stops. There you will settle. Now I must go. But you will have help from the proper deities, from your good spirits. Just keep your own doors open and always remember what I have told you.'

According to the Hopi, this is the world in which we now live. There is much in this narrative that is clearly symbolic and cannot be taken literally – for example, the subterranean ant people. However, we have seen that in general it provides substantial support for our basic theme of spiritual debasement and destruction, and arguably of a catastrophe caused by an axial shift. However, can we take the theme of *multiple* destructions seriously? In my view we should certainly take the apparently advanced technology of the third race with a pinch of salt because of the likelihood that the Hopi traditions have been infected by modern developments, although I will substantiate this rejection further in Part 2. But as to the more general theme, at this stage I feel we must reserve judgment.

THE FIVE SUNS

If we turn now to Central America, and specifically to the Aztecs of Mexico, we have a number of texts written in alphabetic script that date to the middle of the sixteenth century, after the Spanish conquest. The primary source for their world age traditions is the three-part *Codex Chimalpopoca*, translated by Central American specialist John Bierhorst in his *History and Mythology of the Aztecs*. One part, the *Leyenda de los Soles* or 'Legend of the Suns', is summarised in Figure 2.

This brief account is indubitably untrustworthy. Showing clear influences from across the Atlantic, a god tells the flood survivors

Age/Sun	Details
Jaguar	Lasted 676 (13 × 52) years. This age ended with all the people being devoured by jaguars.
Wind	Lasted 364 (7 × 52) years. This age ended when everything was swept away by the wind.
Rain	Lasted 312 (6 × 52) years. This age ended when everything was destroyed by a rain of fire.
Water	Lasted 676 (13 × 52) years. This age ended when everything was destroyed by flood; 'the skies came falling down . . . all the mountains disappeared.'
Movement	Because of its name, it is assumed that an earthquake will bring this, our current age, to an end.

Figure 2: The Aztec Legend of the Suns[9]

to hide inside a hollowed-out cypress tree, and when they emerge and cook a fish the gods are angry.[10] Meanwhile the time periods are clearly extremely short and fall well within our known historical epoch. The first age in this record was dated to only 2513 years before its composition in 1558 – that is, to 956 BC – and given that the first four ages total 2028 years, we would have been 485 years into the current age at the time this account was written. If the other time periods are anything to go by, the volcanic destruction promised for our current race should have occurred at the latest in the middle of the eighteenth century. Of course 364, the length in years of the wind age, is roughly the number of days in a year, while the length of every age is a multiple of 52, the number of weeks in the year. Moreover, the length of the second and third ages combined is the same as that of the first and of the fourth. Accordingly, we can perhaps assume that these numbers have some calendrical and even symbolic rather than factual significance.

Another section of the codex, the *Anales de Cuauhtitlan*, is even less revealing in that it contains no durations, and although the details are broadly the same the ages are in the different order of water, jaguar, rain, wind and then movement.[11] Meanwhile, in a separate source discussed by Mayan specialist Eric Thompson in *Maya Hieroglyphic Writing*, called the *Historia de Colhuacan y de Mexico*, the four preceding ages once again total 2028 years.[12]

Another commentator, Gregory Severin, suggests that these world ages should be equated with the precessional duration of each constellation, which we calculate as 2160 years, and he goes into great iconographic detail in his attempts to validate this argument.[13] However, he has clearly misinterpreted the summaries of the texts provided by other commentators, assuming that *each* age lasted 2028 years, whereas this is of course the stated duration of *all four* previous ages. In any case his suggestion is somewhat invalidated by a further Mexican source known as the *Codex Rios* – also referred to as *Codex 3738* and *Codex Vaticanus A* – in which the total duration of prior ages is considerably larger at 17,861 years, with each age lasting 4008, 4010, 4801 and 5042 years respectively.[14] This text also contains the following interesting passage about the survivors of the first destruction by flood:

> Others say that not only the two inside the tree survived the flood, but that other people found refuge in certain caves, and after the flood they came out and they parted from each other spreading all over the world, and the following populations worshipped them as Gods, each in his nation.[15]

This is very much a part of the postcatastrophe scenario that I painted in an earlier chapter. Moreover, the text also reports that Quetzalcoatl 'effected the reformation of the world by penance, since . . . men had given themselves up to *vice*, on which account it had frequently been destroyed . . .'[16] However, the remainder of the description of world ages in the text is made up of broadly Christian themes, including an early race of giants, a 'tower of Babel', and a 'virgin birth'.

Moving down now to South America, the world age traditions of the Incas of Peru are equally well attested. The accounts of a number of indigenous scholars writing in the sixteenth century are summarised as follows by Hartley Burr Alexander in his Latin American volume of *The Mythology of All Races* – a monumental thirteen-volume work dating to the early part of the twentieth century, which is an invaluable source of traditions from all over the world and one to which we will regularly return:

> Molina, Cieza de Leon, Sarmiento, Huaman Poma tell of the making of sun and moon, and of the generations of men, associating this creation with the lake of Titicaca, its islands,

and its neighbourhood. Viracocha is almost universally represented as the creator, and the story follows the main plot of the genesis narratives known to the civilised nations of both Americas – a succession of world aeons, each ending in cataclysm. As told by Huaman Poma, five such ages had preceded that in which he lived. The first was an age of Viracochas, an age of gods, of holiness, of life without death ... the second was an age of skin-clad giants, the Huari Runa, or 'Indigenes', worshippers of Viracocha; third came the age of Puron Runa, or 'Common Men', living without culture; fourth, that of the Auca Runa, 'Warriors', and fifth that of the Inca rule, ended by the coming of the Spaniards. As related by Sarmiento the first age was that of a sunless world inhabited by a race of giants, who, owing to the sin of disobedience, were cataclysmically destroyed ... [17]

Although we can see that these various Central and South American accounts do contain a degree of support for our main theme, in general they are relatively brief and highly symbolic. Coupled with their huge inconsistency, for example with respect to the duration and nature of each age, I would argue that it is inappropriate to take them too seriously as evidence of multiple races of humankind in antiquity.

COUNTING LONG

So far I have only made passing reference to the Mayan culture that flourished in Central America right across from Mexico to the Yucatán. They too have a world ages tradition of sorts, but this theme takes a strange twist in their most famous sacred book, the *Popol Vuh*, and we will have to wait for a later chapter to consider it properly. In the meantime, this culture also represents a point of crossover between the world age and world cycle traditions, because the Mayans also developed an extremely sophisticated calendar that incorporated the notion of cyclical catastrophes.

Unlike many of their counterparts in other parts of the Americas, the Maya had an extensive literature and a sophisticated form of pictographic writing that used distinctive glyphs. Apart from the *Popol Vuh*, three main Mayan hieroglyphic texts survived the Spanish conquest in the early sixteenth century, during which almost all copies of such texts were avidly sought out and destroyed – all, of course, to the glory of the Catholic Church. They are named after the cities in whose institutions they reside, and Thompson provides a useful summary:[18]

- The *Dresden Codex* is divinatory, taking the form of almanacs, and includes complex and accurate astronomical and calendrical data, for example on lunar cycles and the heliacal rising of Venus.
- The *Madrid Codex* – also known as the *Codex Tro-Cortesianus* and made up of several parts, including the *Troano Codex* – merely contains divinations, and no prophecies or astronomy.
- The *Paris Codex* shares similarities with the others, but is not fully translatable because it is incomplete.

The *Dresden Codex* is thought to date to the twelfth century because its latest dates for astronomical calculations are for this period, while the other two appear to be somewhat later compositions. The only other Mayan texts of note are the *Books of Chilam Balam*, various versions of which have been found because each town had its own copy. Although they are in alphabetic script, they are similar to the codices, but are somewhat distorted by being interwoven with later Christian dogma.

From all these written texts, and various inscriptions on steles and temples, scholars have been able to establish the details of the Mayan calendar system. Their short-count calendar had two types of year: a sacred one of 260 days called a *tzolkin*, and a normal one of 365 days. Any given day was identified by both systems, so that the calendar lasted 52 years or 73 tzolkins before it repeated itself, and this was the Mayan equivalent of a century. It was therefore supplemented by a long-count calendar in which 20 days or *kins* made up a 20-day month or *uinal*; 18 uinals made up a 360-day year or *tun*; 20 tuns made up a *katun* of approximately 20 years; 20 katuns made up a *baktun* of approximately 400 years; and 13 baktuns made up a great cycle of approximately 5200 years; and the end of each great cycle was thought to be marked by a cataclysm. Some commentators suggest that the last great cycle ended on 13 August 3114 BC, and that the current one will end in catastrophe on 22 December 2012.[19]

This long-count calendar allowed the Maya to calculate extremely remote dates in the past and future, and some commentators
have further suggested that its use in predicting regular catastrophes was based on a highly scientific understanding of sun spot
cycles and, for example, their effects on earth's electromagnetic
field – not only in the atmosphere but particularly in its core.[20]
This is an area of growing interest, and I do not suggest that our
scientists fully understand all the complex electromagnetic interactions in our solar system. However, I do believe that those who
suggest such interactions cause cyclical, worldwide catastrophes
have a long way to go in proving their point, and in particular we
will discuss the thorny issue of earth's magnetic field and its
associated polar reversals in Part 2. In any case, we must still
question how the Maya could have developed such knowledge,
which surely requires a scientific understanding and method far in
advance of normal astronomical observation.

The Mayan system leads us neatly on to the most complex world
cycle traditions of all – those of the Far East.

DAYS AND NIGHTS OF BRAHMA

The Indian philosophy of world cycles does not really come to the
fore in the Vedic literature, although it would in my view be a
mistake to suggest that it was newly created in the Hindu epics in
which it is most clearly expounded. This time we will concentrate
on the *Mahabharata*, which contains eighteen main books or
'parvas' including the celebrated 'Bhagavad-Gita'. The full epic was
meticulously translated by Chandra Ray over a period of ten years
at the end of the nineteenth century, and in book three, the 'Vana
Parva', we find the following:

> . . . after the dissolution of the universe, all this wonderful
> creation again comes into life. Four thousand years have been
> said to constitute the *Krita Yuga*. Its dawn also, as well as its
> eve, hath been said to comprise four hundred years. The *Treta
> Yuga* is said to comprise three thousand years, and its dawn,
> as well as its eve, is said to comprise three hundred years. The
> *Yuga* that comes next is called *Dwapara*, and it hath been
> computed to consist of two thousand years. Its dawn, as well
> as its eve, is said to comprise two hundred years. The next

Yuga, called *Kali*, is said to comprise one thousand years, and its dawn, as well as eve, is said to comprise one hundred years. Know, O king, that the duration of the dawn is the same as that of the eve of a *Yuga*. And after the *Kali Yuga* is over, the *Krita Yuga* comes again. A cycle of the *Yugas* then comprises a period of twelve thousand years. A full thousand of such cycles would constitute a *day* of Brahma. O tiger among men, when all this universe is withdrawn and ensconced within its home the Creator himself, that disappearance of all things is called by the learned to be Universal Destruction [original italics].[21]

With echoes of our main theme, but this time broken into multiple ages, the text goes on to describe in great detail how each age becomes successively less enlightened and more debased, how depravity overtakes humankind toward the end of the 'dark' kali age, how that age is destroyed by drought, then fire, then flood, and then how the new 'golden' krita age dawns again.[22]

Then in book twelve, the 'Santi Parva', we find the same details but with more added.[23] First, we are told that 'a year is equal to a day and night of the gods', and, as a result, scholars normally regard the years in the texts as being 'divine', made up of 360 'human' years. We are then told that:

With the commencement of Brahman's day the universe begins to start into life. During the period of universal dissolution the Creator sleeps, having recourse to *yoga*-meditation. When the period of slumber expires, He awakes. That then which is Brahman's day extends for a thousand such *Yugas*. His night also extends for a thousand similar *Yugas* [original italics].

In the succeeding passages we are given detailed descriptions of the processes of creation and destruction at the beginning and end of each day and night of Brahma. It would appear from this that the original view was that, although there are destructions at the end of each yuga, the universe as a whole is only completely 'reabsorbed' back into its primal state at the end of each day of Brahma, or after 4.3 billion years, after which it lies dormant for

Age or Yuga	Dawn (Divine Years)	Age (Divine Years)	Twilight (Divine Years)	Total (Divine Years)	Total (Normal Years)
Krita	400	4,000	400	4,800	1,728,000
Treta	300	3,000	300	3,600	1,296,000
Dwapara	200	2,000	200	2,400	864,000
Kali	100	1,000	100	1,200	432,000
Maha				12,000	4,320,000
Manvantara (14 in day of Brahma)				850,000	308,000,000
Day of Brahma (1,000 maha yugas)				12,000,000	4,320,000,000
Night of Brahma (same length as day)				12,000,000	4,320,000,000

Figure 3: The Hindu World Cycles

an equivalent period. From all this we can piece together the various details that are summarised in Figure 3.

If we now turn to the later *Puranas* that were compiled mainly in the middle of the first millennium, again there are eighteen major works in this group, although most record similar information. Perhaps the best known is the *Vishnu Purana*, and here we find the same themes, but with some new information and also some major amendments.[24] It confirms explicitly that each divine year is the equivalent of 360 human years. It introduces new terminology, in that a complete cycle of the four yugas is referred to as a *maha yuga*, and the length of a day or night of Brahma as a *kalpa*. It also introduces the new concept that each day of Brahma is divided into 14 *manvantaras*, each of which lasts approximately 71 maha yugas or 308 million years.

However, the most profound change is that it introduces the additional concepts of a year of Brahma, made up of 360 days and nights of Brahma, or 720 kalpas, or 3 trillion human years, and of a life of Brahma, which is made up of 100 years of Brahma, or 72,000 kalpas, or 311 trillion human years. According to the Puranic model, it is only at the end of *this* almost inconceivably long period that complete reabsorption takes place.

Although it might be argued that the time periods in the *Mahabharata* are somewhat unbelievable, these modifications lend even less credence to the Puranic model. Many modern commentators have attempted to amend them, with varying degrees of scholarship and success, and even to identify where in the cycles we currently stand.[25] However, all in all I believe that to follow the literal detail of these models in respect of human life on planet earth is, as with so many other world aeon traditions, a mistake. And this view is substantiated by a final *coup de grâce* in the Puranic model in that, with echoes of other cultures' beliefs in races of giants, and of longer life spans, they indicate that in each yuga humankind's longevity and stature – as well as virtue – decrease.

What I think we *can* take from these world cycle traditions is twofold. First, there is no doubt that in general they once again support my main theme of a golden age followed by progressive debasement. Second, the general philosophy of cycles of creation and emergence followed eventually by reabsorption back into the primal state is, when applied on a broad scale to the universe as a whole, and to the whole body of both physical and spiritual entities within it, in my view inherently plausible and indeed philosophically logical. However, I repeat that to attempt to rigidly apply the full details of these universal cycles on a smaller scale, and in particular to *human* existence on *this* planet, strikes me as inappropriate, and I will expand on this view as we go along.

THE WHEEL OF TIME

We have not so far considered the Jain religion, which emerged in India at about the same time as Buddhism in the latter half of the first millennium BC, and was of similar influence. Its doctrine of world cycles is similar to that of the Hindus that we have just considered – but with an interesting twist. It is described briefly by A Berriedale Keith in his Indian volume of *The Mythology of All Races*:

> To the Jain time is endless and is pictured as a wheel with spokes . . . normally with twelve, divided into two sets of six, one of which belongs to the *avasarpini*, or 'descending', and the other to the *utsarpin*, or 'ascending'. In the first of these eras good things gradually give place to bad, while in the latter the relation is reversed. Of these eras the fifth 'spoke', or *ara*, of the *avasarpini* is that in which we live [original italics].[26]

This seems to represent a similar idea to that of the fourteen manvantaras within a day of Brahma, except with only twelve.

Moreover, once again we find that the time periods involved are incredibly lengthy, while the theme of progressively reducing life spans and human stature recurs.[27] However, the Jain tradition can be clearly differentiated in that it suggests that only the first half of the cycle is one of progressive debasement, while the second half is one of upward spiritual progression. This is an important issue to which we will return shortly.

We might also note that a less specific cyclic theme exists in ancient Egyptian tradition. For example, modern Egyptologists John Baines and Geraldine Pinch make the following observation in their essay in *World Mythology:*

> The cosmos would not last forever, the Egyptians believed.
> The time would come when the creator would grow so weary
> that he and all his works would dissolve back into chaos.
> Then the cycle of creation would recommence.[28]

More confusing is the contribution made by the Zoroastrian religion, which dominated the mighty Persian Empire at its height in the first millennium BC, and which we know cross-fertilised with the development of Judaism in the Near East.[29] Joseph Campbell suggests that the Zoroastrians were the first to introduce the concept of a progressive, rather than deteriorating, world cycle.[30] However, we have already seen that the Jains mixed the two ideas, and Campbell himself accepts that their worldview may have started to form long before, during the period of the early Indus civilisation.[31] Moreover, although the Zoroastrians almost certainly contributed to the Christian concept of the second coming, their cycle contains only two rounds of twelve thousand years each, and they are not repeated.[32] As a result, in my view it does not make a significant contribution to the theme of world cycles.

CONCLUSION

It is entirely possible that the world *cycle* traditions in particular have resulted from the inappropriate merging of the theme of human debasement and destruction – which is in my view broadly historical – with a more general original philosophy of universal cycles. On the other hand, in their desire to reflect the microcosm in the macrocosm and vice versa, our ancestors may at some point have mistakenly attempted to apply the same cyclic rules to the mesocosm of the world scale. In my view, either of these approaches would represent a fundamental mistake, and because these concepts can become somewhat confusing I should take some time to explain.

The nature of all life at the microcosmic level is cyclical. Inasmuch as they all have a separate soul of sorts, all physical forms be they vegetable or animal go through a cycle of death and rebirth in the physical realm. In the case of vegetable life in particular, the cycle is particularly obvious in the progression from seed to plant to death to rebirth as seed again. However, these cycles do not in essence conform to any fixed and precisely measurable pattern, and each one is, in relative terms, of extremely short duration. If we then jump to the macrocosmic scale, I find it plausible that the universe as a whole operates in an extremely long-term cycle whereby it periodically emerges into manifestation on the physical level in the form of galaxies and solar systems, and then after an immense time span the whole ensemble ultimately dissolves and is reabsorbed back into the primal state. As for the planets on which physical life resides, I would argue that they operate entirely *within* this overall cycle – in other words, it seems highly unlikely that in any physical sense they are subject to their own planetary subcycles, or days of Brahma, whereby they manifest and dissolve repeatedly during the main cycle of the entire universe, or life of Brahma, as some interpretations of the ancient texts might suggest. As for the physical life forms on these planets, including humans, I would suggest that they develop via orthodox evolutionary mechanisms, and again not according to any subcyclic pattern.

However, apart from the relatively simple principle of the universe as a whole going through immensely long cycles of emergence and ultimate reabsorption, I believe there *is* a valid explanation for the planetary subcycles, but it is a highly spiritual and nonphysical one – so that if I am right it shows just how distorted most versions of the Hindu and Jain traditions that we now have are. And it uses what is most commonly understood as Qabalistic thinking and the various versions of the 'tree of life' as its basis. We will examine this in much more detail in Part 3, but for the moment I will try to provide a brief introduction to the potential underlying principles.

The vital clue comes from the Jain idea that the first half of the 'wheel' involves regression or descent, and the second half progression or ascent. Imagine that various groups of souls are attached to a particular solar system. Imagine that at some point one group emerges from what we might describe as the 'primal unity', and its souls become differentiated. Imagine that they then go through a prolonged series of 'incarnations' in which they gradually 'descend' through the various ethereal realms into the physical realm, and then gradually 'reascend' back through the ethereal realms until they are reabsorbed back into the primal unity. Imagine this group repeating the whole process through a number of cycles. Now, imagine that a whole load of different groups at different stages of karmic advancement are doing the same thing. And finally, imagine that the same process is being repeated in all the solar systems in all the galaxies throughout the universe.

This makes for a pretty mind-boggling scenario, but for those of a spiritual persuasion it makes a good deal of philosophical sense and, in my view, comes closer to explaining the detailed principles on which the Hindu and Jain universal cycle traditions were probably originally based than any other alternative. This is especially true if we argue that the former have been further distorted by only considering the *downward* part of the cycle that, for example, human souls attached to earth are in the process of completing, and then assuming this is regularly repeated.

So, as far as the world or planetary cycle traditions are concerned, on the one hand I have severe reservations about any geological or astronomical mechanism that could produce regular, cyclic catastrophes causing *global* devastation, and on the other I believe that if they are properly interpreted from a more spiritual perspective they are in no sense contradictory to my main themes. Above all, I must reemphasise that any worldview predicated upon predetermined cyclic catastrophes, which wipe out all human life, completely removes karmic choice from the equation. Inasmuch as this is what the Hindu traditions suggest – despite the clear contradiction that karma also underpins their worldview – it is surely right to suggest that the relatively late versions we have are expanded distortions of a far more philosophical original philosophy of *universal* cycles only.

But what of the less rigidly cyclical world *age* traditions? We have seen that they do contain a number of clear distortions but, as we have already mentioned and will discuss further in Part 2, it is now generally accepted that the earth has been rocked by repeated major catastrophes in its history. In particular, it is undoubtedly the case that the various ice ages and interglacial periods must have been allied to significant upheaval, on both a local and sometimes continental and even cross-continental scale. It is just possible that some of these traditions reflect that reality.

We must be very clear, however, that if we broadly accept the theory of evolution as applied to the human race, as I do, then the timescales in which these multiple destructions took place would have to be considerably shorter than is suggested in the majority of the world *cycle* traditions, and considerably longer than is suggested in most of the world *age* traditions. So, although all the traditions that we have considered in this chapter once again provide a degree of support for my general theme of a golden age brought to an end by debasement and destruction, my best guess – and it is *only* an educated guess – is that the realistic timescales of human cultural evolution that we will consider in Part 2 only allow for one previous *worldwide* catastrophe that affected the modern human race and was therefore *karmically* based.

Of course, I know that this conclusion could lay me open to accusations of selectivity in that I may appear to support some elements of various traditions and reject others as distortions. However, I can only hope that it is clear that I do try to justify my approach in each case with reference not only to the broader context of other traditions, but also, where applicable, to the various disciplines of both science and philosophy. That is the best I can do in attempting to pick my way through what is clearly a minefield of information that is extremely difficult to interpret consistently without making some subjective judgments.

7. TAKING ON THE EXPERTS

We are now, at last, in a position to consider the orthodox view of the themes we have been discussing in the last four chapters. Although, in view of the considerable quantity of worldwide detail that we have amassed, it is something of a surprise that the experts in mythology are relatively reticent about them.

CAMPBELL AND CYCLES

If we start with the eminent Joseph Campbell, he reviews the biblical themes of the fall of Adam and Eve and the flood itself in some detail, but the fall of the angels that sits in between – a narrative that I would suggest is of the utmost importance – receives hardly a mention. In fact he hardly comments in any detail on our main themes, despite the huge depth and breadth of his studies, but to the extent that he does his whole attitude towards them is based on a cyclical interpretation, the principle behind which we introduced in the opening chapter. Nowhere does he emphasise this more than when he discusses the flood theme in *The Masks of God*:

> . . . the whole idea of the Flood rather as the work of a god of wrath than as the natural punctuation of an aeon of say 432,000 years seems, indeed, to be an effect of later, secondary, comparatively simple cerebration.
>   Thus the evidence from a number of quarters suggests very strongly that in the earliest known Sumerian mythological texts the basic, mathematically inspired priestly vision has already been overlaid by an intrusive anthropomorphic view of the powers that motivate the world, far more primitive than that from which the earliest high civilisation had emerged; so that the myths that have survived to us represent a certain drop or devolution of tradition, which was either intentional, in the way of all devotional popularisation, or else unintentional following a loss of realisation. And the latter is the more likely, since, as Professor Poebel has let us know, the

Sumerian idiom of these texts 'is no longer that of the classical period'. They are already of a late, epigonous age.

I would suggest, therefore, that the mathematics still evident in certain of the earliest known, yet late, Sumerian documents suffice to show that during the formative period of this potent tradition (which has by now reshaped humankind) an overpowering experience of order, not as something created by an anthropomorphic first being but as itself the all-creative, beginningless, and interminable structuring rhythm of the universe, supplied the wind that blew its civilisation into form. Furthermore, by a miracle that I have found no one to interpret, the arithmetic that was developed in Sumer as early as c. 3200 BC, whether by coincidence or by intuitive induction, so matched the celestial order as to amount in itself to a revelation. The whole archaic Oriental world, in contrast to the earlier primitive and later Occidental, was absolutely hypnotised by this miracle. The force of number was of far greater moment than mere fact; for it seemed actually to be the generator of fact. It was of greater moment than humanity; for it was the organising principle by which humanity realised and recognised its own latent harmony and sense. It was of considerably greater moment than the gods; for in the majesty of its cycles, greater cycles and ever greater, more majestic, infinitely widening cycles, it was the law by which gods came into being and disappeared. And it was greater even than being; for in its matrix lay the law of being.[1]

I entirely agree with Campbell's general assertion that there must have been a significant 'devolution of tradition', that is to say a regression in its quality, at some point in the early history of the Mesopotamian civilisation and before the texts we have left to us were compiled. For that matter, as I have already suggested, I would argue that the same can arguably be said of the traditions of the ancient Egyptian civilisation from a broad spiritual perspective, however much that may be more controversial. This is precisely why I believe the Indian *Vedas* represent some of the least distorted remnants of a great universal philosophy that predated the development of these first major civilisations, although I very much doubt Campbell would either support my rather more spiritual view of the nature of this philosophy, or my assertion that it was first developed on earth tens of thousands of years ago in antediluvian times, and only *reasserted* after the catastrophe. Moreover, I have already made it clear that I totally support the concept of *universal* cycles, even if as far as I am aware there is little concrete evidence to support Campbell's implicit assertion that the specific time spans on which it is based were already established at the time the Mesopotamian and Egyptian civilisations were first flourishing – because as we have seen these were only fully elucidated for the first time in the much later Hindu epics.

However, it would appear from this passage that he somewhat seamlessly merges the concept of these lengthy Brahmanic cycles with that of the lesser cycles of precession, whereas in my view these two are really rather separate ideas. Yes, the Hindu model was applied to life on earth, but I have previously argued that this was already a distortion of the original philosophy on which it was based, and that the ideas of regular emergence or creation and reabsorption or destruction should only be applied to the universe as a whole. Meanwhile, the Nearer Eastern precessional model of 'as above, so below' that was perhaps most developed by the ancient Egyptians can be seen from a philosophical perspective as a model of the 'unity of all aspects of the universe'. However, this really has nothing to do with cycles of creation and destruction – except if applied in the rather simplistic sense of certain stars *appearing* to be destroyed in that they become invisible in the sky at certain periods and then *appearing* to be recreated when they reappear during another part of the precessional cycle. But I do not believe that the people who first discovered and analysed the phenomenon of precession were at all simplistic, even if certain later civilisations' understanding and application of the phenomenon did regress. In any case, I would argue that not only should we be careful to understand these two cyclic models as separate concepts, and to isolate any late distortions they contain, but we should also be wary of assuming too close a link between them.[2] And, for my own part, I regard the universal model as having a significantly greater degree of genuine philosophical importance than the precessional one.

But I digress somewhat. The crucial issue is that Campbell appears to judge at least the flood traditions from the perspective of 'early cyclical models good, later anthropomorphic models bad'. And while I have some sympathy with this approach, I still find it somewhat simplistic, in that it effectively suggests that the bulk of the later traditions that are left to us can contain nothing of any value in terms of possible pointers to a real hidden history. For example, he is clearly arguing that the idea of a single worldwide flood must be seen as an anthropomorphised distortion of the previously dominant cyclic view, rather than entertaining the possibility that the two ideas should be seen as entirely separate and of starkly contrasting derivation: the latter representing a broad esoteric philosophy, while underneath all the distortions the former represents a pointer to a genuine historical event.

Moreover, to the extent that Campbell comments on any of the traditions that are relevant to the current study he has a tendency to dismiss them as, for example, 'part and parcel of the heritage of civilisation itself'.[3] It is fine to suggest that the tendency to view the past through 'rose-tinted spectacles' is an innate human trait, thus explaining the golden age traditions and the idea that things have gone downhill since then. To some extent this is also consistent with a cyclical worldview whereby all things are born or created, and then degenerate until they are destroyed or die. All of this I accept. But in my view these psychological explanations fail to account for the fundamental context of these traditions. We have seen that there is extremely persuasive evidence from across the globe that both the golden age and the degeneration that followed it are described in *highly spiritual* terms. And in an earlier chapter I have already argued that to write off this element too as purely a psychological construct of simplistic people that felt the need to attribute all events to an anthropomorphic god or gods is to totally underestimate their depth of spiritual and esoteric wisdom.

ELIADE AND RENEWAL

Mircea Eliade is a much more specialised commentator, so the fact that he fails to consider my main themes in any great depth is perhaps less surprising. To some extent in his *Myth and Reality* he follows a similar tack to Campbell, but with a few differences. His most pertinent comments come when, after discussing the ritualised theme of *annual* renewal at some length, he attempts to apply this to the idea of world ages:

In other words, the End of the World in the past and that
which is to take place in the future both represent the
mythico-ritual system of the New Year festival projected on
the macrocosmic scale and given an unusual degree of
intensity. . . . But now we no longer have what might be called
the 'natural end' of the World . . . there is a real catastrophe,
brought on by Divine Beings. The symmetry between the
Flood and the annual renewal of the World was realised in
some very few cases (Mesopotamia, Judaism, Mandan). But in
general the Flood myths are independent from the
mythico-ritual New Year scenarios. This is easy to understand,
for the periodic festivals of regeneration symbolically re-enact
the cosmogony, the creative work of the Gods, not the
destruction of the old world; the latter disappeared 'naturally'
for the simple reason that the distance that separated it from
the 'beginnings' had reached its extreme limit.[4]

Although Eliade, too, has much to offer, I would argue that
anyone that finds this particular explanation for the destruction of
a prior race convincing is perhaps somewhat easily pleased. As a
corollary, in his separate work, *The Sacred and the Profane*, he
suggests that flood myths – especially of the submerged and lost
continent type – can be compared to the concept of initiatory death
and rebirth through baptism.[5] This is an interesting observation,
but in my view hardly a convincing explanation for the entirety of
the destruction traditions from across the globe.

As far as the golden age is concerned, Eliade points out that the
Communist and Nazi movements of the twentieth century –
however disparate and secular they appeared, and however
intrinsically evil at least the latter was – were clear attempts to
remember and re-create just such an age, and that this is a
powerful and natural human trait.[6] And it is undoubtedly true that
the 'New Age' movement that, arguably, I am supporting with the
present work, represents a similar desire. However, in my view it
does not automatically follow that the ancient traditions, by
harking *back* to a golden age, are merely manifesting the same trait
in reverse. Moreover, I must emphasise once again that they clearly
and consistently describe a *spiritual* race that became *spiritually*

debased, and in my view this cannot be seen as an automatic human response involving rose-tinted glasses.

CONCLUSION

I trust I have done enough in this chapter to show that modern experts in mythology such as Campbell and Eliade pay scant regard to the traditions from around the world of an antediluvian race that was wiped out, which are in my view perhaps the most revealing of all. Moreover, to the extent that they do comment on them they insist on a primarily psychological explanation based on twin paradigm constraints: on the one hand, the refusal to entertain the prospect that these might have some genuine historical content; and on the other, a severe lack of awareness, or at least acceptance of, the spiritual worldview that arguably allows us to make real sense of them. Whether or not one agrees with my own interpretations, the shortcomings of the experts' approach to these traditions – however much their erudition from a broader perspective is not in doubt – are surely there for all to see.

Moreover, I intend to back up my arguments with reference not only to the high degree of esoteric knowledge displayed in the various origin traditions from around the world, but also to the evidence of archaeology and geology and theoretical science. But before we turn to these issues, there is another theme in the texts and traditions that I would suggest strengthens my arguments still further. We find this new piece of the puzzle in yet more veiled secrets that our ancestors have bequeathed to us in their descriptions of the creation of humankind, and it is these that we will examine next.

8. CREATION CONFUSION

For a long time I struggled with the widespread accounts of the creation of humankind, unable to break the code of what their suggestions of us being fashioned from dust, clay or earth represented, other than the orthodox view that the ancients regarded us as the progeny of the 'Earth Mother'. Some of the traditions are somewhat more complex, however, and just may provide a more meaningful insight to complete our spiritual interpretation.

IN HIS OWN IMAGE

Some of the most detailed accounts of the creation of humankind are to be found in the Mesopotamian texts. Indeed, it is these that Zecharia Sitchin and others have used to promote the idea that humankind was genetically created by visitors from another planet, and if we had no better appreciation of the symbolic and spiritual aspects of these texts we could be forgiven, in this instance, for accepting his interpretations – because the details, at first sight and taken out of context, could support just such a proposition.

The most explicit is the Sumerian *Birth of Man* text, the version we have dating to some time in the second millennium BC. As we have seen so often, this appears to be a composite of two separate original texts that have been merged none too seamlessly. And just as we saw previously in the Akkadian *Atrahasis*, in the first part we find the gods deciding to create humankind to relieve them of their excessive workload in digging and maintaining their extensive network of irrigation and drainage canals – a theme that, incidentally, I believe has no hidden meaning, and is a purely fanciful notion based on the idea that the gods created the world that the Sumerians inhabited, and their localised experience was of the massive effort involved in the annual 'corvée':

To his mother Namma he [Enki] called out:
'. . . When you have drenched even the core of the Apsu's fathering clay . . .

O mother mine, when you have determined its mode of
being, may Ninmah put together the birth-chair
    And when, without any male, you have built it up in it, may
you give birth to humankind!'
    Without the sperm of a male she gave birth to offspring, to
the embryo of humankind.[1]

This emphasis on the mother goddess' creation of humankind
without male assistance can only be taken to mean that it extols
the role of the archetypal Earth Mother in producing humankind
from her own self – that is, the earth or clay – so from this
perspective the text can only support the orthodox view.

The second part of the text is the one more often quoted,
because it describes how Enki and Ninmah get drunk together,
apparently to celebrate the creation of humankind. Ninmah boasts
that she controls the 'build of men', be it good or bad, and Enki
responds with the challenge that he can mitigate any 'badness' that
she produces. So Ninmah makes a variety of beings, described as
the 'man-unable-to-close-the-shaking-hand-upon-an-arrow-shaft -
to-send-it-going', the 'one-handing-back-the-lamp-to-the-men-
who-can-see', the 'hobbled-by-twisting-ankles', the 'moron, the-
engenderer-of-which-was-a-Subarean', the 'man-leaking-urine', the
'woman-who-is-not-giving-birth', and the 'man-in-the-body-of-
which-no-male-and-no-female-organ-was -placed'. Enki then is
able to find a position in society for all these creations, and, after
creating his own being that is literally an abortion because it is not
gestated properly in the female womb, the text ends with Enki and
Ninmah agreeing that both men and women have vital roles to play
in the reproductive process.

Accordingly, we can see that it is hopelessly inappropriate to
suggest that the second part of this text describes genetic
experimentation, when in fact it is clearly a polemic on reproduction
and on the role of the disabled in society. It is also very much out of
step with the first part, which contains the creation theme proper,
while it is also evident that it is set in a time when humankind – for
example, in the form of the detested Subareans – already exists.

In the hope of more interesting revelations, let us now turn to
the Akkadian texts that deal with the creation of humankind. The
most important is the *Atrahasis*:

Enki made his voice heard
And spoke to the great gods,
'On the first, seventh, and fifteenth of the month
I shall make a purification by washing.
Then one god should be slaughtered.
And the gods can be purified by immersion.
Nintu shall mix clay
With his flesh and his blood.
Then a god and a man
Will be mixed together in clay.
Let us hear the drumbeat forever after,
Let a ghost come into existence from the god's flesh,
Let her proclaim it as his living sign,
And let the ghost exist so as not to forget (the slain god).'
They answered 'Yes!' in the assembly,
The great Anunnaki who assign the fates.
On the first, seventh, and fifteenth of the month
He made a purification by washing.
Geshtu-e, a god who had intelligence,
They slaughtered in their assembly.[2]

Now we appear to be getting somewhere, because we have a clear message that humankind was not just created *by* the gods, but *from mixture with* at least one of them. And what is the part of the god that humans receive? His 'ghost', and his 'intelligence'. Would it be so very inappropriate to hazard the guess that this is a veiled description of humankind receiving a relatively advanced soul for the first time? The text continues as follows:

Mami made her voice heard
And spoke to the great gods,
'I have carried out perfectly
The work that you ordered of me.
You have slaughtered a god together with his intelligence.
I have relieved you of your hard work,
I have imposed your load on man.
You have bestowed noise on humankind.
I have undone the fetter and granted freedom.'

This is, of course, the same 'noise of humankind' that, when it became excessive, caused the gods to destroy their creation, and which we struggled to interpret in a previous chapter. If it was 'bestowed' on humans from the beginning, are we simply referring to the proper development of the power of speech? Or is there something more significant here? We will have to wait until later in the chapter for more clues.

In any case, the goddess then goes on to 'pinch off fourteen pieces of clay' and, with the assistance of the 'womb-goddesses', proceeds to create the first seven men and seven women. There follows a recommendation of the rituals that should be performed 'wherever a woman gives birth', and I might note in passing that these are remarkably similar to those followed by the Hopi of North America.[3]

The composite *Epic of Gilgamesh* contains a brief reference to the creation of humans, again involving 'purification' and 'clay', but we find that the being created is Gilgamesh's eventual companion, Enkidu, who is described as follows:

> She created a (primitive man), Enkidu the warrior: offspring
>   of silence . . .
> His whole body was shaggy with hair . . .
> He knew neither people not country; he was dressed as cattle
>   are.
> With gazelles he eats vegetation,
> With cattle he quenches his thirst at the watering place.[4]

The reference to Enkidu being the 'offspring of silence' is surely in deliberate opposition to the 'noise of humankind', but again we will leave this to one side for now. In any case, if we ignore the confusion that in this epic he is himself the being that is created, is this passage not a perfect description of humankind's earlier ancestors before the 'creation' of modern humans – by the first incarnations within the general population of relatively advanced human souls – and its 'civilisation' by the incarnation among it of certain even more advanced angelic souls?

Meanwhile, in the celebrated *Epic of Creation* – also known as the *Enuma Elish* – which dates to the first half of the first millennium BC, a brief reference to the creation of humankind asserts that the 'blood' of one of the gods was involved:

They bound him [the chosen god, Qingu] and held him in front of Ea, imposed the penalty on him and cut off his blood. He created humankind from his blood.[5]

This can surely be taken as a metaphor for the life spirit of the 'god' entering humankind, as in a more 'godlike' soul. Moreover, that is undoubtedly how Berossus interpreted this text, because in reporting it he suggests that it is 'on this account that men are rational and partake of divine knowledge'.[6]

Of course, all this becomes distilled in the first chapter of Genesis into the suggestion that humankind was created in 'the image of God', but we can now see exactly what this brief and veiled reference implies.[7] We should also note the confusion in the biblical account that derives from combining the originally separate Elohist and Yahwist texts. The first Elohist-derived chapter simply says 'male and female created he them' – that is, men and women were created together – while the second Yahwist-derived chapter contradicts this by stating that Adam was created first 'of the dust of the ground', followed by Eve who was fashioned from one of his ribs to act as his 'help-meet' or companion.[8]

As we might expect, Joseph Campbell comments on these texts, and on the biblical variants that derived from them, at some length.[9] As well as ascribing to the standard view regarding the simple symbolism of creation from the 'earth', he discusses the gradual increase in emphasis on the role of the male god or gods in the creation of humans over that of the original mother goddess, resulting from the increasingly patriarchal nature of Mesopotamian society.[10] He also notes the marked philosophical change that results from the introduction of the idea that humankind was created as a servant of the gods.[11] I have no problem with these arguments. Once again, however, I believe that he is failing to pay proper attention to the deeper symbolism of the spiritual message that lies beneath the surface of these creation accounts.

THE MAKER, MODELLER, BEARER, BEGETTER

The Mayan *Popol Vuh*, compiled by native scholars in the middle of the sixteenth century, contains a lengthy description of how a variety of beings were created before a successful human was developed, which is highly comparable to and yet in some ways very different from the world age traditions discussed in a previous chapter.[12] The following description is taken from the translation made by Mayan scholar Dennis Tedlock.[13]

First, the creator deities referred to collectively as the 'Maker, Modeller, Bearer, Begetter' fashioned various animals, but they were unable to speak properly to praise them.

> And then the deer and birds were told by the Maker, Modeller, Bearer, Begetter:
> 'Talk, speak out. Don't moan, don't cry out. Please talk, each to each, within each kind, within each group', they were told – the deer, birds, puma, jaguar, serpent.
> 'Name now our names, praise us. We are your mother, we are your father ... speak, pray to us, keep our days', they were told. But it didn't turn out that they spoke like people: they just squawked, they just chattered, they just howled. It wasn't apparent what language they spoke; each one gave a different cry.

So the deities experimented again, this time:

> ... working with earth and mud. They made a body, but it didn't look good to them. It was just separating, just crumbling, just loosening, just softening, just disintegrating, and just dissolving. Its head wouldn't turn, either. Its face was just lopsided, its face was just twisted. It couldn't look around. It talked at first, but senselessly. It was quickly dissolving in the water ...

And so the first human creation was destroyed:

> So then they dismantled, again they brought down their work and design. Again they talked:
> 'What is there for us to make that would turn out well, that would succeed in keeping our days and praying to us?' they said. Then they planned again ...

After various further consultations, a new human was devised from wood:

The moment they spoke it was done: the manikins,
woodcarvings, human in looks and human in speech.

This was the peopling of the face of the earth:

They came into being, they multiplied, they had daughters,
they had sons, these manikins, woodcarvings. But there was
nothing in their hearts and nothing in their minds, no
memory of their mason and builder. They just went and
walked wherever they wanted. Now they did not remember
the Heart of Sky.

And so they fell, just an experiment and just a cutout for
humankind. They were talking at first but their faces were
dry. They were not yet developed in the legs and arms. They
had no blood, no lymph. They had no sweat, no fat. Their
complexions were dry, their faces were crusty. They flailed
their legs and arms, their bodies were deformed.

And so they accomplished nothing before the Maker,
Modeller who gave them birth, gave them heart. They became
the first numerous people here on the face of the earth . . .

They were not competent, nor did they speak before the
builder and sculptor who made them and brought them forth,
and so they were killed, done in by a flood.

So once again this race was destroyed, this time by the
ubiquitous flood, and a detailed and gory description of their fate,
and the revenge taken on them by the deities they had not praised
and the animals they had not respected, ensues. This is followed
by a highly suggestive passage:

Such was the scattering of the human work, the human
design. The people were ground down, overthrown. The
mouths and faces of all of them were destroyed and crushed.
And it used to be said that the monkeys in the forests today are
a sign of this. They were left as a sign because wood alone was
used for their flesh by the builder and sculptor. So this is why
monkeys look like people: they are a sign of a previous human
work, human design – mere manikins, mere woodcarvings.

Manikins and woodcarvings that resemble monkeys . . . what
can the authors have meant? We have already seen the emphasis

that the ancient texts and traditions place on the tendency of humans in the golden age to pay due homage to their gods, or, in more philosophical terms, to appreciate and respect their spiritual roots. But here we see it placed in the context of the creation itself, and we find that the emphasis is on the early creations not being able to speak in order to 'keep our days and pray to us'. In purely practical terms the prerequisite for the golden race was that humans should have the *intelligence* to appreciate their roots, with the necessary corollary of *speech* in order to be able to communicate with their peers. And now for the moment of truth . . . because I would argue that these more complex creation traditions just *may* be describing the idea that relatively advanced souls may have tried to incarnate in human form *before* our race was sufficiently advanced along the evolutionary path to make the 'experiment' viable. This interpretation is, of course, a corollary to my earlier interpretation of the Enochian traditions of the 'angels' expressing some uncertainty as to the timing of their fall into incarnation, and also of there being several groups of angels that 'fell' at different times and with different results.

Does this suggestion stand up in the continuation of the text? As a final resort, the creators decided to fashion humankind proper from corn:

'The dawn has approached, preparations have been made, and morning has come for the provider, nurturer, born in the light, begotten in the light. Morning has come for humankind, for the people of the face of the earth', they said. . . .
　　And then the yellow corn and white corn were ground, and Xmucane did the grinding nine times. Food was used, along with the water she rinsed her hands with, for the creation of grease; it became human fat when it was worked by the Bearer, Begetter, Sovereign Plumed Serpent, as they are called.
　　After that, they put it into words: the making, the modelling of our first mother-father, with yellow corn, white corn alone for the flesh, food alone for the human legs and arms, for our first fathers, the four human works.

And, this time, the experiment was more of a success:

And these are the names of our first mother-fathers. They were simply made and modelled, it is said; they had no mother and no father. We have named the men by themselves. No woman gave birth to them, nor were they begotten by the builder, sculptor, Bearer, Begetter. By sacrifice alone, by genius alone they were made, they were modelled by the Maker, Modeller, Bearer, Begetter, Sovereign Plumed Serpent. And when they came to fruition, they came out human:

They talked and they made words.

They looked and they listened.

They walked, they worked.

They were good people, handsome, with looks of the male kind. Thoughts came into existence and they gazed; their vision came all at once. Perfectly they saw, perfectly they knew everything under the sky, whenever they looked. The moment they turned around and looked around in the sky, on the earth, everything was seen without any obstruction. They didn't have to walk around before they could see what was under the sky; they just stayed where they were.

As they looked, their knowledge became intense. Their sight passed through trees, through rocks, through lakes, through seas, through mountains, through plains. Jaguar Quitze, Jaguar Night, Not Right Now, and Dark Jaguar were truly gifted people.

This is quite clearly yet another eloquent description of the spiritual awareness that humankind displayed in the golden age, when the first advanced souls were successful in incarnating in human form – and I would argue that it strengthens my contention that the descriptions of failed creation attempts are, underneath all the symbolism and distortion, indicative of similar but unsuccessful previous endeavours.

However, the text then takes a peculiar turn. The deities suddenly decided that the people they had created were *too* good and a potential threat:

'What our works and designs have said is no good: "We have understood everything, great and small," they say.' And so the Bearer, Begetter took back their knowledge:

'What should we do with them now? Their vision should at least reach nearby, they should see at least a small part of the face of the earth, but what they're saying isn't good. Aren't they merely "works" and "designs" in their very names? Yet they'll become as great as gods, unless they procreate, proliferate at the sowing, the dawning, unless they increase.'

'Let it be this way: now we'll take them apart just a little, that's what we need. What we've found out isn't good. Their deeds would become equal to ours, just because their knowledge reaches so far. They see everything . . .' And when they changed the nature of their works, their designs, it was enough that the eyes be marred by the Heart of Sky. They were blinded as the face of a mirror is breathed upon. Their vision flickered. Now it was only from close up that they could see what was there with any clarity.

And such was the loss of the means of understanding, along with the means of knowing everything, by the four humans.

What are we to make of this? In my view one option is to dismiss it as the product of a distorting Christian influence, because it is clearly reminiscent of the account of the 'first fall' in Genesis. In the latter, at the serpent's suggestion Adam and Eve eat the forbidden fruit of the 'tree of the knowledge of good and evil', after which God exclaims 'Behold, the man is become as one of us' and banishes them from Eden.[14] Moreover, we find a striking similarity between this Mayan tradition and that of the Gnostics – as expressed, for example, in the *Apocryphon of John*:

And in that moment the rest of the powers became jealous, because he [Adam] had come into being through all of them and they had given their power to the man, and his intelligence was greater than that of those who had made him, and greater than that of the chief archon. And when they recognised that he was luminous, and that he could think better than they, and that he was free from wickedness, they took him and threw him into the lowest region of all matter.[15]

It is my strong belief that the predominantly Judaeo-Christian theme of the 'first fall' is a late and entirely disingenuous one, developed to support what Campbell refers to as the 'mythic dissociation' of God and humans – whereby, instead of considering ourselves as all being a 'part of God', we are persuaded that the supreme deity is something entirely external to us.[16] Unfortunately, it would appear that this is essentially a political doctrine designed to keep the common people in their place, and it forms the fundamental distinction between the systems of the Occident and the Orient.

In any case, as I have previously suggested, to the extent that any 'falling' occurred at the outset it was undertaken by advanced souls who deliberately incarnated in physical human form. And, of course, this automatically involves a degree of 'restriction of spirit' when compared to life in the ethereal realms.[17] So this is perhaps another way of attempting to interpret the Mayan account of a reduction in humankind's awareness. Meanwhile, the final option is that it represents a distorted memory of the genuine fall into materialism and spiritual debasement of our forgotten race, which is blamed on divine intervention rather than being seen in its true light of an entirely human failure.

THE DAWN OF CREATION

We have seen that the Mayan traditions as portrayed in the *Popol Vuh* appear to confuse the themes of multiple creations with those of world ages, or alternatively to completely omit the latter. By contrast, we find that the Hopi tradition of world ages discussed in a previous chapter is *preceded* by a complementary account of the creation of humankind that again has, to some extent, multiple phases:

So Spider Woman gathered earth, this time of four colours, yellow, red, white, and black; mixed with *tuchvala*, the liquid of her mouth; moulded them; and covered them with her white-substance cape which was the creative wisdom itself. As before, she sang over them the Creation Song, and when she uncovered them these forms were human beings in the image of Sotuknang. Then she created four other beings after her own form. They were *wuti*, female partners, for the first four male beings.

When Spider Woman uncovered them the forms came to life. This was at the time of the dark purple light,

Qoyangnuptu, the first phase of the dawn of Creation, which first reveals the mystery of man's creation.

They soon awakened and began to move, but there was still a dampness on their foreheads and a soft spot on their heads. This was at the time of the yellow light, Sikangnuqa, the second phase of the dawn of Creation, when the breath of life entered man.

In a short time the sun appeared above the horizon, drying the dampness on their foreheads and hardening the soft spot on their heads. This was the time of the red light, Talawva, the third phase of the dawn of Creation, when man, fully formed and firmed, proudly faced his Creator.

'That is the Sun', said Spider Woman. 'You are meeting your Father the Creator for the first time. You must always remember and observe these three phases of your Creation. The time of the three lights, the dark purple, the yellow, and the red reveal in turn the mystery, the breath of life, and warmth of love. There comprise the Creator's plan of life for you as sung over you in the Song of Creation . . .'

The First People of the First World did not answer her: they could not speak.[18]

This tradition undoubtedly has similarities to that of the Mayans, and appears to reinforce my suggestion that they are describing the difficulties encountered when advanced souls first attempted to incarnate in human or even protohuman forms that 'could not speak'. It continues:

Spider Woman explained. 'As you commanded me, I have created these First People. They are fully and firmly formed: they are properly coloured; they have life: they have movement. But they cannot talk. That is the proper thing they lack. So I want you to give them speech. Also the wisdom and the power to reproduce, so that they may enjoy their life and give thanks to the Creator.'

So Sotuknang gave them speech, a different language to each colour, with respect for each other's difference. He gave them the wisdom and the power to reproduce and multiply.

Then he said to them, 'With all these I have given you this world to live on and to be happy. There is only one thing I ask of you. To respect the Creator at all times. Wisdom, harmony, and respect for the love of the Creator who made you. May it grow and never be forgotten among you as long as you live.'

So the First People went their directions, were happy, and began to multiply . . .

Is this, yet again, confirmation that, once they had been 'given' the 'power of speech' that would allow them to 'respect the creator', humankind had at last advanced sufficiently along the evolutionary path to be ready to successfully receive the advanced souls that had been waiting in the wings? Finally, the creation tradition ends as follows:

With the pristine wisdom that had been granted them, they understood that the earth was a living entity like themselves. . . . Thus they knew their mother in two aspects which were often synonymous – as Mother Earth and the Corn Mother.

In their wisdom they also knew their father in two aspects. He was the Sun, the solar god of their universe. Yet his was but the face through which looked Taiowa, their Creator.

These universal entities were their real parents, their human parents being but the instruments through which their power was made manifest. In modern times their descendents remembered this. . . .

The First People, then, understood the mystery of their parenthood. In their pristine wisdom they also understood their own structure and functions – the nature of man himself.

What more eloquent expression of humankind's dual lineage – that of our bodies from our earthly parents and of our souls from the universal and ethereal – could we desire? And is this not consistent with my suggestion that certain angelic souls must have incarnated at the outset of the golden age to educate their fellows about the true nature of the physical and not-so-physical universe, and of the immortality of the soul?

SILENT IN BORNEO

Further examples of multiple creation attempts from the other side of the world are provided in the traditions of various Indonesian tribes, described by Roland Burrage Dixon in his Polynesian volume of *The Mythology of All Races*:

A somewhat different form of origin-myth describes a series of attempts at creation in which different materials are tried, the first trials being failures, although success is finally achieved. Thus the Dyaks of the Baram and Rejang district in Borneo say that after the two birds, Iri and Ringgon, had formed the earth, plants, and animals they decided to create man. 'At first, they made him of clay, but when he was dried *he could neither speak nor move*, which provoked them, and they ran at him angrily; so frightened was he that he fell backward and broke all to pieces. The next man they made was of hard wood, but he, also, was utterly stupid, and absolutely good for nothing. Then the two birds searched carefully for a good material, and eventually selected the wood of the tree known as Kumpong, which has a strong fibre and exudes a quantity of deep red sap, whenever it is cut. Out of this tree they fashioned a man and a woman, and were so well pleased with this achievement that they rested for a long while, and admired their handiwork. Then they decided to continue creating more men; they returned to the Kumpong tree, but they had entirely forgotten their original pattern, and how they executed it, and they were therefore able only to make very inferior creatures, which became the ancestors of the Maias (the Orang Utan) and monkeys.

A similar tale is found among the Iban and Sakarram Dyaks, only reversing the order, so that after twice failing to make man from wood, the birds succeeded at the third trial when they used clay. Farther north, among the Dusun of British North Borneo, the first two beings 'made a stone in the shape of a man but the stone *could not talk*, so they made a wooden figure and when it was made it talked, though not long after it became worn out and rotten; afterwards they made a man of earth, and the people are descended from this till the present day.'[19]

We can see even from such summaries that they contain similar themes, especially the pervasive one of the inability of the earliest 'creations' to talk. And with that we will leave our discussion of the creation traditions.

HORRIBLE HYBRIDS

One final theme from the ancient texts requires some brief comment before we move on to other things, because it too has caused some confusion and led to what are, in my view, mistaken and misleading interpretations. It is the theme of composite beings that are part-human and part-animal.

In a previous chapter I discussed Berossus' account of how Oannes brought civilisation to humankind, and argued that suggestions the sage was part-man, part-fish were purely symbolic. However, the following is Berossus' account of what Oannes himself supposedly wrote concerning the beings that inhabited the 'primeval waters':

> There was a time in which there was nothing but darkness and an abyss of waters, wherein resided most hideous beings, which were produced of a two-fold principle. Men appeared with two wings, some with four and with two faces. They had one body but two heads; the one of a man, the other of a woman. They were likewise in their several organs both male and female. Other human figures were to be seen with the legs and horns of goats. Some had horses' feet; others had the limbs of a horse behind, but before were fashioned like men, resembling hippocentaurs. Bulls likewise bred there with the heads of men; and dogs with fourfold bodies, and the tails of fishes. Also horses with the heads of dogs: men too and other animals, with the heads and bodies of horses and the tails of fishes. In short, there were creatures with the limbs of every species of animals. Add to these fishes, reptiles, serpents, with other wonderful animals, which assumed each other's shape and countenance. Of all these were preserved delineations in the temple of Belus at Babylon.[20]

This account *precedes* Berossus' equivalent description of the Mesopotamian *Epic of Creation*, which itself commences with a description of the 'undifferentiated waters' personified by the goddess Tiamat before she was split into two to create heaven and earth – this origin theme being one to which we will return in Part 3. As a result we can only assume that either Polyhistor, or Berossus himself, or someone before them, had become completely confused about chronology, because the idea that these creatures could have any *physical* form before the earth was even created is clearly ludicrous.

Descriptions of composite beings can also be found in the relatively late works of Pliny, Strabo and Diodorus, among others. One possible source for all these is a Mesopotamian text that Assyriologist Alexander Heidel refers to as *A Prince's Vision of the Underworld*, discovered in Ashur and dating to the seventh century BC. It describes the dream of a certain Prince Kumaya:

Namtar, the vizier of the underworld, the creator of decrees, I saw; a man stood before him; the hair of his head he held in his left, while in his right he held a sword.

Namtartu, his consort, had the head of a *kuribu*, her hands and feet were those of a human being. The death-god had the head of a serpent-dragon, his hands were those of men, his feet were those of (?).

The evil Shedu had the head and the hands of men, he wore a tiara and had the feet of a (?)-bird; his left foot was planted on a crocodile (?). Alluhapnu had the head of a lion, his four hands and his feet were those of men.

Mukil-resh-limutti had the head of a bird, his wings were spread, and he flew to and fro; his hands and feet were those of men. Humuttabal, the boatman of the underworld, had the head of Zu, his four hands and his feet were those of men.

(?) had the head of an ox, his four hands and his feet were those of men. The evil Utukku had the head of a lion, his hands and feet were those of Zu. Shulak was a normal lion, but he stood on his two hind legs.

Mammetu had the head of a goat, her hands and feet were those of men. Nedu, the gatekeeper of the underworld, had the head of a lion, his hands were those of men, his feet those of a bird. Mimma-limnu had two heads; one was the head of a lion, the other the head of (?).

(?) had three feet; the two fore feet were those of a bird, the hind foot that of an ox; he was decked with terrifying splendour. Of two gods – I do not know their names – the one had the head, hands and feet of Zu, in his left hand (?).

The second had a human head, he wore a tiara, in his right hand he carried a club, in his left (?). In all there were fifteen gods; when I saw them, I worshipped them.

Moreover, there was a unique man; his body was black as pitch, his face was like that of Zu, he was clad with a red garment, in his left he carried a bow, in his right he held a sword, and his left foot was planted on a serpent (?).[21]

Some commentators have suggested that these various accounts can be taken literally: that they are either descriptions of visitors from other planets, or represent accounts of hybrids that at one time were part of the evolutionary mix on earth.[22] We will consider these issues in more detail in Part 2, but for now I should say that in my view neither suggestion matches our knowledge of evolution, and nor are they supported by the archaeological record. And, of course, there is a far more subtle but also simple explanation.

The fact that in the above text these creatures exist in the underworld, and some of them are described as gods of it, hints at what I believe to be the proper perspective for these accounts. We all know that the gods of ancient Egypt, and to a lesser extent Mesopotamia, are often depicted with the head of an animal and a human body, or occasionally vice versa as in the Great Sphinx. Moreover, some of the creatures described by shamans during trance states have similar traits, and shamans themselves often dress in animal costume, giving a composite effect. It seems highly likely to me that these composite forms are archetypes chosen, or even imprinted on the universal consciousness at a higher level, because they represent particular characteristics. And the composite beings described in relatively late Mesopotamian and other literature show sufficient similarities that there is little doubt in my mind that this is their derivation, even if the authors of these accounts seem to show little appreciation of the essentially symbolic nature of the originals.[23]

CONCLUSION

I have taken a relatively orthodox stance on the issue of composite beings, but the same cannot be said for my interpretation of the creation texts. I have suggested that the Mesopotamian accounts that emphasise the role that the 'blood', 'intelligence' and 'ghost' of a god played in creating humankind support my theme of the first advanced souls incarnating in human form.

I have further suggested that the multiple-creation traditions of Native American and Polynesian tribes may represent the failed attempts of advanced souls to incarnate in human or protohuman forms that were insufficiently physiologically advanced. Of course, one could argue that these traditions are merely describing what 'humankind' was like before we fully evolved. But it is clear that they are all attempting to describe deliberate 'acts of creation' rather than just some passive process of evolution. Moreover, we also have the possible Enochian theme of disagreements amongst the 'angels' about the right time to incarnate, and of there being several groups of angels that 'fell' at different times. All this suggests to me that my interpretation at least deserves serious consideration.

To close this first section, I have already suggested that two types of advanced souls incarnated when humankind was sufficiently evolved to kick-start the golden age, in that a relatively small number of angelic-type souls incarnated to educate a larger number of human-type souls that were also incarnating for the first time. To clarify exactly why both types are necessary in my hypothesis, in my view it was essential to the karmic development of humankind to bring a conscious appreciation of a spiritual worldview into the physical realm. Now in the ordinary course of events, and certainly before anyone knew anything about such a worldview on earth, this could not be 'summoned out of thin air' because no one would have known how to meditate to make contact with the higher realms, for example, or even had any recollection at all of their roots in the spiritual realms. So the few angelic souls that were sufficiently advanced as to be able to recall their spiritual roots even while in physical incarnation were vital to kick-start the process. Thereafter, the ordinary human-souled people of the golden race would have got used to passing on this information verbally, and also to the practical methods of making contact with the higher realms for themselves. And if we need further confirmation of this hypothesis, we will find that it is almost unequivocally provided when we examine the *Hermetica* in Part 3.

In conclusion, as radical as my interpretation of the creation traditions might seem, arguably it provides the final piece of the jigsaw of our spiritual framework for making sense of the huge variety of texts and traditions that we have considered in this and the preceding chapters. And they only serve to reinforce my general theme of a forgotten race of great awareness that lost its spiritual roots and became obsessed with the material and physical to such an extent that universal karma dictated it must perish.

Moreover, my view that this is arguably a more appropriate interpretation than any that has gone before is as unshakable as my view that, if I am right, it has massive significance for the plight of the modern world.

CONCLUSIONS FROM PART 1

- When analysing the multitude of ancient texts and traditions from around the world, we must be ever aware of the important role that symbolism and archetypes play, as well as many other psychological, religious and political influences. Many passages, however, also contain underlying germs of historical fact.
- Practical research into proofs of reincarnation and past lives is ongoing, but already there is a significant body of evidence that cannot in my view be ignored, and which supports the adoption of a spiritual worldview.
- The texts and traditions contain the consistent theme of a golden age in which a forgotten race led a simple life of great spiritual awareness. I have postulated that this age arose as a result of the first angelic souls being able to incarnate in human form on earth in order to teach their human-souled fellows about the true nature of the ethereal as well as physical universe.
- They also contain the consistent theme that this age was followed by one of progressive debasement and loss of spiritual awareness. The focus of our forgotten race turned toward material preoccupations such as achieving power over others and amassing wealth and possessions.
- This debasement led ultimately to their destruction in a worldwide natural catastrophe. I have interpreted the underlying cause of this as a universal karmic reaction.
- Various knowledge transfer traditions describe how certain highly influential figures, who often came to be regarded as divine or semi-divine, taught important civilising skills to their fellow humans. I have interpreted these on the one hand as accounts of the earliest angelic souls that incarnated on earth to initiate the golden age; on the other as accounts of either more culturally advanced humans who survived the catastrophe, as perceived by their less advanced counterparts, or of further angelic souls that once again decided to incarnate at this time to assist the rebuilding process and reassert a spiritual worldview.

- The multiple world age traditions suggest that such catastrophes have devastated humankind repeatedly, but given the timescales of human cultural evolution I believe there has been only one of worldwide and karmic significance to the modern human race. The similar but contrasting world cycle traditions tend to be mistakenly applied to human life on earth, whereas their real message concerns only the emergence and reabsorption of the entire universe over incredibly long time frames, and the possible planetary subcycles of incarnation of various groups of souls in both the ethereal and physical realms.
- The human creation traditions can be interpreted as describing how the first advanced souls incarnated in human form. Moreover, those that involve multiple creation attempts may be describing how initial attempts were unsuccessful because human intellect and physiology had not evolved sufficiently to serve as an appropriate vehicle for those souls.
- Experts in mythology have not been able to provide cogent symbolic or psychological interpretations of these themes in the ancient texts and traditions, which is why they are deserving of the above reinterpretation.

It is now time to examine the potential corroborative evidence from the scientific fields of archaeology and geology.

PART TWO
CORROBORATION

9. ARE WE SPECIAL?

I believe that the evidence of the orthodox archaeological record is increasingly proving to be broadly consistent with my argument that a highly cultured antediluvian race once existed on earth. I also think it possible that certain relatively nontechnical 'anomalous' artefacts that have been unearthed in the last few centuries but are not as yet accepted by the establishment *may* act as a further confirmation of its existence. All of this will be examined in the next few chapters. Before we look at them, however, it is important that we develop an overall sense of context and perspective.

In particular, this means that we must consider the thorny and always emotive issue of evolution, because we need to establish whether the timescales in which our forgotten race operated are definitely constrained by human evolutionary theory, or if this can be dismissed as irrelevant based on either creationist or Interventionist arguments. Integral to this will be an assessment of whether these nonorthodox schools provide a coherent alternative paradigm with logical and philosophical validity to act as a backdrop for supposedly anomalous evidence of varying kinds. But we must also recognise that to properly assess the various arguments over *human* evolution we have to consider them in the broader context of *global* or general evolution, and this is where we will start.

I should make it clear that in no sense can the following sections be regarded as a definitive review of the arguments. A dedicated volume at least is required to put forward each side, and this has already been attempted by numerous scholars far better qualified than I. Nevertheless, I would like to ensure that the orthodox view receives the fair hearing it is not always accorded in the work of some revisionist authors, and as a result to see if there really do remain any shortcomings that require some other form of explanation.

GLOBAL EVOLUTION

The orthodox theory of global evolution suggests that the earth was formed approximately four and a half billion years ago, that

Million Yrs Ago	Era	Period	Epoch	Evolutionary Steps
4,500				Earth formed
4,000				Single-cell life forms
3,500				Multi-cell life forms
570	Palaeozoic	Primary	Cambrian	Marine invertebrates
510			Ordovician	
440			Silurian	Marine vertebrates
410			Devonian	Amphibians
365			Carboniferous	
290			Permian	Land reptiles
245	Mesozoic	Secondary	Triassic	Sea reptiles
210			Jurassic	Air reptiles
145			Cretaceous	Birds
65	Cenozoic	Tertiary	Palaeocene	Mammals
55			Eocene	
35			Oligocene	Primates
25			Miocene	Hominids
5			Pliocene	Homo
1.7		Quaternary	Pleistocene	Homo sapiens
0.01			Holocene	

Figure 4: Evolution in the Geological Ages[1]

primitive single-cell life forms developed in the primeval chemical cocktail about 500 million years later, and that the first multi-cell forms emerged about another 500 million years after that. Nevertheless, it took another three billion years before life forms of any significant size and complexity developed during the Cambrian explosion of approximately 570 million years ago.

This broad evolutionary chronology is not greatly disputed by any members of the orthodoxy – except in the detail, with which we are not concerned. However, there are fundamental challenges to global evolutionary theory per se, not only from creationists and some Interventionists but increasingly from the relatively new 'Intelligent Design' school.[2]

For example, various critics originally suggested that the archaeological record clearly shows major jumps in evolution at various times, which was regarded as inconsistent with the idea of gradualism inherent in the original Darwinian model. But this challenge was in my view successfully rebutted by the introduction of the idea of 'punctuated equilibrium'.[3]

Allied to this is the criticism that the bulk of the known phyla of the animal kingdom arose suddenly during the Cambrian explosion, with few of the slowly differentiating precursors we might expect. But one of the most recent and in my view eloquent explanations for this apparently quite sudden explosion of diversified life forms is the 'snowball earth' theory.[4] In brief, it centres on the delicate balance of the ecology of this planet, which can produce sudden and exponential changes in temperature until a new equilibrium is reached. A large number of complex environmental factors inter-relate in this model, including the make-up of the atmosphere, the gases given off from any life forms and other chemical processes, the insulation strength of the ozone layer, the reflectivity of ice coverings, and a variety of other factors. In particular, it suggests that when there was only one huge continent centred on the equator, glaciation at the poles was able to spread relentlessly until it covered the entire landmass and the overall temperature plummeted to minus forty degrees Celsius – a process that could only be reversed by a huge build-up of carbon dioxide from repeated volcanic eruptions through the ice sheet.

At a critical point, the theory continues, huge reversals took place, with rapidly melting ice, acidic rains and overall temperature soaring to as much as fifty degrees Celsius. The model suggests that this cycle was repeated perhaps four or five times throughout the earth's earliest history, preventing any significant evolution of life. However, as the single continent progressively broke up and the various segments drifted more towards the poles, the balance was affected and complete glacial coverage could no longer take place. Accordingly, by the start of the Cambrian epoch simple bacteria and algae were able to evolve uninhibited into marine animals, which in turn crawled onto the land and flew into the sky.

And then we have more specific criticisms such as, to take one example, that concerning the complexity of the eye, which supposedly emerged in the earliest advanced marine life and whose broad design has supposedly remained relatively unchanged ever since – suggesting that this could not have occurred as a result of random mutation and natural selection. But let us look at this more closely. The orthodoxy actually suggests that the evolution of the eye in different types of animal commenced with a small light-sensitive spot, then progressed to an indented cup lined with light-sensitive cells, then to a closed cup forming a hollow ball with a pinhole opening at the front, then to a clear immovable lens at the front, and finally to the development of muscles that move the lens for focusing. Moreover, it argues that the human eye, for example, is in fact poorly designed precisely because it has evolved by mutation rather than being perfectly designed from the outset – in that the retina is *behind* the nerves and blood vessels, so that not only is the acuity of our eyesight reduced, but the chances of retina detachment are also increased.

Many other examples are quoted by anti-evolutionists, too numerous to be listed here, but my overriding impression as a nonspecialist is that the evolutionists – while still not having all the answers because theirs is always going to be an evolving discipline due to its inherent complexity – usually seem to be able to provide compelling detailed answers to what often appear to be ill-informed criticisms levelled at their theory.[5]

That having been said, I am open to the idea that some examples of evolution do seem to be somewhat perplexing and unexplainable from a purely neo-Darwinian perspective. Moreover, perhaps the most significant criticism of evolutionary theory for a long time was the issue of how life could have evolved on earth in the first place from a primitive chemical cocktail in a cauldron of primordial soup. As scientists became more familiar with the structure of cells and of DNA, it became clear that the chances of such a combination of chemicals coming together under exactly the right circumstances to create primitive life were so minuscule as to be almost impossible. But then we discovered that meteorites and other cosmic debris can carry these primitive, probably bacterial, forms of life prepackaged within them, and the 'panspermia' theory of the initial seeding of life on this planet was born. In my view this theory is perfectly plausible, but of course from a philosophical perspective it only begs the question of how life emerged on the seeding planet, and so on.

The ultimate question is therefore whether the 'hand of God' lies behind the creation of the entire universe. In my view it does, although I would prefer to avoid such emotive language and to refer to the influence in more archaic, esoteric terms as that of the 'absolute' or 'universal' creative power. This is a fundamental aspect of a spiritual worldview, and I will elucidate it further in Part 3. But if we accept this, then we must ask ourselves about the extent to which perhaps subsidiary ethereal forces intervene in the creation of all life forms on different planets.

It seems unlikely to me that all the day-to-day processes and nuts and bolts of evolution on all planets are predetermined in some sort of detailed master plan; this would seem to go against the laws of karma. However, it seems equally likely to me that various creative ethereal powers can provide a little added impetus at various times if they so choose. And if this seems somewhat illogical, we must wait until the very end of this work to see exactly how this type of intelligent design input might be provided within a spiritual framework.

Overall, then, I think I can safely be regarded as an evolutionist from the practical perspective of accepting orthodox evolutionary timescales, but also as a supporter of intelligent design from a more philosophical perspective.

HUMAN EVOLUTION

Man is nothing more than an advanced ape. Of course when Charles Darwin published *On the Origin of Species* in 1859, he did not explicitly say as much. He concentrated on expounding a global theory of evolution by natural selection and random mutation, and deliberately avoided mention of its implications for humankind, in his own words, 'to avoid adding to the prejudices against his views'. However, he knew full well that these implications were clear to all who cared to consider them, and twelve years later he clarified his position in *The Descent of Man*, as follows:

> We thus learn that man is descended from a hairy, tailed quadruped, probably arboreal in its habits, and an inhabitant of the Old World.[6]

As soon as this explosive idea burst into the world, the intellectual movers and shakers were split into two bitterly opposed groups. The religious community – which was far more powerful and orthodox in Darwin's day – reacted with hysteria and did everything they could to disprove or dilute Darwin's message, especially with respect to the evolution of humankind. After all, they had already been forced to submit to the realisation that the earth was not at the centre of the solar system, and this further blow threatened to remove all vestiges of divinity from humankind. On the other hand, the increasingly influential scientific community hailed it as a final nail in the coffin for nonrationalistic thinking.

This fierce debate still continues, as we would expect, and it has taken many twists and turns in the intervening period. The orthodox position is well summarised by Richard Leakey – who carried on the pioneering palaeanthropological work of his parents Louis and Mary in East Africa – in his highly readable 1994 work *The Origin of Humankind.*[7] The following is a brief outline.

As a committed Christian, Darwin himself assumed not only that the original impetus for all life on earth had been divine, but also that humankind had split off from the apes at a very early stage and quickly developed all the traits we associate with human life – a view that allowed our species to retain a mollifying degree of special status. The three most important of these human traits were bipedalism, technology in terms of tools and weapons, and an enlarged brain, and Darwin argued that they were all linked together in a self-inflating chain reaction.

He was, of course, operating entirely within the realms of theory, because at that time the only fossil evidence of our ancestors consisted of relatively late Neanderthal remains from Europe. But this thinking predominated even as increasing numbers of older specimens were uncovered. A part of the upper jaw of a small apelike creature labelled *Ramapithecus* was discovered in Tertiary sediments many millions of years old in India in 1932 and, although it was immediately reported to have more hominid than ape characteristics, it was surprisingly left somewhat in obscurity while other far less ancient discoveries hogged the limelight. However, that all changed in the early 1960s when Elwyn Simons of Yale University brought it to the public's attention by speculating that it was bipedal and must therefore represent our earliest humanlike ancestor. It was further assumed that these protohumans must have evolved as much as fifteen or even thirty million years ago.[8]

This view was challenged in the late 1960s when two biochemists at Berkeley University, Allan Wilson and Vincent Sarich, adopted a revolutionary approach by comparing the blood proteins of modern humans and apes, arguing that the rate of mutation of their molecular structure acted as a clock. This suggested that their divergence had occurred no more than five million years ago. Palaeanthropologists were slow to accept this new technique, but similar experiments continued to confirm its findings. Finally, the decisive discovery of new and more complete *Ramapithecus* remains in Pakistan and Turkey in the early 1980s indicated that it did continue to live in the trees and was *not* bipedal.

More recent genetic tests have pushed the date for the divergence of hominids from apes back to somewhere between eight and five million years ago, and this figure is now broadly accepted.[9] However, the issue of what caused it remains highly contentious. Darwin's 'linkage' has been proved false, because the earliest signs of stone tools do not appear until about two and a half million years ago, and this *did* coincide with brain expansion sufficient to differentiate the genus *Homo* for the first time, leaving a several-million-year gap back to the time when our earliest hominid ancestors descended from the trees and became bipedal. This latter characteristic, with its associated advantage of freeing the upper limbs and allowing the hands to develop to cope with more intricate tasks, has therefore become the defining mark of the hominid–ape divergence.

There is a broad consensus that this occurred specifically in East Africa sometime after the formation of the Great Rift Valley, which began some twenty million years ago, progressively acting as a natural barrier separating the east and west sides of the continent and, more importantly, their ape populations. The climate and ecology of the eastern side dramatically changed, with dense forest being replaced initially by more sparse woodlands, and finally by grasslands and savannah.[10] There are a number of schools of thought, however, regarding the evolutionary advantages that bipedalism conferred on hominids, which then acted as the impetus to reinforce this significant divergence.

One suggestion is that the freeing of the arms allowed the males to collect more food for the females, who as a result of improved nutrition and diet were able to produce offspring more regularly than their ape counterparts. However this argument has clear weaknesses, implying monogamistic tendencies that are not borne out by the continued divergence in size between the larger males and smaller females at this stage of hominid evolution, a common trait of polygamistic species. Another is that this form of locomotion, although not as swift, was more energy-efficient in the hot climate and required less food. Yet another is that it allowed our ancestors to operate more efficiently when standing in water – which would be advantageous either when crossing the increasingly abundant swamps of the area, or even perhaps when adapting to catch fish by hand in inland lakes and shallow coastal seas.

This area is one of heated ongoing debate among evolutionists themselves. The same level of debate surrounds the issue of whether *modern* humans evolved exclusively in Africa before emerging to populate other continents, or developed in parallel in different parts of the world; and also the issue of the mechanisms and timing of the development of attributes such as language and thought. While we will return to these subjects in the next chapter, it is quite clear that evolutionists do not have all the answers to these questions of human divergence and development – nor even to some of the more global questions. It is also clear that a great deal of their analysis is built around speculation, pure and simple. It is equally clear, however, that our knowledge does slowly improve as new scientific techniques are brought to bear, and as increasing fossil evidence becomes available for scrutiny. All these healthy debates will run and run, as they should.

But is there any sense in which we need to look outside the bounds of human evolutionary theory, as some revisionist researchers suggest? Moreover, are they contributing constructively to the debate by offering a philosophically and logically sound alternative paradigm? We shall now examine the two main revisionist schools of thought that have entered this arena, each from a different perspective.

HINDU CREATIONISTS
The prime exponents of the first anti-evolutionary revisionist school are Michael Cremo and Richard Thompson. Their hugely

influential *Forbidden Archaeology* first appeared in 1993, while an abbreviated version was published under the title *The Hidden History of the Human Race* the following year.[11] They suggest that archaeological evidence of modern humankind's existence stretching back many millions of years has been 'suppressed, ignored, or forgotten because evolutionary prejudice has acted as a knowledge filter in the archaeological community'.[12] Other revisionist researchers have trodden this path before, but not in as much detail and without the broad accompanying philosophy that Cremo and Thompson, at least on the face of it, provide. This is not discussed in the book itself, but they are quite open about it in their introduction:

> Some might question why we would put together a book like *The Hidden History of the Human Race*, unless we had some underlying purpose. Indeed, there is some underlying purpose. Richard Thompson and I are members of the Bhaktivedanta Institute, a branch of the International Society for Krishna Consciousness that studies the relationship between modern science and the world view expressed in the Vedic literature of India. From the Vedic literature, we derive the idea that the human race is of great antiquity. For the purpose of conducting systematic research into the existing scientific literature on human antiquity, we expressed the Vedic idea in the form of a theory that various humanlike and apelike beings have coexisted for long periods of time. That our theoretical outlook is derived from the Vedic literature should not disqualify it. Theory selection can come from many sources – a private inspiration, previous theories, a suggestion from a friend, a movie, and so on. What really matters is not a theory's source but its ability to account for observations. Because of space considerations, we were not able to develop in this volume our ideas about an alternative to current theories of human origins. We are therefore planning a second volume relating our extensive research results in this area to our Vedic source material.[13]

First of all, to avoid confusion I should note that their reference to the Vedic literature is clearly intended to include the later Hindu epics and *Puranas* in which the theory of world cycles is properly expounded, as we saw in Part 1. In any case, they are absolutely right to suggest that their affiliation should not disqualify their work – after all, my own philosophical framework underpins the entirety of this work – although we will find shortly that there may be other more prosaic and factual reasons to question it. It is, however, somewhat disconcerting that they make no real attempt to put their new 'evidence' into the broader context of a detailed alternative to evolution, promising that the full elucidation of the 'Hindu creationist' paradigm will be forthcoming in another book – which, even though a decade has now passed, is yet to emerge. Moreover, in their work they actually spend little or no time criticising the details of the orthodox theory of evolution per se.

Nevertheless what we can say is that, while their work concentrates on providing supposed evidence that counteracts the theory of human evolution in particular, we already know that the Hindu traditions apply a concept of cyclical creationism to all forms of life, and so we must assume that they are by definition creationists on the full global scale. Further information can be gleaned from Cremo's 1998 work *Forbidden Archaeology's Impact*, which includes the entirety of the reviews and correspondence that resulted from the initial publication. In one response to a critical review he offers the following:

Hindu cosmology speaks of cycles of creation and destruction. The basic unit of these cycles, which are of vast duration, is the day of Brahma. During the day of Brahma, which lasts about 4.3 billion years, the earth is manifest. During the night of Brahma, which also lasts 4.3 billion years, the earth is unmanifest. According to the Hindu cosmological calendar, we are about 2 billion years into the present day of Brahma. That would be the age of the current earth. Because life has, according to Vedic accounts, been here since the beginning of the current manifestation of earth, we should therefore expect the fossil record to extend back about 2 billion years. And according to modern palaeontology it apparently does go back about 2–3 billion years, with the age of the earth itself being about 4 billion years. In short, there is rough equivalence between Hindu cosmology and modern geology regarding the age of the earth and the extent of the fossil record.[14]

This is all somewhat confusing. On the one hand he asserts that we are only 'about two billion years into the present day of Brahma', which 'would be the age of the current earth';[15] and on the other that 'the age of the earth itself [is] about four billion years.' The former denies the evidence of geology. The latter – given that the best estimate of the age of our planet is in fact four and a half billion years – suggests that that we are already 180 million years late for our next planetary dissolution and that the night of Brahma should already be upon us; but, as far as I can tell, and for better or worse, mother earth and her various inhabitants are still here.

Nor is it clear whether life having 'been here since the beginning of the current manifestation of earth' includes human life. If it does, we are left with a further conundrum: how were our distant forebears supposed to walk around on the planet for the first few hundred million years of its existence – when it was still being bombarded by cosmic debris from the formation of our solar system, and the atmosphere was almost certainly poisonous?

Of course, whenever this took place, we might also ask the even more obvious question of exactly how humankind arrived on the planet in the current day of Brahma – the implication being that we were somehow created afresh. I have already commented at length on the flaws in the Hindu traditions on which Cremo and Thompson base their philosophy, and I can only reiterate my opinion that it is a massive distortion of the original esoteric wisdom of the theory of universal cycles to suggest that human life on earth, or any physical life on any planet for that matter, are subject to subcycles of manifestation and reabsorption within the universal cycle – and as a result operate outside the orthodox cosmological and evolutionary framework. In any case, until and unless further explanation of their underlying philosophy is forthcoming, it remains a puzzling and somewhat logically unsatisfactory one.

That having been said, how does their supposed physical evidence for the far greater antiquity of humankind stand up? I can only say that however much I was intrigued and excited by their work when I first came across it, upon closer examination I have found that it contains a number of flaws. Although I do not have the space to elucidate these in any detail here, these include the omission of new evidence where it might conflict with their interpretation; a general selectivity in analysing and presenting their evidence that is arguably far worse than that which they accuse the orthodoxy of; the devotion of considerable time to analysing noncranial and simple flint tool evidence that is by far the most contentious; and a tendency to exaggerate and to fail to contextualise the conflicts that undoubtedly exist within the orthodox community.[16]

THE INTERVENTIONISTS

The other main revisionist school of thought that challenges evolutionary theory, again usually only from the human perspective, are the Interventionists – who as we saw in Part 1 argue that humankind was genetically created by visitors from another planet.

Let us commence with a review of the work of arguably this school's most celebrated exponent, Zecharia Sitchin. Never mind that his proposed origin for these visitors is Nibiru, a supposed twelfth planet in our solar system, with an orbit so eccentric that at its aphelion it would be a freezing wasteland receiving only negligible light from the sun, and with a highly variable climate and atmosphere totally alien to our own – hardly an inspired choice for such intelligent and supposedly humanlike beings.[17] Never mind that his general interpretation of Mesopotamian and other Near Eastern texts is, as we have seen, scholastically flawed from the perspective both of grammar and of symbolism. Never mind that his specific interpretation of the Mesopotamian *Epic of Creation* – which is highly literal and from which he derives his story of how earth was created by a collision during one of Nibiru's orbital passes – not only reveals a fundamental lack of understanding of cosmology but also of the context of other similar traditions from other parts of the world, as we will see in Part 3. Never mind that, as we saw in Part 1, his specific and again unduly literal interpretation of the Mesopotamian *Birth of Man* text – from which he primarily derives his support for genetic intervention – again ignores not only the specific polemical content but also the context of other similar but in many cases more revealing traditions from both Mesopotamia itself and from the rest of the world. Let us concentrate on what he has to say specifically about the failure of evolutionary theory to account for humankind's advancement.

This exercise will not take up too much of our time – because in all of his books there are only two chapters in which Sitchin discusses the supposed creation of humans in detail, and in both cases he concentrates on the texts and on modern developments in genetic engineering, but *not* on any analysis of why evolutionary theory might be faulty.[18] In fact it was left to his successor Alan Alford to pick out the nuggets from the human evolution debate in *Gods of the New Millennium*, published in 1996. This work expanded and in some cases amended Sitchin's ideas, although to a large extent Alford has more recently, and with some degree of courage and integrity, publicly disowned it. The other revisionist author to follow up on this theme is Michael Baigent in *Ancient Traces*, published in 1998, and, although he does not support the Intervention hypothesis – indeed his philosophical framework is not disclosed save perhaps for the general principle of attacking orthodox theories wherever possible – he too raises some interesting questions about human evolution.[19]

The first issue they highlight is that our development appears to have been incredibly rapid from an evolutionary perspective. Alford argued that this indicates relatively recent intervention, something like two hundred thousand years ago, while Baigent suggests – like Cremo and Thompson – that this must mean hominids have been around for considerably longer than the orthodox seven million years. There can be little doubt that the advances over the last few million years or so that have resulted in modern humans *are* truly exceptional in evolutionary terms. But while we know that many species do seem to show only minor changes over millions – or even hundreds of millions – of years, we also know that the theory of punctuated equilibrium does seem to provide a reasonable explanation for the sometimes enormous leaps forward in many species – but is this explanation sufficient?

They also suggest that Darwinian thinking dictates that all evolutionary changes, which result from the seeding of originally random genetic changes by natural selection in an isolated environment, will be sufficient only to ensure the survival of the species, and no more. By contrast, they point out that modern humans have evolved far more than is necessary purely for survival, and moreover that we have characteristics that in earlier periods would have been positively *disadvantageous*.

For example, the enlargement of our craniums to carry a bigger brain, coupled with the reduction in size of the female birth canal in our narrowed pelvises as a result of our upright gait, significantly increased the possibility of death during childbirth – while the mechanism we have developed to counteract this, of reducing the length of gestation, merely makes our offspring vulnerable for a longer period. Our 'descended larynx', which is unique among land-dwelling mammals, allows us to make a wider variety of sounds for speech but presents the risk of choking when we attempt to swallow and breath at the same time. We have lost the thick hair covering that formerly protected us from extremes of both cold by night and heat by day – such as are often found in the zones in which we are supposed to have evolved – while our uncovered skin is also relatively fragile. In addition, we no longer have a penis bone that would allow swift copulation in a dangerous environment, while we exacerbate the situation by copulating face to face, a virtually unique occurrence.

What are we to make of all this? At first sight these appear to be perplexing observations. However, with a little thought it becomes clear that Alford and Baigent are approaching many of the issues from a somewhat perverse angle. For example, most evolutionists clearly argue that our gestation period shortened *because* we wanted to retain the more significant advantages of bipedalism and a larger brain; and that our larynx descended *because* we were in the process of developing a wider range of sounds for language – which is perhaps the most significant evolutionary advantage of them all.

Moreover, it is clear that they tend to ignore the additional *cultural* impetus that evolutionists accept is unique to humankind, and to our rapid development well beyond the mere necessity to survive. This can accelerate development far more than any other impetus, and as a prime example we only have to look at how changes in our Western diet and standards of health care in the last century have led to significant and rapid physiological changes in our average stature and longevity. The balance of probability must be, therefore, that all these supposed disadvantages arose entirely from natural evolutionary mechanisms, even if we may never understand the entirety of the intricate details of these processes.

To close this section, I have already indicated that I do not reject the possibility that life exists elsewhere in the universe – indeed I strongly support its statistical likelihood. Nor do I find it inherently implausible that the earth may have been visited, perhaps throughout its history, by intelligent species that have mastered the art of interstellar or even intergalactic travel. However, I must stress that not only do I find the Interventionists' arguments against evolutionary theory unconvincing, but also that *if* intervention has indeed occurred they have not as yet come up with any substantive physical or even textual evidence to support their case.

There is an increasing tendency even among the 'UFO community', however, to accept that many of the encounters and abductions reported are 'interdimensional phenomena' that are perhaps more closely related to spiritual experiences than to actual physical encounters with beings from other planets and their craft – albeit that the stereotypes of our modern culture tend to distort many subjects' interpretation of their experience.[20] This opens up a whole plethora of possibilities that to some extent could bring the Interventionists' position more into line with my own – particularly inasmuch as I do suggest, in a manner of speaking, that modern humans were 'created' by the 'intervention' of more advanced souls. This is an issue that we will explore further at the very end of this work.

CONCLUSION

From a global perspective, a spiritual worldview, if properly understood and applied, removes us from a parochial focus on earth and humans in particular, and allows us to appreciate the broader, universal picture. We then come to realise that all life, both on this planet and in the universe as a whole, is in some sense special and divine, and that it just so happens that in purely earthly terms humankind, given our advanced status as a species, is particularly so – but probably at least as much by luck as by premeditated 'divine' plan. In particular, this worldview does not challenge the fundamental tenets of evolutionary theory – at least from the perspective of earthly timescales – and it certainly does not assume that humankind in particular is somehow aloof from the natural evolutionary process.

However, it does insist that the first simple physical life forms could not have evolved from a complex chemical cocktail purely by accident, wherever in the universe this may have first occurred, and that indeed the same is true of the galaxies and stars and planets that make up the universe as a whole. Some divine creative impetus was clearly necessary, at the very least at the outset.

Moreover, despite my broad acceptance of it, perhaps there are nagging doubts about human evolution. Our advanced intellect and general level of culture is, quite clearly, without precedent on this planet, yet recent revelations from the human genome project have made it clear that our human genes are remarkably undifferentiated from those of even most basic of life forms – far, far less than we could ever have anticipated. When the project started, it was anticipated that we would discover anything from 80,000 to 140,000 human genes, but in fact we find that there are as few as 30,000 to 40,000. In comparison, the humble fruit fly has 13,000, the microscopic nematode worm has 18,000, and the tiny thale cress plant has 26,000.[21] So is there something else more intangible that differentiates the human species?

I must emphasise that my approach is *not* that evolutionary theory has fundamental and fatal flaws, even where humankind is concerned. There are difficulties, to be sure, but they are not necessarily of the magnitude that some commentators would have us believe. However, if we postulate for entirely different reasons that at some point humankind began to play host to more advanced souls, then it is only logical to assume that this would have had a massive and perhaps unprecedented impact on our intellectual and cultural evolution. This, more than any other, is surely the intangible factor that most differentiates the modern human species.

With that, we should put the heated debates about evolution to one side and, accepting its broad chronological premises, investigate the archaeological record in an attempt to establish when and where our forgotten race might have lived on earth.

10. DEFINING THE WINDOW

If we broadly accept evolutionary theory, then clearly the most important place to start in attempting to establish the time window in which our forgotten race lived is with conventional archaeology. So let us begin by briefly mapping out the orthodox view of the human family tree – although, before we do, we should take heed of Richard Leakey's warning about the evidence available:

> My anthropological colleagues face two practical challenges in addressing these problems. The first is what Darwin called 'the extreme imperfection of the geological record'. In his *Origin of Species*, Darwin devoted an entire chapter to the frustrating gaps in the record, which result from the capricious forces of fossilisation and later exposure of bones. The conditions that favour the rapid burial and possible fossilisation of bones are rare. And ancient sediments may become uncovered through erosion – when a stream cuts through them, for instance – but which pages of prehistory are reopened in this way is purely a matter of chance, and many of the pages remain hidden from view. For instance, in East Africa, the most promising repository for early human fossils, there are very few fossil-bearing sediments from the period between 4 million and 8 million years ago. This is a crucial period in human prehistory, because it includes the origin of the human family. Even for the time period after 4 million years we have far fewer fossils than we would like.
>
> The second challenge stems from the fact that the majority of fossil specimens discovered are small fragments – a piece of cranium, a cheekbone, part of an arm bone, and many teeth. The identification of species from meagre evidence of this nature is no easy task and is sometimes impossible. The resulting uncertainty allows for many differences of scientific opinion, both in identifying species and in discerning the interrelatedness of species. This area of anthropology, known as taxonomy and systematics, is one of the most contentious.[1]

EARLY ANCESTORS

We have already seen that *Ramapithecus* is now regarded as more ape than hominid, and certainly did not possess the fundamental characteristic of bipedalism, so it is another genus we must first examine – that of the australopiths. A significant number of their remains have now been uncovered, indicating that a number of species existed; and in fact there is much ongoing debate over exactly how many there may have been and how they are related to each other, as we would expect given Leakey's earlier comments.

For some time, the now considerable remains uncovered in the Hadar region of Ethiopia were thought to be the earliest, and they include the almost complete skeleton of the infamous 'Lucy' – who stood only a little over one metre tall as a mature adult, although the more fragmented remains found at the same location indicate that the males of the species were probably nearly twice the size. It is now almost universally agreed from the shapes of the pelvises and lower limbs that Lucy and her kind were bipedal but retained the ability to climb trees with ease. The Hadar remains were categorised as a single species, *Australopithecus afarensis*, and date from between three and three and a half million years ago. Meanwhile, remains unearthed particularly in South and East Africa have confirmed that a number of other australopith species developed, the earliest just over four million years ago, including *anamensis, bahrelghazali, africanus, garhi, aethiopicus, robustus* and *boisei*.[2] In fact, the latest classifications include a new although similar genus, *Ardipithecus*, which is thought to be slightly older still, and a genus tentatively classified as *Kenyanthropus*, which dates to at least three and a half million years ago.[3]

Although all australopiths and similar genera are thought to have died out by about one million years ago, another branch of the family tree had been developing, although the point at which this forking occurred remains highly debatable.[4] Nevertheless, what we do know, from remains first discovered by the senior Leakeys at Olduvai Gorge in East Africa, is that by at least two and a half million years ago a new species categorised as *Homo habilis* had emerged.[5] It had a significantly thinner cranium, indicating a slighter overall build, and the major reason for accrediting it as the first of the genus *Homo* was its significantly increased cranial capacity – which had more than doubled in this new species from the 450 or so cubic centimetres of australopiths to what is now considered to be an average of 800 for *Homo habilis*.

Associated with the emergence of *Homo* are the first stone tools, small flints with sharp edges referred to as eoliths that required significant skill to produce, and may have been used not just for butchering meat but also to cut saplings and reeds for shelters.[6] Moreover, the development from vegetarian to meat eater significantly increased this species' survival prospects. Then, about 1.6 million years ago a new type of technology emerged, involving larger flints skilfully shaped into hand axes, cleavers and picks – which not only require even more skill and patience to produce, as modern experiments have established, but also seem to indicate a more advanced and not merely opportunistic spatial awareness of the differentiated shapes desired. These tools, termed palaeoliths, are associated with a putative descendant of *Homo habilis* known as *Homo erectus*, a species that appears to have first emerged about 1.9 million years ago.[7] Its cranial capacity had once again increased, to about 900 cubic centimetres, and would eventually reach as much as 1100.

As we have already seen, a significant result of this expansion of cranial size was that offspring had to be born earlier, when their brains were only about one-third of their adult size, in order to squeeze through the narrower birth canal dictated by bipedalism proper. It is now recognised that this was just as much the case with *Homo erectus* as with modern humans, although the position of *Homo habilis* remains unclear because no complete pelvis has yet been found. The implication is that at least the former species must have developed a totally different cultural milieu from that of the apes and australopiths, co-operating in the raising of vulnerable infants over a prolonged time frame just as modern humans do. Moreover, remains of early *Homo* indicate that the huge size differential between males and females had been significantly reduced, signifying a new degree of monogamy, and of co-operation among males rather than competition.

One other significant difference between the genus *Homo* and its more apelike cousins is its bipedal athleticism. It has been proved that australopiths, although bipedal, could not have run in this posture for any length of time because their conical rib cages would have prevented them from being able to lift their thoraxes to breathe deeply. Of course, this combination of mobility *and* agility from having freed-up arms provided yet another evolutionary advantage to *Homo* – the ability to hunt with weapons. The issue of how early this process commenced remains contentious, because the combination of stone tools and animal bones bearing tool marks at ancient sites could merely be indicative of the scavenging of meat killed by other animals. Nevertheless, Leakey for one believes that as much as one and a half million years ago *Homo erectus* had a nomadic hunter-gatherer lifestyle – with all the elements of primitive culture including language, exchange, sharing, kinship and division of labour – that was not too far removed from that of our far more recent ancestors.

THE EMERGENCE OF MODERN HUMANS

Homo erectus is thought to have spread into Europe and Asia more or less from the outset, that is a little less than two million years ago, although in the former the only remains found so far date to no earlier than 800,000 years ago. Meanwhile, from about 27,000 years ago the *only* remains we have anywhere in the world are those of fully modern humans – who by this time are not only distinguished by their slighter build, more upright forehead and less protruding jaw, but also by their more advanced tools and evidence of culture proper. So what happened in the intervening period, and exactly how and when did modern humans emerge?

As Leakey confirms, this is probably the area of most heated evolutionary debate of them all because, despite the relative abundance of evidence compared to more archaic periods, there appears to be more confusion about this period than any other. Nor has the situation been alleviated as much as we might expect by the addition of genetic testing and more advanced dating methods to the tried and tested techniques of analysing remains from an anatomical and tool technology perspective.

One event that we can pinpoint is the emergence of the species *Homo neandertalensis* in Eurasia about a quarter of a million years ago. Initially differentiated most notably by their larger cranial capacity of 1250 cubic centimetres, they reached their zenith with a cranial capacity of as much as 1700 cubic centimetres about 150,000 years ago, and then died out about 27,000 years ago.

However, the picture is complicated somewhat by discoveries of the remains of similar but clearly different species in a number of Eurasian sites dating as far back as half a million years ago, which are referred to as those of *archaic Homo*. The majority view is now that modern humankind was not descended from the Neanderthals, because there is abundant evidence that they coexisted to some degree for at least 70,000 years.

Another marker is that the first modern humans arrived in Western Europe around 40,000 years ago. Usually referred to as Cro-Magnons, they had an even larger brain capacity than the most advanced Neanderthals, at anything from 1600 to 1900 cubic centimetres. Intriguingly, our modern capacity has shrunk somewhat to between 1350 and 1500 cubic centimetres, but we should remember that cranial capacity is not always an accurate indicator of brain size, and that brain size is not always an accurate indicator of intelligence; improved neural connections in the brain could improve efficiency with reduced size, and this may be a relatively late evolutionary development in modern humans. In any case, according to the orthodoxy the arrival of Cro-Magnon man was the prelude to the first evidence of culture proper, especially as displayed by the magnificent cave paintings of the era – although this is a subject to which we will return shortly.

So where did modern humans originally emerge? And how long ago?

The first question provides the main focus for current establishment debate. The 'out of Africa' school argues that, although *Homo erectus* migrated out of Africa into Eurasia nearly two million years ago, modern humans developed relatively swiftly and solely in Africa, from where they in turn migrated. By contrast, the 'multiregional' or 'parallel evolution' school argues that modern humans developed more gradually, and that the process occurred simultaneously in all the parts of the world to which *Homo erectus* had spread. The latter school of thought also tends to apply the term *archaic Homo sapiens* to our non-Neanderthal forebears in Eurasia, suggesting that they were our most likely ancestors.[8] This debate tends to focus on the one hand on DNA evidence that can attempt to highlight a common ancestor of the modern population – of which more later – and on the other on the extent to which modern racially diverse characteristics in different areas remain

Years Ago	Genus or Species	Cranial Capacity
4,400,000	Ardipithecus	?
4,200,000	Australopithecus	375–550
2,500,000	Homo habilis	800
1,900,000	Homo erectus	900–1100
500,000	archaic Homo	1250+
250,000	Homo neandertalensis	1250–1700
200–100,000	Modern man	1350–1900

Figure 5: Hominid Development

consistent when traced back in the archaeological record. New studies continue to appear with great regularity, but as yet neither side seems to have won the argument outright. For our current purposes, however, this debate is not particularly relevant.

As to the more important second question of *when* this occurred, the entire orthodoxy accepts that the remains of modern humans have been found in Africa dating back to 130,000 years ago and in the Middle East dating back to 100,000 years ago.[9] Moreover, most members of the orthodoxy accept that modern humans must have emerged before this, with the out-of-Africa school in particular arguing for an earlier date of 150,000 or, in some cases, even as much as 200,000 years ago, while the multiregionalists tend to dispute the classification of the earliest African finds and prefer a more conservative 100,000 years ago – albeit that this conservatism tends to be refuted by, for example, genetic evidence as we will shortly see. Meanwhile, although none of the *earliest* – that is more than 100,000 year-old – modern human remains have as yet been definitively discovered in the immediate vicinity of evidence of culture proper, there is plenty of orthodox support for the idea that they were sophisticated in their behaviour well beforehand.[10]

GENETIC STUDIES
We saw in the last chapter that modern developments in genetic testing have led to considerable improvements in geneticists' ability to determine when various branches of the hominid family tree diverged. Of particular interest to us now is the fact that a number of researchers have for some time been attempting to use this technique to isolate the period in which the common ancestors of

modern human populations lived. They can do this because certain strands of DNA change over time as human groups drift apart.

The original studies that concentrated on mitochondrial DNA, which is passed on only by women, were conducted by Allan Wilson in 1987. They indicated that the most recent common female ancestor, or 'mitochondrial Eve', lived somewhere between 150,000 and 200,000 years ago, a finding that is of course consistent with the orthodox archaeological view of the emergence of truly modern humans. Although the methodology of these tests has improved enormously since then, the results have remained substantially unchanged.

But researchers have recently developed a technique that uses Y-chromosome DNA to attempt to date the common male ancestor as well. A recent study conducted by biologist Peter Oefner and his colleagues at the Stanford DNA Sequencing and Technology Center has tentatively indicated that 'Adam' lived only about 50,000 years ago.[11] If these results were confirmed, they would imply that earlier male lineages contemporary to Eve died out for some as-yet-unidentified reason, leaving one relatively recent common father.

Another study performed by Stanley Ambrose, a professor of anthropology at the University of Illinois in 1998, suggests that a bottleneck occurred in human evolution at around 70,000 years ago, coinciding with a volcanic winter following the Toba super-eruption.[12] In fact, a multitude of studies are now being conducted, with new findings announced almost weekly. They are still somewhat in their infancy, and it will be some time before the results become more accurate and reliable. It will also take time for the appropriate cross-disciplinary co-operation between archaeologists and geneticists to develop. Nevertheless, they do appear to provide firm evidence that the orthodoxy is operating in the right ballpark when it comes to dating the emergence of modern humans.

CONSCIOUSNESS AND LANGUAGE

For some time the orthodox view persisted that it was when humans first developed self-awareness that their consciousness started to diverge substantially from that of their ape cousins. This view remained unchallenged because historically most anthropologists shied away from such a difficult area of study.[13]

However, in the late 1960s psychologist Gordon Gallup came up with an ingenious test. He painted a red spot on the forehead of various animals, and placed the animals before a mirror. He then waited to see whether they would investigate by touching the curious anomaly on the reflected image, thinking that they were confronted with another animal, or by touching it on their own forehead, which would clearly indicate that they recognised the image as their own. Contrary to the conventional wisdom of the time, he found that chimpanzees and orang-utans tended to touch themselves – although gorillas tended to touch the reflection, and these results were somewhat strange inasmuch as humans are more closely related to the great apes than to chimpanzees.

Modern studies have also revealed that primates that live in large groups tend to have an advanced social awareness of group politics – which appears to require not only some sense of self, but also a sense of one's allies and enemies, of *their* allies and enemies, of how these alliances change over time, and even of the need to deliberately and consciously change them to one's own advantage.

All of this tends to indicate a sufficient degree of self-awareness in certain other primates that it cannot be the major differentiating factor of human consciousness. Some commentators suggest that the difference in humans is our ability not only to predict how others will behave, but also to empathise with how they feel. However, anyone who is close to a dog or a cat will be aware that they can sense mood changes in humans, and that their empathy is, at least at times, more than just manipulation to gain food. Moreover, televised footage of, for example, elephants co-operating to save one of their kin from drowning in a bog, or displaying all the signs of group grief when one of the herd dies, abounds.

Nevertheless, anthropologists have been able to determine that a major evolutionary divergence occurred with the first species of *Homo*, all of whose frontal brain lobes are larger than those at the rear, whereas in apes and australopiths the situation is reversed. So did the emergence of *Homo habilis* some two and a half million years ago mark a major leap forward in the consciousness of humankind? The answer is probably yes, but this does not mean that the species had the kind of fully developed consciousness we now possess.

Is it possible to look for more clues in the link between consciousness and language? The issue of whether language is a *prerequisite* for conscious thought, or a direct *product* of it, has always been hotly contested by philosophers and anthropologists alike, and scholars such as Noam Chomsky, Steven Pinker, Karl Popper and Daniel Dennett, among numerous others, have all made important contributions to this debate.[14] I tend to fall into the latter category, for a number of reasons. First, we all know that some people tend to think in terms of words, but others tend to think in terms of feelings or pictures, and these latter thoughts surely do not require language as a prerequisite even if we tend to express them verbally to communicate them to others. Second, I believe in telepathy – in part based on a degree of personal experience – and I suspect that even if we had no common language or even pictorial symbols we would still get the message. For example, although some species of animal are proving to have relatively advanced audio communications, they are clearly far behind the complexity of human speech; yet the seemingly telepathic ability of certain species suggests that language is not a prerequisite. In fact it would appear that, perhaps as a result of the development of language, our own telepathic abilities have to some extent been culturally bred out of us, or at least lie dormant through general lack of use. So although in general I agree with the consensus that the development of language advanced human-kind's evolution, perhaps it had some drawbacks as well. Third, and partially related to this latter point, is the fact that appreciation of some more esoteric concepts and experiences can be positively hampered by attempts to communicate them in words, because they rely heavily on personal experience – even if, as we will see later, I have little time for those who do everything they can to discuss such issues in obscure language to make themselves seem more in possession of secret wisdom.

These are interesting areas for discussion, but not vital to our quest as, at the very least, it seems likely that in human evolutionary terms the development of consciousness and of language progressed pretty much hand in hand. So can we establish the point at which language was first developed?

In its own right this too is an area of heated debate. Chomsky heads the school of thought that advocates a late and relatively sudden emergence of language, postulating that it arose as a result of the enlargement of the brain. Still, we know that this latter process was gradual and commenced several million years ago, and as a result the majority tend now to side with Steven Pinker's suggestion of a gradual evolution of language that was accompanied by a rewiring of the neural network in the *Homo* brain. This gradualist view is supported by the evidence of anatomical developments in the various *Homo* species. For example, it has been established that the area at the base of the cranium is flat in apes and australopiths but becomes more arched in *Homo*, and it is likely that this is an accompaniment to an increasingly descending larynx.[15] Moreover, an examination of brain shape reveals that in modern humans a portion at the front known as 'Broca's area', which is thought to be associated with language, is accentuated – and there is evidence that this process had already commenced with *Homo habilis* at least two million years ago.[16]

It would appear, therefore, that the development of consciousness and language was a slow and gradual but interlinked process that commenced several million years ago, and went hand in hand with advances in social interaction and tool use.

THE DEVELOPMENT OF CULTURE

Let us now turn our attention to what the archaeological record tells us about the more general cultural development of humankind. We should start by heeding another warning from Leakey:

> We have to remember that the vast preponderance of human behaviour in technologically primitive human groups is archaeologically invisible. For instance, an initiation ritual led by a shaman would involve the telling of myths, chanting, dancing, and body decoration – and none of these activities would enter the archaeological record. Therefore we need to keep reminding ourselves, when we find stone tools and carved or painted objects, that they give us only the narrowest of windows onto the ancient world.[17]

We have already seen that there are a number of significant stages of tool development, commencing with the crude and small eoliths of *Homo habilis* about two and a half million years ago, then ranging through the more advanced palaeoliths associated with *Homo erectus* just over one and a half million years ago and composed of approximately twelve main types, and then continuing on to the further advances of *archaic Homo* about 250,000 years ago, when the toolkit expanded to contain some sixty items. Sometime between these latter two humankind also learned to control fire, with the earliest definitive signs of this occurring at least 700,000 years ago, and more tentative signs perhaps well before that.

We then jump forward to approximately 100,000 years ago and, although there are few examples of this age, the first definitive proof of the deliberate burial of modern humans at a site in Israel accompanied by animal bones which are indicative of some degree of ritual activity.[18] We also find that by at least 75,000 years ago the burial rituals included the deliberate working of skulls – particularly of the bear in Western Europe.[19]

These cultural advances continued in more dramatic fashion in the 'Upper Palaeolithic explosion' that took place about 40,000 years ago, shortly after modern humans entered Western Europe. There is little conventional evidence of what these fully modern humans were doing before this, and we cannot be completely certain even of where they came from, although the consensus appears to be that they had migrated from somewhere farther east. What we do know is that they suddenly gave us evidence of culture proper in abundance.

During the Aurignacian period, which commenced 40,000 years ago, they were not only using an even more complex stone tool kit but had also started to work in other materials and, for the first time, to produce art. Beautiful miniature sculptures of humans and of animals such as the mammoth and horse have been found dating to this period, carved mainly from ivory, and Leakey admits that they are as fine as anything that has come since (see Plate 1).[20] Moreover, music had definitely entered our forebears' repertoire by this stage, because at least one small bone flute dating to this period has been recovered;[21] and – as we will see in Part 3 – the 'language' of music and harmony plays a significant role in esoteric rituals and understanding generally.

On a more prosaic level, at about this time we also find that the use of clothing and body adornment had become widespread, because a multitude of small drilled ivory beads, presumably for adorning garments and for necklaces and other jewellery, have been found in what were clearly specialist manufacturing sites (see Plate 2). In fact recent research has led to the conclusion that body ornamentation was widespread and relatively standardised in Europe, Asia and Africa by at least 40,000 years ago, suggesting the existence of a shared system of communication and probably trading links over wide geographic areas.[22]

These developments were followed in the Gravettian period, which commenced 28,000 years ago, by the regular production of a variety of Venus figurines carved in bone, stone, and ivory (see Plate 3). These figures are usually somewhat stylised, with indistinct faces and imposing breasts and hips, and Joseph Campbell argues that they are indicative of the Mother Earth worship that we considered in Part 1 in connection with gatherer and planter cultures.[23] Moreover, although pottery is normally only associated with the advent of the Neolithic, a site in Moravia has produced thousands of fragments of fired-clay artefacts and figurines that date to this earlier period.[24]

The following period – the Solutrean, which commenced 21,000 years ago – saw the emergence of the magnificent cave paintings that reached their zenith in the Magdalenian period beginning 16,500 years ago (see Plates 4 and 5).[25] These show a marked shift to a more hunter-based and male-dominated society, with un-equivocal evidence of shamanic practices, and they are fast becoming universally recognised as the first definitive proof of modern humans acting in a fully cognitive way that is comparable in its advancement to our own – even if the shaman's worldview is somewhat different to say the least. Recent studies have indicated that shamans in modern South African tribes have described how certain similar but later rock paintings in the Cape represent complex cosmological and shamanic beliefs, and how they would have been used in nightlong rituals to the accompaniment of rhythmic clapping and chanting in order to promote altered states of consciousness.[26] This view is borne out by additional research indicating that, in those areas of the western European caves where the most clearly shamanic paintings are concentrated, the acoustics are enhanced.[27] We will study shamanism and altered states more closely in Part 3.

One other development in the Upper Palaeolithic that is worthy of note is the emergence of geometric patterns in cave paintings and reliefs. These include dots within circles, grids, chevrons, curves, zigzags, nested curves, rectangles and, in one isolated case, a swastika.[28] This type of art becomes even more conspicuous in Neolithic temples and burial mounds all over Western Europe, by which time it has developed to include cups and rings, spirals, linked spirals, mazes and lozenges.[29] As we will see in Part 3, there is every reason to suspect that these patterns had an esoteric significance that reveals just how spiritually aware our Palaeolithic and Neolithic ancestors were. Moreover, some commentators even suggest that a rudimentary symbolic script was used *throughout* the Upper Palaeolithic.[30]

Was there a prior period of development of these artistic and musical skills that we find emerging in such glorious and sudden abundance in Western Europe in this period – the remains of which we have yet to uncover either because we have not yet looked in the right places or because they have been largely destroyed? Almost certainly yes, because new research is unearthing increasing evidence that *archaic Homo* and modern humans may have exhibited a previously unsuspected degree of artistic and ritualistic behaviour well before the Upper Palaeolithic period.

For example, recent evidence from Zambia suggests that as many as six different pigments may have been manufactured in the period from 400,000 to 200,000 years ago; if correct, this would certainly suggest that body painting rituals were conducted at a very early stage.[31] This is backed up by evidence of ochre mining and usage from a variety of South African and European sites dating back to a similar time frame.[32] Even more controversial are recent suggestions that what was thought to be a natural lump of volcanic rock discovered at a site in Israel's Golan Heights dating back to at least 220,000 years ago is in fact the world's earliest-known sculpted figurine, probably of a woman.[33] Finally, multiple circles engraved on the Jinmium rock shelter in Australia's Northern Territory are thought to be at least 58,000 years old, and possibly much older.[34] These various discoveries may require the orthodox view of the emergence of culture proper to be somewhat revised.

Years Ago	Cultural Stage	Cultural Period	Developments
2,500,000	Lower Palaeolithic	Oldowan	Small flints
1,700,000		Acheulian etc.	Stone tools – c. 12 main types
700,000			Use of fire
250,000		Mousterian	More advanced stone tools – c. 60 main types
100,000			Ritual burials
40,000	Upper Palaeolithic	Aurignacian	More complex tools Ivory animal figurines Drilled necklace beads Musical instruments
28,000		Gravettian	Venus figurines Pottery
21,000		Solutrean	Cave paintings
16,500		Magdalenian	Advanced cave art Geometric patterns
11,500	Neolithic	Azilian	Agriculture Stone buildings Urbanisation Protowriting
6,000			City-states
5,000			Pictographic writing

Figure 6: Major Cultural Advances[35]

URBANISATION

According to the prevailing orthodoxy the 'Neolithic revolution', which has historically been thought of as beginning in the Near East about ten thousand years ago and in Europe some two thousand years later, brought the first urbanisation that this planet has ever witnessed. For many years the move away from a nomadic hunter-gatherer to a settled and urbanised lifestyle was symbolised by the infamous town of Jericho in Jordan, which consisted of a number of mud-brick houses when first inhabited some 10,300 years ago, but was then fully developed to include imposing perimeter walls and a colossal stone tower some 10 metres in diameter about 800 years later. However, this is no longer the sole example of early urbanisation. To the northwest in Turkey, the

Anatolian settlement of Catal Hoyuk was first excavated back in 1959; since then a number of nearby sites such as Nevali Cori and Gobekli Tepe have been unearthed. All these settlements contain multiple stone buildings, including not only homes but also communal and ceremonial structures, and have elaborately carved stone columns bearing animal motifs. Each site also exhibits some degree of agricultural activity, although it is now thought that instead of cereal farming these sites tended, at least at first, toward the corralling of domestic animals such as pigs. Their earliest periods of occupation also date back to about ten thousand years ago.[36]

Meanwhile, recent discoveries in Syria not only indicate that Neolithic urbanisation was relatively widespread, but also push the date of its onset back by as much as fifteen hundred years. The most revealing site is that of Jerf el-Ahmar in the north, which was initially occupied as far back as 11,600 years ago (see Plates 6 to 10).[37] Not only that, but the Franco–Syrian excavation team led by Danielle Stordeur that started working at the site in 1995 discovered, at slightly more recent levels, a number of small terracotta plaquettes bearing what they speculate may be mnemonic symbols – etchings that predate the appearance of pictographic writing in Sumer some five thousand years ago by a further five millennia (see Plates 11 and 12).[38] They also uncovered evidence of the cultivation of crops and experimentation with new types of grain that is the earliest proof of formalised agriculture currently accepted by the orthodoxy.[39] Unfortunately, however, both Jerf el-Ahmar and Nevali Cori have already been submerged by the construction of new dams in both Syria and Turkey, while many other sites remain under threat from these and similar projects.

In time these early settlements, which had been repeatedly built upon, were abandoned, and new walled cities sprang up with more imposing and varied communal buildings such as temples, bakeries, breweries and potteries. These emerged approximately six thousand years ago, and not only in Mesopotamia but also, once again, in Syria, where recent excavations at the site of Tell Hamoukar have unearthed an impressive city dating to the same period that covers as much as five hundred acres.[40]

These discussions of the orthodox evidence for the development of culture and urbanisation may or may not have direct relevance to our forgotten race, depending on the timescales that we determine for their emergence and destruction, but either way they provide an important backdrop to our ongoing investigations.

CONCLUSION

There exists an overwhelming weight of archaeological and genetic evidence that fully modern humans evolved somewhere between 150,000 and 200,000 years ago. However, given my interpretation of the ancient texts and traditions in Part 1, my primary aim now is to attempt to establish when the first advanced souls might have 'successfully' incarnated in human form to kick-start the emergence of our forgotten race. We can obviously assume that it was some time after the earliest of these dates. So have we uncovered anything in our examination of the development of consciousness and culture that provides a better clue – a pointer to the sort of significant cultural spur to human evolution that would surely have been the logical outcome of these first advanced incarnations?

In general terms I have already indicated that I support the suggestion that our consciousness and culture evolved relatively gradually, progressively pulling humans clear of their hominid cousins. This is entirely consistent with the suggestion that everything, animate and inanimate, has a soul or at least a life force of some sort, in varying stages of karmic advancement. This gradualist view of nonphysiological developments would tend to suggest that there was no sudden one-off arrival of advanced souls. Moreover, it is supported by my previous interpretation of the creation accounts in Part 1 when I suggested that there may have been multiple waves of incarnation attempts, the first of which were described as to some extent 'abortive' because our race was still insufficiently developed – perhaps more from a psychological and intellectual perspective than a physiological one. Nevertheless, this process would arguably have maintained a gradual evolutionary impetus on the development of consciousness and culture – and, given what we have now learned in terms of context, is one that may conceivably have commenced as much as several hundred thousand years ago, or perhaps even longer.

However, there is one major milestone in the development of human consciousness that unequivocally differentiates us from other species – and that is the awareness of our own mortality that, as we saw in Part 1, plays an essential role in the development of mythology. It does seem pretty certain that, whatever else they may have, no other animal or primate possesses this aspect of self-awareness. Moreover, by contrast to so many of the other issues under discussion, there is one very clear archaeological indicator of this awareness that has not, in my opinion, received the attention that is deserves: and that is deliberate human burial accompanied by ritual activity.

We have seen that the first evidence of such activity dates back to about 100,000 years ago in Israel. If this is the era when it first occurred, it must surely be seen as a pivotal point in human development. After all, it not only represents definitive proof of a groupwide awareness of mortality but must also, surely, be linked to the development of attitudes toward the afterlife. And no mechanism is more likely to have provided this impetus than a newly acquired appreciation of the temporary nature of physical life, and of the eternal nature of the soul – an appreciation that would have arisen when both angelic and human souls were finally able to successfully incarnate in a body that possessed the appropriate mental capabilities. Accordingly, I put forward the hypothesis that the initial emergence of our forgotten race should be traced back to some time around about 100,000 years ago.

However, even if we are able to identify the time window of when our forgotten race first emerged with a reasonable degree of confidence, the issues of how long it would have taken for them to really flourish to the point where the golden age proper commenced, and of how widely they then spread their net, remain far more difficult. The process could have commenced in the Near East and then spread outwards but – given that even the out-of-Africa school would accept that modern humans could have been anywhere in Africa or Eurasia by this relatively late stage – it could just as easily have started simultaneously in other parts of the world, with subsequent developments running in parallel.

11. ANOMALOUS ARTEFACTS

Although I have rejected the supposed evidence of anomalous modern human remains dating back many millions of years, that of anomalous artefacts may yet provide some additional evidence of the level of culture and whereabouts of our forgotten race. The artefacts I wish to consider in this chapter are those that, although potentially advanced for the period in which they appear to have been deposited, are not technologically advanced in the modern sense.[1] In other words, although they might represent something of a surprise to the establishment if they were verified as genuine for the period, inasmuch as they would indicate not just culture proper but advanced culture, they do not take us outside the realms of what fully modern humans can achieve without advanced technology.

There are a number of sources of information on such artefacts, but most of them are relatively old and, sadly, unverifiable. Consequently I ask for a degree of indulgence while we examine evidence that, I freely admit, is of questionable reliability.

DONNELLY'S DAZZLERS

The first source is Ignatius Donnelly, better known as the man who resurrected the modern interest in lost continents in *Atlantis: The Antediluvian World*. His other main work, *Ragnarok: The Age of Fire and Gravel*, was published in 1883 and is in fact a relatively sober and sensible study. He attempts to examine various scientific issues in support of his search for a forgotten race, and in this work at least he does not stray into the realms of fantasy and advanced technology as have so many of his successors.

In any case, the first reports of anomalous artefacts that he presents are of boats and pottery turning up in unexpected places:

> In the seventeenth century Fray Pedro Simon relates that some miners, running an adit into a hill near Callao [Peru], 'met with a ship, which had on top of it the great mass of the hill, and did not agree in its make and appearance with our ships'.

Sir John Clerk describes a canoe found near Edinburgh, in 1726. 'The washings of the river Carron discovered a boat thirteen or fourteen feet underground; it is thirty-six feet long and four and a half broad, all of one piece of oak. There were several strata above it, such as loam, clay, shells, moss, sand, and gravel.'

. . . In the State of Louisiana, on Petite Anse Island, remarkable discoveries have been made. At considerable depths below the surface of the earth, fifteen to twenty feet, immediately overlying the salt-rocks, and underneath what Dr. Foster believes to be the equivalent of the Drift in Europe, 'associated with the bones of elephants and other huge extinct quadrupeds', 'incredible quantities of pottery were found'; in some cases these remains of pottery formed 'veritable strata, three and six inches thick'; in many cases the bones of the mastodon were found above these strata of pottery. Fragments of baskets and matting were also found.[2]

As with the majority of these accounts of anomalous remains, the original sources contain no attempts at dating, partly because the disciplines of geology and archaeology were, relatively speaking, in their infancy. However, the inclusion of depths and details of overlying deposits are attempts to provide a context.

Donnelly also reproduces several drawings of anomalous art, including one of a large black marble statue found 'twelve feet below the surface' when a well was being dug at Marlboro, Stark County, Ohio, and in which the overlying sand and gravel were reported to have been totally undisturbed.[3] He then moves on to an account in a magazine in which reports of 'pavements and cisterns of [that is, resembling] Roman brick now lie seventy feet underground'. On further investigation he established that they were discovered in the vicinity of Memphis, Tennessee, although he provides no further details.[4]

The final account from Donnelly that I would like to consider is his reproduction of a quote from geologist Alexander Winchell regarding the discovery and analysis of an apparently anomalous coin:

I had in my possession for some time a copper relic resembling a rude coin, which was taken from an artesian boring at the depth of one hundred and fourteen feet, at Lawn Ridge, Marshall County, Illinois.[5]

Winchell continues by describing a letter from Mr W H Wilmot of Lawn Ridge, dated 4 December 1871, in which the latter describes the exact nature of the boring and the circumstances of the find, indicating that it could not have come originally from a 'depth of less than eighty feet'. Winchell then describes the coin itself, which was:

. . . about the thickness and size of a silver quarter of a dollar, and was of remarkably uniform thickness. It was approximately round, and seemed to have been cut. Its two faces bore marks as shown in the figure [see Plate 13], but they were not stamped as with a die nor engraved. They looked as if etched with acid. The character of the marks was partly unintelligible. On each side, however, was a rude outline of a human figure . . . around the border were undecipherable hieroglyphics. . . .

This object was sent by the owner to the Smithsonian Institution for examination, and Secretary Henry referred it to Mr. William E. Dubois, who presented the result of his investigation to the American Philosophical Society. Mr. Dubois felt sure that the object had passed through a rolling mill, and he thought the cut edges gave further evidence of the machine-shop. 'All things considered', he said, 'I can not regard this Illinois piece as ancient nor old (observing the usual distinction), nor yet recent; because the tooth of time is plainly visible.'

After indicating his support for the authenticity of the object, Winchell's account closes with details of further anomalous remains discovered nearby:

In Whiteside County, fifty miles northwest from Peoria County, about 1851, according to Mr. Moffatt, a large copper ring was found one hundred and twenty feet beneath the surface, and also something which has been compared to a boat-hook. Several other objects have been found at lesser depths, including stone pipes and pottery, and a spear-shaped hatchet, made of iron.

The majority of the anomalies discussed by Donnelly were discovered in North America, which is a regular source of such reports as we will shortly see. As for the man himself, he was for many years a renowned US politician – although quite what impact that has on his reliability as a compiler of evidence from various sources is a moot point. In any event, some of these cases are valuable if only in that they are rarely mentioned by modern researchers.

WILKINS' WONDERS

The next source is Harold Wilkins, whose work is often quoted by modern revisionist authors. Unfortunately, the most cursory of inspections reveals that, by contrast to Donnelly's *Ragnarok*, there are minimal source references, and much of the content appears highly fanciful – particularly when he discusses Atlantis and its fellow lost continent, Mu, as if his statements were strict fact rather than pure conjecture. Nevertheless, we do find in his *Secret Cities of Old South America*, published in 1950, a few references to anomalous artefacts that follow along similar lines to, and in some cases replicate, Donnelly's. The first accounts that are worthy of note concern, once again, ancient ships – although this time in Europe:

> Giovanni Pontano, an Italian historian and statesman who died at Naples in AD 1503, was one of many persons, who, in his day, on a mountain top high over the sea at Naples, saw, enclosed in the middle of a great boulder brought down by a hurricane, the remains of a great and ancient ship of antediluvian make. It was certainly no old Roman, or Carthaginian galley or trireme. The rock completely enclosed the old ship and it was evident that such a petrifaction must have taken thousands of years. . . .
> Again, in AD 1460, miners digging for metals in the mountains of the canton of Berne, in Switzerland, found, at a depth of 100 feet in the bowels of the earth, a most ancient wooden ship which must have perished untold ages before. It

had carvings and was well-fashioned. By it lay masts, broken and eaten away with secular corrosion. There was an anchor of iron, and what gave the old Swiss miners a horrid turn was the sight in the timbers of the bones and skulls of forty men. Another contemporary account, in Latin, says that the ship had rotted shreds of what looked like sails of some woollen fibre adhering to her masts. Eye-witnesses told the story to old Baptista Fulgosa, Italian writer in forgotten Latin folios of many curious things in nature, read only by curious scholars of to-day.[6]

Wilkins then cites the discovery of a large nail of some sort in Peru:

At Cayatambo, in Peru, in the sixteenth century, there was found by Spanish miners, deep in a silver mine at the eighth stage of its depth, a nail or spike shaped like a cross and embedded in the body of a very hard rock, from which it had to be hacked out with another hard stone, clamped with a sharp point. The nail had been riveted to a piece of wood. It was about 6 inches long and the viceroy, Don Francisco de Toldeo, who wanted it for his cabinet as a curio, was forestalled by an Augustinian monk who took it home to old Spain. The nail, it is said, was as free from rust as if it had only that day been placed in the shaft.[7]

Are the reports Wilkins cites at all reliable? Our confidence is not exactly enhanced when, immediately following the above account, he lists the supposed discovery in California of 'six-toed giants' and 'an amazing human skull of giant size with a double row of teeth'. Be that as it may, they certainly make interesting reading.[8]

STEIGER'S SPECIALS

Moving nearer to the present, the next source that we should consider is Brad Steiger, the prolific author of numerous books on revisionist history and other more spiritual topics. His most important work for our current purposes is Worlds Before Our Own – which was published in 1978, not long after Erich von Däniken and Zecharia Sitchin had gripped the public's imagination with their visions of extraterrestrial visitors in antiquity. Although

Steiger includes an extensive bibliography, it was actually compiled not by him but by a colleague, and the list of 'works cited' is far shorter; moreover, like Wilkins before him, he provides few proper references. Still, in questioning the origins and antiquity of humankind he at least does not follow the extraterrestrial route of his contemporaries, preferring instead to postulate a forgotten race of indigenous giants on earth that may have had advanced technology.

In general, this work of Steiger's represents a mishmash of allegations of conspiracy and cover-up by the Establishment about the antiquity of humankind, mixed in with a healthy dose of questioning of the date and purpose of ancient monuments such as the pyramids in Egypt and the Americas.[9] This heady mixture is not exactly logically consistent if we stand back from it, but it does make for a cracking read.

Because *Worlds Before Our Own* in particular appears to have exerted such a high degree of influence on more recent revisionist writers – who have repeated the formula with great success, as I will confirm in a later chapter – and because it remains out of print at the time of writing, it will be useful for the serious student of revisionist history if I briefly summarise its contents. After all, many modern authors are not the best at admitting that they are largely regurgitating, and only to a small degree expanding upon, books that have been published long before. It includes chapters on, among other things, remains of supposedly modern humans dating back many millions of years;[10] on supposedly modern human footprints preserved in strata that again date back many millions of years;[11] and on textual and physical evidence of ancient aviation, astronomy, medicine, nuclear holocausts and other advanced technology.[12] If only some of these sound familiar at present, the remainder soon will.

In any case, for the moment we should concentrate on Steiger's accounts of nontechnological artefacts that appear to be of anomalous antiquity. The first that I would like to consider involves additional evidence of archaic artistic endeavour in the form of small carvings:

Professor Walter Matthes, head of the College for Prehistorical and Early History Study in Hamburg, discovered the objects on a steep stone bank of the River Elbe. Professor Matthes stated his assessment that the carvings represent 'the oldest man-made likenesses yet discovered' and estimated that the pieces were as much as 200,000 years old.

For the most part, the carvings are no larger than match boxes, and they depict the heads of human beings and Ice Age animals. According to Professor Matthes, the human heads bear few, if any, of the apelike characteristics so commonly associated with Neanderthal man.[13]

Unfortunately, Steiger does not tell us when this find was made. Meanwhile, the next is a more intricate piece of artwork discovered in a mine:

> On April 2, 1897, a very peculiar piece of rock was removed from the Lehigh coal mine in Webster City, Iowa. The slab was found just under the sandstone, which was 130 feet beneath the surface.
>
> The tablet was about two feet long by one foot wide and four inches thick. The surface was artistically carved in diamond-shaped squares, with the face of an old man in each square. Of the faces, all but two are looking toward the right. The features of each of the portraits were identical, with each bearing a strange mark in the shape of a dent in the forehead.[14]

Another account of anomalous art is of a fragment of bone engraved with a representation of a 'horned quadruped' and 'traces of seven or eight other figures' found by a Mr Frank Calvert near the Dardanelles in 1873.[15] If we now turn to Steiger's plates section, we find the reproduction of a drawing of yet another possible piece of art that was found when a well was being dug (see Plate 14):

> In August 1889, near Nampa, Idaho, M. A. Kurtz picked up an odd-looking lump of clay that had been brought up from a depth of 300 feet during a well-drilling operation. When he broke it open, he discovered what he thought looked like a tiny human figure made of clay. The controversy over the apparent antiquity of the Nampa Image has raged ever since.[16]

We then come to a 'metallic vessel' that was blasted out of some rock. And, for once, a photograph is provided because the whereabouts of the original were still known (see Plate 15):

In its June, 1851, issue the *Scientific American* carried an item about a metallic vessel that had been blasted out of an 'immense mass of rock' when workmen were excavating on Meeting House Hill in Dorchester, Massachusetts. 'On putting the two parts together, it formed a bell-shaped vessel, 4 ½ inches high, 6 ½ inches at the base, 2 ½ inches at the top, and about an eighth of an inch in thickness. The body of this vessel resembles zinc in colour, or a composition metal, in which there is a considerable portion of silver. On the sides there are six figures of a flower, or bouquet, beautifully inlaid with pure silver, and around the lower part of the vessel a vine, or wreath, inlaid also with silver. The chasing, carving, and inlaying are exquisitely done by the art of some cunning workman. This curious and unknown vessel was blown out of the solid pudding stone, fifteen feet below the surface. . . . Dr. J. V. C. Smith, who has recently travelled in the East, and examined hundreds of curious domestic utensils . . . has never seen anything resembling this. . . . There is no doubt but that this curiosity was blown out of the rock . . .'[17]

Steiger then goes on to quote from a letter to him by the contemporary owner of the vessel, a Mr Milton Swanson of Maine:

It had been given to Harvard College, but because of its mysterious origin they relegated it to a closet. The building supervisor finally brought it home to Medford, Mass. He sold it to me just before he died in his eighties.

Through the years I have had so-called experts look at it, and no one ever came up with an answer. Its age and use is just unexplainable. It is almost black, but the metal is composed of brass with zinc, iron, and lead. The inlay is pure silver, and I had to put lacquer on to protect it. I always felt that it was a burial ash container.

The Museum of Fine Arts in Boston has the world's finest and most complete laboratory, which was built in cooperation

with M.I.T. I was able to have them run it through every kind
of test for two years. Still no answer as to its period or origin.

Finally, we turn to a case that Steiger mentions only briefly in
his opening chapter, and on which as far as I can tell he does not
elaborate later:

No fabric is supposed to have been found until Egypt
produced cloth material 5,000 years ago. How, then, can we
deal with the Russian site which provides spindle whorls and
patterned fabric designs more than 80,000 years old?[18]

Despite the fact that I do not agree with the entirety of Steiger's
approach, and despite his lack of source references, we can see that
he has amassed considerable evidence of anomalous artefacts that
clearly deserves to be included in my review.

CREMO'S CANONS

Even more up to date is, once again, the work of Michael Cremo
and Richard Thompson. By contrast to Wilkins and Steiger, I have
already noted that their work is well referenced, and whatever I
might have made of their general work in a previous chapter, it
would be an omission not to include their additional cases of
anomalous artefacts here.

They devote considerable attention to reports of a number of
finds made by miners during the Californian gold rush of the
mid-to-late nineteenth century.[19] Although there were a number of
surface finds of uncertain age, many of the more interesting
artefacts were supposedly discovered in the numerous deep mine
shafts that were sunk to reach the auriferous gravels under the
mountains. They included, most notably, spearheads and large
stone mortars and pestles (see Plate 16) – apparently found at
depths of as much as 'several hundred feet' beneath the surface.

These finds caused great excitement at the time, and much is
made both then and now of the extent to which the miners
involved either would or would not have been qualified to judge
them *in situ*. Could they have been intrusions from native Indian
burials? Might they have fallen through cracks and sinkholes long
ago, or been dislodged from higher levels, and so on?[20] Various

geologists visited the sites of the finds, including J D Whitney, the
state geologist of California; Clarence King, who himself found a
stone pestle embedded in the gravel at Table Mountain, although
this was in the recently exposed surface and not underground; and
George F Becker, who submitted reports to the American Geological Society for official consideration. It has nevertheless been
suggested that most if not all of the finds were deliberate hoaxes,
perpetrated either by native Indians or, more likely, by the miners
themselves – who, after all, were nothing if not opportunists. I
must also note that supposedly anomalous human remains, whose
general provenance I have already rejected, were found in
conjunction with them.

Let us now look at certain other anomalous artefacts cited by
Cremo and Thompson.[21] First we have a report from the American
Journal of Science of 1820 of a number of stone columns, wooden
tools and coins discovered by quarrymen in Aix-en-Provence in
France in 1788, at a 'depth of fifty feet'. Apparently they also found
a large fragmented wooden board that, when pieced back together,
was similar to the workboards they used themselves when
quarrying, with the same rounded edges. Moreover, the wooden
artefacts had apparently all petrified into agate.

Next we come to a report by a Scottish physicist, Sir David
Brewster, presented to the British Association for the Advancement
of Science in 1844, regarding an iron nail 'several inches long' that
was found partially embedded in a block of sandstone at the
Kingoodie quarry in Scotland.[22] While in the same year, the
London Times of 22 June reported that quarrymen working on the
banks of the River Tweed near Rutherford mill had found a gold
thread embedded in stone at a 'depth of eight feet'.

The final two cases from Cremo and Thompson's work that I
would like to consider are of artefacts supposedly embedded in the
middle of lumps of coal. The first is that of a gold chain found by
a Mrs S W Culp of Morrisonville, Illinois, in 1891. The report in
the local paper suggested that the chain was about 'ten inches
long', weighed about twelve grams, and was 'of antique and quaint
workmanship'. However, there is a distinct possibility of fraud in
this case, because we find that this lady was none other than the
wife of the newspaper's editor, and the story did appear on the
front page. We should also realise by now that the citizens of the

US had, by the late nineteenth century, been fired up by similar reports for some time.[23] The other is of an iron cup found by a Mr Frank J Kenwood in 1912, apparently in the presence of a colleague, while he was working at the Municipal Electric Plant in Thomas, Oklahoma (see Plate 17). The coal was traced to the Wilburton coal mines, and the circumstances were confirmed by Kenwood in a signed and witnessed affidavit in 1948, a copy of which is still in existence.

BAIGENT'S BOMBSHELLS

In *Ancient Traces* Michael Baigent provides a few additional cases of anomalous artefacts, as well as further commentary on a number of those that we have already considered.[24] The first is a report in *Nature* of 11 November 1886, regarding another block of coal that broke open in an iron foundry in the Austrian town of Vöcklabruck in 1885. This one supposedly contained a small steel cuboid, 'several inches in diameter', with a deep groove running around it and two rounded opposing faces. Some of the experts who examined it thought it might be a meteorite, but further tests are now impossible because only a cast survives in the museum in Linz.[25] The second is the for once relatively recent discovery by a Mr Frederick G Hehr, in California in 1952, of an iron chain embedded in sandstone and found 'thirty-seven feet down the side of a ravine' (see Plate 18).[26]

Baigent's final addition to our compendium is the most recent find of them all: a fragment of wooden plank uncovered at an archaeological site in the northern Jordan Valley in Israel in 1989. Naama Goren-Inbar and her colleagues reported in the respected *Journal of Human Evolution* that it was highly polished on one side, with no tool marks evident, and had one completely straight and deliberately bevelled edge. It was made of willow, and measured about 'ten inches long by five wide' (see Plate 19).[27]

There is one other artefact that is not mentioned in any of the above sources but worthy of consideration, and that is a hammer that was supposedly found in a lump of sandstone on a ledge next to a waterfall in London, Texas, by a Mr Max Hahn in 1934. The iron head was about 'six inches long by one in diameter', and the wooden handle was broken off but protruding from the stone (see Plate 20).[28]

For those of you whose heads are reeling after taking in the details of these numerous cases – as mine was while I was compiling them – I have provided an easy reference summary in Figure 7.

CONCLUSION

There are a number of questions that we have to ask about these artefacts. First of all, how reliable are the numerous reports? There must clearly be some doubts, as Cremo and Thompson, for example, freely admit:

> The reports of this extraordinary evidence emanate, with some exceptions, from non-scientific sources. And often the artefacts themselves, not having been preserved in standard natural history museums, are impossible to locate.
>
> We ourselves are not sure how much importance should be given to this highly anomalous evidence. But we include it for the sake of completeness and to encourage further study.
>
> In this chapter, we have included only a sample of the published material available to us. And given the spotty reporting and infrequent preservation of these highly anomalous discoveries, it is likely that the entire body of reports now existing represents only a small fraction of the total number of such discoveries made over the past few centuries.[29]

It is true that the majority of these artefacts themselves are no longer available for inspection, let alone the exact locations in which they were found. In addition, once again the vast majority of the finds date from the nineteenth century and even earlier, with very few in the last century or so. However, we might argue that this criticism is not as relevant to the discussion of artefacts as it is to that of skeletal remains. Moreover, given that many of them came from well borings, mines and quarries, perhaps the lack of modern finds reflects the higher levels of technology that are now used in such operations – which could ensure that any similar objects would now either be destroyed immediately or fail to be noticed by a human operator.

A number of the reports also appear to come from reputable original sources, or to have been covered by reputable academic

Age or Depth	Artefact	Location	Date	Source
Under hill	Ship	Callao, Peru	1700s	Donnelly
13–14 feet	Large oak canoe	Edinburgh, Scotland	1726	Donnelly
15–20 feet	Pottery, baskets, matting	Louisiana, USA	?	Donnelly
12 feet	Large marble statue	Ohio, USA	?	Donnelly
70 feet	Brick pavements and cisterns	Tennessee, USA	1880s	Donnelly
80–114 feet	Copper coin	Illinois, USA	1870s	Donnelly
120 feet	Large copper ring, boathook, pottery, iron hatchet	Illinois, USA	1851	Donnelly
In large boulder	Large ship	Naples, Italy	1400s	Wilkins
100 feet	Wooden ship with iron anchor	Berne, Switzerland	1460	Wilkins
Stage 8 of mine	Cross-shaped nail or spike	Cayatambo, Peru	1500s	Wilkins
200,000 years	Small human and animal carvings	Hamburg, Germany	?	Steiger
130 feet	Stone tablet with carved human heads	Iowa, USA	1897	Steiger
Miocene?	Bone with animal engravings	Dardanelles, Turkey	1873	Steiger
300 feet	Small human clay figurine	Idaho, USA	1889	Steiger
15 feet	Small decorated metallic vessel	Massachusetts, USA	1851	Steiger
80,000 years	Spindle whorls, patterned fabric	Russia	?	Steiger
Up to 200 feet	Stone spearheads, pestles and mortars	California, USA	1800s	Cremo
50 feet	Stone columns, coins, wooden tools/workboard	Aix, France	1788	Cremo
In quarry block	Iron nail	Kingoodie, Scotland	1844	Cremo
Embedded in stone	Gold thread	Rutherford, Scotland	1844	Cremo
In block of coal	Gold chain	Illinois, USA	1891	Cremo
In block of coal	Iron cup	Oklahoma, USA	1912	Cremo
In block of coal	Small grooved steel cube	Vocklabruck, Austria	1885	Baigent
37 feet	Iron chain	California, USA	1952	Baigent
500,000 years	Fragment of polished wooden plank	Jordan Valley, Israel	1989	Baigent
In lump of stone	Iron hammer with wooden shaft	Texas, USA	1934	Internet

Figure 7: Anomalous Artefacts

journals of the time – though cynics would argue that the standards of such journals were not as high then as now. Nevertheless, we must still consider the likelihood of hoaxes. I have little doubt that, of the full range of cases we have covered, a proportion would fall into this category, although I could hazard no guess as to what proportion or which cases – apart perhaps from having particular suspicions about the reports with no quoted original sources and those from the California gold rush. That said, I have already omitted a number of reports that I felt were especially dubious from the above summary.

We must also ask whether, even if some of the reports and finds are genuine, the evidence itself has been misinterpreted. Again, this cannot be ruled out in some of the cases, and in particular with respect to the dating of the finds. And in that context, there is a whole new can of worms that we have to open.

Most of the artefacts were originally described only as being found at a certain depth under the surface, but this is only the most general of guides because a find at only a few metres down in one geological location can be far, far older than one hundreds of metres down in another – and this is before the issue of possible intrusion from a higher stratum comes into play. Nevertheless, in the most recent case that we examined, that of the Jordanian polished plank, as we would expect the archaeological team have a clear idea of the age of the site – and it is reckoned to be, perhaps somewhat disconcertingly, half a million years old. Moreover, there is one other case in which the discoverer of an anomaly was sufficiently geologically trained to hazard a guess as to its age, and that is the Dardanelles engraved bone, which Calvert dated to the Miocene period that ended a full five million years ago.

And that is not all. As they did with their supposedly anomalous skeletal remains, Cremo and Thompson have sought the advice of modern geologists in attempting to age a number of the other artefacts that we have discussed. The lowest date that they derive is for the Illinois copper coin at 200,000 to 400,000 years old; thereafter their dates become ever more at variance with the orthodox framework for modern human evolution. They derive an age of 2 million years for the Idaho figurine, anything from 9 to 55 million years for the Californian gold-mine artefacts, and then for the Illinois gold chain, Oklahoma iron cup, Rutherford gold thread, Kingoodie iron nail and Massachusetts metallic vessel they derive minimum ages of 260, 312, 320, 360 and 600 million years respectively.

From what little I know of geology, I can suggest with respect to these latter that it may be somewhat misleading to ask geologists for the general age of the strata at a certain depth at a particular site if they have no knowledge of the exact location of the find. For example, localised faults in the rock can easily become filled with younger material from a higher stratum, something that can only be identified by on-site inspection. Moreover, the dating of the Dardanelles bone *could* be prone to error purely on the basis that it was discovered more than a century ago. Nevertheless, we might expect the modern professional team that discovered the Jordanian plank to be reasonably sure of their ground.

To summarise, we have tentative dates of greater than 200,000 years old for 9 out of the 26 cases I have presented. The majority of the remainder are undated. Given my opinion that modern humans did not exist before this time – which I hold, as we have already seen, because of the broader contextual evidence from around the world and because I reject the supposedly anomalous skeletal evidence – it will come as no surprise that I am inclined to think that either the finds supposedly older than this are hoaxes, or the interpretation of their date is erroneous. As to the other undated finds, it is effectively useless to conjecture about their possible age.

Given the dating problems and the possibility of hoaxes in some cases, what are we to make of all this? I would *cautiously* submit that the body of evidence of anomalous artefacts that we have considered is sufficiently substantial that we can apply the 'no smoke without fire' maxim, and accept that *some* of it just *may* provide general support for my contention that our antediluvian race possessed a far higher level of culture than the orthodoxy currently allows – and not only culture proper in terms of artistic works, which we might reasonably expect anyway, but also advanced culture in terms of building large boats, spinning cloth, building in brick and manufacturing sometimes intricate metalwork. And although I find this evidence too unreliable from a dating perspective to amend my previous assertions regarding the time window, with regard to the 'where' question it appears to broaden the scope yet again – inasmuch as the North American continent at least must now be added to Europe, Asia and Africa on our list of contenders for the whereabouts of our forgotten race.

As a final word, I should say that if my insistence on sticking within the current orthodox time frame for modern human existence is ultimately proved to be misguided by a new and stronger body of more archaic skeletal and artefactual evidence, then I will be happy to change my opinion. That said, if any irrefutable evidence of modern humans dating back significantly more than 200,000 years were to emerge, I would be inclined to side with the Interventionists and to preserve my basic faith in evolution, rather than pursue what would be in my view a fundamentally illogical creationist explanation. At the same time, however, I would then expect to see some evidence of seriously advanced technology – after all, interplanetary travellers would be unlikely to favour stone mortars and pestles for the preparation of their food; unless, of course, the 'intervention' was of a more ethereal nature, a possibility we will return to at the very end of this work.

With that, let us now turn to the final area of scientific study that may provide support for my crucial theme of our forgotten race's destruction, and possibly also their whereabouts: that of geology and, especially, catastrophism.

12. CATASTROPHE!

The idea that the earth has been rocked by major catastrophes has been around for a long time. The predominantly Christian movers and shakers in the scholarly community of the seventeenth and eighteenth centuries used primitive geological studies to support the biblical notion of a worldwide flood occurring not long after God had created it. By the early part of the nineteenth century, however, a more rational view of an earth that had been *repeatedly* ravaged over a far more prolonged time frame had begun to emerge. The leading exponent of this new catastrophist school was the gifted French scientist Georges Cuvier, who reached his conclusions by studying the various geological strata that had been laid down in the environs of the Paris basin. He also had what, to me at least, seems a highly enlightened view of the effect a major catastrophe would have had on our ability to trace any ancestors that lived before it:

> I am not inclined to conclude that man had no existence at all before the epoch of the great revolutions of the earth. He might have inhabited certain districts of no great extent, whence, after these terrible events, he re-peopled the world. Perhaps, also, the spots where he abode were swallowed up, and his bones lie buried under the beds of the present seas.[1]

Nevertheless, by the mid-nineteenth century this view had in turn been challenged, with Charles Lyell at the forefront of the new uniformitarian or gradualist school. They proposed that many huge boulders found all over the world had been carried to their current locations not by a worldwide flood but by gradual glacial movement over prolonged periods, and the theory of ice ages was born.

ICE AGES

Geologists are relatively united in their view that the most recent ice age, known as the Pleistocene epoch and which started about 1.7 million years ago, was dominated by cycles of gradual encroachment of the polar ice caps towards more temperate zones, followed by a similar retreat. The extent of glaciation differed in each cycle, as it did on each continent in each cycle. North America and the northern parts of Europe and Asia were most affected, being considerably closer to the North Pole than South America, Africa and Australasia are to their southern counterpart. Analysis of ocean-floor sediments and Greenland ice cores has revealed that as many as two dozen major cycles occurred during this epoch. These were accompanied by significant and rapid temperature shifts of up to seven degrees Celsius in as little as one or two decades.

For our purposes the most important period is the last 100,000 years. The most recent American and European cycles are known as the Wisconsin and Würm glaciations that commenced about 115,000 and 75,000 years ago respectively. Both reached their height about 18,000 years ago, after which a significant retreat began to take us towards the Holocene epoch. Figure 8 reveals that, at its height, glaciation reached as far south as the fiftieth parallel in most parts of northern Europe and the western US, and

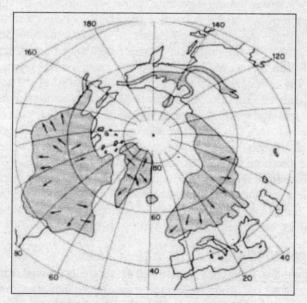

Figure 8: Maximum Glaciation in the Pleistocene[2]

even as far as the fortieth parallel and sometimes less in the eastern US.

So much for the effects. By contrast, geologists are far less united in their theories of the *causes* of the ice ages and their fluctuations. The best that can be said in the short space we have here is that, as with the snowball earth theory of the pre-Cambrian epoch alluded to earlier, a huge variety of ecological, geological and environmental factors have been interacting with each other in a model that is complex and hard to pin down – and moreover sensitive and easy to knock out of equilibrium.

Nevertheless, there is considerable support for the idea that a number of extraterrestrial bodies – either asteroids or comets – may have impacted on the surface of the earth during this epoch, providing the catalyst to disturb the equilibrium. All the evidence suggests that such impacts cause huge disruption, although it is not always made clear that there are two very different scenarios with different effects. On the one hand, an impact on land causes general tectonic upheaval and activates volcanoes, and has two obvious knock-on effects: the mass emission of carbon dioxide from volcanoes tends to produce global warming via the green-house effect, but at the same time the blanket of dust and debris thrown into the atmosphere tends to blank out sunlight for considerable periods and acts to reduce global temperatures. By contrast, an impact in the ocean causes massive tidal waves, and while the immediate consequences for the quality of the atmos-phere are less, the knock-on effects of ocean warming and both initial and longer-term evaporation of sea water are still quite profound. And, of course, the exact effect of both scenarios depends heavily on the location of the impact. Meanwhile, we should also note that vulcanism does not *have* to be associated with extraterrestrial agents, and it is thought to have been particularly prevalent throughout the Pleistocene – with the huge eruption in Toba in the East Indies, for example, having more or less coincided with the commencement of the Würm glaciation.[3]

DESTRUCTION ON A GLOBAL SCALE

Despite the fact that the theory of ice ages initially derived from the gradualist school, from the foregoing we can see that catastrophism has now made a significant comeback – particularly in relation to the end of the Pleistocene. This resurgence commenced in the mid-twentieth century, and although the pioneers had to fight hard to overcome the dominant gradualist view, in the last few decades it has grown from strength to strength. In contemporary academic circles the work of leading modern catastrophists such as Richard Huggett and Trevor Palmer is widely respected.[4]

Still, there is no geological evidence whatsoever for the entire world being flooded and under water at any time since its landmasses first emerged – as suggested, for example, by the biblical flood account. The last time it even approached this situation was about 65 million years ago when large parts of North America, Africa and Eurasia were covered by shallow seas. At this point many commentators suggest that the impact of a huge extraterrestrial body in what is now the Gulf of Mexico led not only to the extinction of the dinosaurs but also to a dramatic fall in sea levels – although not, as far as we can tell, to an ice age.

Therefore, any catastrophic event at the end of the Pleistocene must be more accurately depicted as causing *permanent* flooding only of coastal and low-lying areas, and this is undoubtedly supported by the widely accepted evidence that at this point there was a relatively swift and permanent rise in sea levels of around 100 metres.[5] But was there an even more significant upheaval that accompanied this change? Were higher inland elevations temporarily overcome by huge tsunami tidal waves, causing massive and widespread destruction? Let us examine the evidence.

MASS GRAVES

Although most animal species had managed to survive the Pleistocene relatively unscathed, towards its end – somewhere between 13,000 and 11,000 years ago – as many as 130 species suddenly died out in the Americas alone, compared to only about twenty genera in the previous 300,000 years.[6] These were predominantly large mammals such as mammoths, mastodons and native cats, and the evidence from northern Eurasia is much the same. The gradualists suggest either that this time around the relatively rapid climate and associated habitat changes did not suit them, or more recently that an increasingly proliferating and cultured humankind may have not only hunted these species to extinction but also introduced lethal diseases.

Catastrophists do not find these lines of reasoning persuasive, and reference a body of physical evidence that, in their view, tells a very different story. Perhaps the most celebrated is that of the large numbers of supposedly flash-frozen mammoths that were found in the permafrost of northern Siberia by explorers in the eighteenth and nineteenth century. Some of these were in such a fine state of preservation that their meat was supposedly eaten with no ill effects. Cuvier was one of the first to bring these discoveries to public attention, indicating not only that the Siberian climate must have been sufficiently temperate for such animals to live there *before* the end of the last ice age, but also that they no longer live there despite the fact that the global climate has generally become warmer. Even more perplexing, say the catastrophists, is just how we account for such a sudden demise and freezing of a variety of large animals that died by the tens of thousands. This is what many of them have attempted to explain over the years, but before we consider their views there is additional evidence to examine.

One of the most celebrated leaders of the resurgent catastrophist movement was Immanuel Velikovsky, whose 1955 work *Earth in Upheaval* for the first time gathered together a multitude of old and new evidence into a damning critique of the gradualist approach.[7] He indicated that the Siberian mammoths, some of which had surviving red blood corpuscles that seemed to indicate death by drowning or suffocation, possibly by poisonous gas, were not alone. Twentieth-century gold mining in Alaska had apparently revealed a similar tale of sudden destruction of mammoths and a number of other species, their bones well preserved but thrown about in a catastrophic melee in a layer of muck deposits that in some places reached 45 metres in depth. According to the discoverers, many of the bones appeared relatively recent in that they were not fossilised, and the animals could not have perished in the normal course of events because their partial skeletons were jumbled together, dismembered and disarticulated – nor were there any teeth marks or other signs of them having been the victims of predators. Moreover, the muck was reported to contain masses of twisted and splintered trees to bear witness to the ferocity of the catastrophe that had affected a huge area.[8]

Velikovsky then chronicled apparently similar evidence from all over the world, commencing with various caves explored by leading geologist William Buckland in the early nineteenth century, including in Britain those at Kirkdale in Yorkshire, Brentford near London, Cefn in Wales and Bleadon in Somerset, and in Europe examples such as Breugue and Arcy in France. Not only did many of these sites appear to reveal a similar tale of sudden destruction of animals of all ages, including the young, but they were also reported to include species as diverse as reindeer from Lapland and crocodiles and hippopotami from the Tropics – often found side by side. It was thought extremely unlikely that the latter in particular could turn up in northern Europe as a result of a temporary migration, and yet again most of these remains were, apparently, not yet fossilised.[9]

Velikovsky's final evidence with respect to catastrophic extinctions came from various sites where rock fissures and other crevices and pits were investigated, mainly in the late nineteenth century, and apparently found to be filled with similar debris. British sites included Plymouth and Pembrokeshire; European sites included Kesserloch near Thayngen in Switzerland, Neukoln near Berlin in Germany, central and southern France, Gibraltar, Corsica, Sardinia and Sicily; and US sites included Cumberland Cavern in Maryland, La Brea Asphalt Pit near Los Angeles, Agate Spring Quarry in Nebraska, Big Bone Lick in Kentucky, San Pedro Valley in California, John Day Basin in Oregon and Lake Florissant in Colorado. Meanwhile further similar finds were reported in, for example, Choukoutien near Beijing in northern China, the Siwalik foothills of the Himalayas in India, and the gorges of the Irrawady River in central Burma. All of these sites were reported as containing an incredible density of bones from the broken and dislocated skeletons of numerous large animals, all again relatively recent, for which only a catastrophic explanation appeared to make any logical sense.[10]

The other major catastrophist to emerge at this time was Charles Hapgood, whose *Earth's Shifting Crust* was first published in 1958, and republished under the title *The Path of the Pole* in 1970.[11] He devoted the entirety of his last chapter to a discussion of the frozen mammoths, and added a few apparently pertinent points. For example, he reported that the massive number of animals involved was indicated by an estimate that as many as twenty thousand pairs of tusks were exported from Siberia in the last few decades of the nineteenth century alone, and that this hardly depleted the full stock. He also provided additional arguments in support of the notion that all these animals had been living in a relatively temperate climate when they were suddenly frozen – for example, by analysing the conditions under which both meat and ivory must be frozen swiftly and permanently in order to remain edible and workable respectively.[12] He further provided a table of radiocarbon dates on a selection of mammoth and other animal remains found predominantly in the US, which placed a significant proportion of their deaths in the period from 13,000 to 9000 years ago.[13]

Hapgood also included an extensive quote about the Alaskan muck from Frank C Hibben, a professor at the University of New Mexico who analysed it first-hand:

In many places the Alaskan muck is packed with animal bones and debris in trainload lots. Bones of mammoth, mastodon, several kinds of bison, horses, wolves, bears, and lions tell a story of a faunal population. . . .

Within this mass, frozen solid, lie the twisted parts of animals and trees intermingled with lenses of ice and layers of peat and mosses. It looks as though in the midst of some cataclysmic catastrophe of ten thousand years ago the whole Alaskan world of living animals and plants was suddenly frozen in mid-motion in a grim charade.[14]

Hibben continues by suggesting that extensive vulcanism and hurricanes accompanied the devastation:

One of the most interesting of the theories of the Pleistocene end is that which explains this ancient tragedy by world-wide, earthshaking volcanic eruptions of catastrophic violence. This bizarre idea, queerly enough, has considerable support, especially in the Alaskan and Siberian regions. Interspersed in the muck depths and sometimes through the very piles of bones and tusks themselves are layers of volcanic ash. There is no doubt that coincidental with the end of the Pleistocene animals, at least in Alaska, there were volcanic eruptions of tremendous proportions. It stands to reason that animals whose flesh is still preserved must have been killed and buried quickly to be preserved at all. Bodies that die and lie on the surface soon disintegrate and the bones are scattered. A volcanic eruption would explain the end of the Alaskan animals all at one time, and in a manner that would satisfy the evidences there as we know them. The herds would be killed in their tracks either by the blanket of volcanic ash covering them and causing death by heat or suffocation, or, indirectly, by volcanic gases. Toxic clouds of gas from volcanic upheavals could well cause death on a gigantic scale. . . .

Throughout the Alaskan mucks, too, there is evidence of atmospheric disturbances of unparalleled violence. Mammoth and bison alike were torn and twisted as though by a cosmic hand in Godly rage. In one place, we can find the foreleg and shoulder of a mammoth with portions of the flesh and the toenails and the hair still clinging to the blackened bones. Close by is the neck and skull of a bison with the vertebrae clinging together with tendons and ligaments and the chitinous covering of the horns intact. There is no mark of a knife or cutting instrument. The animals were simply torn apart and scattered over the landscape like things of straw and string, even though some of them weighed several tons. Mixed with the piles of bones are trees, also twisted and torn and piled in tangled groups; and the whole is covered with fine sifting muck, then frozen solid.

Storms, too, accompany volcanic disturbances of the proportions indicated here. Differences in temperature and the influence of the cubic miles of ash and pumice thrown into the air by eruptions of this sort might well produce winds and blasts of inconceivable violence. If this is the explanation of the end of all this animal life, the Pleistocene period was terminated by a very exciting time indeed.

It is debatable whether the animals – and indeed perhaps humans – that met such a devastating and untimely end would have found it 'exciting' themselves, but Hibben's description is undoubtedly vivid. His assessment of the number of animals killed in the Americas alone was as many as forty million.

Velikovsky and Hapgood, although by training a psychoanalyst and a science historian respectively, both used mainly orthodox geological sources for their evidence. However, some of these sources were relatively old even in their day, and, as you might expect, further studies of the various sites mentioned have been undertaken more recently by modern geologists who, quite rightly, do not take the old evidence and reports at face value.

These more recent studies do cast some doubt on particular cases cited by Velikovsky and Hapgood. To take one of the most important examples, investigations into the ten- to twenty-metre-deep muck deposits in the Fairbanks region of Alaska appear to reveal not a jumbled, chaotic mass as suggested by the original reports, but rather a series of seven well-defined geological layers dating back as far as three million years ago. Moreover, apparently the tree remains are limited to three specific layers, and the dislocated state of the animal remains has been somewhat exaggerated. In particular, it would appear that landslides and mud flows created by the melting of the permafrost have created a confused picture in places, which the original investigators failed to place in the more clearly stratified broader context.[15]

Does this mean that the entirety of the evidence for sudden mass extinctions collated by Velikovsky and Hapgood should be dismissed? Some geologists say yes, others say no. What I can say is that no definitive rebuttal of this evidence has yet been produced as a coherent work.

MARINE DEPOSITS

Velikovsky backed up his arguments with another body of evidence – that of marine deposits in unlikely places. He described how the relatively recent skeletons of whales and other large marine animals had been discovered north of Lake Ontario, in Michigan, in Vermont and near Montreal.[16]

These are marine animals that would not have inhabited the extensive freshwater lakes that were created in many parts of North America as the glaciers melted at the end of the last ice age. Admittedly, all of these areas could at one point have formed an inland sea, but all the finds were at altitudes of at least 140 metres above the *current* sea level, which as we know had already risen some 100 metres at the end of the Pleistocene.

Some geologists argue that these remains can be explained away by the geological process known as eustatic rebound. As ice sheets

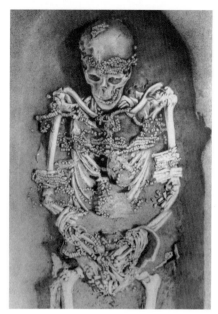

Plate 1 The 'Lady of Brassempouy'. This beautifully-sculpted ivory figurine from France is 25,000 years old. Were such fine artists merely subsisting in cold, damp caves? (Agence Photographique de la Réunion des Musées Nationaux)

Plate 2 One of the 'Sungar Skeletons'. This adult was buried in Russia 28,000 years ago with full regalia, including clothing adorned with hundreds of drilled ivory beads. Would purely nomadic tribes struggling for food have time for such luxuries? (Science Photo Library)

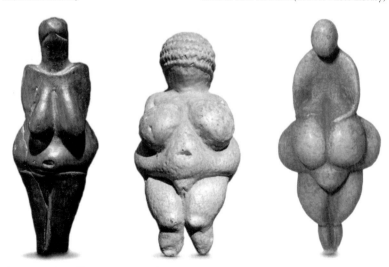

Plate 3 A variety of 'Venus Figurines'. These European examples are as much as 30,000 years old and, although stylised, are carefully sculpted. (Ancient Art and Architecture Collection)

Plate 4 Decorated spear thrower. This beautiful 16,000 year-old example from Le Mas d'Azil in France is carved from bone and shows two fighting bison. (Ancient Art and Architecture Collection)

Plate 5 Bison painting. This fine example of Upper Palaeolithic art comes from the Altamira Caves in Spain. Has anything more realistic been produced in the modern era?

Plate 6 Jerf el-Ahmar. This sizeable settlement in Syria is more than 11,000 years old. Does the fact that it has no precursors prove that it is the work of survivors of the catastrophe?
(Danielle Stordeur/CNRS)

Plate 7 Aerial view of one of the round communal buildings at Jerf el-Ahmar, surrounded by individual houses. Stone has been used throughout for construction, and there are clear signs of early agriculture. Were our antediluvian ancestors engaging in settled agriculture long beforehand?
(Danielle Stordeur/CNRS)

Plate 8 The site of Jerf el-Ahmar about to be flooded by a newly-constructed dam in 1999. It is now buried under 15 metres of water. How much antediluvian evidence was lost in similar fashion when sea levels rose by 100 metres after the catastrophe? How much more have we already destroyed in the modern epoch? And how much more will be lost to future development?
(Danielle Stordeur/CNRS)

Plate 9 Close up of one of the communal buildings at Jerf el-Ahmar. (Danielle Stordeur/CNRS)

Plate 10 Stylised head sculpture from Jerf el-Ahmar. It is interesting that it shows a relative lack of sophistication compared to Upper Palaeolithic art from millennia before. (Danielle Stordeur/CNRS)

Plate 11 Etched terracotta plaquette from Jerf el-Ahmar. Do the symbols represent mnemonics that would assist the recording of antediluvian events? (Danielle Stordeur/CNRS)

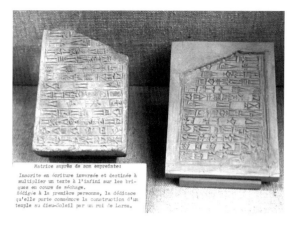

Plate 12 Example of late Sumerian pictographic script, which first emerged some 5000 years ago. Is this merely a development of the mnemonic etchings from Jerf el-Ahmar many millennia before? (Ancient Art and Architecture Collection)

Matrice auprès de son empreinte:

Inscrite en écriture inversée et destinée à multiplier un texte à l'infini sur les briques en cours de séchage.
Rédigée à la première personne, la dédicace qu'elle porte commémore la construction d'un temple au dieu-Soleil par un roi de Larsa.

Plate 13 Drawing of a copper coin found between 80 and 114 feet down a new well-boring in Illinois, USA in 1871. Were our antediluvian ancestors using money? (Ignatius Donnelly)

Plate 14 The 'Nampa Figurine' found 300 feet down a new well-boring in Idaho, USA in 1889. (www.time-travel.com)

Plate 15 Metallic vessel about 4.5 inches tall, blasted out of solid rock 15 feet below the surface during excavations in Massachusetts, USA in 1851. It has defied all attempts to identify its origin. Does this prove that our antediluvian ancestors were highly skilled metalworkers? (Milton Swanson/Brad Steiger)

Plate 16 Stone pestle and mortar found 1400 feet along a mining tunnel under Table Mountain in California, USA in 1877. How far back might reasonably advanced stoneworking go? (British Library)

Plate 17 Iron cup found embedded in a block of coal in Oklahoma, USA in 1912. How far back might reasonably advanced ironworking go? (Creation Evidence Museum/ David Lines)

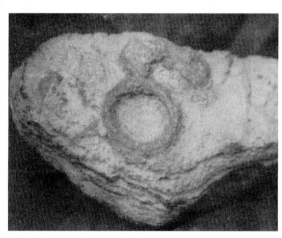

Plate 18 Iron chain found embedded in sandstone 37 feet down the side of a ravine in California, USA in 1952. (Frederick G Hehr)

Plate 19 Wooden plank excavated in the northern Jordan valley, Israel in 1989. It is highly polished, with one completely straight and bevelled edge. The site is thought to be about half a million years old. How far back might reasonably advanced woodworking go? (Elsevier)

Plate 20 Iron hammer head, about 6 inches long and with wooden handle, found embedded in sandstone in Texas, USA in 1934. (Creation Evidence Museum/ David Lines)

Plate 21 Hand-held model of the 'Celtic cross'. Note how the circular bob-weighted scale revolves and is read through holes in the upright. Were our antediluvian ancestors using such a simple but effective device to navigate the oceans? (Crichton Miller)

Plate 22 Full-sized model of the 'Celtic cross' being used by its 're-inventor' to measure the angle of the sun. (Crichton Miller)

Plate 23 The Mitchell-Hedges crystal skull. Discovered in a Mayan temple at Lubaantun in Belize in 1924, it is detailed, life-sized, and has a detachable jaw fashioned from the same block of totally pure piezoelectric quartz crystal. Although it can never be dated, is it possible that it has been programmed with a wealth of knowledge of antediluvian times? (Galde Press/Frank Dorland)

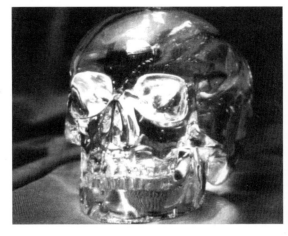

build up, sometimes to a depth of several kilometres, the weight causes the landmass underneath to sink into the underlying mantle – just as a loaded ship sits lower in the water. Then, as the ice melts, it rises again. This argument is somewhat inconclusive, however, because as the ice sheet grows and the crust sinks, so too the sea level falls, and vice versa. So we can see that this is a complex process in which the various influences on sea levels relative to the landmass tend to counterbalance each other to significantly reduce any overall effect. Moreover, it is even harder to use eustasy to explain away the large marine-animal remains that have been found in abundance in more southerly areas that were never affected by glaciation – for example in Alabama, Georgia and Florida.[17]

Consequently these remains appear to provide evidence that tidal waves, of sufficient size and force to carry animals as large as whales in their wake, caused extensive and temporary inland flooding in North America at a time when the ice sheets had *already* receded significantly. This points us towards the *very* end of the Pleistocene epoch.

MOUNTAIN FORMATION

Both Velikovsky and Hapgood devoted considerable time to questioning the orthodox geological view of mountain building, arguing that many of the great ranges in the world developed far more recently than is normally accepted.[18] However, modern geologists are pretty much united in the view that, for example, the Alps were formed between 65 and 25 million years ago, the Himalayas about 2 million years ago, and the Andes more recently again but not as late as the end of the Pleistocene. Accordingly, I am inclined to reject this aspect of their arguments.

Nevertheless, one site on which Velikovsky and many subsequent commentators have concentrated is that of the ancient stone ruins of Tiahuanacu, which borders Lake Titicaca high in the Bolivian Andes – a mountain range accepted as being of relatively recent formation.[19] He argued that it is somewhat implausible to suggest that early cultured settlers in South America would deliberately choose to isolate themselves 3800 metres up in the mountains, where it is now hardly possible to eke out a subsistence agricultural living.

This is a fair point, but Velikovsky's resolution – that the ruins were raised to their current level late in the Pleistocene – seems rather more implausible. The earliest dates for this settlement have been proposed by archaeoastronomers – who use key solar or stellar alignments in temples to gauge the precessional age in which they were constructed. The Kalasaya at Tiahuanacu is a fine candidate for this, and Arthur Posnansky's initial studies in 1945 suggested they might date back as far as 17,000 years ago.[20] This could have supported the notion that they were erected before any major catastrophe at the end of the Pleistocene, but Posnansky's own revisions, and more recent archaeoastronomical and conventional studies, have suggested the site is far younger.[21] Moreover, it would appear highly unlikely that the perfectly preserved integrity of the foundations of the site would have been maintained during a wholesale upheaval. I have my own suggestion to solve the enigma of why such an isolated spot was chosen, but that will have to wait until the very end.

GRADUALISM AND CATASTROPHISM COMBINED

Despite the fact that sound analysis and some more recent studies have clearly revealed some holes in Velikovsky's and Hapgood's physical evidence of a catastrophe at the end of the Pleistocene, a significant proportion of it is still broadly accepted by catastrophists within the professional geological community. The views of Huggett and Palmer have recently been reinforced by, for example, those of Derek Allan and Bernard Delair, and of Robert Schoch, to name just a few of the specialists who have come out in support of the catastrophic view.[22] Moreover some new research, rather than weakening the catastrophists' stance, provides additional support for it – as we will see in the next section.

Overall, therefore, it seems safe to assert that geological, animal and human evolution all have their gradual and uniformitarian side, but have also been punctuated by massive upheavals and catastrophes that have played a significant role. And also that, in particular, some form of devastating catastrophe on a broad scale accompanied the end of the last ice age and massively accelerated the transition from the Pleistocene to the Holocene.

EXTRATERRESTRIAL BODIES

If we now turn our attention to the agency that might have triggered this catastrophe, as we have already seen by far the most popular theory is that an extraterrestrial body or bodies played a part. We have already seen that most orthodox opinion suggests the impact of such a body, some 10 kilometres in diameter, caused the massive climatic upheaval that wiped out the dinosaurs about 65 million years ago; and there are suggestions that an impact of similar size occurred at least once before, about 250 million years ago. Meanwhile the impact of smaller bodies, either on land or sea, can still have devastating consequences, and these appear to have occurred far more regularly in the earth's history. For example, it is now thought that a two-kilometre body impacted somewhere in the Southern Ocean southwest of Chile some two million years ago, while a two- to five-kilometre body struck somewhere in Indochina about 800,000 years ago.[23]

Moreover, although Hapgood had other ideas – as we will shortly see – Velikovsky firmly believed that the repeated catastrophes that had shaken the earth had been caused by 'extraterrestrial agents'.[24] In particular, he noted that clay dredged up from the bottom of the Pacific by oceanographer Hans Pettersson in 1948 contained an abnormally high proportion of nickel and radium, which is clearly suggestive of extraterrestrial residue.[25]

If we now move on to more recent research, and concentrate particularly on the end of the Pleistocene, in their 1990 work *The Cosmic Winter* astronomers Victor Clube and Bill Napier suggest that the modern orbits of the Comet Encke, the asteroid Oljato and the Taurid meteors derive from the disintegration of a giant comet some 9500 years ago – a comet that may have been causing considerable interference with the earth's atmosphere and climate long beforehand. In particular they report on ice-core studies indicating that a significant quantity of dust was deposited in the last years of the Pleistocene, which has been found to have the same chemical content as that deposited in the Tunguska region of Russia by another extraterrestrial body in 1908. Moreover, Napier points out that even an extraterrestrial body as small as two hundred metres in diameter would, if it hit the ocean, result in devastating tidal waves.[26]

In their 1995 work *When the Earth Nearly Died* Allan and Delair follow a similar line, although they suggest that the catastrophe was caused by the close passage of a large extraterrestrial body, possibly even a runaway planet, at the earlier date of 11,500 years ago – which they link to the Greek tradition of the runaway Phaethon. There are two major areas, however, in which I take issue with their work. The first is their highly literal translation of the Mesopotamian *Epic of Creation*, which we encountered briefly in Part 1, and on which they place significant emphasis when determining the path of the extraterrestrial body in question. Not only is this interpretation completely contextually inappropriate in my view, as we will find out in Part 3, but also they appear to borrow significantly from Zecharia Sitchin's much earlier work on the subject without crediting him in their voluminous footnotes.[27]

But by far the more serious criticism is that they devote a substantial proportion of this work attempting to prove that the Pleistocene ice ages never occurred at all, and that all the evidence of glaciation – boulder deposition, underlying rock striation and so forth – was in fact caused by cascades of water from the massive flooding induced by this one event. However, orthodox geologists would point out that the features of relict glaciation that litter northern Europe and North America are directly comparable to those found in modern ice fields, while there are features that usually accompany rock striations – for example, roches moutonnées and drumlins – that are exclusively formed by ice flows and cannot be replicated by water flows.[28] It is perfectly possible that tidal waves played a major part in depositing some boulders in places where glaciation could not have operated, and marine and other remains in places where we would not expect to find them. To extrapolate this evidence into the suggestion that the most recent ice ages never happened, however, is surely a considerable step too far.

Moreover, Allan and Delair tend to follow Velikovsky and Hapgood in questioning the age of various mountain ranges, another theory that, as we have seen, receives little orthodox support. Nevertheless, and despite these shortcomings, in general their work is highly detailed and well referenced, and does undoubtedly provide support for my central hypothesis of a worldwide catastrophe at the end of the Pleistocene caused by an extraterrestrial agent.

Let us move on now to more direct terrestrial evidence of extraterrestrial impacts at this time. The most celebrated is that of the Carolina Bays, which were originally highlighted by Velikovsky.[29] He reported that they are 'oval craters thickly scattered over the Carolina coast of the United States and more sparsely over the entire Atlantic coastal plain from southern New Jersey to northeastern Florida'. They number into the tens of thousands, maybe even as many as half a million according to some estimates, and the very largest are as much as ten kilometres in length. They also display some remarkably consistent features in that they are all to some extent oval, their longest axes are more or less parallel to each other and oriented northwest to southeast, and they all have an elevated rim of earth at the southeastern end.

Even in Velikovsky's day it was accepted that some form of extraterrestrial agent must have been involved in their creation, and the first major study, by Frank Melton and William Shriever in 1932, concluded that they had resulted from the impact of a meteorite shower anywhere from fifty thousand to a million years ago.[30] Then in 1952 William Prouty proposed not only a much more recent date of about 11,000 years ago, but also the idea that they were created by shock waves resulting from the aerial explosion of an extraterrestrial body before it hit the ground.[31] At about the same time, evidence began to emerge of similarly large numbers of elliptical bays, oriented in the same direction, near Point Barrow in the northwest US, at Harrison Bay in Alaska, in the Yukon Territory of Canada, and even down in the Beni region of northeast Bolivia.[32]

In 1961 further studies of the event that shook the remote Tunguska region revealed a number of somewhat similar craters, although they were far smaller, far fewer in number and spread over a far smaller area. The team established that, like the Carolina Bays, they did not contain any obvious meteoritic debris; but they did find tiny spheroids near the epicentre, which on analysis were thought to be the dirt particles from the nucleus of a comet. This led researchers to believe that a far larger cometary explosion may have caused the Carolina and other bays in the Americas. However, it is now thought that the nucleus of a comet may have a more solid core than just the 'dirty snowball' assumed in the past, and that indeed this core may be effectively the same as an asteroid, so we need not get too carried away here with the exact nature of the extraterrestrial agent involved. What is clear is that it is generally accepted that such an agent was responsible for forming the bays, and that – unlike smaller individual meteorites – large-scale extraterrestrial bodies tend to vaporise when they explode, either before or on impact. For example, none of the craters caused by large-scale impacts in previous epochs contain obvious extraterrestrial debris.

Most important for our purposes is to establish whether or not the event that caused the bays' formation occurred at the end of the Pleistocene. To this end, we now turn to an analysis of the sediment at the base of the depressions conducted by a team from Duke University in the 1950s. They found that a layer of bluish clay appeared to have been deposited in some of the bays shortly after their formation, and that the sediments immediately beneath and above this layer yielded radiocarbon dates in the range of 11,000 to 10,000 years ago.[33]

Overall, I believe it is fair to say that there is strong support for a catastrophic interpretation of the end of the last ice age, and that an extraterrestrial agent is likely to have played a major part. But let us now examine certain climatic enigmas that are not easily explained by sole consideration of the mechanisms we have so far discussed.

AXIS SHIFTS AND CRUSTAL DISPLACEMENT

One of the most fundamental problems with any theory of ice ages is that the distribution of glaciation appears to have been extremely inconsistent in terms of latitude. During the Pleistocene we know that in the Northern Hemisphere most parts of North America, Greenland, Iceland and northern Eurasia were glaciated, and in the Southern Hemisphere possibly the south island of New Zealand and parts of Patagonia in South America. This is all to be expected. But how do we explain the fact that, as we have seen, northern parts of Siberia, Alaska and Greenland were not – even at the most recent height of the Pleistocene some 18,000 years ago? Moreover, there is clear evidence of previous glaciation in equatorial regions of the world, such as India, southern Africa, Madagascar, Argentina and southern Brazil. Although this is ascribed to the preceding ice age, which is thought to have occurred towards the end of the

Permian epoch about 250 million years ago, it still provides something of a challenge to geologists attempting to develop a theory of ice ages based at least in part on latitudinal factors.[34]

A similar enigma that geologists are forced to confront is the abundant evidence that corals at one time grew in various polar regions; for example from the island of Spitsbergen in the Arctic Ocean in Alaska, from Canada and from Greenland. These regions are in total darkness for six months of the year and yet, as we all know, coral grows only in tropical waters. Moreover, beds of coal and other evidence seems to indicate that forests once flourished not only in these Arctic regions but also in parts of Antarctica as well.[35]

Ever since Alfred Wegener first proposed the theory of slow continental drift in 1918 – having observed the similarity between the coastlines of South America and Africa – gradualists have insisted that this is the only mechanism required to explain these climatic anomalies. However, although in general this theory remains a bedrock of geology, many commentators have long considered it incapable of explaining them fully, especially those that are clearly quite recent. Indeed, catastrophists suggested early on that the only likely explanation was some mechanism that might change the position of the poles. It is, of course, the offset of the plane of the equator from that of our ecliptic orbit around the sun – currently about 23.5 degrees – that not only creates the seasons but also, if it changed, would alter the configuration of the tropical, temperate and arctic zones of the earth. Cuvier certainly supported the concept of pole shifts, and moreover felt that one must have occurred suddenly in a relatively recent epoch in order to account for the apparently flash-frozen mammoths of Siberia and Alaska.[36]

It has long been recognised that there are two main mechanisms by which a pole shift could occur. On the one hand, the entire earth could shift its axis – a genuine axis shift. On the other, the hard outer crust or lithosphere could move relative to the semimolten mantle underneath – which would *appear* from any surface measurements of the magnetic poles to be an axis shift, and would have the same effect in terms of climate change at a particular location on the landmass, albeit that the angle of the ecliptic would actually remain unchanged. Both mechanisms, however, require a huge amount of force. And although the latter would appear to require somewhat less due to the considerably smaller mass involved, this is offset by the requirement to overcome the frictional attachment between the crust and the mantle, and also to stretch new parts of the mantle over the equatorial bulge.

Although Hapgood is most often identified with this latter theory of crustal displacement in the modern era, others had been discussing it for at least a century before.[37] But his original *Earth's Shifting Crust* made two main contributions. First, he used the evidence of climate change and of ice cores to argue that the poles had shifted position at least three times during the late Pleistocene. Specifically he proposed that about 120,000 years ago the North Pole was located in the Yukon Territory of Canada, shifted to the Greenland Sea some 80,000 to 75,000 years ago, on to the vicinity of Hudson Bay around 55,000 to 50,000 years ago, and finally to its present position about 17,000 to 12,000 years ago. Of course, he also suggested that the position of the South Pole had moved in a corresponding fashion.[38] Second, he proposed a new mechanism by which crustal displacement might have been brought about: that of an 'unbalanced mass within the lithosphere exerting a sufficient centrifugal effect'.[39] In particular, he favoured an asymmetrical build-up of ice at the poles.

Velikovsky preferred the axis shift theory and was somewhat scathing about Hapgood's work, although without mentioning him by name:

> . . . the theory that would explain the displacement of the crust by an asymmetric growth of the polar ice caps, is quantitatively indefensible; this theory uses the same phenomenon – the growing ice caps – as the cause *and* the effect of ice ages.[40]

Perhaps this summary dismissal had something to do with the fact that both these men were vying for the approval of Albert Einstein just before his death.[41] In any case, Velikovsky's observations have been backed up by more recent criticisms of Hapgood's theory – for example those of mathematician Flavio Barbiero, who has recently undertaken considerable analysis of catastrophe mechanisms and also favours the axis shift theory:

[Hapgood's] theory does not explain some of the most significant peculiarities of Pleistocene climate changes, first of all the speed with which these changes appear to have taken place. According to Hapgood it took the north pole at least two thousand years to move from its previous position to the present. The evidence we have, however, is in favour of a definitely much faster climatic change. It was Hapgood himself who underlined the enormous amount of evidence proving the high speed at which the shift of the poles appears to have happened; speed which the mechanism he proposes is unable to explain.[42]

I am personally persuaded that, if the geological and climatic anomalies I have described can only be satisfactorily explained by some form of pole shift, then crustal displacement is not the answer – while an axis shift of the entire globe *is*, as Velikovsky, Barbiero and numerous others suggest. But what catalyst would provide enough energy to cause such a shift?

Remember that, to the extent that I am at least in part attempting to explain inconsistent glaciation in the ice ages, this catalyst must operate not regularly but *sporadically* – after all, there were no ice ages between 65 and 2 million years ago. Moreover, we need to recognise that the glaciers that build up during an ice age are formed of water from the oceans, and in particular that considerable heat is required to evaporate such huge quantities of water until it falls as snow over polar regions and extends the ice caps. So, paradoxically, the initiation of an ice age requires a significant *increase* in temperature, although followed by a rapid and equally significant decrease so that glaciation has the chance to take hold. In other words, neither heat nor cold alone can initiate an ice age. However, we must simultaneously recognise that the termination of an ice age also requires a relatively sudden increase in temperature to melt the glaciers, but this time it needs to be more permanent. Moreover, of course, we still need an explanation for the complete reversal of this latter situation that appears to have flash-frozen the mammoths in Siberia and Alaska at the end of the Pleistocene.

Taking all these factors into account, I am inclined to agree with Velikovsky and the numerous other commentators who suggest that there is only one catalyst capable of (a) causing sufficient swift temperature swings to initiate or terminate an ice age, (b) carrying enough energy to initiate an axis shift that would produce inconsistent glaciation and climate change, and (c) occurring only sporadically, not regularly; and that is the impact of an extraterrestrial body.[43]

This view is strengthened by a lengthy paper prepared by Barbiero, which 'analyses the behaviour of a gyroscope subjected to a disturbing force, and shows that the torque generated by the impact of a relatively small asteroid is capable of causing almost instantaneous changes of the axis of rotation and therefore instantaneous shifts of the poles in any direction and of any amplitude'.[44] The paper contains complex mathematics, at least for a nonspecialist, but it certainly appears to be the most in-depth and scholarly study of this subject undertaken to date.

Nevertheless, is any kind of pole shift really required to explain the climatic enigmas of either recent or more remote epochs? If we concentrate on the more remote epochs first, it is of course possible to argue that they did not result from axis shifts, but from less catastrophic causes. For example, the evidence of equatorial glaciation could have resulted merely from a particularly severe ice age towards the end of the Permian epoch. Similarly, it is perhaps conceivable that, if the evidence of a tropical climate in polar regions is reliable, it prevailed in a period when the entire earth was considerably warmer even near the poles – and that the various trees and corals somehow adapted to an environment that would still have been in perpetual darkness for large parts of the year.

As for the end of the Pleistocene, can we conceive of any other mechanism that could cause such localised irregularities in the northern polar regions? In its own right an extraterrestrial impact – indeed, perhaps the one that created the bays in Carolina and elsewhere – would undoubtedly have a multitude of knock-on effects that would be highly confusing to predict in any detail. However, I find it hard to conceive of how it could produce *permanent* localised climate changes without causing a degree of axis shift as well. Remember this mechanism would ensure two things happened after any short-term disruptions to the atmosphere had died down: on the one hand, some previously temperate zones relatively close to the pole would suddenly become arctic – hence the fate of the frozen mammoths; conversely, some previously-glaciated areas would suddenly be in more temperate latitudes, producing massive, swift and permanent melting. Moreover, although Hapgood was attempting to prove his theory of crustal displacement via imbalance in the lithosphere, his underlying evidence of polar shifts in general does provide support for an axis shift as well.

Above all, whether or not any sort of pole shifts have ever occurred in the earth's long history, we must bring ourselves back to the prime consideration for the present work. That is the abundant evidence that a major catastrophe did occur to accelerate the end of the Pleistocene.

GEOMAGNETISM AND POLAR REVERSALS

One other issue is often raised in conjunction with discussions of catastrophes and pole shifts: the evidence of geomagnetism. Particles of molten rock with any iron content will align themselves with the magnetic poles as they solidify, thereby keeping a permanent record of their position at the time, and Hapgood collated evidence from a number of studies suggesting that the magnetic orientation of the poles had indeed changed several hundred times in the history of the earth.[45] Moreover, such studies have continued in the intervening years, and in particular examination of the volcanic rock that has emerged from the Mid-Atlantic Ridge for millions of years suggests that these shifts in orientation are considerably more frequent than even Hapgood thought – with *complete reversals* in polarity occurring approximately every half a million years.[46]

Many commentators use this as evidence for either crustal displacement or axis shifts, but this approach is surely flawed. The big problem is that scientists still do not know what produces the earth's magnetic field, although they assume that it has something to do with convection currents in the semimolten mantle, and possibly also electromagnetic radiation from the sun as we discussed briefly in Part 1 in connection with the Mayan calendar. Moreover, we all know that the magnetic pole is not in the same position as the axial pole – currently, magnetic north is about five degrees west of true north in the UK, but this varies with time and location. Therefore, apart from all the problems that are in any case inherent in geomagnetic studies, they tell us only about the position of the magnetic pole in distant epochs – and given that we have no idea of the previous relationship between this and the axial pole, to suggest they are a reliable pointer to the latter is surely inappropriate. Moreover, if we do not know what governs the direction of the magnetic field, how can we predict what it would do if there were a crustal displacement or axis shift? Conversely, how can we predict what effect a significant shift in the magnetic pole, or even a complete reversal in polarity, might have on the earth's axis? Many commentators suggest that we are heading for a complete reversal in the near future, but the earth's axial rotation has certainly not been affected so far.

MEMORIES

So much for the physical evidence that the end of the Pleistocene was a time of catastrophic upheaval. It seems highly likely that, wherever in the world our forgotten race had spread to, they could easily have been decimated. But did the survivors manage to pass on a memory of these events to their descendants who had, to a large extent, to begin all over again? After all, all orthodox evolutionists accept that the fully modern humans of this relatively late period would have been sufficiently cultured to discuss such events at length. Moreover, did these memories manage to survive in oral form for thousands of years before being incorporated, sometimes in somewhat distorted form, into the written traditions of the earliest civilisations of the modern epoch?

I have already mentioned the abundance of generalised flood and destruction traditions from around the world. However, concentrating on those that perhaps contain somewhat more pertinent detail, we saw in Chapter 3 how, in the Ethiopian *Book of Enoch*, 'the earth became inclined' as 'destruction approached', 'the earth laboured, and was violently shaken', 'the moon changed its laws', and 'many chiefs among the stars . . . perverted their ways'. And we saw in the Mesopotamian *Erra and Ishum* that Marduk, or originally Enlil, made 'the positions of the stars of heaven change' and 'did not return them to their places'.

In Chapter 5 we saw how, in the Taoist *Essays from Huai Nan Tzu*, 'the four seasons failed', 'thunder-bolts wrought havoc', 'hailstones fell with violence', and 'noxious miasma and untimely hoarfrosts fell unceasingly'.

In Chapter 6 we saw that in *Timaeus*, Plato recounts how the Egyptian priests specifically told Solon that the Greeks' story about Phaethon was a distortion of a true event; and Phaethon is described as the child of the sun who 'harnessed his father's chariot, but was unable to guide it along his father's course', as a result of which there was 'a widespread destruction by fire of things on the earth'. Moreover we saw that, in the Hopi traditions, during one destruction 'the world teetered off balance', 'mountains plunged into seas', 'seas and lakes sloshed over the land', and 'the world froze into solid ice', while during another 'waves higher than mountains rolled in upon the land', and 'continents broke asunder and sank beneath the seas'. This is in addition to the general concept of destructions by flood, fire, volcano, hurricane and earthquake preserved in the various South American world age traditions we reviewed.

Moreover, there are a considerable number of other worldwide sources that can be used to back up these narratives. Mesopotamian texts, for instance, include numerous references to fierce battles conducted by the gods, especially those associated with atmospheric phenomena. They include Ninurta – who is the god not only of war but also of floods, and is further identified with the 'thunderbird' known as Imdugud – and also Ishkur, the storm god.[47] Furthermore they have weapons with similar associations, such as the *abubu* or flood weapon, and the *kasusu* or wind weapon.[48]

One of the finest examples is the Sumerian *Ninurta Myth, Lugal-e*, which dates to the beginning of the second millennium BC and is a composite of three original parts. In the first Ninurta is accompanied by his trusty friend and weapon Sharur – described as 'the one who lays low multitudes' and 'the flood storm of battle' – while engaging in a fierce battle with the enigmatic Azag, an object or creature whose main weapon is its 'dreadful aura'. The translator, Thorkild Jacobsen, suggests that Azag is a tree of some sort, on the basis that it is described in the text as being the product of 'heaven copulating with verdant earth', but arguably this is just as likely to represent an extraterrestrial body that impacted – a similar interpretation to that suggested by Allan and Delair for the Greek Phaethon. This possibility is strengthened when we find

Jacobsen admitting that Azag's description at the end of this part changes enigmatically to 'zalag stone'.[49]

As for the text itself, we find Ninurta's march into battle described thus:

> The evil wind and the south storm were tethered to him, the
> flood storm strode at their flanks, and before the warrior went
> a huge irresistible tempest, it was tearing up the dust,
> depositing it again, evening out hill and dale, filling in
> hollows; live coals it rained down, fire burned, flames
> scorched, tall trees it toppled from their roots, denuding the
> forests. Earth wrung her hands against the heart, emitting
> cries of pain . . . the desert was burnt off as if denuded by
> locusts, the wave rising in its path was shattering the
> mountains.[50]

We then find that when Ninurta attacks Azag 'the sun marched no longer, it had turned into a moon . . . the day was made black like pitch'.[51] Meanwhile, when Azag retaliates:

> . . . it screamed wrathfully, like a formidable serpent it hissed
> from among its people, it wiped up the waters in the
> highland, swept away the tamarisks, it gashed the earth's
> body, made painful wounds, gave the canebrake over to fire,
> and bathed the sky in blood, the interior it knocked over,
> scattered its people, and till today black cinders are in the
> fields, and ever heaven's base becomes to the observer like red
> wool – thus verily it is.[52]

Finally, once the battle is over, we find the following description of the aftermath:

> In those days the waters of the ground coming from below did
> not flow out over the fields. As ice long accumulating they
> rose in the mountains on the far side . . . in dire famine
> nothing was produced . . .[53]

If any literal rather than symbolic interpretation of this text is appropriate, I would certainly propose that it describes a natural catastrophe of some sort – possibly only a localised and more recent one given that we have no broader context, but possibly also our worldwide catastrophe initiated by an extraterrestrial body – rather than, as some commentators have suggested, an aeronautical or even nuclear conflict.[54]

Later Zoroastrian traditions report dramatic climate changes in the transition from the first world age, which was dominated by the benign deity Ahura Mazda, to the next, dominated by his evil counterpart Angra Mainyu. They describe how a temperate climate switched to 'ten months of winter and two of summer', and also how Angra Mainyu 'assaulted and deranged the sky'.[55]

Although I established in Part 1 that the world age traditions of the classical Greek writers are somewhat unreliable, they do in general follow up on the Mesopotamian themes of violent gods associated with severe atmospheric phenomena. In his relatively short *Theogony*, Hesiod does not mention the flood specifically, but his descriptions of Zeus' wars with the giant Titans and also with Thyphoeus – who is clearly the role model for the later Phaethon mentioned by Plato – are highly comparable to those of Ninurta.[56] Meanwhile, in *Metamorphosis* Ovid provides full details of the Phaethon tradition;[57] he also describes the subsidence of the water and the emergence of the hills after the flood in some detail.[58]

It is no surprise that Scandinavian traditions continue in the same vein. For example, at the end of the first part of Snorri's *Edda* we find the passage that describes Ragnarok – the 'twilight of the gods'. This appears to be a forecast of a time to come, but is arguably a distortion or repetition of events that have already taken place long ago:

> Snow will drive from all quarters, there will be hard frosts and biting winds; the sun will be no use. There will be three such winters on end with no summer between . . . the wolf will swallow the sun and that will seem a great disaster to men. Then another wolf will seize the moon and that one too will do great harm. The stars will disappear from heaven. Then this will come to pass, the whole surface of the earth and the mountains will tremble so violently that trees will be uprooted from the ground, mountains will crash down, and all fetters and bonds will be snapped and severed. . . . The sea will lash

against the land. . . . Surt will fling fire over the earth and
burn up the whole world. . . . The sun will go black, earth
sink in the sea, heaven be stripped of its bright stars; smoke
rage and fire, leaping the flame, lick heaven itself. . . . While
the world is being burned by Surt, in a place called
Hoddmimir's Wood, will be concealed two human beings
called Lif and Lifthrasir. Their food will be the morning dews,
and from these men will come so great a stock that the whole
world will be peopled . . .[59]

Finally, even when we get to the admittedly distorted and
relatively late Arab accounts, we still find echoes such as Abd al
Hokm's description of how the flood was anticipated by King
Saurid because 'the whole earth was turned over' beforehand.[60]
Moreover, in addition to all of these relatively ancient textual
records that appear to provide support for catastrophism in the
recent past, there are many similar native traditions in indigenous
cultures around the world – for example, not only in the Americas
but also in Africa, Australasia and Oceania.[61]

Of course, we must be ever vigilant for the symbolism inherent
in many descriptions of battles involving gods, such as are
particularly prevalent in, for example, Mesopotamian, Greek and
Scandinavian texts. Nevertheless, I would maintain that there
remains a sufficiently large and detailed body of textual and
traditional evidence of catastrophe from all around the world that
at least some of the stories are likely to represent genuine memories
based on fact and not fancy – providing a degree of confirmation
that a terrible worldwide destruction did indeed take place in
relatively recent times.

DATING

Let me summarise what we have learned about the dating of the
catastrophe that accelerated the end of the Pleistocene. Figure 9
shows that a date of 11,500 years ago, or 9500 BC, is clear favourite
– although some commentators would shift this several thousand
years either way.

For our broad purposes, attempting to isolate an exact date is
unnecessary. We are more interested in the considerable geological
and textual evidence in favour of a worldwide catastrophe at

Years Ago	Source	Details
13–11,000	Various	Mass extinctions
13–9,000	Hapgood	Radiocarbon dating of various US animal remains
17–12,000	Hapgood	Gradual crustal shift
11–10,000	Duke University	Radiocarbon dating of Carolina Bay deposits
11,500	Allan and Delair	Phaeton disaster
11,500	Various	Ice-core samples[62]
11,500	Plato	In *Timaeus* (see Part 1)
11,000	Prouty	Disintegration of extraterrestrial body
9,500	Clube and Napier	Disintegration of giant comet

Figure 9: Suggested Dates for the Catastrophe

around this time – one that would in all likelihood have wiped out the vast majority of the members of our forgotten race, forcing them to start all over again from scratch.

However, was there only one major catastrophe in the last 100,000 years? Increasingly catastrophists are postulating that there may have been several, and that indeed modern humans – and their earlier ancestors in more distant epochs – may have come close to extinction on a number of occasions. This approach is perhaps confirmed by the genetic studies that, as we saw in an earlier chapter, increasingly appear to indicate that there have been a number of bottlenecks in modern human evolution – particularly around the time of the Toba supereruption about 70,000 years ago, although as yet none point definitively towards the end of the Pleistocene. Moreover, Hapgood postulated three pole shifts in the last 100,000 years, even if I do not agree with his mechanism and some of his evidence. If these theories are correct, then perhaps the multiple world age traditions deserve more credence than I previously gave them. However, this line of reasoning requires considerable speculation, and I am more inclined to play it safe and concentrate on the principle that the major single destruction that dominates *most* of the ancient texts and traditions occurred somewhere around 11,500 years ago.

WHERE ON EARTH?

But where were the members of our forgotten race when they were decimated? We have seen that, even if there was a relatively small axis shift at the end of the Pleistocene, *broadly* speaking the climatic zones of the earth would have been largely unchanged. In addition, even at the height of the Pleistocene significant parts of the temperate zones and the entirety of the tropical zones would have remained free of ice. Admittedly, on current reckoning, temperatures may have been anything from five to ten degrees Celsius colder at times, but this would only serve to make the tropical climate more tolerable.

We have also seen that even *Homo erectus* was mobile across major continents just after two million years ago, so we can assume that more modern counterparts would have had the freedom to travel to any climate, or indeed continent, that suited them – including, I would suggest, having the navigational skills to travel by boat across significant oceans, a subject we will address shortly. I believe we can therefore postulate quite safely that they could have been in any temperate or tropical latitude between, for the sake of argument, forty degrees north and forty degrees south . . . and that we can forget about the idea that prior to the catastrophe they would have only been sheltering in caves wrapped in bearskins. This still leaves an enormous area of search. Is it possible to narrow it down further? And perhaps more to the point, is it possible to suggest locations where any evidence of their settlement would not yet have been discovered?

I would not be the first researcher to suggest that the first place we might look is under water – because, if our forgotten race's main method of travel for trade was by sea, then most of their major settlements would have been coastal. Not only would these be most affected by any tsunamis, but also sea levels rising by as much as one hundred metres would subsequently submerge any that were not initially wiped out. This rise in sea levels leaves a great many possibilities, including not only significant portions of the modern continental shelf in all regions, but also large areas of what are now shallow seas. As we can see from Figure 10, in the temperate and tropical zones this includes, among others, the Persian Gulf; the Yellow, China, and Java Seas; and the seas between Australia and New Guinea.

In this context, a number of underwater structures have been located around the world in the modern era. The most celebrated is the so-called 'Bimini Road' discovered by J Manson Valentine in

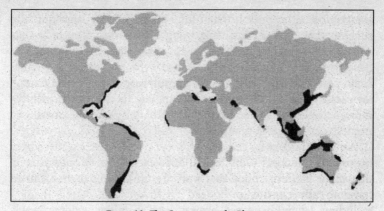

Figure 10: The Continents in the Pleistocene

shallow waters off the island of the same name in 1968, although geologists are split about whether or not this is a natural structure.[63] Then, in 1987, large structures resembling temples with platforms and giant stairs were located in the waters off Yonaguni, the most southerly of the Japanese Ryukyu island chain. But Schoch, who has dived on the site himself, makes the hugely important point that it consists of 'a single piece of solid bedrock' that is 'criss-crossed by many joints and fractures running vertical to the bedding planes', which is what has allowed it to form the right-angled and apparently regular shapes that we now see. In other words, it is not composed of separate human-made blocks, making it almost certain that this too is a natural structure.[64] Moreover, in 2001 a Canadian team searching for underwater shipwrecks off the coast of Cuba reported the discovery of underwater structures that 'resemble pyramids, roads and build-ings' in an 'urban development', though they are in some 700 to 800 metres of water and no one has dived on them yet.[65]

Finally, another discovery in 2001 of 'a grid of geometric structures thought to be the foundations of two cities, each more than five miles wide' has been detected forty metres below sea level in the Gulf of Khambhat or Cambay, forty miles off the coast of Gujarat in northwestern India.[66] This time the retrieval of pottery and other artefacts suggests that this is indeed a man-made site, and Graham Hancock – who has been concentrating on dives in coastal areas for several years now to research his 2002 book

Underworld, an approach that I fully endorse – has been quick to suggest that this is his long sought-after evidence of a late Pleistocene advanced civilisation. However, artefacts from the site have been provisionally carbon dated to only 7500 BC, which is some two thousand years *later* than our best guess for the date of the catastrophe. So, although it appears that the site is considerably more advanced than the smaller conurbations that preceded it in Anatolia and Syria, and although its discovery, if properly verified, does push the date for the development of fully-fledged cities back by several thousand years, it still appears to be a development of the *post*catastrophe epoch that was, presumably for more localised reasons, submerged later.[67]

Overall, then, it would appear that definitive evidence of a submerged *pre*catastrophe culture still awaits discovery. Having said that, a far less well-known enigma comes in the form of the 'Lost Pyramids' of Rock Lake, Wisconsin. A number of reports of these structures have cropped up in the last century, and several divers have described at least one four-sided stone pyramid lying beneath the water. Formed from relatively small rocks but as much as ten metres high and six metres wide at the base, and either rectangular or square, the reported design is clearly not consistent with either North American earth mounds or Central and South American stepped pyramids. Moreover, the lake is thought to have been formed at the end of the Wisconsin glaciation, suggesting that the structures do indeed date to the precatastrophe period.[68]

Let us now turn our attention to land. I must reiterate that I do not support any of the suggestions made by other revisionist authors that definitive proof of antediluvian civilisations has already been found in existing monuments that have supposedly been incorrectly dated by the Establishment – although we must wait for a later chapter to examine these suggestions properly. Nevertheless, are there significant areas of the temperate and tropical zones that have yet to be properly explored?

Of course, the answer is yes. We only need to think of the extent to which the huge expanse of the Sahara is largely uncharted territory. Because it is clear that in the late Pleistocene it provided a temperate climate and abundant vegetation, who can say what lies beneath its numerous dunes? The same might be said of large parts of the Arabian Desert. Moreover, even if we were to argue that Central and South America, western and southern Europe and the Near East have all received more than their fair share of exploration and as yet yielded no advanced cultural sites of late Pleistocene date, surely no one could argue that huge parts of central and southern Asia – including especially the Gobi Desert, which straddles the fortieth parallel – remain largely unexplored.

MISSING EVIDENCE

Most scientists would argue that missing evidence is no evidence at all, and we can do nothing but accept that, at the present time, no definitive evidence has been uncovered of a late Pleistocene culture of the level of advancement that I am advocating for our forgotten race – save perhaps for a few artefacts that have turned up to provide small clues. There is evidence aplenty of the fact that modern humans had developed a reasonably high level of intellectual culture perhaps as long as 100,000 years ago, but none that supports the notion that they built large permanent settlements of the sort that at present we find only at the commencement of the Holocene some 11,500 years ago. Of course, it may be no coincidence that this dating ties in remarkably well with that of the catastrophe, indicating that what we have found increasingly in recent years are settlements in the Near East that represent the *re-emergence* of a cultured race almost immediately after the catastrophe that wiped out their debased predecessors.

It is important to stress that I am not suggesting that all traces of our forgotten race from all around the world must have been completely eradicated. This would be a dangerous approach, because far more ancient but primitive sites of occupation of early *Homo* – in, for example, South and East Africa – remained in the substrata largely undisturbed by whatever catastrophes have affected the planet in the intervening period. Of course, it is possible that the areas in which such early sites have been preserved happened to survive relatively unscathed, while those chosen more recently by our forgotten race happened to be unlucky. It is less speculative, however, to argue that the combination of the catastrophic destruction at the end of the Pleistocene – which is likely to have devastated a significant proportion of the landmass, as well as permanently submerging many coastal areas – *and* the fact that large parts of the globe that our forgotten race might have inhabited remain largely unexplored even today, work in tandem to explain why we have not as yet discovered the definitive evidence of their cultured existence that orthodox science demands.

. The other major issue that we must consider is the materials that our forgotten race were using for their buildings. We all like to think that they may have been erecting huge and impressive stone temples and pyramids similar to those erected by our postdiluvian ancestors in more recent epochs, but I believe that to be realistic we must accept that this *may* not have been the case. The individual buildings may not have been that large, and they may have been constructed entirely from wood or mud-brick, especially in the temperate and tropical regions that we are considering as the primary targets. I think few scholars would argue that these materials do not survive well in the archaeological record when we attempt to go back to between 100,000 and 11,500 years ago.[69] Moreover, they definitely do not survive well when submerged under a hail of volcanic debris, or when ripped apart by ferocious hurricanes, or when submerged under tidal waves or rising sea levels.

Does this have to alter our view of the level of advancement of our forgotten race? I would argue not. After all, many of the residents of modern Switzerland, to take one example, prefer the use of wood for construction of their houses – and yet quite clearly this does not reduce their level of cultural sophistication below that of the rest of the modern world. Nor does this scenario preclude the development of settlements that would be construed as reasonably large even by modern standards. However, it would tend to suggest that the debasement of our forgotten race did not include outright wars between different factions, otherwise we might expect them to have built large fortifications out of stone. Does material debasement necessarily have to include war? I would argue not. In fact, late-twentieth-century attempts to reduce global warfare went hand in hand with the rampant rise of materialism. We must remember that above all this was a *spiritual* debasement.

I am clearly exploring possibilities here, and indulging in considerable conjecture. However, I would argue that the wealth of evidence that I have already collated in the present work demands that we make some educated guesses about our forgotten race – albeit perhaps more conservative ones than are made by many revisionist authors.

CONCLUSION

Despite some weaknesses in the evidence, the argument that our forgotten race was indeed decimated by a major catastrophe at the end of the Pleistocene remains strong. The various worldwide traditions have all the appearance of being reasonably accurate descriptions of what orthodox catastrophists think *did* happen at the end of the Pleistocene. Many of them involve the land being inundated by water, and we not only have the evidence of marine deposits right across inland areas of North America and other carnage in many other parts of the world, but also the fact that – although the degree of complexity of the interactions makes this an extremely general assumption – the end of an ice age is more likely to be brought about by an extraterrestrial body impacting in the ocean rather than on land. So I would argue that the physical and textual evidence all point towards the most likely scenario for the end of the Pleistocene being one in which, around 11,500 years ago, a comet or asteroid sped across northwest America in a southeasterly direction, disintegrating as it went, until it impacted in the ocean off the Carolina coastline, sending huge tsunami waves all around the globe. Moreover, the textual references to changes in the positions of the celestial bodies, combined with the physical evidence of inconsistent glaciation and climate change, seem to point towards an accompanying axis shift of unknown degree.

But was our forgotten race completely destroyed? Clearly not, because the modern human population would not be here if they had been. Some, who knows exactly how many and where, must have been around to commence the rebuilding process, again just as the texts and traditions suggest. But then again, perhaps we do have some clues as to who the most likely survivors were. We all know about Noah and his ark, but in his excellent 2001 work *The Golden Thread of Time* independent researcher Crichton Miller has made the fascinating observation that the people most likely to have survived the catastrophe were indeed ocean navigators. He provides persuasive arguments that long before the catastrophe our forgotten race had mastered the use of a simple bob-weighted, freely revolving, circular angle-measuring dial attached to a right-angled cross for determining their position from the stars and sun with astonishing accuracy – a device that not only could be used for surveying on land as well, but also provided the crucial archetypal symbol on which all later crosses, and especially the Celtic cross, were based (see Plates 21 and 22). He goes on to suggest that any navigators that were at sea at the time of the catastrophe would have been least affected by any tsunamis, which cause only a swell in deep ocean rather than the breaking, destructive waves experienced on the shore. Moreover, as the most advanced astronomers of our forgotten race, they may even have predicted the impact of an extraterrestrial body and set sail accordingly. This of course gives a new, and in my view highly credible, slant to the traditions of flood survivors such as Noah.

I have already suggested repeatedly that, although on the surface the catastrophe was a natural event, underneath it was a karmic one that our forgotten race brought on their own heads by their debased behaviour. But were they culturally advanced enough to be *that* material, and *that* debased, to deserve such a catastrophic karmic reaction? After all, I have suggested that they probably did not even have the level of city-based culture our more recent ancestors possessed some four to five thousand years ago. Again I am speculating, but my answer is, theoretically, yes. If they were advanced enough to be living in reasonably large coastal trading settlements, and navigating the oceans, then they were advanced enough to reach a stage whereby the pursuit of power and material gain could quite easily have become the predominant driving force of their lives, and over a period of time this debasement could have become so thoroughly entrenched that those trying to hang on to the 'old' universal spiritual truths would have been virtually wiped out by persecution. Speculation yes, but also perfectly possible without entering the world of fantasy.

Finally, let us not forget that this is what many of the ancient traditions actually tell us, some in quite frightening detail. The survivors preserved the memory of what had befallen them and passed it down from generation to generation over the millennia, in order that we too can heed the warning of our distant forebears . . . if ears we have to listen.

13. THE THEOSOPHICAL PERSPECTIVE

In the search for corroboration of my interpretation of the ancient texts and traditions regarding our forgotten race, it is now time to move away from the boundaries of science that have so far dominated this part of the work, and on to less reliable but nevertheless related areas of study. The first is the worldview of the theosophists, and in particular of the person who founded their movement in 1875, Madame Helena Petrovna Blavatsky.

I do not have the space here to go into great detail about her life, and in any case a number of excellent reference works are freely available.[1] I should note, however, that she travelled extensively in India and the Far East before returning to England to write her best-known works, *Isis Unveiled* in 1877 and *The Secret Doctrine* in 1888. Both are massive two-volume compilations that stretch to more than fifteen hundred pages each, and they are well referenced. However, they are also extremely hard work to read, not so much because of the length but because of Blavatsky's prose style, a deficiency that can only in part be attributed to the fact that English was not her native tongue. In any case, the latter is broadly accepted as her more definitive masterwork, and it is on its contents that we will mainly concentrate.

Attitudes towards her work have always tended to polarise into either complete and devotional support or total rejection, whereas in my view the correct approach, as we so often find, is to tread a middle path. The rejections, especially in the early days of theosophy, were partly based on a fundamental antipathy to her broadly esoteric and particularly anti-Christian views, and as a result two charges were levelled at her: first, that she was a fraud who pretended to telepathically channel much of her material from Eastern 'masters' who never existed; and second, that she was a rampant plagiarist. Accordingly, if we are to allow any of her material to stand, we must first assess the validity of these accusations.

THE MASTERS

In his 1994 study *The Masters Revealed*, K Paul Johnson uses archive material to demonstrate that Blavatsky's masters were in fact real adepts from all parts of the world, whom she had met on her foreign travels. He also demonstrates that she had very good reasons for concealing their identity. On the one hand, some of her Indian masters were heavily involved in political independence movements, and on the other all genuine adepts have a tendency toward privacy and secrecy. As she herself noted in correspondence:

> Well, I told him the whole truth. I said to him that I had known Adepts, the 'Brothers', not only in India and beyond Ladakh, but in Egypt and Syria – for there are 'Brothers' there to this day. The names of the 'Mahatmas' were not even known at the time, since they are called so only in India. That, whether they were called Rosicrucians, Kabalists, or Yogis – Adepts were everywhere Adepts – silent, secret, retiring, and who would never divulge themselves entirely.[2]

However, her letters also reveal that she and her cofounder of the Theosophical Society, Colonel Henry Olcott, spent considerable time in private accusing each other of being responsible for the exaggeration of the nature of the masters, and of their elevation to godlike and superhuman status. There is little doubt that Blavatsky herself had encouraged this in the early days in order to gain attention for the movement, even to the extent of amazing her followers by 'materialising' supposed letters from the masters in midair, and other trickery. Moreover, it would appear that once the genie was out of the bottle not even she could put it back – although it is impossible to determine whether or not her apparent contrition towards the end of her life was genuine.[3]

PLAGIARIST?

Although late on in her life and in private Blavatsky herself admitted to a degree of trickery, she also emphasised that her works should be taken on their merits alone – and this would appear to be a fair approach for us to adopt. And as a general observation they do not have the appearance of being channelled to any significant degree, replete as they are with footnoted references.

But even if they were not channelled, to what extent were they perhaps plagiarised from a variety of sources in a more prosaic fashion? William Coleman, an ardent spiritualist and contemporary critic of Blavatsky, was the first to suggest that, for example, in *Isis Unveiled* she had referenced some fourteen hundred works even though she only possessed about one hundred in her own library – the latter observation being confirmed by Olcott.[4] In other words, she was being criticised for providing the primary references only, and for not crediting her secondary sources.

However, this is a trait of all authors of scholarly and even nonscholarly works – including, I freely admit, myself. It certainly does not amount to plagiarism. Moreover, the intention is usually to provide the most original source for the interested reader or researcher to check if they so wish. That having been said, I would add two riders to this that are of more general application. First, where a researcher is consistently using a secondary source, it is only proper to give it at least a general credit. Second, and even more important, we should recognise that this practice can lead to errors and inaccuracies being perpetuated. For this reason, if there is any doubt as to the validity of a secondary source, the primary source should undoubtedly be located and consulted – and, where appropriate, the primary source before that, all the way back as far as possible. This is something many revisionist historians in particular would do well to learn and practice more assiduously, because many of their predecessors have not been averse to distortion of source material, or even downright fabrication from scratch, as I have repeatedly discovered.

None of this makes Blavatsky either an outright plagiarist or a complete charlatan. In fact, we might note that she was in her mid-fifties when she decided to work all hours of the day and night to produce *The Secret Doctrine*, having already achieved considerable notoriety with *Isis Unveiled*, and further that she had already come close to death through ill health before and did so again in the middle of this herculean labour. Moreover, arguably the effort did kill her because, after completing a few shorter works, she died only three years later. So, accepting that her underlying motives for her work were probably to a large extent genuine, despite her admitted surface trickery, let us see what she really had to say.

THE BOOK OF DZYAN

Much of *The Secret Doctrine* is based on stanzas from the enigmatic and supposedly extremely ancient *Book of Dzyan* – the provenance of which we will consider shortly – and on Blavatsky's accompanying commentaries. The two volumes are split into 'Cosmogenesis' and 'Anthropogenesis', with the stanzas in the former largely based on the Eastern worldview of the hidden and cyclic nature of the universe as a whole that we have already discussed to some extent and will consider in greater detail in Part 3. In particular, Blavatsky reveals the extent to which a Hindu worldview informs much of her work in that at the time of writing she believed us to be 4989 years into the kali yuga of what she refers to as the *Vaisasvata* manvantara.[5]

In applying this cyclic view to the human race she reveals herself to be categorically opposed to evolutionary theory, and I have already given my reasons for regarding this as a complete misinterpretation of the original esoteric foundation of the cyclic worldview. Nevertheless, the most interesting stanzas from the anthropological section of the *Book of Dzyan*, which describe the 'root races' on which Blavatsky concentrates in her second volume, can, in my view, be reinterpreted and found to have a fair degree of consistency with my main themes – particularly if we adopt the more spiritual and less physical approach to world cycles that I have already expounded in Part 1:

Stanza 5

18. The First were the sons of Yoga. Their sons the children of the Yellow Father and the White Mother.
19. The Second Race was the product by budding and expansion, the asexual from the sexless. Thus was, O Lanoo, the Second Race produced.
20. Their fathers were the Self-born. The Self-born, the Chhaya from the brilliant bodies of the Lords, the Fathers, the Sons of Twilight.
21. When the Race became old, the old waters mixed with the fresher waters. When its drops became turbid, they vanished

and disappeared in the new stream, in the hot stream of life. The outer of the First became the inner of the Second. The old Wing became the new Shadow, and the Shadow of the Wing.[6]

Blavatsky admits that the first 'self-born' race were only ethereal beings with no physical body, which is entirely consistent with our understanding of advanced discarnate souls. As for the second 'sweat-born' race, she suggests in her commentary that they were 'the most heterogeneous gigantic semi-human monsters – the first attempts of material nature at building human bodies'.[7] This is of course reminiscent of the legends of hybrids that I rejected in Part 1, but it is certainly not borne out by the stanzas themselves. However, they do make it clear that they were asexual and were not generated by any normal reproductive means, which in my view suggests that if these stanzas have any validity at all they at least indicate that the second race was also made up of ethereal beings.

Stanza 6

22. Then the Second evolved the Egg-born, the Third. The sweat grew, its drops grew, and the drops became hard and round. The Sun warmed it; the Moon cooled and shaped it; the wind fed it until its ripeness. The white swan from the starry vault overshadowed the big drop. The egg of the future race, the Man-swan of the later third. First male-female, then man and woman.
23. The self-born were the Chhayas: the Shadows from the bodies of the Sons of Twilight.

Blavatsky suggests that this third 'egg-born' race was the first to become fully physically manifest, and then to split into male and female allowing for sexual reproduction. Is it possible that these stanzas should be interpreted to mean that it was during this stage of the evolution of humankind that advanced souls attempted to incarnate for the first time? This view certainly seems to be reinforced by the ensuing stanzas:

Stanza 7

24. The Sons of Wisdom, the Sons of Night, ready for rebirth, came down, they saw the vile forms of the First Third. 'We

can choose', said the Lords, 'we have wisdom.' Some entered
the Chhaya. Some projected the Spark. Some deferred till the
Fourth. From their own Rupa they filled the Kama. Those
who entered became Arhats. Those who received but a spark,
remained destitute of knowledge; the spark burned low. The
third remained mind-less. Their Jivas were not ready. These
were set apart among the Seven. They became narrow-headed.
The Third were ready. 'In these shall we dwell', said the Lords
of the Flame.

25. How did the Manasa, the Sons of Wisdom, act? They
rejected the Self-born. They are not ready. They spurned the
Sweat-born. They are not quite ready. They would not enter
the first Egg-born.

26. When the Sweat-born produced the Egg-born, the twofold
and the mighty, the powerful with bones, the Lords of
Wisdom said: 'Now shall we create.'

27. The Third Race became the Vahan of the Lords of
Wisdom. It created 'Sons of Will and Yoga', by Kriyasakti it
created them, the Holy Fathers, Ancestors of the Arhats.

Stanza 8

28. From the drops of sweat; from the residue of the substance;
matter from dead bodies of men and animals of the wheel
before; and from cast-off dust, the first animals were produced.

29. Animals with bones, dragons of the deep, and flying
Sarpas were added to the creeping things. They that creep on
the ground got wings. They of the long necks in the water
became the progenitors of the fowls of the air.

30. During the Third Race the boneless animals grew and
changed: they became animals with bones, their Chhayas
became solid.

31. The animals separated the first. They began to breed. The
two-fold man separated also. He said: 'Let us as they; let us
unite and make creatures.' They did.

32. And those which had no spark took huge she-animals
unto them. They begat upon them dumb Races. Dumb they
were themselves. But their tongues untied. The tongues of
their progeny remained still. Monsters they bred. A race of
crooked red-hair-covered monsters going on all fours. A
dumb race to keep the shame untold.

These stanzas appear somewhat confusing and self-contradictory, in that one moment they describe the third race in positive terms as 'the sons of will and yoga', and the next as 'mindless' and 'dumb'. However, Blavatsky's commentaries describe a bewildering array of seven subraces within each root race, and seven further branches or families within each subrace – the origins of all of which are not described, except inasmuch as they appear to derive from different levels of advancement in the incarnating 'monads'.[8] In general terms, however, the stanzas seem to bear out the idea of multiple and unsuccessful incarnation attempts that I put forward when discussing the various creation traditions from around the world in Part 1. In particular, we find the ethereal beings arguing over whether or not the human form of this race is 'ready' for them to incarnate into, and also the suggestion that at least some of the race remained 'dumb' – which is highly reminiscent of the other traditions in which, as we have seen, early humans are 'silent' or 'cannot speak to praise their creators'. As for the suggestion in the stanzas that this race bred with animals to create yet more hybrid monsters, and Blavatsky's further assertion in her commentaries that in general it was a race of giants, my view is again that these elements are equivalent to certain aspects of the Hindu and Judaeo-Christian traditions that I have already rejected.

Stanza 9

33. Seeing which, the Lhas who had not built men, wept, saying: –
34. 'The Amanasa have defiled our future abodes. This is karma. Let us dwell in the others. Let us teach them better, lest worse should happen.' They did.
35. Then all men became endowed with Manas. They saw the sin of the mindless.
36. The Fourth Race developed speech.
37. The One became Two; also all the living and creeping things that were still one, giant fish-birds and serpents with shell-heads.

If my previous assumptions are correct, this fourth race that developed speech for the first time must surely be regarded as the 'golden race' that we have already met in so many other traditions

– emerging when modern humankind had finally advanced, intellectually and psychologically, to a sufficient degree to furnish the advanced incarnating souls with an appropriate physical shell. However, as we would expect, the theme of their subsequent debasement rings out loud and clear:

Stanza 10

38. Thus two by two on the seven zones, the Third Race gave birth to the Fourth-Race men; the gods became no-gods; the sura became a-sura.

39. The first, on every zone, was moon-coloured; the second yellow like gold; the third red; the fourth brown, which became black with sin.[9] The first seven human shoots were all of one complexion. The next seven began mixing.

40. Then the Fourth became tall with pride. We are the kings, it was said; we are the gods.

41. They took wives fair to look upon. Wives from the mindless, the narrow-headed. They bred monsters. Wicked demons, male and female, also Khado (dakini), with little minds.

42. They built temples for the human body. Male and female they worshipped. Then the Third Eye acted no longer.

Stanza 11

43. They built huge cities. Of rare earths and metals they built, and out of the fires vomited, out of the white stone of the mountains and of the black stone, they cut their own images in their size and likeness, and worshipped them.

44. They built great images nine yatis high, the size of their bodies. Inner fires had destroyed the land of their fathers. The water threatened the Fourth.

45. The first great waters came. They swallowed the seven great islands.

46. All Holy saved, the Unholy destroyed. With them most of the huge animals, produced from the sweat of the earth.

This contains all the traditions with which we are already familiar: the preoccupation with the material, the loss of the 'third eye' of spirituality, and the eventual destruction by flood, which also eliminates most large animals. Again, however, I would argue against the repeated notion that this race bred with inferiors to produce monsters. Meanwhile, the suggestion that they built 'huge cities' is clearly open to interpretation.

Stanza 12

47. Few men remained: some yellow, some brown and black, and some red remained. The moon-coloured were gone forever.

48. The Fifth produced from the holy stock remained; it was ruled over by the first divine Kings . . .

49. . . . who re-descended, who made peace with the Fifth, who taught and instructed it.

And so, finally, we come to the fifth race. This stanza clearly suggests that there were a number of survivors of the catastrophe who went on to found our current race. Moreover, we appear to have clear confirmation that the first 'divine kings' were a new group of angelic souls that deliberately incarnated at this time to help to rebuild and to reassert a spiritual worldview. This is a possibility that, as we have already seen in Part 1, is additional to and not inconsistent with the more prosaic idea that certain of the physical survivors would have been more advanced and better equipped to lead the rebuilding process.

DISTORTIONS

Apart from the specific distortions in the stanzas and in Blavatsky's commentary to which I have already alluded, there are a number of more important general areas in which I believe she makes fundamental mistakes.

OVERCOMPLICATION

Blavatsky argues that, until the middle of the third root race, there was no normal sexual reproduction. This forces her into all sorts of pseudoscientific contortions about how these evolutionary changes came about. Worse still, she makes out that the change-over to normal sexual reproduction in some way forced 'the creative gods, compelled by karmic law, to incarnate in *mindless* men'.[10] This statement is not explained, but how much easier it is to regard all living things as having separate souls of varying degrees of advancement, which incarnate in physical bodies that are produced by normal sexual means. And to regard the first and second root races as purely spiritual rather than physical entities. End of story, no further complications required.

In a similar vein, certain Eastern and Western schools of thought postulate complex hierarchies of 'angels' and 'demons', or in our terms souls or ethereal beings. This is more or less consistent with my main themes, but the attempts made by Blavatsky and other commentators to explain the various levels – and especially their actions, interrelationships and various disagreements in different epochs and on different planes – leave the head spinning.

Moreover, the same traditions describe humans as having a multilayered constitution, with the soul, spirit and mind all regarded as separate aspects from the physical body. It may well be that personally I have yet to properly appreciate the essential differences between these aspects – particularly between the spirit and the soul – but it seems clear that most modern commentators, Blavatsky included, again manage to tie themselves and their readership into terrible knots with their attempts to explain these differentiations and to apply them in their writing.[11] So again, is it naive to attempt to simplify the whole thing, and merely to appreciate the difference between the temporal physical body and its associated human intellect or mind on the one hand, and the ethereal soul on the other; and also between intuitive 'right brain' awareness – deriving from a connection to a higher self or universal consciousness – and rational 'left brain' thought? How much understanding do we lose by sticking with these simplifications? I suspect not that much, and that for most people the picture is made considerably clearer.

This tendency to overcomplicate is inherent not just in Blavatsky's work, but also in almost all esoteric and occult literature. It seems that the more complications are introduced, and the more obscure the result, the more the author is credited with superior levels of occult wisdom. Despite the fact that we are clearly dealing with sometimes complex issues that do not always lend themselves easily to explanation by the written word, it may be time for us to question this approach – and to suggest that, at least to a certain degree, if writers cannot properly explain themselves, then the chances are that they are obfuscating to conceal their own lack of understanding. Of course, broadly speaking I apply this only to writers of relatively modern times who have not had to code their words to avoid charges of heresy. But this is the motive behind my attempt to differentiate between the basic, relatively uncomplicated 'spiritual worldview', and the more complex 'esoteric worldview' that we examine more fully in Part 3.

TIMESCALES

Although the stanzas make no mention of timescales, Blavatsky suggests that the third, fourth and fifth root races emerged approximately eighteen, five and one million years ago respectively.[12] In some senses it would be possible for us to ignore both the cyclical and the anti-evolutionary aspects of her anthropological interpretations, and to go with these timescales, especially inasmuch as the first two root races were only ethereal beings anyway. Moreover, the suggestion that the third or fourth subrace of the third root race was the first to became fully physically manifest, a full eighteen million years ago, could be seen in terms of them being mere primitive hominids at this stage of the physical evolution process; and she does suggest that this first fully physical race did not, for example, have the power of speech.[13]

However, she argues that their use of telepathy allowed them to build cities, and that the fourth root race – which emerged some five million years ago – went on to develop a fully technologically advanced civilisation. This latter distortion of Blavatsky's apart, we can still see that her timescales, influenced as they are by the Hindu world cycles, are hopelessly out of step with what we know about human evolution and the development of advanced culture; and that we would have to take a much more condensed view of them if we were to attempt to place any reliance on our revised interpretation of the stanzas, which of course make no mention of timescales themselves.

Blavatsky's view of the world cycles as related to humanity are in any case somewhat at odds with the conventional Hindu view in that she suggests that each 'round' or manvantara is 'composed of the yugas of the seven periods of humanity'.[14] If we refer back to Figure 3 this makes little apparent sense, because there are approximately seventy and not seven maha yugas, or yuga cycles, in a manvantara.

Moreover, she suggests that from about the midpoint of the fourth race the previous gradual descent into materiality and debasement is reversed, so that the remaining races become progressively more spiritual again, until the seventh once more consists of ethereal beings only.[15] This has clear echoes of the Jain traditions we reviewed in Part 1, except their 'wheel' has fourteen 'spokes' and not seven, so we see something of a mixture in her work. However, given my views about the way in which modern humanity – although supposedly representing the fifth root race that is on the upward return path – is increasingly repeating the mistakes of its predecessors by focusing on the material at the expense of the spiritual, I regard such a view as wishful thinking in the extreme. This is precisely why I believe it is fundamentally incorrect to think of the progress of souls in terms of rigid calendrical cycles, because I reiterate that the whole issue of karmic advancement is governed by choices and not by predestiny. There may be a general outline karmic plan that, for example and to simplify matters, the group of souls represented by the human race should go through a process of devolving onto the material plane and then gradually evolving back onto the ethereal plane, but I would suggest not only that the timescales are flexible, but also that even the entire outcome could be jeopardised by us making the wrong karmic choices and repeating the degenerative mistakes of our predecessors.

CATASTROPHES

We can see that only *one* flood is described in the stanzas, which is broadly what we would expect given our own view of these themes. However, Blavatsky suggests this was a major flood that destroyed the last large peninsula of Atlantis about 850,000 years ago, and that there have been numerous others. For example, she asserts that the lesser flood of about 12,000 years ago only destroyed the final small island remnants of the continent.[16]

More troubling is the fact that she uses her belief in the Hindu world cycles to postulate that the earth is karmically disrupted by axial shifts at *regular* intervals.[17] I need not comment further on the fact that I do not support the theory of catastrophes occurring at set intervals, whether by axial shift or otherwise.

SCIENCE

Blavatsky is, in general, almost as scathing about the limitations of science and scientists as she is, for example, about the dogmatic and narrow-minded Christian church; but this does not prevent her from attempting to justify her assertions about human evolution and geology on pseudoscientific grounds, quoting the work of scientists when it suits her cause.[18] These attempts are not particularly impressive, however, even allowing for the state of scientific knowledge at the time. Moreover, as we have seen, her views are entirely at odds with the findings of modern archaeology, geology and other disciplines.

FALLEN ANGEL THEMES

Turning now specifically to what Blavatsky has to say about the fallen angels, she suggests that the disagreement between the ethereal beings as to when to incarnate, as described in the seventh stanza of the *Book of Dzyan*, lies behind many of their later negative portrayals.[19] Of course, one aspect of the 'fall' is their descent into materiality, and I have already suggested that it just may be that in the ethereal realms there was some disagreement about the possible consequences for the karmic balance of the 'angels' if they incarnated too early in forms that were not sufficiently advanced. Nevertheless, I continue to emphasise that the other aspect of the fall is the subsequent spiritual debasement of the human race as a whole. As we saw in Part 1, these two are undoubtedly confused in the Judaeo-Christian narratives, and to some extent Blavatsky's analysis supports my attempts to disentangle them.

In her usual style, however, she cannot help but further confuse the issue herself. For example, she suggests that an additional aspect of the fallen angel narratives, based on the inference in the tenth stanza, is that some of the fourth root race bred with the 'wrong stock' – that is, the 'fair to look upon' but 'mindless' ancestors of the more degenerate members of the previous third race – to create yet more inhuman monsters.[20] This is clearly similar to the distorted and negative Judaeo-Christian tradition of the fallen angels 'taking wives' from among the 'fair daughters of men' but she compounds this distortion by portraying the biblical Nephilim as one of the last products of these unholy unions, and describing them as 'hairy, dumb monsters'.[21]

AN ARCHAIC MANUSCRIPT?

Leaving the distortions of Blavatsky's commentaries aside, and concentrating once again on the *Book of Dzyan* itself, it is extremely difficult to assess whether the stanzas are a literary device used by her to provide enhanced impact, or translations of extracts from a genuine ancient text. At the outset she suggests that 'an archaic manuscript, a collection of palm leaves made impermeable to water, fire, and air . . . is before the writer's eye.'[22] She adds:

> The Book of Dzyan is utterly unknown to our Philologists, or at any rate was never heard of by them under its present name. . . . The main body of the Doctrines given is found scattered throughout hundreds and thousands of Sanskrit manuscripts . . .[23]

She then goes on to describe how, despite a variety of religious zealots' attempts to destroy all copies of ancient esoteric works, *all* the most ancient manuscripts ever written are preserved in secret lamaseries in Tibet, and copies of a number of them are in the vaults of the Vatican, although clearly they are inaccessible to the general public.[24] This is an intriguing possibility that I raised previously, but it does not help us particularly with our current quest to establish whether or not the *Book of Dzyan* itself is a genuine source.

In *The Secret Doctrine* Blavatsky mentions 'an old book' that she had referred to at the beginning of *Isis Unveiled* as 'the original work from which the many volumes of *Kiu-ti* were compiled'.[25] Moreover, in an article entitled 'The Secret Books of Lam-Rim and Dzyan' published only after her death, she states the following:

> The *Book of Dzyan* – from the Sanskrit word 'Dhyana' (mystic meditation) – is the first volume of the Commentaries upon the seven secret folios of *Kiu-te*, and a Glossary of the public works of the same name. Thirty-five volumes of *Kiu-te* for exoteric purposes and the use of the laymen may be found in the possession of the Tibetan Gelugpa Lamas, in the library of any monastery; and also fourteen books of Commentaries and Annotations on the same by the initiated Teachers.

Strictly speaking, those thirty-five books ought to be termed 'The Popularised Version' of the Secret Doctrine, full of myths, blinds, and errors; the fourteen volumes of *Commentaries*, on the other hand – with their translations, annotations, and an ample glossary of Occult terms, worked out from one small archaic folio, the *Book of the Secret Wisdom of the World* – contain a digest of all the Occult Sciences. These, it appears, are kept secret and apart, in the charge of the Teshu-Lama, of Shigatse. The *Books of Kiu-te* are comparatively modern, having been edited within the last millennium, whereas, the earliest volumes of the *Commentaries* are of untold antiquity . . .[26]

In 1981 theosophical scholar David Reigle managed to identify the *Books of Kiu-te* as a portion of the Tibetan Sacred Canon known as the *Kanjur*.[27] Blavatsky specifically mentions this work twice in *The Secret Doctrine*, and in particular the *Kala Chakra*, which is the first tantra of it.[28] According to Reigle, this is the only Buddhist tantra that bears any resemblance to the subject matter of *The Secret Doctrine*. However, he has been unable to trace any of the stanzas themselves to the *laghu* or 'abridged' version of the *Kala Chakra*, which is the only one commonly available, and he suggests that the *mula* or 'root' version, which is referred to in other Buddhist writings, probably does contain them but is accessible only to initiates. In other words, it remains deliberately concealed from the general public, just as Blavatsky suggests. We might also note that Blavatsky regularly quotes extracts from supposedly original *commentaries* on the *Book of Dzyan* throughout *The Secret Doctrine*.

CONCLUSION

If the stanzas from the *Book of Dzyan* are of genuine antiquity, I trust that I have done enough to demonstrate that it is possible to interpret them as largely supportive of the themes I expounded in Part 1 – despite the few obvious distortions they contain. If one day Reigle's hopes were to be fulfilled, and the Tibetan lamas were to feel the time was right to divulge their most secret texts – in the form not of commentaries but of the supposedly ancient original stanzas on which they are based – it would be interesting to see if these distortions were still there. If they were, then I would still question their antiquity and degree of insight – because I am firmly of the belief that, if we go back far enough, there would have been adepts who would have known not to mix cyclical cosmology with human evolution and history on this planet, except by introducing the appropriate spiritual and esoteric angle to it. Whether they ever wrote this message down before it became distorted is, of course, a question that may never be answered. However, we in the revisionist history movement can and should do our best to ensure that such distortions are eradicated, and that the potential original message is once again available for consideration.

Of course we are still left with the *possibility* that the stanzas are merely the products of Blavatsky's own pen, created to support a mishmash worldview deriving from Tibetan, Hindu, Jain and many other influences. If this were the case, she has merely managed to exaggerate and perpetuate a number of distortions that, as we have seen, these sources appear to contain. But even then, and however much we may disagree with her views on human history and evolution, there are still a few pearls of esoteric wisdom in her more general cosmological work that are very much consistent with various ideas that we will examine further in Part 3.

14. THE ATLANTEAN CONNECTION

Let us now examine the supposedly lost continent of Atlantis itself, and in particular the supposed nature of its inhabitants and destruction. As we have seen, there are a multitude of more generalised traditions that describe a forgotten race or even races that were destroyed, but it is clear that the oldest – at least universally available – account of Atlantis in particular is that provided by Plato in his *Timaeus* and *Critias*. We also discovered in Part 1 that in the latter he provides a remarkable but rarely quoted description of the inhabitants that is completely consistent with our main theme.

A plethora of books have been written on the subject of Atlantis, although many have tended to concentrate on the relatively prosaic aspect of where this continent may have been located.[1] Researchers have compared a variety of potential physical and geographical evidence with Plato's lengthy descriptions not only of its general whereabouts – that is, beyond the Straits of Gibraltar or 'Pillars of Hercules' – but also of its layout. This included a main acropolis comprising a vast palace with several temples, which was surrounded by concentric rings of land and water – accompanied by bridges, canals, docks and a huge outer wall with dense adjacent housing. This city lay on a large flat plain surrounded by mountains, and the entire island was split into ten districts, each ruled by a separate governor, and was 'larger than Libya and Asia combined'.[2]

The buildings are described as constructed from stone as well as timber, and the walls as sometimes covered with metals such as gold, silver, bronze and tin, and also a metal referred to as 'orichalc'.[3] Moreover, the temples were full of gold statues, there were public baths and gardens and an elaborate water system, the docks contained large trireme ships and were a hive of activity, and there was even a horse-racing course. Finally, Plato provides details of the military and political organisation of the island. In other words, this description sowed the seeds of the idea that the Atlanteans had a relatively high level of technology, at least equivalent to anything that existed in his own time.

Even if we were to accept – despite the obviously artificial political theme of the supremacy of the antediluvian Athenians that we previously mentioned – that Plato's descriptions of Atlantis are based more on genuine history than on literary creativity to reinforce a more general philosophical theme, the most popular theories as to potential locations are nearly all, in my view, flawed. For example, the Greek volcanic island of Santorini or Thera – which erupted around 1500 BC, with disastrous consequences both for itself and Minoan Crete – has been put forward as a possibility, but this is clearly not consistent with Plato's location; nor does it fit with his timescale for the destruction, 9500 BC.[4] The suggestion that a landmass named Atland or Aldland in the North Sea disappeared under the waves circa 2200 BC suffers from similar shortcomings.[5] And the idea that the continent of Antarctica was in what is now the southern Atlantic, and therefore largely free of ice until it was moved to its present location by a crustal shift in the late Pleistocene, is not borne out by geological evidence.[6] Perhaps a more reasonable suggestion is that Plato's account reflects the submergence of a landmass in the Caribbean Sea in the vicinity of Cuba.[7] Finally, the notion that a large continent within the Atlantic Ocean was submerged in recent times is perhaps the most enduring.[8] This is certainly inconsistent with the currently dominant theory of continental drift, which suggests that the Mid-Atlantic Ridge is a tectonic fault line built up by lava flows over millions of years; but this theory itself is now coming in for criticism from some orthodox quarters, and although more research is clearly needed in this area it may yet prove that a significant landmass was indeed submerged in relatively recent times, perhaps in the region of the Azores.[9]

In any case, we have already discussed the potential locations in which our forgotten race might have lived, and I do not want to concentrate unduly on this aspect here. What is more interesting, and has been less well documented in recent decades, is the body of Atlantean work that follows up on the nature of the inhabitants and of their destruction. Much of this material has supposedly been telepathically channelled from ethereal sources, and much of it is relatively old, so it can hardly be called reliable. Nevertheless, it will be instructive to examine it and see if we can draw any conclusions as to its consistency or otherwise with my central themes. Above all, I should emphasise that, given my worldview, I do not reject such 'evidence' out of hand. Still, there is ample scope for delusion, and indeed downright trickery, when we cross the threshold into this contentious field.

In the course of this investigation we will also encounter descriptions of other lost continents, such as Lemuria, Mu, Hyperborea and Shambhala. These, too, have tended to receive less attention in recent decades, and we will see whether or not this has been appropriate.

DEVELOPING THE THEME

In his excellent 1954 compilation of Atlantis traditions, Lyon Sprague de Camp chronicles the various references to Plato's account in the work of his mainly Greek and Roman successors. Then as now, they were clearly split between believers and sceptics, but they added nothing new from any other ancient source.[10]

Then, from about the sixth century, all discussion of Atlantis disappeared until it began to be resurrected after the Spanish conquest of South America in the sixteenth century. Initially the favoured suggestion was that the Americas themselves were Plato's Atlantis, but increasingly it was found that certain Native American traditions suggested their ancestors had arrived from the East after their home continent sank, and the Atlantic Ocean itself became the focus of attention. These traditions were first recorded by Diego de Landa, a Spanish priest who became bishop of Yucatán after the conquest and was personally responsible for burning many original Mayan books – but then, in something of an about-face, decided to learn and record as much about the Mayan alphabet, calendar and texts as he could. However, his interpretation was that the Mayans' ancestors were the 'ten lost tribes of Israel'; worse still, he managed to frighten the natives into furnishing him with a completely false translation alphabet.[11]

Records of this latter remained lost until 1864, when Charles-Etienne Brasseur de Bourbourg discovered it in a library and attempted to use it to translate the *Troano Codex*. Coupled with his hugely fertile imagination, this produced a mangled tale of a lost continent from a work that, as we saw in Part 1, is now known to be largely divinatory. Far worse, he managed to establish that there were two symbols he could not translate that vaguely resembled de Landa's *m* and *u* and, with a massive leap of logic, he concluded that they spelled out the name of the continent in question: that is how the name Mu entered the equation.[12]

I mentioned briefly in a previous chapter that Ignatius Donnelly is credited with the resurrection of the Atlantis tradition in the modern epoch, with the publication of *Atlantis: The Antediluvian World* in 1882, and from the exoteric perspective this is largely true. He places the continent in the Atlantic, and asserts that it was here that modern civilised humans developed before the survivors of its destruction went on to found the early civilisations in, for example, Egypt and South America. I have already noted that further geological analysis may yet prove this to be a realistic scenario, but Donnelly does also rely on various other observations – such as the supposedly 'sudden' emergence of the ancient Egyptian civilisation, and the arguably coincidental and only highly generalised similarity between, for example, Egyptian and South American pyramids and hieroglyphs – which in my view prove nothing in their own right.[13] Because many more modern researchers continue to adopt these arguments we will return to them in the next chapter.

Donnelly's contemporary, Augustus Le Plongeon, compounded these errors by following up on Brasseur's false translation of the *Troano Codex* and, with the assistance of various other Mayan inscriptions from the ruined city of Chichen-Itza, derived a tale of Queen Moo of Atlantis or Mu who fled from the devastation to Egypt, where she had the Great Sphinx built as a memorial. He also quoted the work of various contemporary 'pyramidiots' who insisted that these monuments too had been erected at about this time.[14] All of this flies in the face of sound archaeological evidence, as we demonstrated in *Giza: The Truth*. In fact, as we will discover, I use the dating of the Giza pyramids as an important yardstick with which to judge the reliability or otherwise of any supposedly esoteric or channelled material.

One final piece of theme development needed before we can continue is the origin of the name Lemuria. A number of geological and archaeological studies in the mid-nineteenth century led to the proposition that at one time there was a landmass connecting Africa and India, although the only remains still above water in the

Indian Ocean are the Maldives, the Seychelles and Madagascar. Based on what is now known to be an incorrect assumption about the distribution of lemurs, the zoologist Philip L Sclater proposed the name of Lemuria, which has stuck ever since.[15] However, again current orthodox geology suggests that if such a landmass ever existed, it sank or broke up considerably before modern humans ever arrived on the scene.

OCCULT ATLANTISM

Just as it was Donnelly who really set the more prosaic Atlantean train in motion in the modern epoch, it was Helena Blavatsky who fired up the occult side. Albeit that lost continents are not mentioned specifically in the *Book of Dzyan*, her commentaries add considerable detail about them.

BLAVATSKY SETS THE PACE

Although the details of the nature of the subraces within each root race – particularly the third and fourth – are sprinkled liberally and somewhat confusingly all over the second volume of *The Secret Doctrine*, in broad terms Blavatsky places the main root races in the following context:[16]

- *The First Race*, although ethereal, inhabited the 'Imperishable Sacred Land' of which 'little can be said', although 'the pole star has its watchful eye upon it'.
- *The Second Race* resided in Hyperborea, named after the Greek traditions of a continent in the north, which at one time 'stretched out its promontories southward and westward from the North Pole' and 'comprised the whole of what is now known as Northern Asia'.
- *The Third Race* inhabited Lemuria, following Sclater's terminology, although Blavatsky identifies the continent with the entirety of the present Indian Ocean, right across to Sumatra and on down to Australia; it emerged sometime before eighteen million years ago, and sank about five million years ago.
- *The Fourth Race* then migrated to *Atlantis*, which is implied to have been somewhere in the Atlantic and originally an extension of Lemuria; the bulk of Atlantis was submerged in stages from about two to one million years ago.

There is insufficient space here to go into great detail, though plenty is provided by Blavatsky – much of it confusing and contradictory. What we can say is that these aspects of her work are completely at odds with modern archaeology and geology, and that, as we have already seen in the previous chapter, any distortions present in the Hindu and other traditions to which she refers in her commentaries are further exaggerated in her detailed descriptions of Lemuro-Atlantean giants and chimeric monsters.

The picture is also distorted by Blavatsky's insistence that various ancient monuments should be redated, and that the Lemuro-Atlanteans were highly technologically advanced – a stance that, as we will see in the next chapter, continues to be maintained by a number of modern revisionist authors, despite substantial evidence to the contrary. For example, she too commits the fatal mistake of suggesting that the Great Pyramid was built by the last remnants of the Atlantean civilisation, perhaps as long as 78,000 years ago.[17] Moreover, she indicates that they may also have been responsible for the pyramids at Angkor Wat in Cambodia and for those in Central and South America – whereas we now know that, at least for the most part, these structures are only between one and two thousand years old.[18] And she places the icing on the cake by being one of the first to suggest, even in 1888, that the Indian epics contain descriptions of aeronautics – a skill supposedly taught to their ancestors by the Lemuro-Atlanteans.[19]

So much for Blavatsky's distortions. We should inquire, once again, into her sources for the Atlantean and Lemurian material that she presents. It is clear that, as well as quoting regularly from Plato, she makes extensive use of relatively prosaic contemporary sources such as Donnelly's *Atlantis* and Louis Jacolliot's works on Hindu traditions – which he interprets as containing descriptions of a former continent in the Pacific rather than the Indian Ocean called Rutas.[20]

This hardly explains the source of the significant body of more occult material that she bombards us with, however, and one of the major contemporary sources for this that she openly and repeatedly references is the work of her fellow theosophist Arnold P Sinnett, whose *Esoteric Buddhism* had been published in 1884. Still, in a somewhat competitive mood Blavatsky claims that she herself taught him what he knew, so, although it remains something of a mystery as to why she would need to quote so extensively from his work unless he had other 'teachers', we end up in something of a cul-de-sac.[21] In fact, arguably it is even harder to establish the real provenance of her occult Lemuro-Atlantean material than it is to establish that of the stanzas of the *Book of Dzyan* – which, as we have seen, contains only the merest hint of it, but on to which she grafts a great deal.

GILDING THE LILY

Another major player in the development of occult Atlantism was another theosophist, W Scott-Elliot, who broadly follows Blavatsky's narrative in his 1896 publication *The Story of Atlantis and the Lost Lemuria*. However, he manages to exaggerate a few of her distortions still further. For example, he suggests that the two large Giza pyramids were erected by Atlantean evacuees just before a catastrophe that occurred as long as 200,000 years ago, 'partly to provide permanent Halls of Initiation, but also to act as treasure house and shrine for some great talisman of power during the submergence which the Initiates knew to be impending'.[22] Perhaps he had come across our old friend King Saurid in the course of his research – who can say? He also goes on to add considerable detail about the construction and power sources of the 'aerial boats' used by more important Atlanteans for transport;[23] and a physical description of one of the Lemurian subraces that, while to some extent reminiscent of an early hominid, suggests they had a 'third eye' in the back of their heads, and again emphasises their giant stature of 'between twelve and fifteen feet' tall.[24]

What were Scott-Elliot's sources? There are no references, but a casual perusal consistently reveals what appear to be mere embellishments of not only Blavatsky's but also Plato's descriptions in a number of areas – the most obvious being his reference to the metal 'aurichalcum', which is clearly the same as 'orichalc'.[25] We are also told, however, that Scott-Elliot was 'allowed access to some maps and other records physically preserved from the remote periods concerned', and that the Atlantean maps consisted of 'a globe, a good bas-relief in terracotta, and a well-preserved map on parchment, or skin of some sort', while those of Lemuria consisted of 'a broken terracotta model and a very badly preserved and crumpled map'.[26] Six reproductions of these maps are included in his work, and they purport to show the positioning of the major continents of the world at the time when Lemuria was at its greatest extent and then somewhat smaller in a later epoch, and also as the continent of Atlantis was progressively destroyed by supposed catastrophes of 1,000,000, 800,000, 200,000, and 80,000 years ago. However, although they show detailed contours of landmasses and islands superimposed on the current world map for comparison, the positioning of the continents does not even begin to match any history of them put forward by professional geologists in modern times. And even if current theories in this area do prove to require substantial revision, his timescales are totally out of step with what we have learned about the evolution of modern humans.

On top of all this, in the foreword to Scott-Elliot's work Sinnett explicitly reveals the method by which much of it was supposed to have been composed:

> There is no limit really to the resources of astral clairvoyance in investigations concerning the past history of the earth, whether we are concerned with the events that have befallen the human race in prehistoric epochs, or with the growth of the planet through geological periods which antedated the advent of man. . . . Meanwhile the present volume is the first that has been put forward as the pioneer essay of the new method of historical research. . . . Every fact stated in the present volume has been picked up bit by bit with watchful and attentive care, in the course of an investigation on which more than one qualified person has been engaged, in the intervals of other activity, for some years past.[27]

On the face of it, this suggests that 'astral clairvoyance' had not been used by Sinnett and Blavatsky in preparing their own previous volumes, but we cannot be certain. In any case, I have already indicated that I do not automatically reject this method as a source of information, but Scott-Elliot's continuation of Blavatsky's distortions, and the addition of a few more of his own, hardly suggests that this 'new method' was reliable in this instance, even if it was genuinely what he and his colleagues attempted – something which is in itself open to question.

This approach was also adopted by Rudolf Steiner in his *Atlantis and Lemuria*, first published by the Theosophical Society in 1911 and then republished in broadly similar form in 1923 by the Anthroposophical Society – a breakaway movement that Steiner formed after various disagreements. In the introduction he discloses that 'such history as this is written in very different letters from those which record the everyday events of past times, for this is Gnosis – known in anthroposophical speech as the Akashic Records.'[28] However much this may sound impressively esoteric, in this work he broadly follows the lead of his predecessors, except in that he adds a few details about the mental capacities of the various races. He suggests that the Lemurians had no reasoning or memory faculties, but used something akin to telekinesis to control nature, while the Atlanteans did develop memory but not reasoning, and also the ability to control the forces of nature by occult means – including mastering the magical power of words.[29] There may be some nuggets in this that are consistent with my own interpretation of Blavatsky's third and fourth root races, but they are still interspersed with multiple distortions.

These reflections of the early theosophists continue to hold great influence in occult circles, for all that they appear to contain manifest and multiple distortions. Moreover, it would appear that they have exerted a profound influence on a number of other lost continent theorists who have no direct connection with the theosophical school, as we will now see. In the sections that follow we will review what I believe to have been some of the most influential contributions to the more esoteric and nonlocational aspects of the lost continent debate in the intervening years, accompanied, as always, by my own views.

MU

James Churchward, who designated himself 'Colonel' in later years, left it until he was in his seventies before producing a number of now well-known works, including *The Lost Continent of Mu* in 1926 and *The Sacred Symbols of Mu* in 1933. The latter is certainly a well-meaning treatise on the common origin and universal meaning of a number of 'religious' symbols that function as archetypes operating through the universal consciousness – an approach with which I have considerable sympathy. Moreover, in the earlier work he describes the pre-Atlantean lost civilisation of Mu, which he suggests flourished on a large continent in the Pacific from somewhere around 50,000 years ago until it was destroyed about 12,000 years ago, and this is clearly a more sensible time frame than that adopted by the theosophists.[30]

However, his works are not referenced properly at all, and are supposedly based on two sets of ancient tablets. He suggests that the 'Naacal' set were composed in Burma or even in Mu itself, and were shown to him by a temple priest in India after which the two of them proceeded to decipher them together, he having studied the 'dead language' with the priest for two years before. From his interpretations they appear to contain little more than a basic esoteric view of world origins that is common to most Eastern and in fact Western traditions, as we will discover in Part 3; they certainly contain no obvious references to Mu itself.[31] So not only can we not corroborate the existence or interpretation of these tablets, but in any case they appear to contain nothing particularly unique or revelatory.

The other set of tablets, which Churchward came across subsequently and incorporated into a second edition of The Lost Continent in 1931, are described as having been discovered not long before by William Niven in Mexico. There were as many as 2600 of them, but again they appear to contain relatively standard Mayan glyphs, and would almost certainly not date to more than 12,000 years ago as he suggests.[32] In any case, he appears to use these only as vague support for his far heavier reliance on Le Plongeon's distorted interpretations of the Troano Codex and other Mayan inscriptions that we discussed above.[33] Finally, despite his apparently more sensible timescales, he reveals that he is nevertheless a creationist – which does not exactly enhance my view of the reliability of his work.[34] Overall, even if one were to believe that Churchward was sincere in his endeavours, there can be little doubt that he was somewhat misguided.

Nevertheless, to return to more prosaic locational issues for a moment, Churchward does record details of a number of megalithic stone structures that are still standing on Pacific islands. These include the infamous and enormous stone statues on Easter Island; an enormous decorated arch on Tonga-tabu – the pillars weighing about 70 tons each, and the lintel about 25 tons – even though it is a coral atoll with no indigenous stone; slender stone pyramids in the Gilbert and Marshall Islands, and in the Kingsmill Islands; in the Caroline Group a great open-air temple – measuring 100 metres by 20 metres, with walls still 10 metres high and 2 metres thick – on Panape Island, a pyramid on Swallow Island, an 11-metre-tall tower on Kusai Island, and a series of walls 7 metres high and 4 metres thick – which abound in vaults and passages and enclose large regularly-shaped areas – on Lele Island; a 50-metre-square and 7-metre-deep stone platform on the top of a hill on one of the Navigator Islands; a series of stone columns – as much as 7 metres high, on bases as much as 6 metres round, and with large hemispherical capstones – on the island of Tinian in the Mariana Group; a series of stone terraces comprised of perfectly worked square blocks of a minimum of 1 metre in diameter on a hill at Kukii in Hawaii; and various other megalithic structures on the Cook Islands and the Marquesas.[35]

Although it is by no means clear how many of these Churchward visited himself, he includes a number of photographs and drawings. Moreover, more recently the explorer David Hatcher Childress has chronicled these monuments and more in his *Lost Cities* series.[36] Both authors suggest that their apparent complexity and distribution indicate that they were erected when all the islands were part of one huge landmass.

This concept is undoubtedly echoed in the traditions of many of the Pacific islands. For example, the Samoan islanders maintain the following: 'The sea . . . arose, and in a stupendous catastrophe of nature the land sank into the sea. . . . The new earth arose out of the womb of the last earth.'[37] On Tahiti, they say that 'in ancient times Taaroa . . . being angry with men on account of their disobedience to his will, overturned the world into the sea, when the earth sank into the water, excepting a few projecting islands which remained above its surface . . .'[38] Meanwhile, Hawaiian tradition is that there was once 'one great continent, stretching from Hawaii, including Samoa, Rarotonga and reaching as far as New Zealand, also taking in Fiji, and there were some lowlands in between these higher lands'.[39]

We have seen in a previous chapter that the land around East China, Malaysia, Indonesia and northern Australia was indeed submerged in this way by the rise in sea levels of some one hundred metres at the end of the Pleistocene. However, when we turn to the main body of the Pacific Ocean, just as with that of the Atlantic, current orthodox geology simply does not bear out a 'great continent' scenario. A casual perusal of any atlas of the Pacific reveals that the sea is only less than one hundred metres deep in the immediate environs of all these islands. It is therefore likely that some of them may have been connected before that time, but there seems little possibility of a single landmass of any significant size – unless, again, further research into the Pacific Ocean floor were to prove that a significant revision of our geological understanding is required. Moreover, although relatively little professional dating work has been performed on these Pacific Island monuments, preliminary work on Easter Island suggests that the most recent roadways used to transport the statues from the quarries are no more than five hundred years old.[40]

THE ARCANE TRADITION

Lewis Spence's work on Atlantis is in many ways more sensible than that of most other commentators in that his timescales are practically short, he does not question evolution, and he attempts to pay at least some attention to the realities of orthodox archaeology. In his 1926 work, *History of Atlantis*, he proposes the gradual destruction of two landmasses in the Atlantic, Antillia in the east and Atlantis in the west.[41] He also suggests that the Aurignacian and Azilian cultures, which ushered in the Upper Palaeolithic and Neolithic eras respectively, were two successive strains of Atlantean refugees who colonised Europe, the first wave being more advanced than its degenerate successor. This is an interesting proposition, although I do not accept his suggestion that there is no evidence they emerged from the East.[42]

Spence also turned his attention to the Pacific in his detailed 1932 work *The Problem of Lemuria*, but again, although his timescales are more reasonable, as yet modern geology does not support his theory that two former landmasses existed in the Pacific – inhabited, supposedly, by a blond-haired white-skinned race that built the various monuments that survive to this day.[43]

In fact, Spence's work would hardly fit into the context of my review of the more esoteric and nonlocational aspects of Atlantism were it not for his publication in 1943 of another work, *The Occult*

Sciences in Atlantis. It is here that he really plays conjecture to the full, but without resorting to unduly unconventional sources other than ancient texts and traditions and, more especially, the information he gleaned about what he refers to as the 'Arcane Tradition' as a member of a secret fraternity that he does not name. This information came from a set of their manuscripts – which he suggests are kept by all such fraternities and which all initiates are allowed to inspect, although they cannot make notes or copies – and also oral communications.[44]

The most interesting aspect of this work is his description, taken from a number of what appear to be medieval French and Spanish manuscripts, of Atlantean occult practices that are reported to include astrology, alchemy, prophecy, necromancy and divination. He also describes how these practices were primarily restricted to the higher priestly and indeed royal class, although the lower castes at some point began to practise their own degenerate 'black magic', which is what led to the downfall of the civilisation. He certainly does not appear to take everything he reads in his sources at face value, and is certainly not credulous when it comes to what he regards as clear distortions introduced every time the material was recompiled or translated from what he believes to be, originally, Egyptian sources.[45]

I hesitate to proffer this material as any sort of evidence for the spiritual advancement and subsequent degeneration of our forgotten race. As Spence readily admits, because of the nature of secret fraternities much of his most interesting material cannot be referenced or checked by outsiders. Nor can we be at all certain as to the reliability of this source material itself. Moreover, I not only have clear reservations about some of the more prosaic aspects of his work, but also believe that certain aspects of his interpretation of the 'ancient mysteries' are misguided when compared to the esoteric worldview I will develop in Part 3. Nevertheless, I have a certain sympathy for the general nature of his references to the practice of occult science in the precatastrophe epoch, and it just may provide interesting additional support for my main theme.

THE AUTOMATIC AUTHOR

H C Randall-Stevens supposedly had no previous history of channelling and 'little interest in occult matters' when he received his first communication from two ancient Egyptian initiates who called themselves Osiraes and Oneferu in 1925.[46] According to eyewitnesses, he recorded these communications using a sort of 'automatic writing and drawing' that was likened to the operation of a modern facsimile machine. They were published in a number of works known as the *Osirian Scripts*, the first of which appeared in 1928; these were then bundled together along with some new material and commentary in *From Atlantis to the Latter Days*, published by his own 'Knights Templars of Aquarius' in Jersey in 1954.

His supposed sources provide detailed reports of Atlantis, and even a genealogical tree of humankind's earliest ancestors.[47] His material, however – whatever its source – does not pass the 'Giza test'. He suggests that all three pyramids were erected in great antiquity after the destruction of Atlantis.[48] Moreover, he describes a network of underground passages and chambers under the pyramids and Great Sphinx that is, in my view, a complete fabrication.[49] Not only that, but there is a possibility that his detailed drawings of the underground temples in the vicinity of the Sphinx were plagiarised from a Rosicrucian source.[50] Accordingly I believe that although his work is still regularly quoted, it is insufficiently reliable to merit further consideration.

THE SLEEPING PROPHET

In the early twentieth century J B Leslie supposedly interviewed a variety of 'Atlantean spirits' via a medium, and collated this material into an 805-page work that included tables of Atlantean letters, numbers and musical notations.[51]

This work is now hardly ever mentioned, however, whereas that of Leslie's contemporary Edgar Cayce – the American seer often referred to as the 'sleeping prophet' – forged for him a worldwide reputation as a psychic, healer and prophet.[52] While in a meditative trance he performed thousands of readings for his subjects, and although he was himself unaware of the contents at the time, they were invariably transcribed. Much of his reputation was gained as a result of his ability to make holistic medical diagnoses, which subsequent developments have proved to be soundly based.[53] However, something of the order of 20 per cent of his readings, which spanned five decades until his death in

1945, suggested that a significant number of his subjects had enjoyed previous incarnations in Atlantis. These were collated by his son Edgar Evans Cayce in *Edgar Cayce on Atlantis*, published in 1968.

In brief, they have much in common with the theosophical perspective, and Blavatsky's in particular.[54] They report that the earth was first populated ten and a half million years ago by spiritual entities, which only gradually took physical form and then split into males and females; that we are the fifth root race of humankind; that the Atlantean civilisation, which emerged at least fifty thousand years ago, was repeatedly destroyed; that its history was forged by conflicts between the 'Sons of the Law of One', who attempted to remain true to the righteous path, and the 'Sons of Belial', who indulged themselves in the material world and abused their power and technology; and that the latter gradually gained the upper hand until, aware of their imminent destruction, a number of the more enlightened Atlanteans made their escape to all parts of the globe. It was these refugees who supposedly brought civilisation to, for example, Egypt – where they built the Great Pyramid and Sphinx in about 10,500 BC – and who set up a number of Halls of Records around the world to preserve their ancient wisdom and warn humankind of the fate that had befallen Atlantis.[55] Cayce himself was supposed to be the reincarnation of one of the more important of these, a priest by the name of Ra-Ta. Finally, his readings also stress the advanced technology angle, including reports of aerial and submarine craft and the 'terrible mighty crystal' or 'firestone', the abuse of which by the Belialians led to the last destruction.

Again we have a few aspects of this material that fit well with my own themes, including the timescales for the emergence and destruction of Atlantis, and the clear debasement theme. However, we can see also that it contains all the distortions that we have, unfortunately, come to expect in its genre, as well as a few additions. Nevertheless, many of Cayce's supporters have always stressed that he had no interest in or exposure to theosophical writings, and was a devout Christian all his life who was often troubled by the contents of his readings – which would, of course, suggest that he was providing independent corroboration of theosophical views. However, once again K Paul Johnson – whose investigation of Blavatsky's masters we discussed in the last chapter – has been able to shed some light on this enigma, his 1998 work *Edgar Cayce in Context* being one of the few serious studies to be produced by someone largely independent of the organisation founded to preserve and promote Cayce's work, the Association for Research and Enlightenment or A.R.E. He reveals that the Atlantean material only started to emerge in 1923, when a prosperous printer by the name of Arthur Lammers came to Cayce for a reading.[56] In fact, even one of the A.R.E.'s own biographers, Thomas Sugrue, reveals the following:

> He [Lammers] mentioned such things as the cabala, the mystery religions of Egypt and Greece, the medieval alchemists, the mystics of Tibet, yoga, Madame Blavatsky and theosophy, the Great White Brotherhood, the Etheric World.[57]

Not only this, but Cayce then stayed with Lammers for several weeks, though the association was apparently short-lived. The crucial issue here is that Lammers had read extensively on theosophical topics, and clearly discussed them at length with Cayce during this period.[58] Moreover, at about this time Cayce also struck up a close friendship with a financier by the name of Morton Blumenthal who, according to Johnson, was also an avid theosophist. This collaboration lasted for seven years, and Blumenthal was closely involved in both the running and the financing of various Cayce projects at the time. Johnson even reveals that Cayce had given a lecture to the Birmingham Theosophical Society in 1922, the year *before* he met Lammers, although admittedly on medical rather than Atlantean matters.[59] If we also consider that his readings were prompted by questions from his subjects, we have the very real possibility that Cayce was merely regurgitating from his subconscious that which had already entered his conscious mind, with a few additions and distortions that would inevitably arise.

This is not to suggest that Cayce was in any way faking anything, merely that his readings may indeed have been influenced by information imparted to him by acquaintances and subjects. At the very least it lays bare the myth that he had no interest in, or knowledge of, theosophical doctrines. Moreover, even if his readings were not influenced in this way, we can only conclude once again that his ethereal sources – whoever they were – were feeding him distorted information.

TEACHINGS FROM SHAMBHALA

Just to show that this type of information is still being passed on to this day, a more recent example is provided by Jon Peniel in his 1998 work *The Lost Teachings of Atlantis*. While on his travels he apparently discovered a legendary ancient monastery in Tibet whose initiates are supposedly members of an ancient sect of Atlantean survivors called the 'Children of the Law of One'. Peniel acknowledges the acute similarity of his historical material with that of Cayce, even down to the name of the sect, but he maintains that he had little knowledge of said material before he published his work.[60]

Whatever may be the truth of Peniel's sources, once again his work must be largely discounted on the grounds of the evident distortions it contains. These include the usual suggestions that humankind did not evolve but was created, and that the Great Pyramid and Sphinx were built long ago by Atlantean survivors. This time, however, we have the even more exaggerated suggestions that the first fallen angels that incarnated as part-animal beings were the flesh-and-blood figures on whom the Egyptian gods were based; that the Great Pyramid was a power generator; and that Thoth's 'airship' remains hidden underneath the Sphinx to this day, waiting to be found and used by modern initiates if the need arises.[61]

The idea of an advanced sect operating in secret somewhere in Central Asia has been around for a long time, lying at the heart of Tibetan traditions of the 'hidden kingdom' of Shambhala. It clearly influenced Blavatsky's work, with her talk of secret lamaseries, and even more that of certain of her theosophical successors like Annie Besant.[62] According to some, Shambhala is supposed to exist somewhere between the Gobi Desert and the Himalayas, although opinions vary as to whether it is a physical land in the normal sense or a more etheric land whose inhabitants can manifest as desired. Of course, the more exaggerated versions of these traditions include all the paraphernalia of special aircraft and advanced technology, while a number of travellers claim to have discovered Shambhala itself.[63]

Suffice to say that, in my view, there are only two aspects of these traditions worthy of any possible consideration. The first is that this whole area of Central Asia is, as we have already seen, a possible location for our forgotten race, albeit that its inhabitants would not have been navigators and traders and may even have deliberately holed up there to escape the increasing materialism of their fellows. The second is that there just may be certain monasteries in remote parts of this region that do continue to preserve records of extreme antiquity – perhaps because some of the more advanced survivors of the catastrophe remained there like their predecessors – and in which the lamas and other initiates may still be able to perform what most of us would regard as supranormal acts of, for example, levitation.[64] However, this latter possibility has undoubtedly been reduced in recent decades by the brutal Chinese occupation of Tibet.

In any case, with its doctrine of unselfish love and its emphasis on the loss of spiritual understanding, Peniel's work is clearly well intentioned and may have many useful messages for modern seekers after the truth. The same might also be said of some of the other works we have reviewed in this chapter. Unfortunately, however, those seeking a more accurate historical and indeed spiritual perspective will, in my view, need to look elsewhere.

CONCLUSION

We have covered a variety of material in this chapter. However, while there have been various aspects that provide a degree of potential corroboration of my main themes, the only addition of any real value is Spence's arcane evidence of the occult practices that our forgotten race may have developed – of both the white and black magic variety. As far as physical lost continents in the Atlantic or Pacific are concerned, I do not entirely reject the possibility that these may have existed at some point even in the relatively recent past, but modern geology has yet to confirm such a view.

Meanwhile, we have also seen that the bulk of the material about Atlantis and other lost continents is massively distorted and misleading. To recap, these distortions include – among numerous other things – the following ideas: that humans were created rather than evolved; that we developed through multiple root races stretching back many millions of years, some of which consisted of giants and even part-human, part-animal hybrids; that the later races possessed advanced technology such as aerial machines; and that the Giza pyramids and Sphinx were built in a remote epoch by Atlantean survivors. Moreover, most of the locations suggested for these lost continents are totally incompatible with the evidence of modern geology.

But let us investigate in a little more detail why these distortions might be so prevalent. I have already indicated that I believe many of the commentators whose research we have examined were well intentioned, although this does not necessarily preclude the possibility of them falsifying their supposed sources to embellish their message. Still, I accept that at least some of them were accurately reflecting the information passed on by their sources – whether ethereal or otherwise. Accordingly, in my view, we have no option but to conclude that these sources have led them a merry dance.

If we start with Plato, debate has always raged as to the extent to which he fabricated his material to act as a vehicle for a philosophical and, to some extent, political message. Nevertheless, we have seen that his description of the Atlanteans' 'fall from spiritual grace' is remarkably consistent with other traditions from around the world and my own main theme, which to me suggests at least a kernel of historicity. As for Blavatsky, she seems to have mistakenly mixed Plato's account with the root-race idea in the *Book of Dzyan* and with a host of other jumbled traditions. Was this all her own work, however, or were these distortions already firmly embedded in her masters' secret sources? Indeed, did the Egyptian priest who informed Plato's Solon really exist, and if so did he take his line from a similarly suspect, albeit less distorted, source of 'ancient wisdom'?

Similarly Churchward, Spence and Peniel all purport to have had access to secret and ancient material of one form or another. To the extent that these claims are true, and the distortions are not of their own invention or copied from their contemporaries, we can only assume that they too may have been perpetuated for many hundreds or even thousands of years – and that the modern 'teachers' are merely passing them on without knowing any better.

If we now turn to the supposedly ethereal sources, and we assume that Scott-Elliot, Randall-Stevens, and Cayce really were communicating with beings from another dimension, who were they, and why were they peddling such gross distortions? At first sight, this seems to be an incongruous and perhaps even remote possibility.

However, we must all be awake to the possibility that some ethereal sources may not be as reliable as we might assume. On the one hand, they may be genuinely mistaken themselves, a possibility that will be verified particularly well in Part 3. On the other, their own integrity must sometimes be called into question. In their 1999 work *The Stargate Conspiracy*, Lynn Picknett and Clive Prince discuss exactly this issue in some detail, and in particular a group of entities called the 'Council of Nine'.[65] In portraying themselves as the original members of the Egyptian Ennead, they say they were extraterrestrials who intervened on earth many millennia ago and who will soon be making a return. Moreover, there appears to be an unpleasantly racist tone to much of their propaganda.

They communicated originally with a private group set up by Andrija Puharich in the late 1940s to investigate psychic phenomena, but it was only in the early 1970s that they really opened up to his reformed research group – which by then had backing from the CIA and the Stanford Research Institute.[66] The group came to involve such notable authors and researchers as Uri Geller, Phyllis Schlemmer, James Hurtak, Bobby Horne, Lyall Watson, Stuart Holroyd, David Percy and David Myers.[67] Not only do many of their works contain distortions similar to those I have already described in this chapter, but the Nine's spokespeople further intimate that they might have had some involvement with early theosophists – if not Blavatsky herself, then at least her successor Alice Bailey.[68]

Picknett and Prince go on to suggest that either these entities are real and are attempting a coup backed by the 'select and chosen few' followers with whom they have been in communication, or that they are the deliberate creations of an entirely terrestrial but well-connected movement whose channelled communications are manufactured by sophisticated mind control. Although I do not necessarily agree with the entirety of Picknett and Prince's conspiracy allegations, it does seem clear that communications from the ethereal world are not always to be trusted – in my view especially when they involve suggestions that the human race is a mere pawn in some much larger universal game over which we have no control or influence. Whether as a result of some larger conspiracy or not, writers such as Erich von Däniken and Zecharia Sitchin, and now many others who increasingly mix ufology with ancient texts and traditions, have all contributed to this notion that we are helpless bystanders, prey to some hidden hierarchy of extraterrestrials that has always dictated our destiny. As I have already said, it is my fervent hope that the present work, even if it achieves nothing else, will help to bury what I regard as a highly destructive and ill-founded notion.

By contrast, if we look to the future it may be that one day we will face the threat of takeover from a non-benign extraterrestrial civilisation with superior technology. It may even be that the ufologists and conspiracy theorists are right, and that preparations for such an event are already in motion – I have not personally studied this most difficult and contentious of areas sufficiently to form a view. However, my overall stance is that as long as this supposed threat remains largely unverified we should continue to believe in our ability as the human race to control our own karmic destiny – because it just may be that all the threats to our future are effectively terrestrial, and involve our own headlong dash to repeat the mistakes of our predecessors.

On the other hand, it is equally possible that any current or future contact will be with an extraterrestrial race that is entirely benign. In fact one present-day channeller suggests from his supposed contact with just such a race that they have emphasised the only way they were able to advance beyond the stage at which humanity currently finds itself was by becoming much more spiritual – and this is a message that is obviously far more to my personal taste.[69] Above all, I must emphasise that in my view an ethereal interpretation of many supposedly physical extraterrestrial phenomenon is arguably far more appropriate, and this is an issue to which we will return at the very end of this work.

All of this having been said, we cannot escape the fact that Atlantean and occult research has always attracted more than the average share of entirely human cranks and charlatans over the years. Accordingly, in my view, well-meaning devotees and inexperienced researchers would do well to adopt a more critical and less credulous attitude to much of this material if any real progress outside of the standard scientific domain is to be made in the future.

15. ADVANCED TECHNOLOGY?

We have already seen that there are a number of schools in the revisionist camp that tend to place the emphasis on advanced technology. Even the early theosophists of the late nineteenth and early twentieth centuries were discussing how the Atlanteans had aeronautic vehicles. Not long afterward, Edgar Cayce's readings reached new heights by suggesting that they had destroyed themselves by abusing their crystal-based technology. And in the 1950s writers like Harold Wilkins helped reinforce these views, since when the preoccupation has grown.

In this chapter we will examine the supposed evidence that our distant forebears were technologically advanced, and see how well it stands up to close scrutiny. First, however, I will provide a little background on the two main modern revisionist schools of thought that promote these ideas.

THE ANCIENT ASTRONAUT AND INTERVENTIONIST SCHOOLS

I have previously referred to both the Ancient Astronaut school and to the subset known as Interventionists whose specific proposition is that these extraterrestrial visitors genetically created humankind.

We have already seen how in 1969 Erich von Däniken employed a radical reinterpretation of various ancient statues, reliefs, steles, wall paintings, monuments and texts to promote this school in *Chariots of the Gods*, while in 1976 Zecharia Sitchin followed this up by concentrating in particular on the Mesopotamian texts in *The Twelfth Planet*. I have also already rejected their arguments based on what I believe to be serious flaws in their scholarship.

A number of lesser-known writers also followed this line at the time: for example, in his 1968 work *Gods and Spacemen in the Ancient East,* W Raymond Drake reinterpreted a great deal of the ancient textual material that was subsequently used by Sitchin, and in fact his work is better referenced. However, his disclosure of sources is still inadequate and, on close inspection, much of his material again appears to have been somewhat manipulated and distorted. Meanwhile, in the early 1970s Peter Kolosimo in *Not of this World* and *Timeless Earth*, and Andrew Tomas in *We Are Not the First* and *On the Shores of Ancient Worlds*, both showed a similar lack of scholarship by failing to provide proper references for much of their material.[1]

Moving more up to date, while Sitchin has remained relatively prolific with a number of books in his *Earth Chronicles* series that are frankly even more fanciful than the first, other writers have continued in much the same vein. For example, we have already seen that Alan Alford followed his lead with *Gods of the New Millennium* in 1996, but has since effectively abandoned the Intervention hypothesis. In addition, in his highly regarded 1976 work *The Sirius Mystery* Robert Temple suggests that we were visited by beings from the Sirius star system about five thousand years ago. However, there is strong evidence that the major foundation on which this theory was built – the supposed traditions of the Dogon tribe of West Africa – was somewhat exaggerated by one of the Western anthropologists who originally spent time with the tribe.[2] To make matters worse Temple goes as far as to suggest that the erosion of the walls of the bedrock enclosure from which the Great Sphinx of Giza was sculpted – the feature that many commentators have used to suggest that it should be redated, as we will see in the next section – occurred when it was originally filled with water by these beings, because they were amphibious.[3] Despite the fact that I have a good deal of respect for Temple's more recent work, as we will shortly see, not only does this earlier work ignore the composite being and especially fish symbolism that we discussed in Part 1, but it also defies logic when viewed in the context of the layout of the Sphinx enclosure and the Giza Plateau in general.[4] Meanwhile, another recent contributor to these themes is Laurence Gardner, whose 1999 work *Genesis of the Grail Kings* to some extent follows Sitchin's interpretation of the Mesopotamian texts.[5]

THE REDATING SCHOOL

In Part 1 I also introduced what I refer to as the Redating school. In broad terms its efforts to ascribe a much earlier date to ancient monuments tend to go hand in hand with suggestions of advanced technology – although the proposed level of advancement varies significantly between different authors, as we will see. Moreover, although much of the evidence that the Redaters present is the same as that adduced by the Ancient Astronaut and Interventionist schools, they do not draw the same conclusions.

We saw in an earlier chapter that Brad Steiger's 1978 work *Worlds Before Our Own* not only questioned the age and purpose of the Egyptian and American pyramids, but also purported to provide textual and physical evidence of, for example, ancient aviation and nuclear holocausts. A number of modern writers have continued with these and similar themes.

For example, in his 1998 work *The Giza Power Plant* Chris Dunn not only argues that the ancient Egyptians used ultrasonics to drill hard stone like granite, but also that the Great Pyramid was built as a huge power plant. The former argument is highly suspect, however, because recent experiments have indicated that drill cores identical to those from ancient Egypt can be produced using nothing more than a bow drill incorporating a copper tube, with a sand slurry as the cutting agent.[6] As for his power plant theory, because he *does* in fact accept that the Great Pyramid is contemporary with the other Fourth Dynasty monuments at Giza and elsewhere, it is clear that it ignores the funerary and ritual context of all these edifices. Nowhere is this more clearly in evidence than in the temples and subsidiary tombs that form an essential part of the layout of all the pyramid complexes of the time, and also in the *Pyramid Texts* found inscribed on the burial chamber walls of the kings from the Fifth Dynasty onward.[7]

In any case, at the forefront of the less outlandish Redating school are Graham Hancock, Robert Bauval and John Anthony West. West's *Serpent in the Sky* was first published in 1979, and in general it represents a fine attempt to follow up on the work of radical Egyptologist René Schwaller de Lubicz, who explored the esoteric symbolism of the ancient Egyptians in his 1961 work *Sacred Science*. West suggests in his introduction that he regards their 'science, medicine, mathematics and astronomy' as being of 'an exponentially higher order of refinement and sophistication than modern scholars will acknowledge'. At the time this may have been true, and there is little doubt that his pioneering work, supported by Hancock and Bauval, has led to a far greater public awareness of the extraordinary achievements of the ancient Egyptians and indeed other early civilisations.

However, West also makes it abundantly clear that he regards such sophistication as having no apparent development period, and that 'Egyptian civilisation was not a development, it was a legacy' that 'proves Atlantis'.[8] This, of course, is the 'no overnight development' argument that, as I have already suggested in my introduction, is invalidated both by a simple look at the techno-logical progress made in the modern world in just a handful of centuries, and by its failure to acknowledge the development period that does exist in the archaeological record. Nevertheless, this theme continues to underlie much of the Redating school's work.

But the most stubborn and enduring element of West's work, which forms the fundamental bedrock for the entire Redating school, is his attempt – in conjunction with Robert Schoch – to ascribe a far earlier date to the Great Sphinx than the circa 2500 BC suggested by Egyptologists, using the evidence of water-weathering on its enclosure walls. The full evidence is presented in a 1993 update of *Serpents* and in a number of more recent papers by both men. This is an issue that we considered in detail in *Giza: The Truth*, and I have already indicated in Part 1 that I believe it *may* be older than the orthodox date, but if so by no more than at the very most one or two millennia. In my view it certainly does not date back as far as 10,500 BC, the date originally suggested by West and supported by Hancock and Bauval in, for example, their 1996 work *Keeper of Genesis*. I believe that this choice of date was to a large extent influenced by Cayce's readings on the subject, and that they bolstered it with what is in my view a largely spurious astronomical argument regarding the position of Orion's belt stars and of the star Regulus in the constellation of Leo at the time – which they refer to as the 'first time', their dubious interpretation of which I have already discussed in Part 1. To make matters worse, West has more recently suggested that, given the supposedly inhospitable climate in Egypt at the end of the last ice age, the monument should be dated to the *previous* precessional age of Leo, circa 36,000 BC.[9]

If we turn now to the age of the Great Pyramid itself – and ignore the distorted speculations of the early theosophists and others that we discussed in the last chapter – it was Sitchin who set the modern agenda with his totally groundless accusation that Colonel Richard Howard Vyse faked the 'Khufu quarry marks' in the relieving chambers of the edifice. The evidence is overwhelming that these are genuine, and they prove beyond all reasonable doubt that it was built by the said Fourth Dynasty king, again around 2500 BC.[10] Moreover, even Hancock and Bauval have accepted this date, despite their somewhat confusing argument that the ground plan of the three Giza pyramids was *laid out* to reflect the position of Orion's belt stars in 10,500 BC.[11] This confusion is made worse by their apparent support for Sitchin's assertions, which seems to have been incorporated – with scant regard for the logical flow of their arguments – merely to bolster their regrettable hostility towards orthodox Egyptologists.[12] In fact the only modern, 'nonchannelling-inspired' researcher who has continued to argue for an earlier date for the Great Pyramid in his recent work is Alan Alford – and he is, quite rightly in my view, somewhat out on a limb on this issue.

Moving farther afield, Hancock in particular has always had a broader scope than just ancient Egypt, and the book that launched him into the spotlight of revisionist history research in 1995, *Fingerprints of the Gods*, contains a great deal of discussion about, for example, the Central and South American pyramids and other ruins. He suggests that some of these are far older than the orthodoxy allows, and were built by an advanced antediluvian civilisation. However, American archaeologists are as insistent about their dates of between 500 and 2000 years old for these various structures as their Egyptologist counterparts, and there is every reason to trust the professionals in this instance as well.

Moreover, because he is forced to accept that many of these structures may *not* have been built in a remote epoch, just as the professionals suggest, Hancock also changes tack and repeats Ignatius Donnelly's suggestion of more than a century ago that the fact that they are all pyramidal in shape indicates that the ancient Americans and Egyptians learned their skills from a common source – the survivors from a prior civilisation. However, this argument is just as flawed as its counterpart of 'no overnight development' – the two usually being used in tandem. The square-based pyramidal shape is an obvious choice for a large and imposing structure, and, whereas the American pyramids are all 'stepped', the only Egyptian pyramid that corresponds to this design is the first, Djoser's at Saqqara, while all its successors had smooth sides formed from casing stones that are now missing in most cases. Hancock attempts to reinforce this 'common origin' suggestion with the fact that the Mayans, for example, also had a hieroglyphic form of script. This is totally unlike any Egyptian script, however, and again, the use of pictorial symbols in early writing is hardly a great surprise that requires a common origin explanation.

To be clear, despite my own view that our forgotten race may well have crossed the Atlantic before the catastrophe so that these similarities *could* have come from a common source, I do not ascribe cultural innovations such as large pyramids and complex hieroglyphs to them. Moreover, I do not necessarily reject the possibility that earlier structures were erected at the Giza Plateau, and perhaps also at other sacred sights of the postdiluvian epoch around the world – the postholes of earlier wooden structures recently discovered at the celebrated site of Stonehenge in southern England are indicative of exactly this. Indeed, I do not totally reject the possibility that some of these sites might even have been occupied before the catastrophe. But I do strongly suggest that *if* this were the case, any previous structures may well have been considerably less sophisticated and imposing.

In any case, these members of the Redating school *do* still ascribe a relatively high level of technological advancement to their lost civilisation, and nowhere is this better proved than in their attitude toward the construction of the Egyptian and American pyramids and various other megalithic structures around the world. If we take the Great Pyramid as the prime example, Hancock and Bauval suggest that it would have been impossible for the ancient Egyptians to have constructed the edifice with nothing more than simple stone and copper tools and a plentiful supply of labour – the inference being, of course, that they used a technology handed down by the survivors of the lost civilisation.[13] And while they tend to use Dunn's arguments about the use of ultrasonics to provide support for this position, we have already seen that these are flawed. Moreover, we spent considerable time in *Giza: The Truth* examining the logistics of the Great Pyramid's construction; and we reached the conclusion – as have professionals who have examined the evidence properly – that although it represents an incredible piece of engineering and project management that would never even be attempted today, it was nevertheless achievable with the relatively simple tools and labour, and above all dedication and mind-set, of the ancient Egyptians.[14] Of course, some of the anomalous artefact evidence that we discussed earlier *may* provide evidence that our forgotten race worked with more than just copper tools – using iron for example – and were this to have continued postcatastrophe the job of constructing such monuments in the modern epoch would have proved far easier; but there is virtually no contextual evidence to support this idea at Giza, save for a small iron plate discovered in the outlet of one of the Great Pyramid's enigmatic shafts that appears to have formed part of the original construction.[15]

In fact, while the largest blocks in the Great Pyramid weigh 70 tons, those used to construct all levels of the walls of many of the ancillary temples at Giza weigh as much as 200 tons, and it was these that most perplexed us at the time of our original investigations. However, more recent research into the mechanics of their construction suggests that even these could have been erected using sand ramps; while, as for the question of *why* the blocks should be so large if this made the builders' life much more difficult, a sensible suggestion is that their size would reduce the likelihood of earthquake damage.[16] Another often-touted example of 'impossible' construction is that of the 'Trilithon', the three massive 800-ton blocks in the walls of the Temple of Jupiter at Baalbek in the Lebanon – but, again, proper research reveals that all is not as complex as it seems.[17]

Before we leave the subject of redating, several hundred pyramids are thought to exist on the Qin Chuan plains of central China. Although it would appear that they are made of clay and earth rather than stone, most of them range from 25 to 100 metres in height – and one, the Great White Pyramid, is reported to be a full 300 metres high. Hartwig Hausdorf visited the area twice in 1994, and his report suggests that they are 'very old' and date to earlier than 3000 BC. However, given that he also accepts the local lore that they were built by 'visitors from outer space', it seems that we should wait for professional archaeologists to attempt a proper dating before rushing to any outlandish conclusions.[18]

There is much that I admire in the Redaters' work, not least their ability to reach and enthuse a huge audience. They do not follow the extraterrestrial route, and, like me, in accepting the constraints of evolutionary theory they tend to place the emergence of their lost civilisation in the late Pleistocene.[19] All of this we have in common. However, the method by which we reach these conclusions could not be more different. They *primarily* use a combination of inappropriate attempts to assign an earlier age to various ancient monuments mixed with the 'no overnight development' and 'common origin' arguments that are, in my view, equally without foundation; the evidence of the ancient texts and traditions is then brought in as a support. By contrast, I come *primarily* from the perspective that we must trust what the ancient texts and traditions tell us about our forgotten race, especially regarding their loss of spiritual awareness and resulting destruction, and I am happy to underplay their levels of technology unless and until proper evidence to the contrary emerges. Moreover, I believe that to the extent we *have* found any physical evidence of their level of advanced culture already, it is represented by the few anomalous but only relatively nontechnological artefacts and perhaps also the small but enigmatic 'Lost Pyramids' of Rock Lake, discussed in earlier chapters.

EXAMINING THE EVIDENCE

We will now turn our attention to some of the other most celebrated examples of artefactual evidence that are regularly used to support revisionist claims of advanced technology in antiquity.

ANCIENT WEAPONRY AND AIRCRAFT

I mentioned in a previous chapter that many revisionist authors have attempted to interpret passages in ancient texts as descriptions of aerial and other advanced warfare, even of extraterrestrial craft. They particularly cite the Mesopotamian texts such as, for example, the *Ninurta Myth* that we reviewed earlier, and the *Epic of Anzu*;[20] certain biblical passages;[21] and, above all, the Indian epics such as the *Mahabharata* and *Ramayana*.[22] I do not have the space to go into detail here, but in my view there is no contextual support for these interpretations, and it is far more appropriate to look at such passages from the perspective of symbolism and literary creativity – except perhaps those cases that, as I suggested earlier, *may* represent memories of the natural catastrophe at the end of the Pleistocene.

These interpretations have been backed up by, for example, a small wooden model in the Cairo Museum that appears to represent a glider with a wingspan of 18 centimetres, which was found in a tomb at Saqqara dating to around 300 BC.[23] Although this has supposedly proved to be aerodynamically sound, I would still argue that contextually it is more likely to represent a stylised bird – especially given that it has eye sockets, although it lacks any other decorative details. In any case, even if it was a genuine replica of a full-scale glider, because it is not particularly ancient it allows us to infer nothing about our forgotten race. As for other suggestions that certain models and reliefs represent *powered* aircraft or even, in one case, a helicopter, I think we can rule these out contextually on the grounds that, if such technology had been available to our postdiluvian ancestors, genuine hints of it at least would have turned up in the archaeological record.[24]

COMPUTERS, BATTERIES AND SPARK PLUGS

In 1958 Derek de Solla Price became the first person to properly investigate the 'Antikythera computer' in the Athens museum. It was found in the wreck of a Greek ship off Crete, and its inscriptions date it to the first century BC. He estimated that when complete it consisted of between 20 and 40 interlocking bronze gears; those that survive are only 2 millimetres thick, while the largest has 240 teeth each only just over a millimetre high. Moreover, he established beyond doubt that it was an astrolabe that could accurately predict the position of the sun and moon.[25]

However, again we can see that this device – as complex and advanced as it was for the time, and however much it may have forced scholars to revise their thinking about technology in the Classical period – is relatively recent and proves nothing about our forgotten race. As it happens, I believe they would have had high levels of astronomical and navigational knowledge, as we will shortly see, but whether or not they would have been able to refine it into this type of advanced mechanism in a much earlier epoch remains seriously open to question.

Another similar enigma is the 'Baghdad battery'. It consists of a clay vase about fifteen centimetres high, into which was inserted a copper tube and an iron rod. Archaeologists have been forced to the conclusion that it is a simple battery, and indeed replicas containing nothing more than an acidic grape-juice solution immediately produced half a volt of electricity. It appears that there is a slight possibility that this artefact is in fact quite recent, but if we ignore this it would be quite stunning to think that the Parthians had developed a rudimentary electrical device some two thousand years ago.

But what does this really mean? Most revisionist commentators give the impression that our forebears were running around with power tools and goodness knows what else, whereas a more sober reflection is provided by the archaeologist who performed the experiments with the replicas, Arne Eggebrecht. Having come across a number of ancient Egyptian statuettes that have such a thin layer of gold plating that he felt it unlikely to have been administered by hand, he suggests that this is what the device was used for, and has backed his argument up with further experiments.[26] So we can see that the level of advancement, as surprising as it is, may not be quite what many commentators would have us believe. If these ancient civilisations did develop other electrical applications, which is admittedly what we might expect given our own more recent experience, we can nevertheless assume that we would have some more definitive proof of this by now. But we do not. And once again, in any case, this is a relatively recent find that tells us nothing about our forgotten race.

By contrast, a supposedly ancient artefact that has led many people a merry dance, and still does despite its having been proved to be totally erroneous, is the 'Coso artefact'. Three mineral hunters discovered what appeared to be an ancient geode near Olancha, California, in 1961, but when they cut the specimen in half the interior revealed what appeared to be a replica of a spark plug. Subsequent investigation, however, has proved this to be no great surprise, because this was no ancient geode, and its enigmatic contents have now been matched perfectly to a spark plug made by the Champion Company in the 1920s.[27]

STONE SPHERES

Another genuine set of enigmas is the 'Costa Rican stone balls'. Hundreds of these were discovered by workmen clearing the jungle in the Disquis delta region in the 1930s; they range in size from a few centimetres to two and a half metres in diameter. Carved from hard granite, which is apparently not locally available, photographs clearly indicate that they are perfectly spherical. They were originally placed in linear or triangular groups of as many as 45 at one site – although a number have now been removed to serve as monuments in private gardens. As to their date of construction, the fragments of pottery found underneath them are of mixed although not particularly ancient date, some being sixteenth century.[28]

Once again, we can only marvel at the collective mind-set that went to so much trouble to transport and carve these stones. However, just as with much pyramid-related technology, there is no need to assume that their architects must have used sophisticated machinery. These relatively recent ancestors would have been perfectly capable of manufacturing templates and using pounding stones and then a sand slurry to whittle the surface down to its perfectly spherical shape, even if their patience and perseverance would be anathema to our modern outlook. Moreover, once again, these balls appear to be relatively recent, and therefore tell us little about the capabilities of our forgotten race.

CRYSTAL LENSES AND SKULLS

If we now turn our attention to some of the crystal-based artefacts that have been uncovered by archaeologists over the years, first we find that a number of optical lenses, which have been precision-ground from rock crystal, have now been located in museums all over the world. Although a few of these have been discussed at least since von Däniken's time, Robert Temple – whatever I might think of his previous work – has exhaustively tracked down a large number over several decades and presented the results in his 2000 work *The Crystal Sun*. The oldest lens, however, dates only to the Old Kingdom in Egypt, so although this evidence proves that many of our ancient cultures in the modern epoch had mastered magnification technology – which would hardly have been credited by the orthodoxy several decades ago – it does not, yet again, tell us anything definitive about our forgotten race.

What about the enigmatic 'crystal skulls', a number of which are located in various parts of the world, all supposedly of Native American origin? In *The Mystery of the Crystal Skulls*, published in 1997, Chris Morton and Ceri Louise Thomas explain how they arranged for four of them to be tested by the British Museum, and although the testers initially suggested that at least two were fakes manufactured using a modern jeweller's cutting wheel in the last two hundred years, investigation of other artefacts has indicated that rotary cutting technology may have been around in the Americas in the pre-Columbian era.[29]

Whatever the status of these skulls, arguably the most interesting specimen is the one reputedly discovered in a Mayan temple at Lubaantun in Belize in 1924 by Anna Mitchell-Hedges, the daughter of the famous explorer Frederick, who now lives near Toronto in Canada. This skull is life-sized, is anatomically detailed, and even has a detachable jaw (see Plate 23). Scientists from Hewlett-Packard's laboratories tested it in 1970 and not only found that it appeared to have been manufactured by hand from natural, high-quality quartz crystal, but also suggested that hand-carving it would require some three hundred man-years of effort – and that even then the likelihood that it would fracture before it was completed was extremely high. Moreover, the jaw was found to have been carved from the same block of quartz as the main skull – indicating that the separation of the two pieces would have been an incredibly complex and potentially disastrous procedure.[30]

Morton and Thomas describe a Native American tradition that thirteen of these skulls exist in various places, and that encoded into them is 'important information about the origins, purpose and destiny of humankind and answers to some of the greatest mysteries of life and the universe'. It also suggests that they will all be discovered and brought together to reveal their collective wisdom only when the human race is sufficiently evolved, both morally and spiritually, that it will not abuse this knowledge.[31] Moreover, in Lubaantun the Mitchell-Hedges' were apparently told that Mayan priests believed their skull to be more than a hundred thousand years old.[32]

Is it possible that our earliest spiritually advanced ancestors created the Mitchell-Hedges skull, and perhaps a number of others? After all, the timescales are more or less in keeping with those that I have postulated for the emergence of our forgotten race. And if so, did they do so to store information that could one day be retrieved? We all know that quartz crystal – especially piezoelectric quartz, from which this skull is made – has inherent capabilities that we are perhaps only rediscovering in the modern era, one of which is its ability to act as an information store.[33] Is it possible that such storage could be programmed more by telepathic than technological means? The very fact that this skull was made by hand and *not* using any sort of advanced technology suggests to me that we would be wrong to completely reject the possibility that it is, indeed, a time capsule of sorts prepared by our spiritually advanced ancestors. But on the other hand, all this does tend to suggest a level of cultural advancement in our forgotten race that, while not exactly technological, is still rather more advanced than I have normally proposed in this work.

More enigmatic still is the information that in recent decades Canadian psychic Carole Wilson has supposedly gleaned from the Mitchell-Hedges skull by channelling. In brief, the results are similar to the native traditions, but with the additional suggestions that it was made by 'thought form'; that it has been on earth for seventeen thousand years; that it was designed as a telepathic link to other dimensions to inform us of our past, and warn us of an impending catastrophe that will be brought about by our own misuse of technology; and that the beings that made it left the earth and returned to their original dimension when they realised that so many people had forgotten their 'original purpose of incarnation into this physical dimension', and had cultivated a 'mind of separation'.[34]

This is heady stuff, and to some extent can be seen as consistent with my main theme, especially inasmuch as Wilson's channellings do not contain exaggerated timescales; indicate that these beings were not extraterrestrial in a normal physical sense – as in 'from another planet' – but were from other more ethereal dimensions; and emphasise the idea of a loss of spiritual roots. However, her revelations also raise a number of alarms, such as suggestions that the coming catastrophe will be brought about by an axis shift and changes in the magnetic field that are somewhat scientifically implausible in the detail; and specific references to the earth 'undertaking great changes' and 'discoveries near Bimini', which exactly match Cayce's earlier predictions. Most enigmatic is her suggestion that these beings – although not from another physical planet – did not incarnate in human form as part of the normal karmic process, but merely 'took a physical form' that was 'recognisable to us'.

This latter again tends to suggest a degree of intervention by a more advanced race, an idea taken to its full extraterrestrial extent in the further 'readings' of this and other skulls by several part-Native Americans, including Harley Swift-Deer and Jamie Sams. They purport to reveal the ancient truths about the skulls that are meant to be handed down only to fully initiated native shamans, but these include the all-too-familiar suggestions that the beings that made the skulls were extraterrestrials from the Pleiades, Orion and Sirius systems that genetically created humankind.[35]

The Mitchell-Hedges skull in particular is a fascinating enigma that, so far, appears to have defied all attempts to date or falsify it. It *could* represent a product of our forgotten race, thereby testifying to their advanced level of culture. Alternatively, it *could* have been created by some very special angelic beings to store information; but if it was, we will have to wait until the very end of this work to find out who these beings might have been, and how they might have operated.

ANCIENT MAPS

Our final evidence in this section is less about advanced technology, and more about attempts to prove that our ancient forebears were sufficiently advanced to have sailed to and mapped the continent of Antarctica *before* it was icebound. This suggestion was originally made in 1956 by Captain Arlington H Mallory after he had investigated the infamous Piri Re'is map of 1513. It was then expanded upon by Charles Hapgood in his 1966 work *Maps of the Ancient Sea Kings*, in which he examined a number of other medieval maps and portolans, including the Oronteus Finaeus map of 1531.[36]

In a previous chapter we saw that modern researchers have suggested that Atlantis was the ice-free continent of Antarctica before it was shifted southward by a crustal displacement at the end of the Pleistocene; the main proponents of this theory, Rand and Rose Flem-Ath, were extrapolating from Hapgood's ideas when they produced their 1995 work *When the Sky Fell*. We have also seen that I do not believe that a crustal displacement was the cause of the catastrophe; nor do I accept that any pole shift at the time was sufficient to move Antarctica from what is now the southern Atlantic to its present position. But did Hapgood nevertheless have a strong basic case about the maps?

Unfortunately, the answer must be a resounding no, as Robert Schoch cogently argues in his 1999 work *Voices of the Rocks*.[37] He admits that there are arguments in geological circles about when Antarctica last benefited from higher global temperatures that rendered it significantly less icebound, but the conflicting estimates range from 23 to 3 million years ago. In other words, for 3 million years at the very least Antarctica has been largely icebound, and any pole shifts or other disturbances appear to have only tampered at the edges. In any case, because there was no *major* pole shift at the end of the Pleistocene that significantly altered the overall position of this huge continent, it is almost certain that for the most part it became *less* glaciated at this time, not more as Hapgood and the Flem-Aths suggest.

As for the maps themselves, Schoch rightly points out that the relevant portions do not 'match' the Antarctic coastline – glaciated or unglaciated – to anything like the degree that Hapgood proposes. Moreover, it is often overlooked that classical Greek scholars such as Aristotle and Ptolemy theorised that there must be a landmass in the southern seas that acted as a counterbalance to those that lay predominantly in the Northern Hemisphere; and while the former was the first to coin the term Antarctica for this land, the latter referred to it as *Terra Australis Incognito* or the 'unknown southern land' – which is exactly the label we find on some of these medieval maps.[38]

Accordingly, even though I strongly suspect that our forgotten race were indeed fine seafarers and possibly cartographers, we can see that the evidence provided by Hapgood and his followers in support of this claim contains considerable flaws.

REALISTIC SCIENTIFIC SKILLS

A number of orthodox and revisionist authors are now concentrating on revealing the less fanciful scientific skills that our ancient forebears developed in the postcatastrophe epoch, and this approach has undoubtedly led to a more balanced view of their significant cultural achievements.

For example, we are increasingly aware of just how astronomically sophisticated the earliest civilisations of the modern epoch were. For this we can be thankful to pioneers like Sir Norman Lockyer, who set the tone in his 1894 work *The Dawn of*

Astronomy. He suggested that the layout of a variety of ancient monuments around the world indicated that they had been deliberately aligned to the sun or to certain stars at one of the equinoxes or solstices, thereby acting as extremely accurate calendars. Moreover, he realised that these alignments could be used to date the monuments. The discipline of archaeoastronomy that he founded as a result, which I referred to briefly in a previous chapter, works on two different bases: in the case of stars, their position changes significantly with precessional movement; in the case of the sun, its position changes much less but still perceptibly over time due to the gravitational pull of other planets changing the angle of the earth's tilt by approximately one degree every seven thousand years. Moreover, he established that changes to the layout of many of the monuments were clearly introduced to allow for these changes over time, and also that sun orientations were preferred because less frequent adjustments were required.[39]

Although in itself Lockyer's work did not prove that the ancient astronomers completely understood the totality of the 25,920-year precessional cycle, subsequent pioneering work based primarily on a symbolic interpretation of various ancient texts and reliefs has provided strong support for this argument. Carl Jung and Schwaller de Lubicz were pioneers of this approach, but it was brought to full fruition by Giorgio de Santillana and Hertha von Dechend in their 1964 work *Hamlet's Mill*. Since then, a number of authors have attempted to reinforce this view, a development that in broad terms I strongly support.

However, this is not to say that certain researchers have not become somewhat overexuberant in their application of this evidence. Nowhere is this more apparent than in Hancock's attempts to apply knowledge of precession, and in particular the 'marker' of the 'first time' date of 10,500 BC, to the layout of every monument he encounters – including, for example, the many temples at Angkor Wat in Cambodia that were actually constructed between the ninth and thirteenth centuries.[40]

Nevertheless, we can say with some certainty that the astronomer-priests of the ancient civilisations of the Near and Far East and the Americas did have an advanced knowledge of astronomy – as did their Celtic counterparts, even though their monuments at first sight appear less sophisticated. I have already mentioned the ancient megalithic site of Stonehenge, which clearly has a combined ritual and calendrical function, but much recent attention has been focused on sites such as Maes Howe in the Orkneys and New Grange in Ireland. For example, in their 1999 work *Uriel's Machine*, Christopher Knight and Robert Lomas suggest that these were also sophisticated calendars that used Venus' highly accurate eight-year cycle, and were developed by the 'Grooved Ware' people of the fifth to third millennia BC.[41] Meanwhile, other recent research has concentrated on the possibility that all the major sacred sites of the ancient world were laid out to a geometric blueprint that suggests, at the very least, an advanced geodesic knowledge.[42] And in a previous chapter we have already referred to Crichton Miller's research into the use of the 'Celtic cross' as a navigational and surveying instrument.

Above all, all of this indicates that these ancient astronomers knew that the earth was round and that it orbited the sun. And yet, although there is indisputable proof that, for example, Classical Greek astronomers retained such knowledge up to a relatively late stage, it apparently became lost to the Christianised Western world – which introduced the primitive idea that the earth was flat and at the centre of the universe, with everything else revolving around it. Indeed, the truth was only rediscovered in the West by Nicolas Copernicus at the beginning of the sixteenth century, nearly one and a half millennia later, and even then he only agreed to publish his work on his deathbed – while his successor Galileo was put under house arrest by the Inquisition for the last years of his life. This amply proves, as if we did not have enough evidence already, just how distortive and destructive an influence dogmatic religion can be.

If we turn now to the field of mathematics, there is ample evidence that by at least the second millennium BC the ancient Egyptians had a thorough appreciation of geometry and especially the value of *pi*.[43] Meanwhile, the quasi-sexagesimal number system of the Mesopotamians – which forms the basis for our measurement of time in units of 60, and of angles in units of 360 – was equally advanced, and their records included tables of reciprocals, squares, cubes, square roots and cubic roots, and of the areas of rectangles and circles.[44]

Finally, in the field of medicine evidence is increasingly available that not only did these early civilisations use a wide variety of natural plants and fungi to concoct advanced and effective remedies, in addition to sometimes adopting a holistic mind-and-body approach to health and healing, but they also engaged, for example, in relatively complex brain surgery and dentistry.[45]

Although once again all the evidence for these areas of expertise is from the modern epoch, I have little hesitation in suggesting that they are the sort of scientific skills that are most likely to have been possessed by our forgotten race – and new, relatively orthodox analyses of Upper Palaeolithic culture are increasingly supporting this view.[46]

CONCLUSION

In the course of this chapter we have repeatedly seen that the physical evidence normally presented in support of claims of a lost civilisation with advanced technology in fact only dates back four or five thousand years at the very most – and none of it can be definitively proved to have been passed down from precatastrophe times. In support of this view I have argued that those who suggest such technology could not 'develop overnight' are being misleading at best, because we have only to look at the exponential technological progress we have made in the last few hundred years of the modern era to see just how quickly it can develop, while there is in any case a contextual build-up of sophistication in the postcatastrophe archaeological record that is often overlooked. I have further argued that the accompanying 'common origin' assumption is equally ill-founded. Accordingly, I have concluded that much of this evidence is intriguing, even astonishing, in its own right, but it allows us to extrapolate nothing about the level of technological advancement of our forgotten race.

Moreover, we have seen that much of this evidence is used to exaggerate the technological progress made by our forebears in the modern epoch. Where it is genuine, I would argue that most of it in fact falls within my definition of 'advanced' but not 'technologically advanced' culture that I established at the outset.

It is important that I re-emphasise that my main yardstick when evaluating this evidence is that of context, and I make no apologies for this. If the Great Pyramid stood alone without an accompanying complex laid out for clearly ritual and funerary purposes, and without other pyramids inscribed with ritual and funerary texts, I would be more prepared to accept that it might have some other function. But it does not. Similarly, if all the ancient paintings, reliefs and statues that are interpreted by some commentators as showing people wearing spacesuits and helmets, or inside rockets, were backed up by even a small degree of genuine physical evidence of such advanced technology, then I would be more prepared to consider a literal rather than a ritual, stylistic or symbolic interpretation of them. But they are not.

I should also emphasise that the corollary to this approach is a requirement for discernment. We need to be able to stand back from any evidence and assess it and its implications calmly, without diving in and resorting to huge leaps of faith and logic. And I would argue that such leaps are *not* required by my postulation that our forgotten race may well have possessed relatively advanced scientific skills in the fields of, for example, astronomy, navigation, mathematics and medicine.

To sum up, there is no definitive physical, textual or contextual evidence to support the suggestion that our forgotten race, or even the ancient civilisations of the postcatastrophe epoch, were technologically advanced in the true sense of the term – and my best guess is that none is ever likely to emerge, although I remain open to investigating any new leads. Nor, however, is there any widespread and definitive physical evidence of the relatively advanced level of nontechnological culture that I propose for our forgotten race at this point – although fragments are perhaps provided by some of the anomalous artefacts we reviewed previously, while other evidence is increasingly being uncovered and accepted even by the orthodoxy. Nevertheless, I would argue that we might be permitted a degree of contextual extrapolation of the advanced scientific skills of our postcatastrophe ancestors back to our precatastrophe forgotten race.

Above all, as unsatisfactory as it is from any scientific perspective to have to work primarily from textual rather than physical evidence, I believe that we have no alternative but to let the overwhelming and consistent message of the ancient texts and traditions from all around the world be our principal guide. This message, of the original spirituality, subsequent debasement and eventual destruction of our forgotten race, is crying out to be heard in its proper spiritual and nontechnological context.

Still, if only we could date that Mitchell-Hedges skull . . .

CONCLUSIONS FROM PART 2

- There are no thoroughly credible challenges to evolutionary theory, although a degree of 'Intelligent Design' is inherent in a spiritual worldview. It is only logical, however, to suggest that when the first advanced souls successfully incarnated in human form this would have acted as a significant spur to our intellectual and cultural evolution.

- It is generally accepted that modern humans emerged somewhere between 200,000 and 150,000 years ago. However, the fact that an awareness of an afterlife had developed by around 100,000 years ago is amply demonstrated by the first indications of deliberate human burial. This would appear to be a huge and often underestimated cultural change that, in my view, is as reliable a pointer as we could wish for to the timing of the first successful incarnations of advanced souls.

- The evidence of anomalous nontechnological artefacts that appear to predate the catastrophe may provide support for my main theme, although there are a number of problems with their dating and authenticity.

- There is a strong body of evidence that the end of the last ice age was accelerated by a sudden worldwide catastrophe. Most of it points towards a date of around 11,500 years ago, and the agent was most likely some sort of extraterrestrial body whose impact, probably in the ocean just off the southeast coast of North America, caused a relatively small shift in the earth's polar axis. The devastation would have been almost total, although there would have been pockets of human survivors.

- Although such a catastrophe would probably eradicate most traces of even a highly cultured race, especially if it mainly used degradable materials for its buildings and artefacts, there are temperate and tropical parts of the globe that would have been perfectly habitable during the ice ages and have not been properly explored. The same is true of the coastal areas that were submerged after the catastrophe as sea levels rose, and in which our seafaring forgotten race most probably built its main settlements.

- It is possible that the main ancient source text of the theosophists is genuine, and if so then to some extent it reinforces my main themes when properly interpreted. It also contains several inherent distortions, however, which the theosophists themselves exacerbate.

- The bulk of nonlocational material that has been written about Atlantis and other lost continents is equally distorted. Where this represents genuine channelled material, or genuine teachings of supposed initiates ancient or modern, we can only conclude that these sources themselves are peddling the distortions unwittingly – although there can also be little doubt that some of the material has been *knowingly* distorted or fabricated. Above all, the unproven suggestion that humankind is under the control of an extraterrestrial master race ignores the extent to which as a race we ourselves represent an order of higher beings with an intrinsic karmic right to control our own destiny for better or worse.

- There is no valid evidence that our forgotten race, or even our ancient civilisations in the postcatastrophe epoch, developed genuinely advanced technological capabilities. There is some evidence to suggest, however, that our forgotten race possessed relatively advanced scientific skills in the fields of astronomy, navigation and medicine.

The one major topic that I have only touched upon so far is the level of more advanced esoteric knowledge that our forgotten race is likely to have possessed. We might guess that it would be relatively high, given what has already been established about their level of broad spiritual understanding prior to their downfall. But in order to assess this properly we must return to the ancient texts and traditions themselves, because they have yet more surprises in store for us.

PART THREE
ESOTERICA

16. ORIGINS

I have repeatedly referred to the concept of universal cycles whereby, over time frames longer than most of us can contemplate, the universe as a whole goes through cycles of emergence from 'nothing' followed ultimately by reabsorption back into 'nothing'. I have also indicated that any attempts to apply this profound philosophy at the mesocosmic level, to particular species such as humankind on particular planets such as earth, are relatively late distortions to what was originally part of a more 'universal wisdom' – albeit that some of the more complex aspects of the surviving traditions may well be better understood as planetary subcycles involving groups of souls in the ethereal as well as physical realms.

But is it likely that this sort of wisdom was originally possessed by our forgotten race, and passed on by the more enlightened survivors of the catastrophe so that it could be reinforced in the modern epoch? Well, what if we were to establish that it seems to be prevalent in the most ancient and revered traditions of virtually every culture around the world, once the inevitable distortions and contextual differences are removed? Would that not be strongly indicative that they all came from a common source after the catastrophe?

Incredibly, this is what I found when I carefully traced, examined and compared all the 'origin myths' from around the world. Even more incredibly, it became apparent that orthodox interpretations of these almost always ignore the fundamental esoteric wisdom that lies behind them, concentrating instead on what the gods in these 'myths' supposedly represent, and other more prosaic aspects – all of which in my view are 'regressive' or 'devoluted' distortions introduced by people who had lost any understanding of the original message. One consistent distortion is that nearly all these traditions appear to be describing the origins or creation of the earth, but it should soon become clear that they are in fact echoing a universal esoteric wisdom concerning the creation of the universe as a whole out of nothing. Thus in my view it is more appropriate to refer to them as cosmogony traditions than origin myths.

IN THE BEGINNING

Let us first remind ourselves of the biblical narrative at the very beginning of Genesis:

1. In the beginning God created the heaven and the earth.
2. And the earth was without form, and void; and darkness was upon the face of the deep. And the Spirit of God moved upon the face of the waters.

This continues by describing God's separation of heaven and earth from the waters – but if we transpose the specific terms 'heaven' and 'earth' into the more general terms of 'the ethereal planes' and 'the physical plane' we may be somewhat closer to the original message. The second verse is clearly describing a time when there was a formless void that had connotations of water, depth and darkness, and which contained the spirit of God. This undoubtedly sets the tone for the other traditions that we are about to review, many of which are older and more explicit. Indeed, the Hermetic and Gnostic texts – which are more or less contemporary with the biblical traditions in terms of both time and location – expand on this theme considerably, and to such an extent that I will have to leave them for the next chapter.

MESOPOTAMIA

Unfortunately, the Mesopotamian texts are again somewhat deficient in this area, revealing only the faintest traces of original wisdom. In part this may be explained by the fact that the only real origins tradition that survives is the relatively late *Epic of Creation* that I referred to briefly before – although it is likely that the missing opening to the earlier Sumerian text, the *Eridu Genesis*, would have contained something relevant. In any case, the following are the opening lines of the former:

When skies above were not yet named
Nor earth below pronounced by name,
Apsu, the first one, their begetter
And maker Tiamat, who bore them all,
Had mixed their waters together,

But had not formed pastures, nor discovered reed-beds;
When yet no gods were manifest,
Nor names pronounced, nor destinies decreed,
Then gods were born within them.[1]

All we can really extract from this is that at one time there existed only the primeval waters of Apsu and Tiamat, and that nothing else was manifest until the gods were born from them. As to the remainder of this text – which, as I noted in Part 2, has been used by Zecharia Sitchin and others as the basis for fantasies about stray planets and comets – we will return to it later.

EGYPT
A summary of ancient Egypt's cosmogony is provided once again by John Baines and Geraldine Pinch in their essay in *World Mythology*:

Before the gods came into existence there was only a dark, watery abyss called the Nun, whose chaotic energies contained the potential forms of all living things. The spirit of the creator was present in these primeval waters but had no place in which to take shape. . . .
    The event that marked the beginning of time was the rising of the first land out of the waters of the Nun. This primeval mound provided a place in which the first deity could come into existence. He sometimes took the form of a bird, a falcon, a heron, or a yellow wagtail, which perched on the mound. An alternative image of creation was the primeval lotus, which rose out of the waters and opened to reveal an infant god. The first deity was equipped with several divine powers, such as Hu ('Authoritative Utterance'), Sia ('Perception') and Heka ('Magic'). Using these powers, he created order out of chaos. This divine order was personified by a goddess, Ma'at, the daughter of the sun god. The word Ma'at also meant justice, truth and harmony. The divine order was constantly in danger of dissolving back into the chaos from which it had been formed.
    The first deity became conscious of being alone and created gods and men in his own image and a world for them to

inhabit. Deities were said to come from the sweat of the sun god and human beings from his tears. The power of creation was usually linked with the sun, but various deities are also named as the creator [Ptah in the Memphite tradition, Ra-Atum in the Heliopolitan, and Amon-Ra in the Theban]. At the temple of the sun god in Heliopolis, the Benu bird . . . was said to be the first deity. Depicted as a heron, the shining bird was a manifestation of the creator sun god, and brought the first light into the darkness of chaos. When it landed on the primeval mound, it gave a cry that was the first sound.[2]

As with the Near Eastern traditions we see that the concept of waters is to the fore, here with connotations of an abyss. In addition, we explicitly encounter the idea of order being created out of chaos, which is a regular theme in many translations of ancient origin myths. I believe that to some extent this theme has been misunderstood since the classical Greek era, because under the Orphic system the god Chaos – from whose name we now derive the word for 'disorder' – in fact represented 'the yawning void'.[3] To that extent this theme surely conveys the idea of creation of an 'order' of energy and life forms out of a 'chasm' of nothingness. This interpretation, and the assumption of the cyclical nature of the universe as a whole on which it is based, is reinforced by the clear symbolism of the primeval lotus – a flower that closes its petals at night and draws back into the water, only to re-emerge and unfold in the dawn – and of course we saw in Part 1 that the ancient Egyptians did have a cyclical worldview. On the other hand, we will find in a later chapter that this theme of order competing with chaos has a far more complex side to it as well.

Moreover, we encounter here the other fundamentally important ideas that the waters contained the *potential* for all forms of life, and that the first deity was equipped with the gift of 'authoritative utterance'. The latter is clearly intended to convey the idea that the Word or thought of the supreme deity is sufficient to trigger the emergence and creation process.

But we can also see here the way modern commentators tend to concentrate on somewhat distracting descriptions of the various guises that the gods took – the various bird forms in the extract above being a fine example. Nevertheless, if we desire confirmation of the underlying themes from an original text, and in particular of the idea that the supreme deity originally created a variety of nonphysical 'forms' out of nothing, I have been fortunate enough to locate one that is rarely mentioned and that perfectly illustrates the point without undue clutter. The following is an extract from the *Book of Knowing the Genesis of the Sungod*:

The Master of Everything saith after his forming:
'I am he who was formed as Khepri.
When I had formed, then only the forms were formed.
All the forms were formed after my forming.
Numerous are the forms from that which proceeded from my
    mouth.
The heaven had not been formed,
The earth had not been formed,
The ground had not been created
For the reptiles in that place.
I raised myself among them in the abyss, out of its inertness.
When I did not find a place where I could stand,
I thought wisely in my heart,
I founded in my soul.
I made all forms, I alone.
I had not yet ejected as Shu,
I had not spat out as Tefenet,
None else had arisen who had worked with me.
Then I founded in my own heart;
There were formed many forms,
The forms of the forms in the forms of the children,
And in the forms of their children.'[4]

INDIA

Moving farther east, I suggested in Part 1 that the original Indian *Vedas* are some of the finest philosophical texts known to humankind. Nowhere is this more clearly demonstrated than in their conception of cosmogony, which is described with great eloquence in the *Rig Veda*:

1. There was neither non-existence nor existence then; there was neither the realm of space nor the sky which is beyond.

What stirred? Where? In whose protection? Was there water, bottomlessly deep?

2. There was neither death nor immortality then. There was no distinguishing sign of night nor of day. That one breathed, windless, by its own impulse. Other than that there was nothing beyond.

3. Darkness was hidden by darkness in the beginning; with no distinguishing sign, all this was water. The life force that was covered with emptiness, that one arose through the power of heat.

4. Desire came upon that one in the beginning; that was the first seed of mind. Poets seeking in their heart with wisdom found the bond of existence in non-existence.

5. Their cord was extended across. Was there below? Was there above? There were seed-placers; there were powers. There was impulse beneath; there was giving-forth above.

6. Who really knows? Who will here proclaim it? Whence was it produced? Whence is this creation? The gods came afterwards, with the creation of this universe. Who then knows whence it has arisen?

7. Whence this creation has arisen – perhaps it formed itself, or perhaps it did not – the one who looks down on it, in the highest heaven, only he knows – or perhaps he does not know.[5]

Could we ask for a finer description of the creative power of the ineffable, unnamable, unknowable, infinite, immanent and transcendent life force of the universe, which slumbers in the 'night' void that contains nothing and yet – at the same time – the *potential* for everything?

CHINA AND JAPAN

This theme is expanded in the following particularly philosophical extract from one of the Taoist *Essays from Huai Nan Tzu*, from which I have already quoted in Part 1:

(1) There was the 'beginning': (2) There was a beginning of an anteriority to this beginning. (3) There was a beginning of an anteriority even before the beginning of this anteriority. (4)

There was 'the existence'. (5) There was 'the non-existence'.
(6) There was 'not yet a beginning of non-existence'. (7) There
was 'not yet a beginning of the not yet beginning of
non-existence'.[6]

This is followed by a commentary that forms part of the original
text:

(1) The meaning of 'There was the beginning' is that there was
a complex energy which had not yet pullulated into germinal
form, nor into any visible shape of root and seed and
rudiment. Even then in this vast and impalpable void there
was apparent the desire to spring into life; but, as yet, the
genera of matter were not formed.
(2) At the 'beginning of anteriority before the beginning' the
fluid of heaven first descended and the fluid of earth first
ascended. The male and female principles interosculated,
prompting and striving among the elements of the cosmos.
The forces wandered hither and thither, pursuing, competing,
interpenetrating. Clothed with energy, they moved, sifted,
separated, impregnated the various elements as they moved in
the fluid ocean, each aura desiring to ally itself with another,
even when, as yet, there was no appearance of any created
form.
(3) At the stage 'There must be a beginning of an anteriority
even before the beginning of anteriority', Heaven contained
the spirit of harmony, but had not, as yet, descended: earth
cherished the vivifying fluid, but had not ascended, as yet. It
was space, still, desolate, vapoury – a drizzling humid state
with a similitude of vacancy and form. The vitalising fluid
floated about, layer on layer.
(4) 'There was the existence' speaks of the coming of creation
and the immaterial fluids assuming definite forms, implying
that the different elements had become stabilised. The
immaterial nuclei and embryos, generic forms as roots, stems,
tissues, twigs and leaves of variegated hues appeared.
Beautiful were the variegated colours. Butterflies and insects
flew hither and thither: insects crawled about. We now reach
the stage of movement and the breath of life on every hand. At

this stage it was possible to feel, to grasp, to see and follow outward phenomena. They could be counted and distinguished both quantitatively and qualitatively.

(5) 'The non-existence' period. It was so called because when it was gazed on no form was seen: when the ear listened, there was no sound: when the hand grasped, there was nothing tangible: when gazed at, it was illimitable. It was limitless space, profound and a vast void – a quiescent, subtile [sic] mass of immeasurable translucency.

(6) In 'There was not yet a beginning of non-existence', implies that this period wrapped up heaven and earth, shaping and forging the myriad things of creation: there was an all-penetrating impalpable complexity, profoundly vast and all-extending; nothing was outside its operations. The minutest hair and sharpest point were differentiated: nothing within was left undone. There was no wall around, and the foundation of non-existence was being laid.

(7) In the period of 'There was not yet a beginning of the not yet beginning of non-existence', Heaven and Earth were not divided: the four seasons were not yet separated: the myriad things were not yet come to birth. Vast-like even and quiet, still-like, clear and limpid, forms were not visible.

Although the chronological order of these commentaries is somewhat confused, they nevertheless represent a highly subtle attempt to describe the way in which the universe emerges into its various forms. In particular, they try to describe the different vibrational energies that go to make up the various stages of the emergence process, and which also differentiate the various dimensions – both ethereal and physical – and the forms they contain. Moreover, another essay provides us with the following:

> . . . the divinities Yin and Yang were separated . . . the hard and soft being mutually united . . . creation assumed form. The murky elements went to form reptiles: the finer essence went to form man. Hence, spirit belongs to Heaven and the physical belongs to Earth. When the spirit returns to the gate of Heaven and the body seeks its origin, how can I exist? The 'I' is dissolved.[7]

Whether or not the attempted differentiation between reptiles and humans is useful, this passage emphasises an important new concept – the idea of the *unity* of our ethereal souls in the highest dimensions. In other words, true wisdom is gained when we realise that at these higher levels, we are all one, all part of the pulsating universal energy that goes to make up the entirety of the universe on all its levels. Which, of course, is what we would expect if all things living and supposedly inanimate, material and ethereal, come from the same original source, and are ultimately reabsorbed back into it.

On the other hand we also see in this passage, with its mention of Yin and Yang, the fundamental principle of duality that underlies so much esoteric thinking. They represent opposing but also in some senses complementary principles that have to be balanced – such as male and female, positive and negative, and light and dark. In this context the implication is that during the night of Brahma the void remains completely undifferentiated and unitary, whereas at the commencement of the day of Brahma – or year, or life, the terminology really does not matter – the first thing that the creative power does is split into two, which is why the emphasis on duality is so all-pervasive in the universe. In many traditions this is represented as the supreme creator recognising that he is alone, and becoming so frustrated that he creates one or more companions for himself.[8]

Meanwhile, we find that Japanese cosmogony is entirely consistent with this view. Their two most sacred ancient texts, the *Kojiki* or 'Record of Ancient Matters' and the *Nihongi* or 'Chronicles of Japan', were compiled in the early part of the eighth century with similar content. The opening lines of the latter are as follows:

Of old, Heaven and Earth were not yet separated, and the In (Yin) and Yo (Yang) not yet divided. They formed a chaotic mass like an egg which was of obscurely defined limits and contained germs.

The purer and clearer part was thinly drawn out, and formed Heaven, while the heavier and grosser element settled down and became Earth.

The finer element easily became a united body, but the consolidation of the heavy and gross element was accomplished with difficulty.

Heaven was therefore formed first, and Earth was established subsequently.[9]

This passage again emphasises the idea of the different levels of vibrational energy on the different planes of existence, with the physical earth, or more generally all suns and planets, representing the 'grossest' or most dense level.

GREECE

In Greek cosmogony we find that, while many accounts contain the somewhat prosaic distortions we have come to expect, traces of the original wisdom still shine through in places. For example, the following view is provided by Ovid in the opening lines of *Metamorphosis*:

Ere land and sea and the all-covering sky
Were made, in the whole world the countenance
Of nature was the same, all one, well named
Chaos, a raw and undivided mass,
Naught but a lifeless bulk, with warring seeds
Of ill-joined elements compressed together.
No sun as yet poured light upon the world,
No waxing moon her crescent filled anew,
Nor in the ambient air yet hung the earth,
Self-balanced, equipoised, nor Ocean's arms
Embraced the long far margin of the land
Though there were land and sea and air, the land
No foot could tread, no creature swim the sea,
The air was lightless; nothing kept its form,
All objects were at odds, since in one mass
Cold essence fought with hot, and moist with dry,
And hard with soft and light with things of weight.

This strife a god, with nature's blessing, solved;
Who severed land from sky and sea from land,
And from the denser vapours set apart
The ethereal sky; and, each from the blind heap
Resolved and freed, he fastened in its place
Appropriate in peace and harmony.

The fiery weightless force of heaven's vault
Flashed up and claimed the topmost citadel;
Next came the air in lightness and in place;
The thicker earth with grosser elements
Sank burdened by its weight; lowest and last
The girdling waters pent the solid globe.[10]

We can see that this passage contains the idea of the undifferen-tiated nature of the void, and makes an admittedly somewhat distorted attempt to describe the different levels of energy vibration on the various planes of existence.

Moreover, once again we find that Plato provides a great deal more information, which we will consider alongside the Hermetic and Gnostic texts in the next chapter.

POLYNESIA

If we now turn to native tribal traditions from around the world, Roland Burrage Dixon provides the following entirely consistent overview of Polynesian cosmogony in *The Mythology of All Races*:

... the essential elements of this form of the myth may be stated as follows. In the beginning there was nothing but Po, a void or chaos, without light, heat, or sound, without form or motion. Gradually vague stirrings began within the darkness, moanings and whisperings arose, and then at first, faint as early dawn, the light appeared and grew until full day had come. Heat and moisture next developed, and from the interaction of these elements came substance and form, ever becoming more and more concrete, until the solid earth and overarching sky took shape and were personified as Heaven Father [Rangi] and Earth Mother [Papa].[11]

So, for example, one Maori tradition reported by Dixon begins as follows:

Io dwelt within the breathing-space of immensity.
The Universe was in darkness, with water everywhere,
There was no glimmer of dawn, no clearness, no light.[12]

Another is even more revealing:

> From the conception the increase
> From the increase the swelling
> From the swelling the thought
> From the thought the remembrance
> From the remembrance the consciousness, the desire.
> The word became fruitful:
> It dwelt with the feeble glimmering
> It brought forth night;
> The great night, the long night,
> The lowest night, the loftiest night,
> The thick night, the night to be felt,
> The night touched, the night unseen.
> The night following on,
> The night ending in death.
> From the nothing, the begetting,
> From the nothing the increase
> From the nothing the abundance,
> The power of increasing, the living breath;
> It dwelt with the empty space. . .[13]

Meanwhile, the cosmogony traditions of the Society Islands, for example, are highly similar:

> He existed. Taaroa was his name.
> In the immensity
> There was no earth, there was no sky,
> There was no sea, there was no man.
> Taaroa calls, but nothing answers.
> Existing alone, he became the universe.
> Taaroa is the root, the rock's foundation.
> Taaroa is the sands.
> It is thus that he is named.
> Taaroa is the light.
> Taaroa is within.
> Taaroa is the germ.
> Taaroa is the support.
> Taaroa is enduring. . .[14]

We can see that these Polynesian traditions in particular emphasise the nature of the creative power in the void, and how it contains the potential germ or seed of all things that will eventually emerge.

AMERICA

How do the native traditions of the Americas compare? First, let us hear once again from the Hopi Indians of the north:

The first world was Tokpela (Endless Space).

But first, they say, there was only the Creator, Taiowa. All else was endless space. There was no beginning and no end, no time, no shape, no life. Just an immeasurable void that had its beginning and end, time, shape, and life in the mind of Taiowa the Creator.

Then he, the infinite, conceived the finite. First he created Sotuknang to make it manifest, saying to him, 'I have created you, the first power and instrument as a person, to carry out my plan for life in endless space. I am your Uncle. You are my Nephew. Go now and lay out these universes in proper order so they may work harmoniously with one another according to my plan.'

Sotuknang did as he was commanded. From endless space he gathered that which was to be manifest as solid substance, moulded it into forms, and arranged them into nine universal kingdoms: one for Taiowa the Creator, one for himself, and seven universes for the life to come.[15]

We can see that this tradition tends to anthropomorphise the nature of the powers in the void right from the outset, by personifying them as a 'supreme creator'. But we can also see quite clearly that this does not prevent it from containing the same fundamental message as the other traditions we have reviewed, especially in terms of the nature of the void and the creation of multiple universes – or, as I normally refer to them, dimensions or planes.

Meanwhile, the Mayan traditions described in the *Popol Vuh* contain similar themes:

Now it still ripples, now it still murmurs, ripples, it still sighs, still hums, and it is empty under the sky.

Here follow the first words, the first eloquence:

There is not yet one person, one animal, bird, fish, crab, tree, rock, hollow, canyon, meadow, forest. Only the sky alone is there; the face of the earth is not clear. Only the sea alone is pooled under all the sky; there is nothing whatever gathered together. It is at rest; not a single thing stirs. It is held back, kept at rest under the sky.

Whatever there is that might be is simply not there: only the pooled water, only the calm sea, only it alone is pooled.

Whatever might be is simply not there: only murmurs, ripples, in the dark, in the night. Only the Maker, Modeller alone, Sovereign Plumed Serpent, the Bearers, Begetters are in the water, a glittering light. They are there, they are enclosed in quetzal feathers, in blue-green.

Thus the name, 'Plumed Serpent'. They are great knowers, great thinkers in their very being.[16]

The Mayan tradition continues by describing specifically how 'the earth arose because of them, it was simply their word that brought it forth'. Thus again we find an emphasis on the creative powers being exercised merely by the thought or Word of the supreme deity.

AFRICA

As Roy Willis points out in his essay on Africa in *World Mythology*, many of its native traditions tend to contain the idea of a 'cosmic egg' that is also found in other parts of the world. But what does this egg contain? The Dogon, whom we discussed in Part 2, describe it as being 'the seed of the cosmos' that 'vibrated seven times, then burst open'.[17] Meanwhile, Willis also indicates that their neighbours the Bambara have one of the most philosophical cosmogonies in Africa:

In the beginning emptiness, *fu*, brought forth knowing, *gla gla zo*. This knowing, full of its emptiness and its emptiness full of itself, was the prime creative force of the universe, setting in train a mystical process of releasing and retracting energy . . .[18]

The consistency of these traditions with those of the other parts of the world hardly requires emphasis from me.

MISSING THE POINT

I have deliberately selected only those origin traditions in which I believe at least some of the original esoteric wisdom comes through, but as we can see we have still amassed evidence from pretty much every part of the globe. Even then, a number of the traditions that I have quoted continue by describing how either the supreme deity – or various other deities created by him – proceed to separate heaven and earth from the waters, place the stars in their proper positions in the sky, arrange the seasons, and so on. A fine example of this is the Mesopotamian *Epic of Creation*, which goes on to record how Tiamat is cut into pieces to form heaven and earth. The folly of Sitchin's interpretation of this as an account of the destruction wrought by a stray planet winding its way through our solar system is demonstrated by the similarity of the other traditions in which a god is sacrificed so that his body can be broken up and used to create heaven and earth. This also happens, for example, to P'an Gu and Ymir in Chinese and Scandinavian traditions respectively, while we have already seen that the Mesopotamian conception of the creation of humankind has a similar theme.[19]

Moreover, this failure to appreciate the broader context seems to extend to orthodox interpretations of Mesopotamian cosmogony, in which scholars suggest that they regarded the earth – Ki – as a flat disc that was separated from heaven – An – by the atmosphere – Lil – with the whole ensemble immersed like a gigantic bubble in the primeval waters of Tiamat.[20] Not only does this interpretation fundamentally ignore the esoteric significance of the primeval waters – which may or may not be a fair reflection of the Mesopotamians' own understanding – but it also appears somewhat at odds with the advanced astronomical skills that we saw they possessed in Part 2.

In any case, these are the relatively prosaic or exoteric aspects that only serve to demonstrate how much the original wisdom had become lost or distorted by the time these traditions as we now have them were composed. And, as I suggested at the outset, it is on these that scholars of mythology have always tended to concentrate, instead of properly examining, distilling, and comparing their highly consistent underlying content and placing it in its proper esoteric context.

It is perhaps to be expected that modern encyclopaedias and compendia of mythology should follow this route – they are, after all, aiming at a broad audience.[21] They also tend to insist on a clear distinction between 'creation myths' that involve a supreme creator who inhabits the void, and those that describe the powers within it in more philosophical terms. But we have seen quite clearly that this is a somewhat misleading distinction that ignores the consistent fundamental message in these traditions – irrespective of the extent to which they anthropomorphise.[22]

However, it is somewhat surprising that the more in-depth studies of experts such as Joseph Campbell and Mircea Eliade should similarly fail to appreciate the true esoteric message of these traditions; and yet this is indeed what we find. For example, in *The Masks of God* Campbell suggests that all except the 'most rarefied' origin myths involve a creator, and that this is a by-product of the simple childhood response of regarding everything as being created by someone. Moreover, he appears to dismiss the 'power of names' – for example, the pronunciation of the name of God or YaHVeH in Qabalistic tradition, and of the supreme Word AUM in Indian tradition – although this concept is fundamental to much esoteric thought, not least because of its link to the creative power in the void. Campbell prefers to explain it as a by-product of another simple childhood response by which the name of an object or animal is intrinsically tied up with its very being.[23]

So what does Campbell have to say about the 'more rarefied' origin myths? He does not specifically tell us which these are, but it is clear that the more esoteric native traditions from around the world are not included. For example, the only American origin myth that he covers in any detail is that of the Apache Indians of New Mexico, which is one of the more prosaic versions anyway.[24] He does not discuss the far more philosophical Hopi and Mayan origin traditions in any of the four volumes of his masterwork, and the African and Polynesian traditions that we have reviewed are similarly ignored. Moreover, for all that on occasion he appears to respect the highly philosophical content of ancient Indian and Chinese traditions – and despite the fact that he discusses their general themes at some length – nowhere does he discuss their origin myths or cosmogonies in any detail.[25]

All that we are left with, therefore, are Campbell's deliberations on the cosmogony of the ancient Egyptians. He begins with something of a contradiction to his earlier more general remarks noted above, by appearing to praise the philosophical leap made by the Memphite priests of the Old Kingdom in according to the deity Ptah the power of creation by the Word. He then compares this with the Heliopolitan tradition in which the deity Atum's creative powers tend to be represented in a more physical and far less psychological way, in that the other gods come into being as a result of his 'taking his phallus in his fist'.[26] However, this is as far as he goes, and we are left uncertain about his real views on the degree of esoteric wisdom possessed by the ancient Egyptians, and indeed other ancient cultures – and about whether or not he believes their worldviews to be nothing more than artificial psychological constructs. Although we must clearly accept that Campbell's aim was not to concentrate on origin myths per se, as I am here, nevertheless I found these omissions somewhat dispiriting after devoting days of study to his extensive but intricate work.

Eliade's most relevant work, *Myth and Reality,* is considerably shorter, so he can perhaps be rather more excused for failing to examine the esoteric consistency of the various origin traditions. In fact he does devote a whole chapter to them, but he concentrates entirely on their magic and prestige in tribal cultures: for example, how they are used to reinforce and celebrate any new act of creation – the birth of a new chief, or the initiation of a young adult – by reference back to the original creation; or to assist in healing the sick or the passing on of the dying.[27] To my knowledge, in none of his various works on mythology does he investigate the more esoteric aspects of these traditions, or of those of the more advanced ancient civilisations.

CONCLUSION

It would appear that while various scholars of mythology have noted certain similarities between certain origin traditions, they have nevertheless concentrated on the more prosaic aspects of them at the expense of the esoteric. As a result, they have in my opinion completely failed to appreciate their real meaning and importance.

In every part of the world these traditions contain a number of esoteric themes that are repeated regularly, even if every tradition does not contain full details of every theme. My interpretation is that, although they contain varying degrees of distortion, they clearly derive from a universal stock of ancient esoteric wisdom that almost certainly emerged long before the catastrophe, and can be summarised as follows:

- During the night of Brahma the universe remains completely dormant. In the more philosophical traditions it is conceptualised as a void, although it is often more prosaically described as a chasm, as an abyss, as the deep or as the primeval waters.
- The dormant creative power within the void is described in the more philosophical traditions in abstract terms such as the One, the All, the Universal or the Absolute, although the more prosaic traditions anthropomorphise it into a supreme creator deity.
- This power contains the potential germ, embryo or seed of all forms that will be created in the universe when a new day of Brahma commences.
- At this latter point the potential is actualised by the mere will or Word of the creative power. The energisation process can perhaps be conceptualised as the blow of a hammer on an anvil, which scatters sparks and energy waves in all directions. Descriptions of light emerging from darkness are attempts to convey the same concept.
- The energy that is initially dissipated by this cosmic trigger then starts to coagulate into a variety of vibrational states, creating the various dimensions and the forms that inhabit them. Some remain ethereal – which is what is meant by the concept of the heavenly dimensions – while over time others solidify fully into the dense physical forms of galaxies and solar systems, and ultimately planets like the earth with its innumerable inhabitants.
- At the highest levels of the ethereal dimensions there is no sense of individuality, only a sense of belonging and totality. This is because the ethereal constituent of everything and everyone is a tiny integral part of the pulsating universal energy from which

it emerged – and back into which it will, ultimately, be reabsorbed.

In the next chapter we will see just how well these concepts fit into a broader esoteric worldview that has been handed down by enlightened initiates throughout the modern epoch. In the meantime, we should recall that it is these depths of esoteric insight in the various cosmogony traditions from around the world that support my view, expressed in Part 1, that to *completely* write off as superstitious nonsense the accompanying traditions regarding our forgotten race – which were in many cases recorded by the same authors in the same documents – is far too simplistic.

17. AN ESOTERIC WORLDVIEW

We have already fully discussed what I refer to as a 'spiritual worldview', based on the principles of reincarnation and karma. These are still the fundamental principles on which what I refer to as an 'esoteric worldview' is founded, but it also extends into somewhat more complex issues. In part it involves a fuller consideration of the concept of universal cycles, in terms not only of the universe's repeated creation or emergence from nothing and ultimate reabsorption back into nothing, but also of the nature of the various ethereal realms and the 'forms' that inhabit them, and of the methods that we as incarnate humans might use to gain experience of or become more 'connected' to these realms. But, following on from the idea of the ultimate 'unity' of all ethereal forms, it also involves somewhat more scientific concepts such as that of universal energy or even consciousness, and of the interconnectedness of everything in the various realms or dimensions. We laid the foundation for much of this discussion in the last chapter, and those that remain will be devoted to further elucidation of this broader esoteric worldview.

We have already seen that the major modern religions of the West and nearer East – Christianity, Judaism and Islam – are not based on the principles of reincarnation and karma. Still, such an observation ignores the increasing impact on the West not only of Eastern religions such as Hinduism and Buddhism, but also of the 'mystery schools' that have survived and in some cases proliferated in the West and nearer East sometimes for several millennia. A number of authors have devoted attention to these schools in recent decades, but it must be said that often their focus is on their more prosaic aspects: on the links between them; or on their origins in, for example, ancient Egypt; or on their leading figures; or on their exalted bloodlines that can be traced back to remote times; or on the treasures they might have hidden. Similar attention has been paid to interpretations of the symbolism they employed, and although this is certainly a more esoteric area of study, nevertheless we are rarely given any sort of contextual overview of what these sects actually believed in and, above all, of how these beliefs might fit into a wider overall esoteric worldview.

In this chapter I aim to rectify this deficiency. We will examine the key original texts of these schools wherever possible to investigate the extent to which they share common principles.

ANCIENT EGYPTIAN BELIEFS

Clearly any review must commence with the ancient Egyptians, not only because so many commentators attempt to trace the roots of the mystery schools back to them, but also because they continue to exert a huge fascination for modern 'seekers of truth'. Moreover, I have already mentioned their extensive use of symbolism, which is clearly displayed in the subtlety of their hieroglyphs, and the extent to which their astronomical, mathematical and medicinal knowledge has now been proved to be considerably more advanced than scholars once assumed. We have also seen that they appear to have believed, to some extent at least, in the principle of universal cycles.

All this is very well; but what was their view on the basic concepts of reincarnation and karma? I suggest in Part 1 that although they were hugely preoccupied with the afterlife there is no firm evidence of a widespread belief in reincarnation and that the ancient Mesopotamians were very much the same. On the face of it, their conceptualisation of what happened in the afterlife, and of how the life one lived on earth affected one's fate there, appears for the most part to have been somewhat primitive.

Let us look at this in more detail, because such a view may seem somewhat controversial – indeed, I risk coming under severe fire from those that have been indoctrinated into a belief that the ancient Egyptians can do no wrong. In Part 1 I mentioned the multitude of funerary texts that have been found, and although different influences affected these texts in different regions at different times, the broad underlying principles are the same. The oldest date to the Old Kingdom – more specifically to the last king of the Fifth Dynasty, Unas, circa 2350 BC – although it is commonly agreed that the contents were based on much older traditions. These are known as *Pyramid Texts* because they were inscribed on funerary chamber walls, and only the king and possibly the highest-ranking priests benefited from them. In the

Middle Kingdom, which commenced around 2000 BC, the rather easier practice of inscribing the texts on wooden inner and outer sarcophagi became more frequent, hence the name *Coffin Texts*. Finally the advent of the New Kingdom in about 1550 BC brought the even more accessible use of papyrus, and the wealthy would select from an ever-increasing number of 'magical spells' that make up the *Book of the Dead*.

The principle was that the existence of these texts in the burial chamber would help the deceased to overcome the manifold dangers and rigours of the journey through the 'underworld' and arrive safely at the 'abode of the blessed'. Clearly the number of people who could afford the assistance of their own copy increased over time, but nevertheless it was hardly a democratic right that was freely available to all. It is difficult for us to determine with any certainty how the fate of the ordinary and less wealthy people of ancient Egypt in the afterlife might have been conceived, but there would appear to be a strong suggestion that only the rich and powerful would gain the blessed abode – and this is our first demonstration of the somewhat distorted and materialistic nature of at least their exoteric religious beliefs. Moreover, their considerable efforts in mummifying their dead bodies, and in providing important material possessions and even food and drink for the journey, leaves us in little doubt that they had a strangely corporeal image of the nature of the afterlife.[1] Meanwhile, they also held the somewhat prosaic belief that the blessed abode was located either, in the stellar cults, somewhere in the region of the circumpolar stars or 'imperishable ones', or, in the solar cults, in the eastern horizon where the deceased was born again in the afterlife with the rising sun god; nor did they have any problem with mixing these two opposing ideas.

The underworld or *duat*, through which the deceased had to journey in order to arrive at the blessed abode, was thought to contain twelve divisions. The trials and tribulations that had to be confronted in each are described in great detail in the *Book of What is in the Duat* and the *Book of Gates*, the most crucial being the 'weighing of the heart' by Osiris – who made the final judgment about whether or not they could proceed to the blessed abode. Unfortunately those who gained an adverse judgment were immediately cast into a fiery abyss – although at least they were thought to be destroyed at once, and it was only the later Christian theologians who would come up with the idea of *eternal* damnation to keep the masses under their strict control. Nevertheless, we can see why even kings were anxious to practice and learn the spells and magical incantations that would allow them to pass these trials, and this, more than anything else, seems to indicate that reincarnation was simply not on the agenda.

What else can I say? Admittedly, the progress through the various gates of the duat might represent the distortion of an original concept of the initiatory trials of any neophyte under esoteric instruction while in incarnate life – something we will study more closely shortly; and the weighing of the heart is suggestive of a karmic appraisal after death. However, in the broad philosophical context of the current review there is little else to mitigate against the view that the ancient Egyptian worldview was, at least as far as the general populace were concerned, somewhat materialistic and unphilosophical.[2]

PLATONIC IDEAS

The theological and cosmological ideas that Plato developed in the fourth century BC were most fully expressed in the *Timaeus*, and they are also commonly believed to have exerted a significant influence on esoteric thinking for many centuries to come. However, we have already noted that many commentators believe he spent several years in Egypt being initiated into the sacred mysteries by their priests. If the original source of much of his thinking is Egyptian – and if the origins of Hermeticism and Gnosticism also owe much to ancient Egypt, as most commentators assume – how can we square this with my broad rejection of ancient Egyptian religious beliefs?

My own view is that, *if* these assertions are correct, certain esoteric schools of thought must have existed in ancient Egypt – presumably right through the dynastic period – that held ideas and beliefs only hinted at in the various publicly available funerary texts. In effect, they would have known that these texts were something of a blind. Moreover, if the priestly initiates of these esoteric schools were the very ones who compiled and propagated the public texts, as seems likely, they were engaged in a continuous and extensive act of deception. What would have been the motive for such an approach? I can only suggest that the overbearing dominance of a political system that required the king to be all-powerful, and indeed the physical personification of the god Horus, could have spawned such elaborate skulduggery.

On the other hand, we also know that to a large extent Plato was picking up on themes that had been developed by his own Greek predecessors. The Orphic Mysteries contain some gems of esoteric insight, and they had already been influencing Greek thinking for some time – although because the identity of Orpheus himself is somewhat confused, with a number of influential authors of that name historically documented, it is difficult to point to any one set of texts as definitive. Moreover, Pythagoras' mathematical work was another major influence on Plato.[3]

As for the contents of the Timaeus itself, after Critias' introductory descriptions of Solon's account of multiple catastrophes and of Atlantis that we reviewed in Part 1, Timaeus picks up the theme of the nature of the universe and everything within it. This lengthy dialogue includes discourses on cosmology, on the nature of the four elements and of the human soul and senses, and on the physiology of the human body and the diseases that can affect it.

This is a complex dialogue, but the first thing we must note is that, in a number of cases, Plato's attempts to use 'rational thought' to explain these features of nature fall a long way short. A fine example is his explanation of the motion of the heavenly bodies. Although he knows that the earth is round and does appear to hint at more complex phenomena such as precession and the retrograde motion of certain planets, it is somewhat surprising to find – especially given the context of other Classical Greek texts – that he clearly suggests that the sun, planets and stars all revolve around the earth.[4] There are a number of similar examples of explanations of other features of nature that are clearly inaccurate and highly simplistic, being neither particularly scientific nor particularly esoteric, although it would be ineffectual to list them all here.

Still, his explanations of some features do appear to have a strong esoteric undercurrent, even if sometimes his language is veiled and the context is confused. For example, on several occasions he appears to hint at the mathematical and geometric basis of the entire universe, and he links this with music and harmonic frequencies.[5] Moreover, he does suggest that a universal energy underlies all things in the universe, both physical and ethereal, that it only changes its 'form' to create new 'receptacles', and that it is 'invisible and formless, all-embracing, possessed in a most puzzling way of intelligibility'.[6] Meanwhile, the following passage provides his basic thoughts about reincarnation:

> To ensure fair treatment for each at his hands, the first incarnation would be one and the same for all and each would be sown in its appropriate instrument of time and be born as the most god-fearing of living things; and human-kind being of two sexes, the better of the two was that which in future would be called man. After this necessary incarnation, their body would be subject to physical gain and loss, and they would all inevitably be endowed with the same faculty of sensation dependent on external stimulation, as well as with desire and its mixture of pain and pleasure, and fear and anger with the accompanying feelings and their opposites; mastery of these would lead to a good life, subjection to them to a wicked life. And anyone who lived well for his appointed time would return home to his native star and live an appropriately happy life; but anyone who failed to do so would be changed into a woman at his second birth. And if he still did not refrain from wrong, he would be changed into some animal suitable to his particular kind of wrong doing, and would have no respite from change and suffering until he allowed the motion of the same and uniform in himself to subdue all that multitude of riotous and irrational feelings which have clung to it since its association with fire, water, air and earth, and with reason thus in control returned once more to his first and best form.[7]

From this we can see that reincarnation and karma are a clear and fundamental part of Plato's philosophy. However we can also see that – even if we ignore the appallingly sexist tone of his time – his conception of them is extremely simplistic and formulaic. Moreover, he also suggests that humankind was 'created' first, and that all other animals were created subsequently to act as physical receptacles for humans who had to reincarnate at a lower level because they did not follow the proper karmic path.[8]

Another strong theme throughout Plato's work is the representation of the macrocosm in the microcosm, in particular in relation to how the human body is a replica of the universe as a whole. He introduces the idea of the soul being split into 'divine reason' located in the head, 'mortal emotion' in the breast, and 'mortal appetite' in the stomach.[9] Although his explanation once again appears somewhat simplistic and distorted, there is a clear link between this and the Eastern idea of 'body chakras'. We will also see the extent to which Qabalistic thinking elaborates on the important macrocosm–microcosm issue shortly.

However, we cannot escape the fact that – even allowing for possible misunderstandings in the English translations from the original Greek, and for a degree of coded meaning – Plato's work is, overall, nowhere near as full of esoteric inspiration as many modern commentators suggest. This is further illustrated in his lengthy discussion of the 'transmutation' of the elements of fire, air, water and earth from one form into another.[10] Transmutation in general is a central theme of many esoteric traditions, and the medieval alchemists were pursuing a similar line of inquiry, as we will shortly see. However, we must recognise that Plato himself is once again making rather clumsy attempts to explain the nature and origin of a number of common physical substances of all varieties – gas, liquid and solid – and that if there is any underlying and coded esoteric message it has, almost certainly, already become severely distorted. As to what the real underlying doctrine of transmutation might be, again we will have to wait until later in the chapter to discuss this fully.

Apart from the celebrated work of his pupil Aristotle, Plato's ideas were most fully developed by the later Neoplatonists. This school of thought was founded by Plotinus in the first half of the third century, and subsequent key figures included Porphyry, Iamblichus and Proclus. Its main thrust was to emphasise the importance of the soul, to such an extent that all physical life was regarded as mere illusion, although its proponents varied in the extent to which they advocated complete withdrawal from the physical world.[11]

I do not have the space here to review the works of the Neoplatonists in any detail. Still, Plotinus' description of those who are obsessed with the physical world at the expense of their spiritual roots, taken from his essay *Concerning the Beautiful*, provides an eloquent rebuke to those who persist in this course that is as relevant now as it was a millennium and a half ago:

> Let us suppose a soul deformed, to be one intemperate and unjust, filled with a multitude of desires, a prey to foolish hopes, and vexed with idle fears; through its diminutive and avaricious nature the subject of envy; employed solely in thought of what is mortal and low; bound in the fetters of impure delights; living the life, whatever it may be, peculiar to the passion of body; and so totally merged in sensuality as to esteem the base pleasures, and the deformed beautiful and fair. But may we not say, that this baseness approaches the soul as an adventitious evil, under the pretext of adventitious beauty; which, with great detriment, renders it impure, and pollutes it with much depravity, so that it neither possesses true life, nor true sense, but is endued with a slender life through its mixture of evil, and this worn out by the continual depredations of death: no longer perceiving the objects of mental vision, nor permitted any more to dwell with itself, because ever hurried away to things obscure, external, and low? Hence, becoming impure, and being on all sides snatched in the unceasing whirl of sensible forms, it is covered with corporeal stains, and wholly given to matter, contracts deeply its nature, loses all its original splendour, and almost changes its own species into that of another: just as the pristine beauty of the most lovely form would be destroyed by its total immersion in mire and clay.[12]

Moreover, Plotinus also provides a glimpse of how the worthy soul is able to develop sufficiently to be able to perceive the true beauty of the divine:

> Recall your thoughts inward, and if, while contemplating yourself, you do not perceive yourself beautiful, imitate the statuary; who, when he desires a beautiful statue, cuts away what is superfluous, smoothes and polishes what is rough, and never desists until he has given it all the beauty his art is able to effect. In this manner must you proceed, by lopping what is luxuriant, directing what is oblique, and, by

purgation, illustrating what is obscure; and thus continue to polish and beautify your statue, until the divine splendour of Virtue shines upon you, and Temperance, seated in pure and holy majesty, rises to your view. If you become thus purified, residing in yourself, and having nothing any longer to impede this unity of mind, and no farther mixture to be found within, but perceiving your whole self to be a true light, and light alone; a light which, though immense, is not measured by any magnitude, nor limited by any circumscribing figure, but is every where immeasurable, as being greater than every measure, and more excellent than every quantity; if, perceiving yourself thus improved, and trusting solely to yourself, as no longer requiring a guide, fix now steadfastly your mental view, for with the intellectual eye alone can such immense beauty be perceived.[13]

I need add nothing to Plotinus' description of the loftier spiritual aims that we would all do well to pursue. So, in conclusion, although we have seen that Plato's own ideas are far less secure as a supposed foundation for many of the mystery schools that sprang up after his death than is normally supposed, there is much in both his and his followers' philosophy that is consistent with our emerging esoteric worldview.

HERMETICISM

The *Hermetica* are a body of texts dating to the second century although, just as with the *Book of Enoch*, the suggestion that they contain divine revelations made to the original Hermes or Thoth himself has led many commentators both ancient and modern to argue for their far greater antiquity. They are of Greco-Egyptian origin, and are separated into two broad categories, the 'philosophical' and the 'popular' or 'technical' treatises. Although certain texts appear to contain elements of both, broadly speaking the latter include astrological, alchemical and magical works.[14] However, it is the philosophical texts that we will concentrate on here, comprising the seventeen treatises of the Greek *Corpus Hermeticum*, plus the Latin *Asclepius*.[15]

I can make a number of general observations about this body of work. There are considerable inconsistencies between the various texts, and these must surely have arisen because of their repeated editing in antiquity, and also because of a somewhat haphazard approach to their compilation as one body of work. In particular it seems likely that the versions we have were based on shorter works that were repeatedly added to in the form of commentary. However, for the most part these inconsistencies need not concern us greatly.[16] As to the consistent general themes that do emerge, there are some that are again fundamentally incorrect – for example, the texts incorporate many of Plato's flawed concepts about the nature of the cosmos and the creation and physiology of humankind.[17] A number of the themes, however, are broadly consistent with the generalised esoteric worldview that I am in the process of setting out, even if certain distortions have, as usual, crept in at some stage.

So we find that reincarnation does form part of the Hermetic worldview: 'Do you see how many bodies we must pass through, my child . . . in order to hasten toward the one and only?' says Hermes Trismegistus, the 'thrice great' who is the main protagonist in the dialogues, to his son Tat.[18] This is, as we might expect, backed up by the principle of karma – although, as the following extract shows, to some extent the *Hermetica* also display a belief in preordained destiny and fate, along the lines of astrology and oracle reading, rather than in karmic choice: 'Everything is an act of fate, my child, and outside of it nothing exists among bodily entities. Neither good nor evil comes to be by chance.'[19] Nevertheless, we once again meet the concept of the earthly karmic round, and the aim of release from it:

Is not the prize our parents had, the one we wish – in most faithful prayer – may be presented to us as well if it be agreeable to divine fidelity: the prize, that is, of discharge and release from worldly custody, of loosing the bonds of mortality so that god may restore us, pure and holy, to the nature of our higher part, to the divine?[20]

In both the Hermetic and Gnostic traditions this release is gained by achieving 'gnosis', or understanding, although as I suggested in Part 1 perhaps *wisdom* is a more appropriate word than *understanding*, as it implies something based on more than just rationality and logic. The gaining of gnosis is described in the texts as an initiatory ascent through various ethereal realms that involves progressively leaving behind the fetters of the material and physical world:

First, in releasing the material body you give the body itself over to alteration, and the form that you used to have vanishes. To the demon you give over your temperament, now inactive. The body's senses rise up and flow back to their particular sources, becoming separate parts and mingling again with the energies. And feeling and longing go on toward irrational nature. Thence the human being rushes up through the cosmic framework, at the first zone surrendering the energy of increase and decrease; at the second evil machination, a device now inactive; at the third the illusion of longing, now inactive; at the fourth the ruler's arrogance, now freed of excess; at the fifth unholy presumption and daring recklessness; at the sixth the evil impulses that come from wealth, now inactive; and at the seventh zone the deceit that lies in ambush. And then, stripped of the effects of the cosmic framework, the human enters the region of the ogdoad; he has his own proper power, and along with the blessed he hymns the father. Those present there rejoice together in his presence, and, having become like his companions, he also hears certain powers that exist beyond the ogdoadic region and hymn god with sweet voice. They rise up to the father in order and surrender themselves to the powers, and, having become powers, they enter into god. This is the final good for those who have received knowledge: to be made god.[21]

So we can see that the ultimate objective is to 'return to the source' and once again become one with that which spawned us – which is described in these translations as 'god', but which is arguably far better thought of as a universal energy or conscious-ness of some sort. This idea is reinforced by the reconfirmation of the associated idea that, in the highest ethereal realms, 'all are one':

There above, then, beings are not different from one another. . . . All think one thought, and all have the same foreknowledge; they have one mind, the father. One sense works in them, and the charm that brings them together is love, the same love that makes one harmony act in all things.[22]

Now, we need to clarify a few points about this because it can become somewhat confusing. The suggestion of this highly esoteric schema is that we do not achieve gnosis and a return to the ultimate source simply through one incarnation that is ended by the death of the physical body and the passing of the soul into the ethereal realms, as a one-off process; rather we attain it by achieving full karmic advancement over repeated incarnations. Nevertheless, the *Hermetica* seem to imply that *any* incarnate human being can choose to make the full ascent through sufficient initiatory practice, whereas I would argue that the reality is rather more complex. I would suggest that not only must a person already be at a relatively advanced stage of karmic development from previous incarnations, but that also, unless they are of sufficient advancement that they have already escaped from the earthly round and only reincarnated by choice, they are unlikely to be able to ascend or make connections with anything more than the first few rungs of the 'ladder' of the ethereal realms. In this respect we can surmise that the degree of unity increases as we ascend the ladder, that the *ultimate* source is only at the very top, and that experience of the higher realms can only be achieved by karmic advancement within these realms themselves rather than while in physical incarnation. These ideas are explored further in the Qabalistic thinking that we will consider shortly.

In any case, the *Hermetica* themselves contain few practical descriptions of *how* all this is to be achieved, except that there are repeated suggestions that shutting out the distractions of the physical world and contemplating the nature of the universe and of the divine will lead to gnosis, and an inference that *intuition* will lead the seeker forward.[23] We will discuss intuition more later on, because it is extremely important. However, there is a clear suggestion that to understand God, neophytes must make themselves like him:

Make yourself grow to immeasurable immensity, outleap all body, outstrip all time, become eternity and you will understand god. Having conceived that nothing is impossible

to you, consider yourself immortal and able to understand
everything, all art, all learning, the temper of every living
thing. Go higher than every height and lower than every
depth. Collect in yourself all the sensations of what has been
made, of fire and water, dry and wet; be everywhere at once,
on land, in the sea, in heaven; be not yet born, be in the
womb, be young, old, dead, beyond death. And when you
have understood all these at once – times, places, things,
qualities, quantities – then you can understand god.[24]

Moreover, a number of passages describe a 'vision of the unity
of all things' that is a fundamental aspect of all experiences of the
divine, as we will later discover:

. . . in an instant everything was immediately opened to me. I
saw an endless vision in which everything became light . . .[25]

Meanwhile, the nature of those who have achieved gnosis and
are effectively 'twice-born' is described in some detail:

. . . seeing within me an unfabricated vision that came from
the mercy of god, I went out of myself into an immortal body,
and now I am not what I was before. I have been born in
mind. This thing cannot be taught, nor can it be seen through
any elementary fabrication that we use here below. Therefore,
the initial form even of my own constitution is of no concern.
Colour, touch or size I no longer have; I am a stranger to
them. Now you see me with your eyes, my child, but by
gazing with bodily sight you do not understand what I am; I
am not seen with such eyes, my child.[26]

By contrast, those who do not achieve gnosis, and 'do not know
the purpose or the agents of their coming to be', are described as
follows:

These people have sensations much like those of unreasoning
animals, and, since their temperament is wilful and angry,
they feel no awe of things that deserve to be admired; they
divert their attention to the pleasures and appetites of their

bodies; and they believe that humankind came to be for such purposes.[27]

As for their fate, the 'irreverent soul' is 'not allowed to fall down into the body of an unreasoning animal', but their mere addiction to the physical world, the pain that always accompanies the undue courting of material pleasures, and their resulting continuance in the earthly karmic round, is regarded as sufficient punishment in itself.[28] We have already seen that I find this view eminently reasonable, and far more philosophical than either the Christian concept of hell or the distorted idea that karmic regression involves reincarnation as a lower form of species.

Two highly practical implications of the Hermetic worldview are worth emphasising. The first, repeatedly mentioned, is that the person who appreciates the roles that reincarnation and karma play *has nothing to fear from death*, whether it be premature or otherwise – because it is not an end but a new beginning or, more accurately, merely a *change* from one energy or vibrational state into another.[29] The second is the assertion in certain of the texts that, even if physical life on earth is not totally abhorrent, nevertheless it is still an illusion, and the only true reality is that which involves perception of the higher realms.[30] We have already seen that this was a fundamental tenet of Neoplatonic thinking, and it is one with which I am largely in agreement. However I should add the rider that in my view not everyone should feel forced to lead the life of an ascetic. We have already seen that it is an essential part of karmic development that souls incarnate in a variety of physical bodies specifically to experience the material or dense realm, and the variety of sensations that go with it, and that in no sense is this contrary to 'karmic law' provided that at least we humans are aware of and honour our spiritual roots. So I would argue that any decision to live the life of an ascetic is purely one of personal karmic choice to be made only when an individual feels fully ready to go down that route, and arguably because their 'inner voice' is crying out that it has completely had enough of physical sensations and experiences.

If we now backtrack somewhat to examine the *Hermetica* for support of the main themes from Part 1, not only do we have the excellent descriptions above of the difference between those who follow a spiritual path and those who do not, but we also find the possible idea that a loss of spiritual roots led to a previous catastrophe: 'choosing the lesser [path] has been humankind's destruction'.[31] Moreover, there is a suggestion that humankind would go down this route again:

They will not cherish this entire world, a work of god beyond compare, a glorious construction, a bounty composed of images in multiform variety. . . . They will prefer shadows to light, and they will find death more expedient than life. No one will look up to heaven. The reverent will be thought mad, the irreverent wise; the lunatic will be thought brave, and the scoundrel will be taken for a decent person. Soul and all teachings about soul (that soul began as immortal or else expects to attain immortality) as I revealed them to you will be considered not simply laughable but even illusory.[32]

Is this not exactly the state of affairs that the dominance of rationalism and logic in the last few centuries has produced? Meanwhile, although for the most part these texts suggest in a relatively prosaic way that humankind was created at the beginning of the world, an interesting angle on a possible original message more in keeping with my suggestions about the first advanced incarnations lies in the following description of what happened after the creation of the universe:

Nature took spirit from the ether and brought forth bodies in the shape of the man. From life and light the man became soul and mind; from life came soul, from light came mind, and all things in the cosmos of the senses remained thus until a cycle ended and kinds of things began to be.[33]

Does this suggest that the relatively advanced souls of 'humankind' remained purely ethereal for a long time before they ever incarnated in physical form? Another passage seems to confirm this interpretation:

. . . when the man saw in the water the form like himself as it was in nature, he loved it and wished to inhabit it; wish and

action came in the same moment, and he inhabited the
unreasoning form.[34]

Meanwhile, another text describes how a variety of 'classes' of
ethereal souls came into being before humankind and even the
physical world were created, and also reveals how:

> . . . when he [the divine creator] decided to reveal himself, he
> breathed into certain godlike men a passionate desire to know
> him, and bestowed on their minds a radiance ampler than that
> which they already had within their breasts, that so they
> might first will to seek the yet unknown God, and then have
> power to find him. But this . . . it would not have been
> possible for men of mortal breed to do, if there had not arisen
> one whose soul was responsive to the influence of the holy
> Powers of heaven. And such a man was Hermes, he who won
> knowledge of all. Hermes saw all things, and understood what
> he saw, and had power to explain to others what he
> understood . . .[35]

These descriptions surely provide considerable support for my
suggestion that certain angelic souls had to incarnate in human
form in order to bring a spiritual worldview into the physical
plane.

Turning now to the origin of the universe itself, we find the
following wonderfully descriptive passage:

> In the deep there was boundless darkness and water and fine
> intelligent spirit, all existing by divine power in chaos. Then a
> holy light was sent forth, and elements solidified out of liquid
> essence. And all the gods divided the parts of germinal
> nature.[36]

The same sense of awe pervades the multiple descriptions of the
ultimate creative power, and of the universal energy that makes up
the universe, in the *Hermetica*:

> The monad, because it is the beginning and root of all things,
> is in them all as root and beginning . . . the monad contains

every number, is contained by none, and generates every number without being generated by any other number.[37]

This is the god who is greater than any name; this is the god invisible and entirely visible. This god who is evident to the eyes may be seen in the mind. He is bodiless and many-bodied; or, rather, he is all-bodied.[38]

. . . god, who is energy and power, surrounds everything and permeates everything, and understanding of god is nothing difficult, my child. . . . If matter is apart from god, my son, what sort of place would you allot to it? If it is not energised, do you suppose it is anything but a heap? But who energises it if it is energised? We have said that the energies are parts of god. . . . Whether you say matter or body or essence, know that these also are energies of god . . . And this is god, the all.[39]

Finally, the Hermetic texts include some interesting observations about memory, and the question of why, if we reincarnate, we do not automatically remember either our previous lives or our experiences of the ethereal realms between them. The following extract appears to represent a plea from the first advanced souls that incarnated on earth:

Ordain some limits to our punishment . . . make us forget what bliss we have lost, and into what an evil world we have come down, and so release us from our sorrow.[40]

Although this is placed in the distorted negative context of punishment, it does tend to suggest that if we did not forget our experiences of the bliss of the ethereal realms we would never be able to suffer the comparable torment of physical incarnation. This is an interesting adjunct to the idea reported by Michael Newton's subjects that memories of past lives would limit our potential for action.

Overall, then, we can see that although the philosophical *Hermetica* have their deficiencies, they are full of useful insights that are consistent not only with the main themes in Part 1 but also with our broader esoteric worldview. Moreover, they allow us to place considerably more flesh on the skeleton of this worldview of reincarnation, karma, ethereal realms and a universal consciousness from which we all sprang, of which we all form part, and to which we all return after achieving full gnosis.

GNOSTICISM

I have already referred to the fourth-century Gnostic texts that were compiled into what is now referred to as the *Nag Hammadi Library*, especially in Part 1 when I examined extracts that, albeit in somewhat distorted form, appear to support certain of my main themes. They are similar to the *Hermetica* in that as a body of literature they contain many inconsistencies, and the close link between the two is proved by the fact that the Gnostic texts include four Hermetic tractates – three of which were previously unknown but can be identified because they are dialogues in which Hermes Trismegistus takes the lead role.[41]

I would argue, however, that this is about as far as the comparisons with the *Hermetica* go, because as much as these two sets of traditions are often spoken about in the same reverential tones, the Gnostic texts are in my view significantly behind in terms of their philosophical insights. Some of the Hermetic texts do contain the idea that divine spiritual entities – intermediaries between the highest realm of the original source and the lowest physical realm of earth – were responsible for the creation of the latter. However, the Gnostic texts are dominated by the idea that one particular 'lesser god' created the physical world and everything in it because of his arrogant assumption that he himself was the ultimate creative power, and due to his ignorance of the true power above him.[42] Accordingly, in this schema the whole physical world is regarded as a mistake and an abomination that should never have arisen, and this oppressively negative view pervades the whole Gnostic corpus. This is in many ways comparable to, although even more severe than, the Judaeo-Christian theme of the first fall from grace that I dismissed as a distortion in Part 1, and at its heart lies a similarly unphilosophical attempt to account for the evil in the world.[43]

The only quest for the Gnostics is once again a release from the bondage of physical incarnation by achieving gnosis, but – and this is perhaps not surprising given the Egyptian heritage of much of their material, which has then been given at least a partly Christian veneer – nowhere is this placed in the context of reincarnation and karma. As a result, the implication appears to be that unless salvation is achieved in the current life, the soul is doomed. And, of course, we have already noted that only those from the 'immovable race' appear to have this opportunity in any case.

Another of the main problems with the Gnostic literature is the extent to which it concentrates on highly specific and lengthy descriptions of the hierarchies of angels and demons that inhabit the various ethereal realms, and on their responsibilities. This approach is found to some extent in Eastern traditions, but it appears to have been given greater prominence by the Zoroastrians, who in turn influenced the development of Judaism – and as we will see shortly, it is in the Qabalah that these hierarchies reach the nadir of their importance. As I suggested in Part 2, my own view is that undue concentration on these hierarchies – although it may well have some validity for advanced occult work if properly understood and applied – is not, for the less advanced seeker, conducive to a clear focus on the overriding philosophical issues that can help to produce real enlightenment.

This emphasis is amply demonstrated by the Gnostic text that reveals most detail about the ethereal realms, *Zostrianos*. Named after a relative of the Persian Zoroaster, it describes how he left his physical body and journeyed through these realms. The gaps that result from this being one of the less well-preserved texts do not assist its readability, but even then we find that it is encumbered by lengthy descriptions of the hierarchies in each realm, and that significant study is required to work out whether it is revealing anything of more general value about them. In fact, a simple summary is that between the highest realm of the 'Invisible Spirit' and the lowest of physical earth, there is a realm called 'Barbelo' that is divided into three 'aeons': 'Kalyptos, the veiled aeon'; 'Protophanes, the first-appearing aeon'; and 'Autogenes, the self-begotten aeon'.[44]

This description shares some common features with Qabalistic thinking, as we will see in the next section, but it can also be contrasted with that in the *Discourse on the Eighth and Ninth*, which is one of the Hermetic texts that the Gnostics decided to incorporate into their own body of literature. This framework is more Platonic, taking as its starting point the seven 'spheres' of the sun, moon and principal five planets that supposedly encircle and control the fate of the earth, and then postulating that beyond this are two divine realms or spheres, attainment of which is the reward for those who have achieved gnosis. Hermes Trismegistus' description of his attainment of the highest realms is one of the more inspiring passages in the Gnostic collection:

> Let us embrace each other affectionately, my son. Rejoice over this! For already from them the power, which is light, is coming to us. For I see! I see indescribable depths. How shall I tell you, my son? [Missing] How shall I describe the universe? I am Mind and I see another Mind, the one that moves the soul! I see the one that moves me from pure forgetfulness. You give me power! I see myself! I want to speak! Fear restrains me. I have found the beginning of the power that is above all powers, the one that has no beginning. I see a fountain bubbling with life. I have said, my son, that I am Mind. I have seen! Language is not able to reveal this. For the entire eighth, my son, and the souls that are in it, and the angels, sing a hymn in silence. And I, Mind, understand.[45]

Moreover, despite all their shortcomings, the Gnostic texts do at least contain esoteric descriptions of the origins of the universe and the nature of the ultimate creative power. At the commencement of *On the Origin of the World* we find the following:

> How well it suits all men, on the subject of chaos, to say that it is a kind of darkness! But in fact it comes from a shadow, which has been called by the name darkness. And the shadow comes from a product that has existed since the beginning. It is, moreover, clear that it existed before chaos came into being. . . .
> When the ruler saw his magnitude – and it was only himself that he saw: he saw nothing else, except for water and darkness – then he supposed that it was he alone who existed. His [missing] was completed by verbal expression: it appeared as a spirit moving to and fro upon the waters.[46]

Here we see all the ideas of the possible misrepresentation of chaos, of the deity being alone, and of the power of the Word that we discussed in the previous chapter. It is even more intriguing that the ultimate creative power is described in the *Tripartite Tractate* as 'a spring which is not diminished by the water which abundantly flows from it', and as something that 'cannot be grasped: nor is it possible for anyone else to change him into a different form or to reduce him, or alter him or diminish him . . . who is the unalterable, immutable one . . .'[47] It is worth reminding ourselves that under normal circumstances energy cannot be destroyed but can change form. Is it going too far to suggest that this passage is attempting some sort of comparison between that state of affairs and the 'immutable' nature of the ultimate creative energy source of the universe when in its 'dormant' state?

On the Origin of the World also contains some intriguing passages concerning the creation of humankind:

And when they had finished Adam, he abandoned him as an inanimate vessel, since he had taken form like an abortion, in that no spirit was in him. . . . He left his modelled form forty days without soul, and he withdrew and abandoned it. . . .

Sophia sent her daughter Zoe, being called Eve, as an instructor in order that she might make Adam, who had no soul, arise so that those whom he should engender might become containers of light. . . .

Now the first Adam, Adam of Light, is spirit-endowed and appeared on the first day. The second Adam is soul-endowed, and appeared on the sixth day, which is called Aphrodite. The third Adam is a creature of the earth, that is, the man of the law, and he appeared on the eighth day . . . which is called Sunday.[48]

Despite the distinctions between spirit and soul that I have already admitted leave me somewhat baffled, and the fact that all this is placed in a somewhat confusing context – not least the references to forty days and then the eighth day – surely this can only represent a somewhat distorted appreciation of the fact that the soul of 'humankind' existed completely independently of the evolution of the physical body, and that these two did not come together at the moment of 'creation' but at some later time. I would therefore suggest this is further confirmation of my underlying interpretation of this and many similar traditions concerning the first incarnations of advanced souls.

To summarise, as with certain other of the ancient and supposedly esoteric traditions, the Gnostic texts contain a few gems but are in general, in my view, far less revealing than modern commentators often suggest.

ALCHEMY

The rise of alchemy in medieval Europe was intimately connected with the emergence of the Renaissance movement in the fourteenth century, and with a revival of interest in Hermeticism and Neoplatonism. The exoteric aspect of the art of alchemy was the search for the 'Philosopher's Stone' that could transmute base metals into gold or silver, and there is little doubt that this branch of the art laid the foundations for the modern science of chemistry. However, there is also little doubt that there was a far more esoteric side to the work of many alchemists, and exactly what they were searching for – and in a few cases perhaps found – remains a subject of intense speculation.

One of the problems with attempting to analyse the alchemical texts is that even those that may contain genuine spiritual insight *were* inevitably encoded to avoid accusations of heresy from the dominant and paranoid Christian church. Therefore, for example, the *Short Tract, or Philosophical Summary* of the fourteenth-century alchemist Nicholas Flammel, regarded by many modern commentators as one of the leading Hermeticists of his day, appears on the face of it to be nothing more than a largely exoteric description of the transmutation of various metals. If this is indeed a cleverly coded esoteric tract it would take a finer scholar than me, and one with a lot more patience and time to indulge in speculation, to decipher its true meaning.[49]

On the other hand, an anonymous tract of probably similar date entitled *The Glory of the World ... Namely the Science of the Philosopher's Stone* is somewhat more enigmatic, and contains repeated references to healing, which is more in keeping with the work of the leading sixteenth-century alchemist Paracelsus.[50] Ultimately, given their connections with Hermeticism and other esoteric movements, I take the view that the more spiritually minded alchemists were attempting to effect an entirely human transmutation whereby the soul could be released from the bondage of the physical body without physical death – which is, of course, the true experience of gnosis while still physically incarnate.

Whether they ever achieved this aim is also a subject of speculation, however, because there seems little doubt that a fair proportion of even those who were attempting a spiritual transmutation were basing their attempts on material that had been handed down from the earlier mystery schools – much of which was probably already corrupted or distorted from any true wisdom that might at one time have been possessed by, for example, the true hierophants of ancient Egypt. As a result of this, and perhaps their own misinterpretations of such earlier material, it may be that many alchemists had a reasonable appreciation of the ultimate aim, but tied themselves in knots trying to work out the practical means of achieving it.[51]

With that, we will now move on to consider some of the esoteric movements that are very much active to this day.

QABALISM

The Qabalah has its roots in interpretations of original Judaic texts on the basis, at least in part, of gematria or number symbolism – whereby each letter of the Hebrew alphabet is assigned a number, and combinations of letters that have the same numerical total can be interchanged to reveal a hidden meaning. These texts include the *Torah*, *Sefer Yetzirah* and *Zohar*, and the latter two in particular are almost incomprehensible in straightforward English translations of the original Hebrew. However, unlike many texts whose hidden messages have produced multiple and conflicting interpretations, the development of the Qabalah has produced a relatively stable and consistent mystical framework that also includes practical advice on spiritual development – which many people in all parts of the modern world are increasingly following.

It would be of little use even to attempt to trace the origins of the modern system back to the Judaic texts, or to examine the coded work of leading occult and Hermetic Qabalists of past centuries such as, for example, John Dee and Eliphas Levi; for once it is more appropriate that our review should be based on modern explanations.[52] Two of the finest sources are Dion Fortune's 1935 work *The Mystical Qabalah*, and her former pupil Gareth Knight's 1965 follow-up *A Practical Guide to Qabalistic Symbolism*.

The fundamental basis of the Qabalah is the diagram of the 'Tree of Life', which is designed to be interpreted from two different perspectives: first, as a view of the different levels of the macrocosm of the universe, and indeed as an explanation of how it progresses in various stages from a night of Brahma into full manifestation; and second, as a view of the microcosm of humankind's spiritual physiology, and in particular of the initiatory paths through the various ethereal realms that we must follow if we are to achieve enlightenment and, ultimately, full gnosis. Accordingly, the reflection of the macrocosm in the microcosm is implicit, and the idea that humans were created 'in the image of God' takes another interesting turn. Figure 11 depicts the basic Tree, which comprises the ten 'sephiroth' – with an eleventh, Daath, that is not numbered – and the twenty-two 'paths' between them, each of which has its own characteristics and influence according to the context.

In order first to apply the symbolism of the Tree to the macrocosm, let us look at Figure 12. Although I do not have the space to go into this in great detail, the general principle is one of different levels, dimensions or planes of existence – which we have already repeatedly encountered. The highest is the most sublime realm of the 'Great Unmanifest' itself, and, as we can see from the descriptions at the top, the idea is of the primeval *limitless* void from which the *light* emerges. The uppermost sephiroth, Kether, lies within the 'archetypal world', indicating that it contains the *potential* for everything that will come into being. Thereafter, in the 'creative world' the primeval *forces* start to sow the seed for the ideas of *forms*, which are then created, corrected, diversified and concreted until they receive their proper patterns in the 'formative world'. Finally, these forms become manifest in the 'physical world' of the lowest plane of Malkuth. All of these ideas are consistent with the conclusions that I reached in the last chapter.

Let us now see how the Tree is applied to the microcosm, humankind itself. Figure 13 again depicts the different realms, and the principle is that what I have so far called souls or spiritual

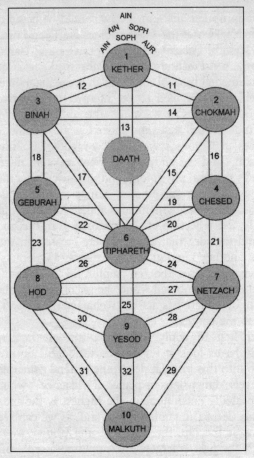

Figure 11: The Qabalistic Tree of Life

entities occupy these planes primarily according to their level of karmic advancement. Looked at from the perspective of the neophytes who hope to accelerate their development while incarnated in a physical body, the path to advancement and gnosis leads away from the sensations of the physical world in Malkuth, and upwards through the stages of instinct and intuition in Yesod and Tiphareth. At this latter point they have progressed from their 'incarnatory personalities' through to their 'individual souls', after which point lies the realm of the pure 'spirit'. I have said previously

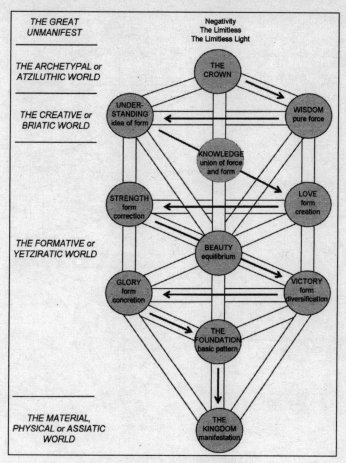

THE GREAT
UNMANIFEST

Negativity
The Limitless
The Limitless Light

THE ARCHETYPAL or
ATZILUTHIC WORLD

THE CROWN

THE CREATIVE or
BRIATIC WORLD

UNDER-
STANDING
idea of form

WISDOM
pure force

KNOWLEDGE
union of force
and form

STRENGTH
form
correction

LOVE
form
creation

THE FORMATIVE or
YETZIRATIC WORLD

BEAUTY
equilibrium

GLORY
form
concretion

VICTORY
form
diversification

THE
FOUNDATION
basic pattern

THE MATERIAL,
PHYSICAL or ASSIATIC
WORLD

THE
KINGDOM
manifestation

Figure 12: The Tree of Life as Macrocosm

that I find these distinctions in particular unclear, but in this case
they do not appear to detract unduly from the clarity of this
description of the attainment of ever-higher levels of awareness,
advancement and, ultimately, reunification with the original source.

During this process a number of hurdles are met that test
neophytes' determination to continue, in the form of the 'gulf', the
'hurdle' or 'veil' and the 'abyss', and Qabalists interpret a number
of passages in ancient texts as descriptive of such initiatory trials
in which the subject feels isolated and alone, and longs to return

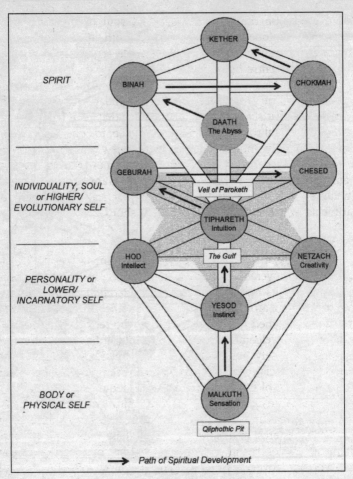

Figure 13: The Tree of Life as Microcosm

to the security of familiar surroundings. It is highly likely that this is the original or underlying meaning of the trials that are described in the Egyptian duat – except that arguably they must be attempted by the neophyte both in incarnate life and after physical death – and this theme of trials and testing is common to all descriptions of initiation into the sacred mysteries. Meanwhile, we can also see the six-pointed 'Star of David' superimposed on the Tree, composed of two overlapping triangles, one upright, the other inverted, which symbolise the perfectly balanced soul of the twice-born adept that can operate equally well in both an upward and a downward direction – with Tiphareth, the sephiroth of equilibrium, as their centre point.

I have little space to elucidate further on Qabalistic thinking except to confirm that, despite its clearly Judaic origins, modern Qabalists at least seem to have little doubt that reincarnation and karma play a vital role in this framework.[53] So, in conclusion, when explained simply and clearly it is in my view a highly revealing worldview that is entirely consistent with the more general one that I am developing here. Moreover, we will examine how modern Qabalists apply this worldview to the practical achievement of karmic advancement and enlightenment shortly.

ROSICRUCIANISM

The 'Fraternity of the Rosy Cross', more commonly known as the Rosicrucian movement, came to prominence in 1614 with the publication of its manifesto, the *Fama Fraternitatis*. This school is still very much around today, and is another that continues to provide enlightened instruction to those who seek it. Unfortunately, although it welcomes anyone into its fold, it has always kept its teachings a closely guarded secret from outsiders, while all the original Rosicrucian material that has ever been published is either too bland to be of interest or, once again, requires decoding.[54]

Still, it is quite clear that seventeenth-century occultists, alchemists, Hermeticists and Qabalists either were also Rosicrucians or at least had an interest in their work, and all these various movements interacted so closely that they may as well be considered as one at that time. Moreover, there is sufficient detail in some Rosicrucian works to reveal that its broad tenets are exactly in keeping with the general esoteric worldview that I am developing in this chapter and will summarise at the end.[55]

Above all, it would appear that the modern movement provides practical advice and training about the ways of achieving varying degrees of enlightenment, and that it attempts to keep its methods up to date to keep pace with cultural changes in society – something for which it should be commended. Moreover, it is democratically open to all who truly wish to seek a spiritual path, and as such avoids the elitism of many of the more secretive movements.

ALTERED STATES

We can see that the basic idea that there exists a higher level of consciousness that we can at least tap into pervades all esoteric thought. Some commentators, such as Jung, emphasise the universal nature of this consciousness, which is clearly consistent with the concept that in the higher ethereal realms the self becomes redundant and the soul merges with the original source. On the other hand, others emphasise the higher consciousness of the individual soul. Broadly speaking, both ideas have their place in an esoteric worldview, and for the most part the distinction makes little practical difference.

Seekers have used various ways of tapping into this consciousness to assist their spiritual development, and to achieve the 'altered states' that allow them to so do. However, before we examine these, I should place the discussion into context and assess what can be achieved by such actions, because the practical objectives can vary significantly. For example, some seekers are desirous of full gnosis, and the complete personal transmutation that it produces. As I have already suggested, on a practical level this requires a considerable degree of commitment and preparedness to remove themselves from the everyday pressures and distractions of physical life, and full gnosis clearly cannot be achieved overnight; indeed, it may not even be achievable in one lifetime, depending on how karmically advanced the individual is from previous incarnations. The ultimate goal is, of course, escape from the karmic round and the necessity of physical reincarnation.

However, in my view less-committed seekers can still make fundamental and huge strides in their karmic development while advancing at their own pace. The objectives of this less ambitious approach can vary enormously: for example, some may want to attempt to gain at least a glimpse of the 'vision of unity' that, as we have seen, underlies most mystical experiences; others might want to attempt to gain some idea of their past lives; most common of all, many just want to 'open up their channels' and synchronise their intuitive abilities as best they can.

This latter is important because to be candid, and in the hope of encouraging others, I can say that I have never been a particularly 'aware' person; but my own personal efforts over the last few years, as modest as they have been, have had two significant results. First, my intuition is far more noticeable and, more important, I *listen* to it far more than I used to – and few students of esoterica would disagree with the suggestion that intuition is the most obvious sign of communication with the higher self, and that it is also by far the easiest advance to achieve. Second, and related, is the fact that once we are more attuned we become aware of synchronicities that we might otherwise ignore – especially on the admittedly rare occasions that these are *so* statistically unlikely that even the most ardent sceptic ought to sit up and take notice. As Newton's subjects indicated in Part 1 such synchronicities are never merely coincidence, and they happen for a karmic reason that often forms part of our life plan – either to teach us something, or to put us in touch with someone, or to give us some other message – but in all cases to provide an opportunity for karmic advancement. Of course, we are free to ignore these signs – which sometimes come in dreams as well, given that these are just another method by which our higher consciousness communicates – and we can do this precisely because karma involves *choice* and not *destiny*. However, if we do ignore them we clearly fail to take advantage of the opportunity presented to us.

It should also be quite clear that those who proselytise about 'positive thinking' are merely talking about progressive karma, and the principle that if we think positively about a particular desire or result we karmically and automatically attract it – unless it is something that is actually 'not meant to be', in which case the trick is to work out the karmic dynamics of why this might be the case. The flip side, of course, is that those who adopt a negative outlook also attract exactly what they predict, in that they miss their opportunities for advancement and remain stuck in a regressive karmic rut – and this, in my view, is the true nature of 'hell on earth'. To clarify further, when discussing karma I deliberately use the words *progressive* and *regressive* rather than *positive* and *negative* or *good* and *bad*, because there is no moral imperative in all this. To be totally unaware of the concept of karma is *not* to be intrinsically evil, and indeed such a person may well be progressing their karma quite well without knowing it, just by doing the right things automatically. Nor is someone with regressive karma in any sense evil, but in my view they provide their own punishment; because our higher selves continually bombard all of us with opportunities and messages, which if we continually ignore them grow into full-scale disasters. I would argue that whenever we face major problems in life they are there to teach us some sort of lesson as to how to avoid the same in future; and if they are serious problems that come all at once on a number of fronts – personal, professional, financial and so on – they are there to act as a major wake-up call. If we still ignore the message the disasters will be repeated, not only in this life but perhaps even over many lives, until we do wake up. And in my view such 'groundhog days' are indeed the true nature of hell.

The foregoing analysis is necessarily somewhat simplistic, and ignores certain complications. For example, any one person may have progressive and regressive karma at work in different aspects of their lives at the same time. This means that even the most spiritually aware positive thinkers will on occasion attract the most appalling experiences, and like it or not these will be ones that are karmically necessary for one reason or another. Of course, the hardest aspect of all this is again working out the karmic dynamics of why these appalling things happen, something that may well only become clear long, long after the event in question. But we would do well to remember that if life was always easy we would learn nothing.

In any case, now that we have some idea of *what* we are trying to achieve, we are ready to examine *how*, in practical terms, we can attain higher or altered states of consciousness that will improve our connectedness to the ethereal realms and allow us to take more control over our karmic development. Every esoteric school or religion advocates one fundamental approach, and that is meditation.[56] I will not attempt to go into any practical detail on this – there are numerous books and classes on the subject – except to observe that almost all approaches tend to involve the use of symbols. For example, Qabalists focus on the Tree of Life and the Tarot – inasmuch as each of the 22 'Trumps Major' of the 'Greater Arkana' is associated with one of the paths on the Tree. By contrast Buddhists, especially in Tibet, use 'mandalas' as a source of meditational focus. The reason for this use of symbols is partly that many of us find it extremely difficult to 'clear the mind' of unwanted conscious distractions, at least as beginners; but in addition, despite their disparity that arises from different cultural 'impressions', they are still effectively archetypes within the universal consciousness that act as catalysts for the awakening process. Moreover, all schools of thought indicate that controlled breathing is essential, while some even advocate mild hyperventilation as a means of increasing awareness. And in certain approaches various mantras are also chanted, especially in group situations, which is tied into not only the power of the Word but also the fact that harmonics are closely linked to energy vibrations, as we will see in a later chapter.

There is one other potential avenue available to those who wish to explore higher and altered states of consciousness, and that is hallucinogens. A number of seekers have gone down this route in a variety of ways and with a variety of results, and the works of Aldous Huxley, Timothy Leary, Carlos Castaneda, Stanislav Grof, Robert Anton Wilson, Terence McKenna and Alexander Shulgin all provide fascinating insights.[57] Some of them have reported intriguing experiences that have many similarities with divine visions, and a balanced view seems to be that the use of especially natural rather than man-made hallucinogens can act as a catalyst to speed up an initial increase in awareness, after which the real 'hard yards' must be gained by unassisted meditation.[58]

SHAMANISM

Of course a discussion of hallucinogens leads neatly on to shamanism, because they are a fundamental part of the shamanic experience, and a number of anthropologists have worked closely with shamans in native tribes in various parts of the world to experiment with them. Of particular interest is the work of Jeremy Narby, whose experiences with a tribe of Peruvian Indians are recorded in The Cosmic Serpent, first published in English in 1998. He describes how he first became intrigued by the shamans' use of the drug ayahuasca when he established the extent of their amazing knowledge of the properties of various of the eighty thousand species of plants in the Amazonian jungle. For centuries they have used amazingly effective healing remedies derived from the extracts of these plants – often combining two or more of them, which makes the statistical likelihood of finding them by trial and error pretty remote – and they maintain that such knowledge is revealed to them by the entities that they encounter when they take ayahuasca itself.

Narby's own view of this, having experimented with the drug and having encountered two huge serpents that he describes as communicating with him by telepathy, is that they were symbols for the double helix of DNA – and that the entwined serpent imagery of so many ancient cultures reveals a common experience that involves the transfer of biochemical and other knowledge directly through the DNA of the recipient. I am not necessarily convinced by the latter argument, although it is a fascinating one. The serpent imagery is clearly important, but the form that the entities take is likely to be largely subjective and, arguably, is culturally impressed – particularly because we know that shamans who use other hallucinogens or even induce trance states by hyperventilation conjure up different images. It is particularly striking that Narby's predecessor, Michael Harner, had seen 'bird-headed people' when he experimented with another group of Peruvian Indians.[59] Harner himself recognised their obvious similarity with the animal-headed gods of the ancient Egyptians, and such a link comes as no surprise when we realise that the latter were themselves no strangers to the use of hallucinogens – particularly the blue water lily or lotus plant that was also, as we have seen, symbolic of the primeval emergence.[60]

My own view is, therefore, that hallucinogens can allow subjects – especially those who have been through the rigorous training, attunement and initiation of the professional shaman – to make contact with an ethereal intelligence, which may represent either their own higher self or some form of universal consciousness. Of course, we cannot avoid the possibility that this contact may also be with ethereal entities such as those that work through channellers, who as we saw in a previous chapter are not averse to playing games, but here at least some of the information supplied – concerning healing remedies, for example – seems to have been pretty reliable.[61]

While on the subject of shamanism, we saw in Part 2 how the cave paintings of the Solutrean period are regarded as having been used in shamanic rituals that also involved acoustics. In fact, important new research by acoustics expert David Elkington in his excellent 2001 work *In the Name of the Gods* has suggested that the chambers in many ancient pyramids and temples of the postcatastrophe epoch were deliberately designed with acoustic properties that, when brought into play by chanting and other ritualised music, would have produced an altered state of consciousness – and it seems clear that this knowledge would have derived from the experiments of their precatastrophe ancestors. We also noted the emergence of geometric patterns in the art of the Upper Palaeolithic; archaeologist David Lewis-Williams believes that these patterns derive from images perceived in the early stages of shamanic trance, and I find this a highly convincing argument.[62] Moreover, it seems to me that, for example, the circle with a dot, and the spiral, are exactly the sort of archetypes from the universal consciousness that would be used to activate a deep esoteric understanding of the underlying workings of the universe on all its planes – and this view will be reinforced in the next chapter.

There are a number of other ways in which shamanic beliefs and methods correlate with the broad esoteric worldview that I have now almost fully developed. For example, the Hopi Indians describe five 'centres of vibration' within the axis of the human body that correlate well with the Eastern idea of chakras.[63] Moreover, the shamanic experience is universally one of initiatory death and rebirth – often accompanied by the extremely distressing perception of dismemberment of the physical body while in trance – and the various preparations and trials faced by the apprentice shaman have clear and close parallels with those of the neophyte seeking gnosis.[64] Finally, the shamanic concept of the 'dream time' of old, to which everything must be referred back, is arguably related to the concept of the higher ethereal realms in which all time is suspended and earthly preoccupations are ignored, and also from which we all originally derived.[65]

CONCLUSION

We have covered a great deal of ground in this chapter. We have seen that certain of the mystery schools or their progenitors were somewhat less enlightened than they are often made out to be, and that the excuse that many of their works were coded to avoid persecution is somewhat overplayed when they are properly viewed in the context of the entire work rather than just selected passages – even if this excuse is probably valid in a few instances.

Nevertheless, we have also seen that not only do a number of these schools provide a good deal of confirmation of my main

themes from Part 1, but also that their teachings are either based
firmly on a universal set of esoteric tenets or, in a few cases, can
be argued to be distortions based on the same original roots. In
addition to the concepts that I summarised in the last chapter
concerning the origins and cyclical nature of the universe as a
whole, and its combination of ethereal as well as physical planes,
the most important of these tenets are as follows:

- A belief in reincarnation and in a framework of ethereal realms
  inhabited by souls in various stages of karmic advancement.
- A belief that the fundamental karmic aim is to transcend the
  purely physical world, and that *ultimate* transcendence reunites
  the adept with the original source.
- A belief that such transcendence involves entering a higher or
  altered state of consciousness that is more often than not
  achieved by meditation.
- A belief that such transcendence, often termed gnosis, can only
  be *fully* achieved after a great deal of preparation, and many
  initiatory trials and tribulations designed to test the commitment
  of the neophyte.

We have also seen that it is not necessary to be committed to
achieving full gnosis in order to gain significant benefits in life from
gradually moving toward a more esoteric worldview. Even small
steps, such as taking time out for proper contemplation and a
degree of meditative effort, can lead to a significant enhancement in
our ability to put our lives and existence into a more philosophical
and meaningful context. In particular, if we concentrate on
developing our intuition, recognising synchronicities and attracting
positive karmic energy, we improve our ability to control and direct
our lives towards more fulfilling and pleasurable ends, and also to
cope with and understand apparently negative karmic experiences.

Moreover incarnate life is, broadly speaking, a game that can be
better played if we know the karmic rules; and the fundamental
rule is that physical 'reality' is not reality at all, but a set of limited
sensations and experiences over which we can, if we choose, exert
a high degree of control. When realisation of this dawns, relief
from what had seemed to be impossible torments and unbearable
burdens can be swift and effective.

Above all, the fact that these common tenets of an esoteric worldview remain at the heart of all the most enlightened philosophies of both East and West suggests strongly to me that within them lies the path to true enlightenment. And we can see that we learn far more by concentrating on their essential similarities and common factors than on their differences.

18. THE COSMIC DOCTRINE

In the last chapter I briefly mentioned Dion Fortune when discussing Qabalism. However, I did not discuss what is in my view her most important work, *The Cosmic Doctrine*, because I feel it deserves a chapter of its own for the extent to which it allows us to investigate some of the more complex aspects of an esoteric worldview. She and her followers considered it too dangerous for general public release when it was first composed, and it was only published privately three years after her death, in 1949. A full and unabridged general edition has only recently been made available.

The first thing I should note about it is that she claims that it was entirely channelled from certain 'Masters of Wisdom' that occupy the ethereal realms – which, given my comments on Helena Blavatsky and others in Part 2, initially raised alarm bells. Indeed, Fortune admits that her whole interest in occult philosophy derived from a reference by the later theosophist Annie Besant to the 'Brotherhood of the Great White Lodge, the Hierarchy of Adepts who watch over and guide the evolution of humanity', and she was herself a member of the Theosophical Society before she broke away to found the 'Society of the Inner Light'.[1] Her down-to-earth and nondogmatic approach is extremely refreshing, however, and in fact she completely endorses the conclusions I reached in Part 2 concerning the reliability of channelled material:

> Do not think that because a piece of information is obtained in an abnormal way it is bound to be true, any more than a thing is bound to be true because it is printed in a book. . . . A spirit communication may come from a perfectly genuine spirit, and yet be valueless. Even if a man survives bodily death, dying is not going to cure him of being a fool; if he had no sense on the physical plane, he will not have any more on the astral.[2]

This point is in fact emphasised by one of her 'communicating entities' while discussing his fellows:

They are different entities. They are what they purport to be ... they do not tell you lies about themselves. All the same, communications may vary in accuracy and completeness. In the present case variation is more likely to be in completeness than accuracy.[3]

This passage demonstrates another of the major differences between this work and others of its genre. The language is free flowing, easy and grammatically sound, despite the fact that Fortune insists that these communications have not been altered in any way other than the insertion of punctuation, and that each of the 31 chapters was dictated in 45 to 75 minutes with no other work going into them whatsoever.[4] This is in stark contrast to the stilted and halting nature of the communications channelled by, for example, Edgar Cayce at about the same time.

This is, of course, no proof of the work's reliability, and Fortune insists it must be judged by its 'intrinsic worth, not its sphere of origin'.[5] And in this respect it does not disappoint. Although there are many similarities with, for example, some of the more esoteric aspects of Blavatsky's work, it contains no explicit references to advanced prior races of impossible antiquity, nor to advanced technology or pyramids being built in remote epochs – all of which were the 'acid tests' that I used in establishing the extent to which other similar communications were distorted in Part 2. So what does it say?

The communicating entity quoted above begins with an extremely interesting discussion of the process by which such communications are effected, comparing it to telepathy between two incarnate beings except that in this case he and his fellows are discarnate. With clear echoes of the Jungian concept of universal archetypes, he indicates that the principle is the use of 'thought-forms' that have an underlying geometric basis, although he emphasises that in all the communications symbolism and analogy must be used in their attempts to describe difficult and abstract concepts that must be to some extent turned into mere words. The main trick is for the more advanced channeller to be able to separate off a portion of their higher consciousness and leave it 'unformed' so that it is capable of receiving any pattern of thought-form. He also suggests that – because the forms are at heart images and symbols that act on the higher consciousness – the person that is receiving the communications cannot process any images that they have not already assimilated, albeit that this may have occurred in past incarnations or on other planes. In effect, the best receivers have a huge stock of images that are not fixed into preconceived combinations, but are fluid and can be recombined to receive a complex new message; indeed, perhaps this is a true description of that horribly overworked expression, *open-minded*.

In more general terms, the communicating entity also provides some interesting observations on the afterlife that correlate well with our review of Michael Newton's work in Part 1. He reports that souls that have recently vacated their physical body often *try* to make telepathic contact with the still-incarnate, but many cannot because they do not yet have the requisite skill. Moreover, he says that 'ghosts' tend to be seen in familiar guise, in terms of clothes and activity, because they are projected according to how they see *themselves* – and it is only the more advanced or longer-departed souls that revert to their true nature so that they are perceived by us as a 'formless mist', coloured according to the nature of the force with which they operate, which we interpret as loose 'draperies'.[6]

After this introduction there are two sets of communications that describe the evolution of the universe or cosmos as a whole, and then that of individual solar systems, and we will deal with each in turn. I will summarise and paraphrase their contents as best I can, although they do become somewhat complex in places. Above all, please bear in mind that the bulk of the important words and phrases I use are those of Fortune and her communicating entities, and they are only approximations and guides to concepts that are not always easy to put into words.[7]

THE EVOLUTION OF THE COSMOS[8]

The evolution of the cosmos begins with the prime movement of a current in space, which, because of the interaction of momentum and inertia, is slightly curved rather than straight. Eventually this curvature causes the current to revert to its original position, having completed a huge circle, and it continues to follow this circular path for a long time. The movement of this current causes a momentum to build up in the surrounding space, which is

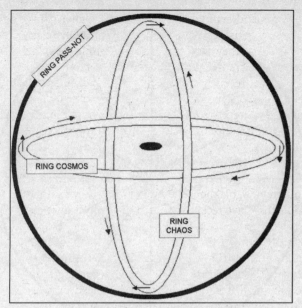

Figure 14: The Cosmic Primal Trinity

eventually translated into another circular current at right angles to the first. These are called the 'Ring Cosmos' and the 'Ring Chaos', and their combined movement eventually gives rise to another ring that encircles them both called the 'Ring Pass-Not'. These three are the primal trinity, and their continued movement eventually evolves the first two into 'solid discs' and the third into an 'encompassing sphere' – as shown in Figure 14.

The nature of the Ring Cosmos is evolutionary and focused on the space within it, and it attempts to extend its centre and cement or solidify any forms within it. For this reason it is regarded as the fundamentally 'good' and forward-looking influence of the cosmos. By contrast, the Ring Chaos is dissolutionary and focused on the outer space beyond the Ring Pass-Not, attempting to diffuse forms back into their primal state in the unmanifest. Accordingly, it is regarded as the fundamentally 'evil' and backward-looking influence of the cosmos, although just as with 'negative' karma in this context the word *evil* does not have the full pejorative associations that it normally would, and it is far better to think of the two rings

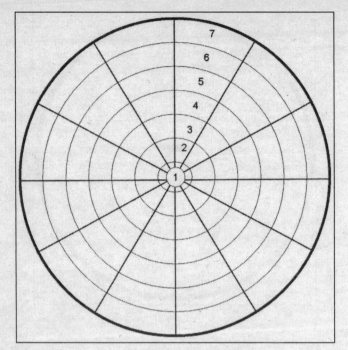

Figure 15: The Cosmic Rays and Planes

as balancing opposites in, for example, the form of the yin and yang of Chinese tradition. This clearly mirrors the notion of order versus chaos, but in a far more complex framework than is normally conceived. The cycles of the cosmos are determined by the interaction of the Rings Cosmos and Chaos, with each being the dominant influence in turn, but all held in check by the ultimate balancing influence of the Ring Pass-Not. This 'holy trinity', then, represents the *primary* stage of cosmic evolution.

Ultimately the continued movement of these three rings sets up new stresses and momentums again, and within the circumference of the cosmos a series of twelve radial 'rays' emanate from the centre, while a series of concentric circles split it into seven 'planes' – as shown in Figure 15. This is the *secondary* stage of cosmic evolution.

Further interactive movements within the circles and rays now give rise to tangential flows that bounce off them at various angles, ultimately setting up localised vortices of interacting forces that circle each other and produce primal atoms – although it would be wrong to think of these as the physical atoms that we all learn about at school. Depending on the number of forces interacting, these atoms take on a geometric pattern that rises in complexity from three to nine sides. Ultimately these primal atoms are centrifugally deposited to the various planes according to their complexity, so that the first or innermost plane contains the simplest triangular atoms only, the second both these and quadrangular atoms, and so on until we reach the seventh or outermost plane, which contains atoms of all types and is the only one to contain nine-sided atoms. This is the *tertiary* stage of cosmic evolution.

At the end of each evolutionary stage an equilibrium of forces and movements is reached, which pertains for a while with no alteration. This is one aspect of a night of Brahma in the cosmic sense, when the Ring Chaos is in the ascendancy but its desire to actively effect dissolution is held in check by the ultimate balance of the Ring Pass-Not. Gradually, though, the cycle moves on until the influence of the Ring Cosmos is once more ascendant, and evolution proceeds. So, overall, that which has already evolved is not dissolved or even disrupted during these cycles, only added to.

At the end of the tertiary stage, all the primary atoms return to the central stillness of the cosmos, and after a period of slumber and equilibrium they emanate and follow the paths of the rays. On their journey they attract and bond with atoms of the same complexity or geometric form and aggregate into composite atoms, while at the same time attracting any atoms of lesser complexity into their general vicinity as they continue outward through the cosmic planes. Ultimately this process leads to the formation of solar systems, with their central suns and surrounding planets, and these systems exist on each plane according to its complexity, with those of the seventh plane such as our own being the most complex and physical. This is the *quaternary* stage of cosmic evolution.

THE EVOLUTION OF A SOLAR SYSTEM[9]

Because a solar system or 'logos' is initially only a reflection of the macrocosm – which is another take on the axiom 'as above, so below' – its evolution commences with the development of its own primary three rings and secondary twelve rays and seven planes – although in this case it is easier to reverse the mental model in line with the Qabalistic Tree and to think of the seventh plane as the 'highest' or 'outermost' and most ethereal, and the first plane of physical manifestation as the 'lowest'. Up to this point the logos contains only disorganised atoms moving in chaotic fashion. However, at a certain point its primitive consciousness becomes aware of its own existence, and projects this thought-form onto the atoms within its own sphere, thereby creating organisation and order among them.

As to the relationship between the controlling entities of a solar system and the cosmos as a whole, the ultimate or absolute in cosmic terms is reflected in the ultimate or absolute in logoidal terms, and in the domain of its own sphere of influence the solar logos is all-powerful, albeit that in the cosmic sense it is inferior to and evolved from the great unmanifest cosmic power that is the only one that can be truly described as infinite and omnipotent. Moreover, whereas the normal consciousness of the logos is aware of its own sphere of influence only, its subconscious is aware of its cosmic origins, and thereby the influences of the cosmos as a whole continue to have an effect.

As a copy of the macrocosm, the solar logos also has its own days and nights of Brahma, except obviously of significantly shorter duration than those that apply on a cosmic scale. During the nights, the logos reflects on the experiences it has had previously, which in the early stages are all cosmic to the extent that it was previously a cosmic atom, and it is these experiences that define its habitual conditions – or effectively determine the 'natural laws' that govern the given logos. During the days, it puts these experiences to effect in the way it evolves, and clearly this is karma operating on a logoidal scale. As its evolution progresses, each new projection by the logos causes a reaction, which it then assimilates before projecting anew – in a manner something akin to the reflections in two mirrors. In fact it is its ability to *memorise* this ever-growing set of reciprocal reactions that gives the logos its consciousness as opposed to mere reactive awareness.

There are three sets of 'life swarms' that initially evolve in the logos. The first are the 'Lords of Flame', and they lead the way in working down through the seven planes and acting as a force that attunes the vibrations of each; the second, the 'Lords of Form', follow one plane behind developing the appropriate forms for that plane; and the third, the 'Lords of Mind', come last. However, because the length of time for a full phase of evolution to be completed on each plane decreases significantly from the first group to the last, the Lords of Mind spend a great deal of time waiting around before they can move on down from each plane to the next, and it is during these periods that they, unlike their predecessors that have a group consciousness only, develop individual consciousness and ultimately separate personalities. Of course, it is they who are most able to assist the life swarms that come after them, either by telepathic contact or by actual incarnation in a form suitable to the plane that the swarm is on.

The ultimate goal of all life swarms is to complete their evolutionary cycle on the planes, moving down through each and then back up to finally remerge with the logoidal consciousness. However, having achieved this remerger, the 'Divine Sparks' of the first three swarms may have to re-emerge from time to time to assist the evolution of a particular aspect of the logos.

HUMANITY AND THE ROLE OF THE PLANETS[10]

A third section of the communications deals with the various influences that affect the evolution of humanity, and therefore to a large extent its purpose is to inform students how the occult powers in the solar logos operate, and how they can be controlled or evoked to assist a particular occult task. As a result it discusses aspects of both sidereal, or cosmic, and planetary astrology that are too complex to cover in any detail here.[11] Meanwhile the explanation of the evolution of humanity itself is somewhat incidental, so we are left with a number of gaps in our understanding.

Nevertheless, the communications suggest that successive life swarms emerge from the logos during each evolutionary stage, and pass down through all the planes and back up, just as the three types of Lords did initially. Each plane is associated with a particular planet, as we can see from Figure 16, so the highest seventh plane is associated with the Sun; then, in order, the sixth down to second planes are associated with Jupiter, Mercury,

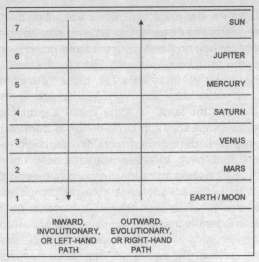

Figure 16: The Realms of the Solar Logos

Saturn, Venus and Mars respectively; finally the lowest or most physical first plane is associated primarily with the moon, although it is inferred that the old moon at some point split to form the current earth and moon.

Irrespective of the validity of this latter assertion, this picture is somewhat confused when we find that the first plane is the *only* one that is manifest in the physical world.[12] The inference appears to be that certain life swarms of our solar logos have inhabited, and continue to inhabit, the other planets, but not in any physical sense. Perhaps the best way to conceptualise this is that they inhabit the 'astral plane' of these planets, much as Newton's subjects described in Part 1, but I am only making an educated guess here and these questions are not fully answered in the communications. Further questions arise from wondering why Uranus, Neptune and Pluto are completely ignored, and how this logoidal model would work in solar systems with completely different numbers of planets.

Moving on to human evolution, a number of these communications affirm the view I have already elucidated concerning reincarnation and karma. Others describe how all life swarms develop only by gradually becoming more and more manifest as they involute down the planes on the 'left-hand path' until they become fully physical in the first plane of earth, and then only properly evolve by moving back up the planes on the 'right-hand path' until they are again at one with the solar logos. This has a clear similarity with the Jain 'wheel of time' that I discussed in Part 1, except it also confirms my more spiritual and philosophical take on that inasmuch as only two segments involve the material plane. Again, an educated guess would suggest that as humanity we are part of one or perhaps even several life swarms, and that our repeated reincarnation as individual souls on earth over many thousands of years is indicative of the amount of time required for just one small part of one life swarm cycle to be completed, at least on the physical plane. However, again this aspect is not properly clarified in the communications.

It is also slightly worrying that, although the concepts of Atlantis, Lemuria and root races are not mentioned at all in the main three sets of original communications, an 'afterthoughts' section contains a number of subsequent communications that do mention these dreaded words. However each is only mentioned once, and then only briefly, with no explicit suggestions about what these races actually were, or when or where they operated, so perhaps we need not let them detract unduly from the positive lessons we can learn from the main body of the communications. Moreover, the reference to Atlantis suggests that we are currently in a similar state of turbulence to the last days of that race, tending to confirm my suggestion that 'it is happening all over again'.[13]

Meanwhile, the last seven chapters of the third section deal with a number of stereotyped 'laws' that have been built up by previous stages of the evolution of our solar system, and which represent major influences on humanity. These are the Laws of Action and Reaction, of Limitation, of the Seven Deaths, of Impaction, of Polarity, of the Attraction of Outer Space, and of the Attraction of the Centre. Although I do not have space to examine these in detail here, they are worthy of further study – as indeed is the entirety of The Cosmic Doctrine.

CONCLUSION

Leaving the possible areas of misunderstanding about the planets and about humanity to one side, these communications contain a number of positive confirmations and genuinely esoteric further explanations of concepts and themes that we have already discussed – as well as of a number of others from ancient texts that we have not had the space to examine – all of which have often been badly misinterpreted in the past.

For example, we can now see that the descriptions of the forces emanating from the void in various origin traditions are applicable to the early stages of both cosmic and logoidal evolution, and we also get a sense of the true meaning of descriptions of deities recognising they are alone, of order being created out of chaos, and of a host of other aspects of these traditions. It is also interesting to note that the images and diagrams used to support Fortune's work have many similarities with the geometric spiral and concentric ring patterns of Upper Palaeolithic art, reinforcing my suggestion in the last chapter that these are symbols from the universal consciousness.[14] Moreover, although I suggested previously that the descriptions of the various levels of gods, angels and demons in many ancient texts tend to make their proper interpretation harder and their meaning more obscure, here we find far more useful explanations of various life swarms and their relation to the various stages of cosmic and logoidal evolution, and to the various planes.

In addition, despite the gaps regarding human evolution, there is a clear esoteric message concerning how more advanced souls can incarnate to assist evolution on earth, and also concerning how neophytes can attempt to accelerate their individual evolution by making contact with and effectively dwelling in higher planes even while in a human incarnate body. Meanwhile, my suggestion that karma can operate on a group as well as an individual level is also clearly reinforced by the message of the karmic reflection of the logoidal consciousness.

As for the days and nights of Brahma, the communications repeatedly mention them in different contexts. It would appear that in logoidal terms the 'lesser' nights of Brahma are only resting periods of equilibrium, just as they are at longer intervals for the cosmos as a whole. It is only in a 'major' night of Brahma that complete dissolution of any solar system occurs, and this happens only after the logos has cycled through a full set of its evolutions. And there is no suggestion that such a solar system re-emerges at some point thereafter, or at least not on the physical plane.

Meanwhile, complete dissolution on a cosmic scale only occurs after a far lengthier period, and this is perhaps the true meaning of terms such as 'years' and 'lives' of Brahma. Above all, my repeated insistence that the cyclical worldview of the East needs to be understood within an ethereal and not purely a physical framework appears to be vindicated.[15]

It is also interesting that Fortune's communications, and Qabalistic thinking in general, share a great many similarities with certain information deriving from Newton's subjects. For example, although most of them seem to have little understanding of such complex issues, some do seem to hint at the idea that other 'worlds' exist in higher, more subtle dimensions.[16] Moreover, they report that the 'place of all knowing', which is occupied by only the most advanced souls, is the 'ultimate mental world of planning and design' in which 'content and form are blended'. In this respect it appears to mirror the notion of the archetypal and formative worlds of the Qabalah in which force and form are combined; however, to the extent that it is also described as 'the final destination of all thought' it seems at the same time to mirror the idea of the Akashic library.[17] Finally, they also report that each solar system has its own 'creator' that is responsible for all the planes or dimensions of that system, and this is again remarkably consistent with what we have just discussed.[18]

Overall, then, the communications in Fortune's *Cosmic Doctrine* appear to have broken new ground in providing us with keys to unlock some of the most sacred mysteries of an esoteric worldview. Everything in the universe, on both the physical and ethereal planes, can be seen to have its proper place in a never-ending series of cycles, subcycles, and sub-subcycles, and to be an 'as above, so below' reflection of the ultimate macrocosmic whole on a smaller scale or different plane. I would argue that this framework at last allows us to really appreciate what the Vedic and Hindu teachers were trying to describe, and also many other commentators since then, and as a result it deserves considerably more attention than it has received to date. Moreover, my attempts to summarise and interpret the communications are likely to be flawed by my own lack of understanding, and it would be interesting to see if others can pick up the baton and explain some of the areas of apparent confusion that I have highlighted.

As if the material within these communications were not enough, we should not forget their demonstration of the extent to which channelled material does not have to be full of distortions, and nor does it have to purport to come from extraterrestrial inhabitants of other planets who are in total control of us. Above all, they also confirm that such information may well have been gleaned by many a learned esoteric initiate in past millennia, indicating how the messages of the incarnate spiritual teachers who originally civilised humankind at the start of the golden age, and assisted the postcatastrophe re-education process, could have been substantially reinforced over prolonged periods.

19. ESOTERIC SCIENCE

Our final area of esoteric interest is that of theoretical science, and in particular physics and cosmology. For the last century, advances in these disciplines have increasingly led to the development of theories that are stunningly consistent with the esoteric worldview we have been studying. Indeed, I would argue that modern scientists are reconfirming, although from a far more technological perspective, universal truths that have persisted for tens of millennia. I am no formally trained scientist, but I will do what I can to explain the basic principles underlying these consistencies as I understand them, under a variety of headings.

EVERYTHING IS ENERGY

The first confirmation of an esoteric worldview comes from Albert Einstein's work. His initial formulation of the special theory of relativity produced the now infamous equation $e = mc^2$, which shows that energy is equal to mass times the square of the speed of light. In the very broadest of senses this tends to suggest that all mass, or matter, is nothing more than *energy*. This is exactly what an esoteric worldview suggests when it describes physical matter as being only a manifestation of energy at a particularly dense level of vibration, and that in more ethereal dimensions the energy vibrates at a higher level that does not produce matter-based physical forms.

MATTER IS AN ILLUSION

We can now take this observation a step further, because modern particle physics has shown us that not only is all matter energy, but in fact it has no fundamental *physical* building blocks at all. To appreciate this, we need to recap on a little history.

Isaac Newton's formulation of the theories of mechanics at the end of the seventeenth century laid the foundation for the study of the physical sciences for the next two hundred years. He reinforced the classical Greek view of Democritus and others that all matter is made up of fundamental particles or atoms, but he also attempted to explain the force that held them together as that of gravity.

By the beginning of the twentieth century, however, it was becoming clear that gravity, while operating on a macroscopic level as the attractive force exerted by any objects of considerable size such as planets and stars, did not explain what was going on at the microscopic level inside atoms. At this time Ernest Rutherford identified that an atom is actually made up of a central nucleus and electrons that occupy various orbits around it and that, rather than being solid, the bulk of the atom is just space. In time it was established that the nucleus itself is made up of protons and neutrons, themselves surrounded by considerable space. Various other elementary particles have now been discovered, although most of these can only be observed in high-speed accelerators that cause them to collide and transform into energy and other particles.

Nevertheless, the fundamental flaw in the Newtonian view was only fully revealed when it became apparent that all subatomic particles sometimes behave like particles, and sometimes like waves. This paradox was solved by the combined work of Einstein, Max Planck, Niels Bohr, Werner Heisenberg and Paul Dirac, among others, in the postulation that the particles are energy waves emitted in packets, or quanta. Moreover, they also discovered that these quanta only show 'tendencies to exist' at a particular place, and that their interactions only show 'tendencies to occur' at a particular time, both of which are measured in terms of probabilities – so that in fact we should envision them as 'probability waves' or, more recently, 'quantum fields'.

All of this, of course, supports the view that matter does not actually exist in any physical sense at all. Atoms and their nuclei do not contain any fundamental building blocks of matter, as had previously been thought, and solid physical form is merely a *sensory perception* of humans and presumably other sentient animals. This perception is underpinned partly by the various quanta showing a marked stability under normal unchanged conditions, not only in the atomic but also in the molecular sense, and partly by the incredible speed with which they revolve in their orbital confinement, thus giving all matter its apparent solidity. Again, such findings are entirely consistent with an esoteric worldview, which suggests that not only is the physical world of relative unimportance, but also that it is actually an *illusion*.[1]

EVERYTHING IS INTERCONNECTED

Another fundamental principle of quantum theory is the fact that the observer in any experiment is not an objective bystander but a fundamental participant. This is revealed by Heisenberg's 'uncertainty principle' which states, for example, that the more accurately observers attempt to measure the momentum of a 'wave packet', the less certain they become of its position, and vice versa. Similarly, the more accurately they attempt to measure the energy of a quantum interaction, the less certain they become about the time at which it occurs, and vice versa. Consequently, we can see that observers choose in an entirely subjective and involved way how they want to observe the process, and what aspect of it they want to measure – which is tantamount to saying that they are an integral part of the process.[2]

Again, we have seen that an esoteric worldview particularly stresses the unity and interconnectedness of all things; under this schema the enlightened realise that their own physical and spiritual being is not separate from, or independent of, anything and everything else in the physical or ethereal worlds, but rather that 'all are one'.

EVERYTHING HAS CONSCIOUSNESS

As an extension to the idea that everything is interconnected, more recent developments in theoretical physics have led to the postulation that consciousness has to be included in any all-inclusive theory about the workings of the universe. For example, this idea is fundamental to the 'bootstrap' theory expounded by Geoffrey Chew, which suggests that there are no fundamental 'laws of nature', and that any such laws developed by scientists are mere reflections of their perception of the world. Instead, we must postulate that the universe operates as a dynamic web of countless interconnected events, and that none of the properties of any part of this web is more fundamental than any other. Moreover, what keeps the whole set of processes dynamically balanced is their self-consistency; and a part of that consistency is by definition – given, for example, the participative interactions involved in quantum experiments – human consciousness.[3]

So much for human consciousness being an integral part of the whole. But what about a broader consciousness? One of the major areas of study in recent decades has been that of 'nonlocal connections' – those events at the subatomic level that appear to occur instantaneously and cannot be categorised as a response to a localised cause. Such phenomena were first discussed in the context of the 'EPR experiment' devised theoretically by Einstein in his attempts to counteract Bohr's postulation of such connections, and to show that all events *must* have a deterministic local cause. However, in the hands of John Bell this experiment went on to provide a vehicle for a theorem that totally rebutted Einstein's view.

In order to understand a highly simplified version of Bell's theorem, we require a little background. Any electron has a spin, which for the sake of this discussion may be regarded as a spin about its own axis. This spin is always of a fixed value, but it can be in either a clockwise or anticlockwise direction. Moreover, although the axis of spin is another of those variables that cannot be predicted in advance with any certainty, as soon as the experimenter chooses an axis in order to take a measurement of the spin, it will be found to be in one direction or the other around that axis. In other words, it is the very act of measurement that gives the electron a definitive axis of rotation, even though this could not have been predicted beforehand.

Armed with this knowledge, Bell's theorem says that two electrons can be given opposite spins so that their combined spin cancels out to zero, even though the individual directions of spin are unknown. If these two electrons are caused to move apart from each other, even to the extent of one ending up on the moon while the other remains on earth, all external influences aside their combined spins will still be zero. Now, if a measurement of the spin of the electron that remains on earth is taken about a given axis, immediately the other electron on the moon is *given* the exact opposite spin about that same axis, *even though it had no means of knowing in advance what axis would be chosen*. This kind of nonlocal and instantaneous reaction cannot even be regarded as the result of a signal of some kind being sent, because it occurs faster than the speed of light. In other words, the interconnections between all parts of the universe not only appear to be instantaneous, but also can only be viewed in the light of a degree of interconnected consciousness residing in all quanta. These findings are, surely, advancing towards the esoteric view that not only can we speak of a 'universal energy', but that in fact this must also be viewed as a 'universal consciousness'.[4]

THE PART IS THE WHOLE

The implications of Bell's theorem – which was finally proved by experiment in 1982 – are still being considered, but one theoretical physicist in particular who took them to their next logical step was David Bohm. He postulated that the fundamental interconnectedness of everything in the universe means that we make a mistake when we look at anything within it as a separate part, and that its 'wholeness' has an 'implicate order' in which all aspects of the whole are 'enfolded' in all the parts, and vice versa. Therefore, for example, the only parts of an electron that we detect are those that 'unfold' into our 'explicate order', and they appear to move as a result of an interactive series of enfoldings and unfoldings between the two orders. This also explains why particles sometimes change into others, and sometimes into pure energy, and vice versa.

As a result Bohm likened the universe to a hologram, which contains the whole of a three-dimensional image even if we perceive only one part at a time. This view allows us to better conceive how the nonlocal reactions of Bell's theorem work, because in a hologram all ideas of location are redundant. However, in order to express the fundamental dynamism of the universe Bohm coined the term *holomovement*, in which consciousness and matter are interdependent and mutually enfolding projections of a higher reality.

Bohm's work surely suggests that to some extent all 'forms' are not so much a tiny part of the 'original whole' or 'source', but rather a *complete reflection* of it. Moreover, he himself drew the implication from his work that all matter and energy is conscious and, to some extent, alive.[5]

ALL TIME IS RELATIVE

The fundamental aspect of Einstein's special theory of relativity that I have not yet mentioned is his demonstration that the Newtonian concept of absolute and independent space and time dimensions – which were assumed to act as a stable and dependable backdrop for all events – was fatally flawed. Einstein proved that while one observer might witness two events simultaneously, another might see them as temporally separated as a result of his having a different velocity relative to the two events. These differences are due to the time taken for visual signals to arrive, which is dependent on the speed of light, and they only really come into play when massive velocities or distances are involved. Nevertheless, Einstein proved that space and time measurements are relative both to the observer and to each other, and that we must consider space-time as a four-dimensional continuum. Moreover, he made it clear that space-time references or co-ordinates are merely artificial constructs used by an observer to describe their environment.

Einstein then went on to extend his work into the general theory of relativity by bringing in the Newtonian concept of gravity. He showed that the gravitational force exerted by massive bodies such as planets and stars has the effect of bending or curving the three-dimensional space around them. This may best be conceived by considering how the rules of Euclidian geometry – which allow us, for example, to accurately draw a square on a two-dimensional plane by marking off right angles – no longer apply on the surface of a three-dimensional sphere. In the same way, gravity warps the space around a massive object so that normal three-dimensional geometric laws no longer apply. Moreover, because time and space form a related continuum, time is also warped in the locality of massive objects, and can therefore be seen to flow at different rates in different parts of the universe.

Astrophysicists were not able to study black holes during Einstein's lifetime, but they provide one of the finest examples of warped space-time. A black hole is formed when extremely large stars collapse in on themselves, and matter is sucked into an increasingly small space in which it becomes ever more compacted. As a result, they exert a massive gravitational attraction, which is what causes them to suck in any matter that strays into their vicinity. The effect of this huge gravitational field is to slow time from the perspective of the external observer, so that, for example, if we could observe an atomic clock flashing a signal back to earth as it approached a black hole, the time it displayed would slow down relative to our own time to such an extent that once it crossed the 'event horizon' – beyond which the force of gravity is so strong that not even light can escape – time in the black hole would be seen to come to a complete halt from our external perspective. But of course from the perspective of the clock and the black hole themselves, time is still flowing at the same rate it always has.[6]

In an esoteric worldview, one of the primary objectives of neophytes searching for enlightenment is to transcend not only their physical limitations but also those of time, and especially in the East time has always been regarded as an artificial construct whose limitations can be overcome. However, this view is reinforced in certain of the Western esoteric texts. For example, in the *Hermetica* we find the suggestion that 'it is for the sake of body that place and time and physical movement exist'.[7] Plato also strongly infers that time does not really exist in any absolute sense, but rather as a concept that provides us with a reference point with which to make sense of the physical world:

> . . . we use such expressions as what is past is past, what is present is present, what is future is future, and what is not is not, none of which is strictly accurate, though this is perhaps not a suitable occasion to go into the question in detail.[8]

Moreover, we have seen Michael Newton's subjects report that perceptions of time in the ethereal realms are totally different from those on the physical plane.

THERE ARE OTHER DIMENSIONS

The search for a 'theory of everything' that will unite quantum and relativity theory has been the holy grail of theoretical physicists ever since the two components were put in place, because although they respectively explain the microcosmic and macrocosmic worlds almost perfectly, they have not yet been successfully integrated. Moreover, several examples show that such a quantum–relativistic bridge needs to be built. In the nuclear world, the speeds of rotation of the protons, nucleons and other quanta are so high that they approach the speed of light, so relativity theory comes into play. Meanwhile, although the force that binds the elements of a nucleus together – known as strong attraction – is so strong that gravity is normally negligible in quantum theory, in the world of the black hole the compression of so many quanta into an increasingly small space creates, as we have seen, a huge mass and huge gravitational forces.

A number of quantum–relativistic theories have been developed in recent decades, one of the most developed and publicised being 'string theory'. A number of versions of this theory exist, but they all work on the principle that the various quanta that we observe are in fact vibrating strings that have some inherent tension, and whose varying states of excitation produce the quanta that we are able to measure. Above all, almost all versions propose that there are at least ten space-time dimensions in total. String theory has many opponents, not least because it has yet to be experimentally verified, but widespread efforts are being made to rectify this deficiency.[9]

We can see that this theory has certain similarities with Bohm's notion of enfoldment, in that its fundamental approach is that there is much going on in other 'nonphysical' dimensions or planes that we are not directly aware of, and about which we can only postulate. This is, of course, entirely consistent with an esoteric worldview.

VIBRATION AND HARMONY RULE
One of the clear implications of string theory is that vibration lies at the heart of all energy forms, although to a large extent this view is implicit in most modern theoretical physics. However, string theory in particular suggests that different configurations of strings effectively produce different 'harmonic chords', and this leads us into familiar esoteric territory in which certain harmonies attune to the fundamental vibrations of the universe. For example, this is the principle behind the power of the Word that we have encountered in a previous chapter, and also behind the chanting and mantras that are often used to precipitate a higher state of consciousness.[10]

BIG BANG WAS A DAWN OF BRAHMA
When, in the 1920s, Edwin Hubble observed that all galaxies appear to be moving apart from each other, it became clear that the universe is expanding. Two theories were then developed to account for this – the 'steady state' view that has now been largely

discredited, and the 'big bang' theory of the origins of the universe that most cosmologists now support. The latter postulates that all the matter in the universe was originally compressed into a 'singularity', a point of zero size but infinite mass, which then exploded – sending its contents spinning off into the universe to form stars, planets and galaxies. Of course, our comprehension of the singularity is perhaps assisted if we regard its contents as pure energy rather than compressed matter, and if we accept that we are not able to comprehend its extended dimensionality.

In attempting to devise a theory of quantum gravity that can successfully describe black holes, Stephen Hawking has made a huge contribution to our understanding of big bang in recent decades, because the increasing concentration of matter in the centre of a black hole has many obvious similarities to the singularity from which the universe exploded. Moreover, our understanding of this event is increasing with the development of ever-more-sophisticated orbiting space telescopes such as the Hubble, which allow cosmologists to see ever farther into the far reaches of the universe. Because of the time taken for such distant signals to arrive on earth at the speed of light, the farther out we observe, the younger the stars and galaxies become, bringing us ever closer to the condition of the universe just after big bang.

These observations, and the various cosmological models that are still under consideration, predict a variety of values for the age of the universe – although they normally vary between ten and twenty billion years. Considerable debate still exists as to whether the universe will continue to expand forever, or will at some point start to contract until it eventually becomes a singularity again. This latter view of an 'oscillating universe' tends to be preferred, and, yet again, we can see that it is highly consistent with the esoteric explanations offered in the ancient texts and traditions from all around the world that we considered in a previous chapter. A number of these suggest that any big bang is just one point in an infinite succession of days and nights of Brahma – in this case the point being the 'dawn' of the current day – although of course it might be more appropriate to talk of lives and deaths of Brahma in this universal context. Moreover, this worldview clearly answers the philosophical question of what happened *before* the big bang, to which the continued-expansion theorists have no real answer.

Within this analysis perhaps lies another clue to the nature of the subcycles within the universal cycles, inasmuch as the development of a solar system and its eventual collapse back into a black hole may be seen as part of a subcycle. However, I must reiterate that there is no reason to suppose that this would happen more than once for any given solar system on the physical plane in a given universal cycle.

THE PARANORMAL IS JUST NORMAL

One of the by-products of the increasingly holistic scientific view of the universe is that an increasing number of researchers are using the new theories of theoretical physics to attempt to explain phenomena that have hitherto been labelled paranormal. These include phantom replays of past events, extrasensory perception, telepathy, precognition, psychokinesis, telekinesis, remote viewing, out-of-body experiences, experiences of the ethereal realms, energy fields and auras and their interactions, and psychic healing.[11]

Moreover, it seems increasingly likely that the predominantly sceptical attitude of scientists towards many of these phenomena will have to change, and that in the future they will receive the widespread professional attention that an esoteric worldview suggests they deserve.[12] In time, it is to be hoped that their *para* prefix will be dropped, and – in a return to a worldview that I would suggest was initiated during the golden age of our forgotten race, and resurrected for a time after the catastrophe – they will be regarded once again as perfectly natural phenomena. And if we can achieve this, we might even in time be able to reverse the cultural repression of these natural skills in our species, and return to encouraging their development.

CONCLUSION

We can see that twentieth-century progress away from the mechanistic Newtonian view of the universe to a more process-oriented view has reconfirmed virtually all of the major tenets of an esoteric worldview that has survived in various Eastern and Western schools of thought for millennia. Indeed, the extent of confirmation is quite startling.

I am not of the opinion that we can belittle this as merely the *rediscovery* of a set of universal truths that have been known all along, because it is quite clear that, although the esoteric and scientific worldviews have both been built up from observation and experiment, the two approaches have nevertheless been fundamentally different. The former has relied on direct revelation and experience of these truths while in a higher state of consciousness, and to some extent on continued observation of the underlying nature of the universe after such insights have been gained, while the latter has relied on an empirical experimentation that is incomparably more technologically advanced than anything that has preceded it. Hence my preference for the term *reconfirmation*.

Nor should the modern scientific approach be underestimated, even by those who are largely sceptical of it, because there can be little doubt that in its modern guise it has the potential to take us beyond anything our predecessors achieved, if used in the right way. Indeed, I might even suggest that the natural dynamic flux of polar opposites, of the Yin and Yang, is nowhere better demonstrated than in the swing from the domination of intuitive appreciation to that of the rational intellect – which has now arguably ruled supreme, in the West at least, for several millennia. If the pendulum is now swinging back again to the former, but with a more advanced rational foundation underneath it, then so much the better.

Above all, rather than holding back or even reversing our spiritual progress, as scientists have indeed done in the past, theoretical physicists at least now would appear to be in the vanguard of ushering in a new, more spiritual era – one in which it is to be hoped that our finest brains will, rather than restricting themselves to the partial view of the single scientific discipline, once again pride themselves on considering the philosophical whole.

CONCLUSIONS FROM PART 3

- The ancient texts and traditions from all around the world contain remarkably consistent esoteric descriptions of the origins of the universe in terms of a void that contains the potential for all forms. This potential is actualised by the mere will or Word of the ultimate creative power, releasing energy that coagulates into a variety of vibrational states, creating the various ethereal and physical dimensions and their forms.

- The most esoteric traditions of both East and West include a belief in reincarnation and karma, in a framework of ethereal realms inhabited by souls in various stages of karmic advancement, and in the karmic aim of transcending the purely physical world and reuniting with the original source. Such complete transcendence can be achieved only after a great deal of preparation, and involves repeatedly entering a higher or altered state of consciousness by meditation or, in some cases, the use of hallucinogens.

- Even small steps, such as taking time out for proper contemplation and a degree of meditative effort, concentrating on developing our intuition, recognising synchronicities and attracting positive karmic energy, can significantly improve our ability to direct our lives. The fundamental rule of the karmic game is that physical reality is not reality at all, but a set of limited sensations and experiences over which we can exert a high degree of control.

- At least one twentieth-century source of channelled material has provided extremely lucid esoteric explanations of the evolution and workings of the entire universe and of the solar systems within it, and of the various planes of existence and levels of souls within a solar system. This source contains few of the distortions normally associated with such material, and especially does not purport to come from more advanced extraterrestrial species who are in control of earth.

- Modern theoretical science is moving ever closer to reconfirmation of an esoteric worldview with the propositions that everything is energy, that matter is an illusion, that everything is interconnected, that everything has consciousness, that the part is the whole, that all time is relative, that there are other dimensions, and that vibration and harmony rule. Moreover, these developments increasingly suggest that supposedly paranormal phenomena are in fact perfectly normal when placed in the context of an esoteric worldview.

EPILOGUE

SINGLE SOURCE?

Let us return briefly to the issue of *why* the various universal themes that we have encountered display such incredible consistency across huge geographic and temporal boundaries. The orthodox approach to mythology allows for two possibilities: diffusion from a common original source, and separate but parallel development in each location. In accepting the commonality of many of the themes of myth, Joseph Campbell discusses these issues repeatedly in *The Masks of God*, and he is primarily a diffusionist – as indeed are most modern scholars.[1] In my view, however, the situation is somewhat more complex than they suggest.

If we first examine the consistent traditions about our forgotten race – concerning their original spirituality, subsequent debasement and eventual destruction – these must primarily represent a genuine human memory of former times passed down orally and built up piece by piece by every generation, from the initial time when the first advanced souls incarnated on earth right down through the catastrophe until they were put into written form perhaps only about five thousand years ago. This is essentially diffusion at work, except that unlike Campbell I am suggesting that a degree of genuine historical information is involved.

When we consider the equally consistent universal truths of an esoteric worldview concerning, for example, the origins of the universe and the nature of the ethereal realms, I have postulated that the first advanced souls would have carried such knowledge with them when they incarnated, as would any that reincarnated to assist humankind's development thereafter, both before and after the catastrophe. But I have also suggested that any neophyte, in any part of the world and at any time, can access a store of esoteric wisdom in the universal or higher consciousness that allows direct revelation – and to some extent personal experience – of such truths. Again, I disagree with Campbell in that I do not believe these transcendental experiences produce merely subjective, human, psychological constructs, but rather that they, in some cases at least, represent contact with an objective and universal source of wisdom. I would therefore argue that these truths have been spread by a combination of diffusion and parallel development.

Of course, this is not to say that there are not problems with this latter method of transmission, just as there are with oral and written information handed down over many millennia. The true transcendental experience should, especially if regularly repeated by any individual or group, produce a relatively reliable and consistent view, as should any view passed on by a genuine incarnate adept or master. However, we have seen that information about both human history and the general nature of the universe *can* be distorted in channelled material, and that the distortions *can* be present in the ethereal source itself. Meanwhile, it is equally apparent even genuine human mediums can be operating in a cultural or religious context that is so far removed from that of the original universal truths that any ethereal messages are subjectivised and distorted to a quite horrible degree.

But can we say that all the religions and philosophies of the modern era sprang from a single source? With reservations, and making due allowance for the universal consciousness as a single source in its own right, I would argue that we can. I believe that the spiritual worldview that emerged when the first advanced souls incarnated has had a massive and all-pervasive historical influence that has not only survived the catastrophe, but also, to a large extent, all attempts to distort it.

MORE FROM NEWTON

I have already mentioned Michael Newton's research repeatedly. I will now point out that I only came across it after the bulk of this work had been completed, when it was suggested that I should provide further evidence to back up my spiritual worldview. We have seen how successfully it achieved that objective. But I was not prepared for the extent to which it would back up a number of the other themes that I have developed. For example, his subjects state quite clearly that certain of the more advanced souls do indeed reincarnate to assist humankind, even though they are under no obligation to do so because they have escaped from the karmic round; better yet, they actually refer to them as 'sages' or 'watchers'.[2] But it gets better still, as Newton himself reports:

> A few of my more advanced clients declare that highly advanced souls who specialise in seeking out suitable hosts for young souls evaluated life on Earth for over a million years. My impression is these examiner souls found the early hominid brain cavity and restricted voice box to be inadequate for soul development earlier than some 200,000 years ago. . . . Within the last 100,000 years, we find two clear signs of spiritual consciousness and communication. These are burial practices and ritualistic art . . .[3]

This is, in my view, superb confirmation of my arguments in Part 1 regarding the repeated attempts of advanced souls to incarnate in humanoid form, of the reasons why these were unsuccessful, and also of the timing of their eventual success.

It is also interesting to note that, while most of his subjects do not provide any information of lives in Middle or Upper Palaeolithic times that would corroborate my theories regarding the level of advancement and eventual demise of our forgotten race per se, a few do apparently mention incarnations in land masses that deviate from earlier continents and which Newton is unable to identify. While he rejects the idea that any advanced race existed substantially before 100,000 years ago on the basis that this would go against the evidence of evolution, and I agree with him, there is another intriguing possibility that he does not discuss. Is it possible that these reports are of incarnations either on another physical planet similar to earth, or even on one in a more ethereal plane? As strange as this may sound, such planets are discussed by his subjects, and this might just be the derivation of, for example, theosophical descriptions of Atlantis and Lemuria. It just may be that a number of the reports of lost continents and even aspects of technology may relate to the original sources' memories of incarnations in other realms that are related to, but not the same as, earth; memories whose real context has become confused over time.

This brings me on to another important aspect of Newton's revelations. It is abundantly clear that when we accept there are dimensions beyond the physical we face considerable difficulties in distinguishing between extraterrestrial and spiritual phenomena. I have previously suggested that it is not inconsistent with a spiritual worldview to postulate that extraterrestrial races exist on other planets that have not only mastered the art of interstellar travel, but are also far more spiritually advanced than us and can therefore 'manipulate' the boundaries between the physical and the ethereal far better than we can. And I cannot totally reject the possibility that in some way such a race might have kept an eye on planet earth, and even tried to assist both its and our evolution in some way, as so many other sources, especially channelled communications, seem to suggest. But *if* that is the case, then I would still argue that the means of such 'intervention' and 'assistance' would have been far more spiritual than physical.

These are again words that I wrote before I discovered Newton's work; and, yet again, his subjects provide confirmation of just such a view.[4] They talk about 'worlds of creation and noncreation', which this time appear to be normal *physical* planets, and at least one of these is supposed to more or less mirror our earth even though it is described as 'larger, somewhat colder, and with less ocean'. While they make it clear that other similar worlds exist that mirror other inhabited planets not similar to earth, 'earth 2' in particular is apparently not even in our galaxy, and it has no permanent human-type inhabitants, only relatively small animals with little intelligence. Instead it is described as a place of quiet and relaxation that more advanced souls connected to earth visit between earth incarnations, and we may assume that they do not actually physically incarnate when they visit it but dwell on its closest ethereal plane. But what is more startling is that they also go there to train in the *art of creation* itself.

They describe being initially instructed in how to create inanimate objects such as rocks, which they do by taking the basic chemical constituents that already exist and combining them into the appropriate form by focusing their energy. The more advanced subjects also describe training to create more complex organic structures such as plants, although none of the subjects was sufficiently advanced to be working on animal replication to a more advanced stage than that of fish. What we can infer is that this is indeed the way in which the 'hand of god' or 'Intelligent

Design' plays a part in assisting evolution on any planet. It would appear that at any stage in its evolution, highly advanced souls can visit its closest ethereal plane *without* physically incarnating – useful in the early stages of a planet's evolution when no advanced physical life form is available for them to incarnate into – and, using the building blocks already available, give the evolution of new vegetable and animal forms a push in the right direction simply by focusing their energy.[5] Again this may seem a little far-fetched at first sight, but when we consider what they are saying we find that they are not creating life forms out of nothing, merely using materials already available and their own directed energy to transform existing combinations into new ones. We are not even talking about genetic engineering in any physical sense, merely a focusing by a discarnate, highly intelligent energy that helps evolution on its way. When Newton provoked one subject with 'I thought nature did those things?' he replied with a laugh: 'What do you think nature is?' Newton also describes how 'students are encouraged to create miniature planetary micro-habitats for a given set of organisms which can adapt to certain environmental conditions', and this seems to indicate how life on any planet is seeded in the first place.

All this seems to mirror the contents of certain supposedly extraterrestrial communications, except that we are not talking about mother ships carrying huge stocks of plant and animal life around the universe like some giant Noah's ark, but about the normal process of evolution receiving a little added energy-directed impetus at various times. This is exactly what I would expect given that we have not found even the smallest amount of definitive artefactual proof of technologically advanced physical intervention. Moreover, this more spiritual approach allows us to remain true to the fundamental message of the ancient texts and traditions, and indeed to the message that comes across in some channellings from supposed extraterrestrials, regarding the fact that our spiritual growth as a race, and our future karmic fate, is entirely under our own control.

But at this point I want to return to the enigma of the Mitchell-Hedges crystal skull. It obviously exists, and can and has been inspected. It also appears to have defied attempts to understand how it was crafted, given that not only does modern technology *not* appear to have been involved, but that it would be hard to replicate it even if such technology was used. It is hard to conceive of any method by which it might be dated, and therefore we may never know whether it is a product of the pre or postcatastrophe epoch. But we also know that the quartz from which it is made is particularly well suited to data storage. Was it indeed created by 'thought-form' and planted on earth by some of the most advanced, discarnate, angelic-type entities associated with our planet – perhaps even by the 'Masters of Wisdom' with whom Dion Fortune was in communication? Does it indeed represent a store of information beyond our wildest dreams? Who can say? But these explanations are as logical as any others I can come up with based on current evidence and pending further revelations.

A NEW HISTORICAL PARADIGM

We have seen that, throughout history, most scholars have tended to dismiss as myth any ancient records that do not fit the prevailing orthodoxy – preferring, perhaps understandably, to wait until a mass of archaeological evidence has been collated before accepting any major revision. Such was the case with the late-nineteenth-century discoveries of Troy by Heinrich Schliemann, and of the Minoan civilisation of Knossos on Crete by Sir Arthur Evans, proving that settlements had existed at both sites since about 3000 BC and forcing a complete revision of orthodox thinking about certain Greek traditions. The same can be said of the multiple cities unearthed in Mesopotamia around the same time, which as we have already seen proved that a mass of biblical tradition was indeed based on fact. These revelations were provided by dedicated explorers who refused to accept the conventional wisdom.

Increasing archaeological effort, allied to more advanced methods and technology, continues to be applied all around the world. Most recently, we have seen that in Anatolia and Syria advanced settlements with houses and temples dating back to the early Neolithic period are being unearthed in increasing numbers. These discoveries are forcing a major re-evaluation of orthodox opinion about the earliest signs of civilisation in the modern epoch. But we also find that there appear to have been no real intermediate stages of development from hunter-gathering to agriculture to urbanisation in the more advanced of these settled communities. Now, I dismissed the 'no overnight development' argument as applied to the flowering of our earliest major civilisations in the modern epoch, that is in Mesopotamia and Egypt, precisely because we *do* see a gradual development from these urbanised settlements in the Near East that existed millennia before. But what of, for example, Jerf el-Ahmar? Here we find a sizeable stone-built settlement with communal buildings and settled agriculture dating back to 11,500 years ago. *And as yet we have found absolutely no precedents for this.* So are we finally discovering the survivors of the catastrophe – and if so, what does that tell us about the level of advancement already achieved by their predecessors, our forgotten race?

It is also interesting to note that many of the Near Eastern traditions report that the early civilisers of humankind lived in the highlands or even in mountain regions, and some alternative commentators use this to suggest either that they were extraterrestrials or that they had to protect some sort of special secret. But, if these are records of survivors of the catastrophe and not of the original civilisers in the golden age, there is a far more prosaic explanation. If you wanted to keep your group intact and to rebuild after such an event, would you not want to be as isolated from anarchic marauders as possible? Where would you go if you feared further flooding and destruction? Might you not also consider fortifying your settlements by building in stone for the first time? And does this also provide an answer to the enigma of why – if the site was indeed first selected not long after the catastrophe – the settlers of Tiahuanacu decided on such a remote and mountainous region?

In any case, important sites in the Near East have already been lost to the floodwaters of new dam construction, and many others are under threat. How much archaeological evidence will we lose, never to be recovered? How much have we already lost all around the world that might have proved that a forgotten, culturally advanced race inhabited the earth before the catastrophe? Moreover, despite the likelihood that the latter would have wiped out most traces of even technologically advanced prior civilisations, has some evidence of their advanced culture actually survived, waiting for mavericks to properly interpret it?

We have already seen in Part 2 that evidence is mounting that technical skills in astronomy, navigation and medicine may well have been more advanced in the Upper Palaeolithic than was previously suspected, while cultural developments such as the use of pigments, the production of abstract and esoteric art, and ritual burials can be traced back even farther.[6] All this is gradually being accepted in orthodox circles. Meanwhile, we have also seen that a number of anomalous artefacts have been unearthed that could provide tantalising evidence of the even greater level of cultural advancement of our forgotten race – despite there being undoubted problems with the authenticity and dating of some of them.

My 'bottom-line' assertion about the level of culture that our forgotten race eventually achieved is that it must have included the widespread trading of goods, most likely by sea, and the development of reasonably sized permanent settlements – which in turn implies settled agriculture. These factors alone would be sufficient to allow my interpretations of the texts and traditions in respect of their increasing material preoccupation and lust for power, and resulting loss of spirituality, to stand. No definitive evidence of even this level of culture has yet been forthcoming dating back to more than 11,500 years ago, but despite the havoc wrought by the catastrophe it may still be only a matter of time.

A NEW PHILOSOPHICAL PARADIGM

In my view, the widespread re-adoption of a spiritual worldview offers great hope for the human race. Its universal truths can be seen to lie at the heart of all religions and philosophies that have not been hopelessly distorted. This can only serve to reinforce the view that the supposedly religious conflicts that continue to plague our world are struggles for power and cultural identity that have nothing whatever to do with any fundamental philosophical truths.

Meanwhile, it is abundantly clear that people in the West are becoming increasingly aware of the absurdity of living to work, instead of working to live, and of focusing on amassing material possessions that they never even have time to enjoy. In their search for a deeper meaning, they are showing a marked tendency toward a personalised 'mix and match' religion that takes elements from East and West, ancient and modern. This is an admirable development, not only because everyone has the inalienable right to find their own path in their own way and in their own time, but also because the distorted dogma of the Western orthodox religions is increasingly being seen for what it is and always has been – primarily a political control mechanism that is far removed from the original wisdom from which it sprang. However, in my view this tendency has also arisen out of the lack of a coherent and simply explained spiritual framework that uses original and universal truths to answer *all* the big questions. I hope that in this work I have done what I can to show that such a framework exists.

Moreover, I have done everything in my power to prove that such a spiritual framework is not just a construct developed by the weak and insecure to give themselves something to believe in, but is to a large extent a genuine, objective and true 'reality' that is being increasingly confirmed by orthodox science. The rationalist argument, that any belief in notions of divinity and soul is by definition irrational, is looking increasingly insecure.

THE FUTURE

It is now time for us to consider what is undoubtedly the most important issue of all in this work, and that is my contention that the human race of the modern era is following the same path to annihilation that our predecessors took. It is quite clear that, in the West at least, our focus on the material world – of possessions, of physical pleasures and of supposed power and prestige – at the expense of any contemplation of our spiritual roots, has been increasing from century to century, from decade to decade, from year to year, and now even from day to day. This gradual but intensifying progression is almost certainly the same as the one that enveloped our forgotten race.

But is our situation really comparable with theirs? In particular, did we start all over again after the catastrophe with our spiritual worldview reasserted? Or has there just been a continual and steady decline from where our debased predecessors left off, for which we can hardly take the blame? I am strongly of the view that the former is the case, and that we can and must take the blame for history repeating itself. The transcendental philosophy of the *Vedas* – which, despite some deficiencies, are perhaps the most refined and original version of the universal truths that still survive, as well as having perhaps the oldest heritage – could not have arisen from the ashes of the catastrophe if we had not been offered a second chance. That chance was, I believe, presented to us by the influx of a new wave of advanced souls who incarnated at that time to put us back on track, and who reasserted a spiritual worldview based on the universal truths. And, if I am right, it can only mean that once again we are in the process of squandering our birthright.

But can it be argued that this is just our karmic destiny, part of the eternal interplay between the Yin and the Yang, and something that we can do nothing about? Should we not just carry on as we are, and await the destruction that is our destiny too? In my view it is most assuredly not. If there is one thing that the rules of karma tell us, it is that nothing is preordained, and that our fate as a race is entirely in our own hands. Both on an individual and on a universal level, karma is not about fate, it is about *choice*.

But do we still have the capability to resurrect our spiritual nature to its proper degree? Undoubtedly, yes. Broadly speaking, we have the same physiology that our more spiritual predecessors had. All we have done is culturally suppress our instinctive and spiritual nature, and we can reverse this process – although not necessarily overnight. Indeed, some of Newton's subjects report that human amnesia about past lives and the ethereal realms has been deliberately increased to a significant degree in the last few millennia, making it far harder to incarnate here – despite the fact that, as we saw, total recall is not regarded as appropriate; they further suggest that a revolt is in progress in the ethereal realms, and that the powers that be may need to change the rules back to how they were before.[7] If this is true and it happens, it can only represent a change for the better.

So, finally, what is our fate if we do fail to heed the warnings and are, once again, destroyed by the decree of universal karma? I do not believe this would be the end for planet earth, or indeed for humankind. But how much patience does our logos have, and how many chances will we get? Is it our long-term karmic destiny to evolve as a race to the point that we no longer physically incarnate, and to collectively return to the source, as many esoteric traditions suggest? If so, is there a time limit, and will we exceed it if we keep going down the wrong path? Or should we just relax and enjoy the unique experience of physical incarnation, because everything will turn out right in the end?

Whatever we might think of their multiple world age traditions, perhaps the Hopi Indians have the answer: 'With this wisdom they understood that the farther they proceeded on the Road of Life and the more they developed, the harder it was. That was why their world was destroyed every so often to give them a fresh start.' If cultural and technological progress is part of the 'plan of creation', as I suspect it must be at least to some extent, then perhaps the Hopi are right to suggest that this is all unavoidable?

But before we become too complacent, let us not forget the closing words of their god Sotuknang to the chosen survivors of the flood when they emerged into our current 'fourth world':

'What you choose will determine if this time you can carry out the plan of Creation . . .'

your bank balance means nothing . . .
only your karmic balance matters

NOTES

INTRODUCTION

1. A multitude of ancient texts and traditions from every continent on the globe record such an event, although we will not examine the detail of all of these in the current work because they have been comprehensively chronicled by others – and, in any case, we will meet with many of them in due course as we progress. For comprehensive lists see, for example, Allan and Delair, *When the Earth Nearly Died*, Part 3, Chapter 1, Table 3A, p. 150; Hancock, *Fingerprints of the Gods*, Chapter 24, pp. 204–12; and Filby, *The Flood Reconsidered*, Chapter 3, pp. 48–58. There are also a number of websites documenting flood myths; one of the best is at <www.best.com/%7Eatta/floods.htm>.
2. Campbell, *Primitive Mythology*, Introduction, p. 27.
3. Jung, *Psychology and Alchemy*, Prefatory Note to the English edition, p. v.
4. For an excellent discussion of ancient Egyptian myth and symbolism, see West, *Serpent in the Sky*, pp. 127–34.

CHAPTER 1: MYTHS IN THE MAKING

1. See Campbell, *Primitive Mythology*, prologue, pp. 14–15, and Mircea Eliade, *The Sacred and the Profane*, Chronological Survey, pp. 229–32.
2. For a full exposition see Campbell, *Primitive Mythology*, Part 1.
3. For a full exposition see ibid., Parts 2 and 3.
4. Ibid., Chapter 3, pp. 146–7.
5. Ibid., Chapter 10, pp. 403–4.
6. Ibid., Conclusion, p. 462.
7. Ibid., Chapter 4, p. 164.
8. Campbell, *Occidental Mythology*, Chapter 3, p. 95.

CHAPTER 2: A SPIRITUAL WORLDVIEW

1. Some of the earliest and most comprehensive research into near-death experiences, performed by psychiatrist Raymond Moody, was first collated in his 1975 work *Life After Life*. During his initial research and prior to its publication the experiences described above were not common knowledge, and so the possibility of precon-ditioning that could clearly prejudice any later studies was considerably reduced.
2. See the bibliography for details of his other works.
3. See Stevenson, *Children Who Remember Past Lives*, Chapter 3. He mentions that one of the finest cases involving hypnotic regression is documented in detail in Bernstein's *The Search for Bridey Murphy*, first published in 1956 and updated in 1965, and that those who suggest this case has been exposed as a fraud have not examined the most recent evidence and rebuttals.
4. See ibid., Chapter 1, pp. 21–3 for further definition of these terms. With respect to the ability to speak foreign languages fluently, termed *zenoglossy*, Stevenson specifically cites the cases of Swarnlata Mishra, Jensen, Gretchen, and Uttara Huddar; see ibid., Note 32 to Chapter 5, p. 292.
5. Ibid., Chapter 4.

6. Ibid., Chapter 5.

7. Ibid., Chapter 10, p. 219.

8. As a trained psychiatrist Stevenson devotes a whole chapter to various behavioural traits that may be better explained by reincarnation than any genetic or cultural influence; see ibid., Chapter 9.

9. Ibid., Chapter 7.

10. Stevenson's methods of research are explained in ibid., Chapter 6.

11. Ibid., Chapter 7, p. 158.

12. Newton, *Journey of Souls*, Introduction, p. 4.

13. The descriptions in the following sections are a more or less chronological summary of the succeeding chapters in ibid.

14. Stevenson reports that in most of his cases the children had a tendency to incarnate in the geographical vicinity of where they previously *died*, even if much of their previous life had been led elsewhere, but we must remember that these cases of sudden death are not the norm; see *Children Who Remember Past Lives*, Chapter 11, p. 247.

15. Ibid., Chapter 5, pp. 110–11.

16. Newton, *Journey of Souls*, Chapter 10, p. 162.

17. Ibid., Chapter 12, pp. 202–3.

18. However, the subjects do report that there is a 'place of transformation' where they can temporarily experience what it would be like to incarnate as the soul of an animal or even a plant, or even to feel the 'energy vibration' of a rock; see ibid., Chapter 10, p. 168. I do not believe that a rock has a soul as such, but it almost certainly forms a part of the integrated energy or even consciousness of the universe. These issues will be explored in Part 3.

19. Ibid., Chapter 11, p. 193.

20. The origins of Hindu beliefs about karma and reincarnation, for example, can be found in the 'Bhagavad-Gita', one of the books of the epic *Mahabharata* that we will discuss in more detail in a later chapter.

21. A prime example of a subject who chose to incarnate in the body of a girl that she knew would lose the use of her legs in an accident, which choice was in no sense a punishment but a learning experience, is provided in Newton, *Journey of Souls*, Chapter 13, pp. 227–9.

22. For discussion of extraterrestrial incarnations see ibid., Chapter 3, p. 41, Chapter 10, p. 157, and Chapter 11, pp. 190–3.

CHAPTER 3: DEBASEMENT AND DESTRUCTION

1. For a discussion of the various texts known to have formed the basis for the Torah we now have, see Campbell, *Occidental Mythology*, Chapter 3, pp. 100–2.

2. See the lengthy paper entitled 'Long Live the King' on my website at <www.ianlawton.com/guindex.htm> for a fuller discussion of this issue.

3. See ibid.

4. Fagan, personal communication, 23 February 2001.

5. This verse, although not central to my current argument, has caused a great deal of confusion. A similar passage from the Dead Sea Scrolls, however, sorts it out: 'In the four hundred and eightieth year of Noah's life, he came to the end of them, and God said, "My spirit shall not dwell with man forever, their days shall be determined to be one hundred and twenty years until the waters of the flood come." ' This fits in with Noah being six hundred years old at the time of the flood,

as reported in Genesis 7:6. See Wise et al., *The Dead Sea Scrolls*, Part 2, Section 44, p. 275, and also Saint Augustine, *The City of God* 15.24.

6. von Däniken, *Chariots of the Gods*, Chapter 4, p. 61.

7. Ibid., plates section.

8. I might note that Sitchin uses the '120 years' in Genesis 6:3 to date the arrival of the Nephilim to 432,000 years before the flood, interpreting these years as 'sars' of 3600 years each; see *The Twelfth Planet*, Chapter 8, pp. 227–9. I have already discussed the proper interpretation of this verse in a previous note, which indicates that Sitchin's version is a nonsense.

9. Although there is insufficient space to provide detailed support for these strong allegations here, I do provide it in a number of papers published or referenced on my website at <www.ianlawton.com/mesindex.htm>. It is worth pointing out that, as far as I am aware, Sitchin has never deigned to respond to any of his linguistic critics in any detail at all.

10. The finest example of this is Sitchin's suggestion that Howard Vyse faked the infamous 'Khufu quarry marks' in the Great Pyramid – which appears to be largely a fabrication of his own that other authors continue to perpetuate in attempting to justify an older date for the edifice. We will discuss this more in Part 2.

11. We will discuss the age of the Sphinx in more detail in Part 2. Note that Collins, while still believing the orthodox dating to be wrong, is now more circumspect about exactly how old it might be; nevertheless he continues to support his 'out of Egypt' hypothesis.

12. For a summary of his chronology see Collins, *From the Ashes of Angels*, Chart 3, pp. 345–6. I should also note that prior to this, in his 1985 work *The Genius Of The Few* and the follow-up *The Shining Ones*, exploration geologist Christian O'Brien devoted considerable time to reinterpreting in particular the little-known Mesopotamian *Kharsag Epics*, along with various other better-known Mesopotamian and Judaic texts, from which he postulates that a well-educated group of fair-skinned Atlantean survivors settled in South Lebanon and began the post-catastrophe rebuilding process. While I have similar chronological and contextual problems with this analysis, I must point out that O'Brien's attempts at retranslation *do* appear to be of a high scholastic standard, and also that, while he tends towards a somewhat technological interpretation of their achievements, unusually he combines this with a high degree of respect for their spirituality. Further research and reprinting of his work is being undertaken by researcher Edmund Marriage – for more information see <www.goldenageproject.org.uk>.

13. Genesis 4:16–24.

14. Ancient History of the Jews 2; see Murray, *History of the Jews*, Volume 1, pp. 26–7.

15. *The City of God* 15.22; a full translation is available at <www.ccel.org>.

16. See Laurence's introductory notes to his 1883 translation of *The Book of Enoch*, pp. iv–vi.

17. All these texts contain a messiah figure who is described and acts in very similar ways to Jesus, but clearly predates or at least is not the same person as him. This, of course, casts severe doubt on the Christian insistence that he was the uniquely divine 'saviour of humankind'.

18. *The City of God* 15.23. The original Latin is 'ob nimiam antiquitatem'. Madame Blavatsky, whom we will meet properly in Part 2, makes this and a number of other interesting points in *The Secret Doctrine*, Volume 2, Part 2, Chapter 21, p. 535.

19. 1 Enoch 7; see Laurence, *The Book of Enoch*, pp. 5–7.

20. 1 Enoch 8; see ibid., pp. 7–8.
21. Collins, *From the Ashes of Angels*, Chapter 1, p. 3.
22. The Ethiopian and Slavonic versions are normally referred to as '1 Enoch' and '2 Enoch' respectively. Meanwhile the Enochian *Book of Giants* is a fragmented text forming part of the Dead Sea Scrolls, and in that it appears to distort any original message by accusing the fallen angels of bestiality, emphasising the giant stature of their offspring, and even naming one of them, intriguingly, as Gilgamesh, it has little relevance to our current discussion; see Wise et al., *The Dead Sea Scrolls*, Part 2, Section 33, pp. 246–50.
23. These ideas are expounded in the descriptions of Enoch's visionary trip to, in particular, the second and fifth 'heavens' in 2 Enoch 7 and 18, and even more in the footnoted commentary that accompanies it; see Morfill and Charles, *The Book of the Secrets of Enoch*, especially pp. 20–2.
24. Further familiar descriptions of the forthcoming flood can be found throughout the text – for example, in 53:7–11. Still, as a whole it contains virtually none of the details of the ark and its contents, of the duration of the flood, and of what happened when the ark came to rest that are found in Genesis and elsewhere.
25. 1 Enoch 10:1–5; see Laurence, *The Book of Enoch*, p. 10.
26. 1 Enoch 10:6–29; see ibid., pp. 10–13.
27. 1 Enoch 82:4–10 and 83:5–8; see ibid., pp. 118–19 and 120–1.
28. 1 Enoch 90:6–7; see ibid., pp. 146–7.
29. This idea of multiple destructions is echoed in 2 Enoch 35; see Morfill and Charles, *The Book of the Secrets of Enoch*, pp. 49–50.
30. 1 Enoch 54:1–3; see Laurence, *The Book of Enoch*, p. 61; see also Genesis 9:8–17.
31. 1 Enoch 64:1–3 and 9; see ibid., pp. 78–9.
32. 1 Enoch 79:3–7; see ibid., pp. 110–11.
33. For more information, see editor Robinson's introduction to *The Nag Hammadi Library*, which is the most recent compilation of scholars' translations of the various tractates.
34. Ibid., pp. 121–2. Although it adds nothing of interest, the only other Gnostic text to directly describe the fallen angels' perversion of humankind is *On the Origin of the World*; see ibid., p. 186.
35. Ibid., p. 121.
36. This idea is expressed in, for example, *The Hypostasis of the Archons*; see ibid., p. 169.
37. More details about the background to ancient Mesopotamia, the excavations, the decipherment of the various scripts, and the pantheon of gods are available in a number of papers that I have prepared on my website at <www.ianlawton.com/mesindex.htm>. I have also prepared summaries of the various Sumerian and Akkadian literary texts, which are too numerous to list here. The main source for translations of the former is Thorkild Jacobsen's 1987 work *The Harps That Once . . . Sumerian Poetry in Translation*, and of the latter Stephanie Dalley's 1991 work *Myths from Mesopotamia*.
38. For confirmation of the fact that Marduk only emerged as a major deity under the Babylonians see Dalley, *Myths from Mesopotamia*, p. 229.
39. Ibid., pp. 9–35; see especially pp. 18–24.
40. Jacobsen, *The Harps That Once . . .*, pp. 145–50.
41. Dalley, *Myths from Mesopotamia*, pp. 109–16.
42. Erra and Ishum 4; see ibid., p. 306.

43. Erra and Ishum 3; see ibid., pp. 299 and 301.

44. Ibid., Glossary (s.v. Seven Sages), p. 328.

45. Erra and Ishum 1 and 2; see ibid., pp. 291 and 294.

46. Ibid., Glossary (s.v. Apsu), p. 318.

47. Erra and Ishum 1 and 5; see ibid., pp. 291 and 311.

48. Erra and Ishum 1; see ibid., p. 290.

49. Campbell, *Oriental Mythology*, Chapter 4, p. 155.

50. Campbell, *Primitive Mythology*, Chapter 10, p. 435, and *Oriental Mythology*, Chapter 4, p. 206.

51. Campbell, *Oriental Mythology*, Chapter 4, pp. 200–6.

52. See Feuerstein et al., *In Search of the Cradle of Civilisation*. Chapter 9 deals with the Aryan invasion theory; Chapter 2 emphasises the importance and antiquity of the *Vedas* and contains a fine introduction to the various categories of Indian text; and Chapter 7 discusses the Indus script.

53. Prasad, *The Fountainhead of Religion*, Conclusion, p. 171.

54. Ibid., Chapter 5, p. 87, Footnote 1.

55. See, for example, O'Flaherty, *The Rig Veda*, p. 37, Note 11: 'The Asuras are the ancient dark divinities, at first the elder brothers and then the enemies of the gods (Devas).' Also p. 212, Note 9: 'Asura not in its later sense of "demon" but in its earlier sense of sky god.' And finally, p. 29, Note 9: 'The two opposed masses are armies, the polarised forces of gods and demons (Asuras) . . .'

56. Prasad, *The Fountainhead of Religion*, Chapter 5, p. 87, Footnote 1.

57. Rig Veda 10.124; see O'Flaherty, *The Rig Veda*, pp. 110–12.

CHAPTER 4: THE ARTS OF CIVILISATION

1. 1 Enoch 64:6; see Laurence, *The Book of Enoch*, p. 78. See also 1 Enoch 64:10, 68:10, and 68:20, ibid., pp. 79, 85, and 86.

2. The various commentaries on Berossus' work were compiled by Cory in 1832 in *Ancient Fragments*, and are also reproduced by Temple in the 1998 edition of *The Sirius Mystery*, Appendix 3, pp. 548–63. See in particular the Polyhistor fragments on pp. 551–2.

3. Ibid., Appendix 3, p. 562.

4. Collins and others have suggested that Oannes is the Greek for Enki himself, via his Akkadian name Ea. Dalley, however, is quite clear that the name Oannes is the Greek form of Uan, another Akkadian name for Adapa, and that he is to be thought of as Enki's son. See Collins, *Gods of Eden*, Chapter 19, p. 293, and Dalley, *Myths from Mesopotamia*, Glossary (s.v. Adapa and Oannes), pp. 317 and 326.

5. Dalley, *Myths from Mesopotamia*, pp. 182–8.

6. Ibid., p. 2.

7. Erra and Ishum 2; see ibid., p. 292.

8. Kramer, *The Sumerians*, Chapter 4, p. 116. He provides a full list of the translated *me's*.

9. Campbell, *Primitive Mythology*, Chapter 10, pp. 454–5.

10. This is discussed in ibid., Chapter 10, p. 457.

11. Berossus fragments recorded by Polyhistor; see Temple, *The Sirius Mystery*, Appendix 3, p. 554.

12. Ancient History of the Jews 2; see Murray, *History of the Jews*, Volume 1, p. 29.

13. Ibid., Volume 1, 'Autobiography of Flavius Josephus', p. 1.

14. Robinson, *The Nag Hammadi Library*, pp. 396–401.

15. 2 Enoch 40; see Morfill and Charles, *The Book of the Secrets of Enoch*, pp. 53–5.

16. Hall, *The Secret Teachings of All Ages*, 'Freemasonic Symbolism', p. 173. I am at a loss to establish the original source of Hall's more detailed information, however, either from his own work or from anyone else's. See also Collins, *From the Ashes of Angels*, Endnote 10 to Chapter 2, pp. 384–5, in which he discusses the background to Enochian traditions in Masonry. In addition, Madame Blavatsky once again has much to say on the topic of Enoch and the knowledge he preserved in *The Secret Doctrine*, Volume 2, Part 2, Chapter 21, pp. 529–35.

17. Lawton and Ogilvie-Herald, *Giza: The Truth*, Chapter 1, pp. 16–17.

18. Ibid., Chapter 5, pp. 223–37.

19. This is described at the outset of the *Kore Kosmu*; see Scott, *Hermetica*, Stobaeus Excerpt 23, pp. 179–80; and also p. 191.

20. Reymond, *The Mythical Origin of the Egyptian Temple*, Chapter 1, p. 9. She also references Boylan, *Thoth, the Hermes of Egypt*, pp. 92–7.

CHAPTER 5: THE GOLDEN AGE

1. Ancient History of the Jews 2; see Murray, *History of the Jews*, Volume 1, p. 28.

2. 2 Enoch 31:2; see Morfill and Charles, *The Book of the Secrets of Enoch*, p. 44.

3. Jacobsen, *The Harps That Once . . .* , pp. 181–204, and especially pp. 185–6. Kramer, in *The Sumerians*, Chapter 4, pp. 147–9, suggests that the original paradise might have been conceived as somewhere far to the east, perhaps in India, which perhaps ties in with the theosophical perspective that we will consider in Part 2 that this is where a spiritual worldview was most reintroduced *after* the catastrophe – although we should not lose sight of the fact that all the golden age traditions place it in an *antediluvian* context. As an aside he also draws some interesting comparisons between this text and the biblical version of the creation of Eve from Adam's rib.

4. The major breakthrough came when Jean François Champollion managed to decipher the multilingual Rosetta Stone in the early nineteenth century.

5. Translations of all these are readily available. For the first two see Wallis Budge, *The Egyptian Heaven and Hell*, and for the remainder see the translations by Faulkner under the original titles.

6. Rundle Clark, *Myth and Symbol in Ancient Egypt*, Chapter 8, pp. 263–4. In *Keeper of Genesis* the Egyptian phrase is rendered as *zep tepi* instead of *tep zepi*, for reasons unknown.

7. Reymond, *The Mythical Origin of the Egyptian Temple*, Chapter 1, pp. 6–11.

8. See the essay on Egypt by Baines and Pinch in Willis, *World Mythology*, p. 41. Although the name of the source text is not provided, it is apparently inscribed on one of the shrines in the tomb of Tutankhamun, and also on the walls of later royal tombs.

9. Campbell, *Oriental Mythology*, Chapter 6, p. 327.

10. Ramayana 1; see Dutt, *The Ramayana and the Mahabharata*, pp. 1–3.

11. See Legge, *Sacred Books of China*, 'Confucian Texts', Parts 1–4 in Müller, *The Sacred Books of the East*, Volumes 3, 16, 27, and 28; and ibid., 'Taoist Texts', Parts 1–2 in ibid., Volumes 39 and 40.

12. Kwang Tze 12; see ibid., Volume 39, pp. 325–6.

13. Kwang Tze 9; see ibid., Volume 39, p. 278.

14. Morgan, *Essays from Huai Nan Tzu*, pp. 35–6.

15. Ibid., pp. 80–2.

16. Works and Days 108–122; see West, *Hesiod: Theogony and Works and Days*, p. 40.

17. Metamorphosis 1:88–111; see Melville, *Ovid: Metamorphosis*, pp. 3–4.

18. Edda 1; see Young, *The Prose Edda*, pp. 37 and 40.

19. It is interesting to note, however, that the prologue to Snorri's *Edda* seems to have been written as a sop to Christianity that is in complete contrast to the convoluted and more indigenous tradition of multiple world ages contained in the main body of the work. It still appears to follow up on the Enochian theme of two world catastrophes, the first being 'Noah's Flood', but by contrast the second is reported as already having taken place since then in history. However, it does contain references to how the second race 'left off paying homage to God', 'lost the very name of God', and 'had not been given spiritual understanding', which, although apparently distorted out of their proper context, are hardly unrelated to my main theme. See ibid., pp. 23–4.

20. Critias 5; see Lee, *Plato: Timaeus and Critias*, p. 145.

CHAPTER 6: ROUND AND ROUND WE GO

1. Works and Days 123–201; see West, *Hesiod: Theogony and Works and Days*, pp. 40–2.

2. Metamorphosis 1:112–162; see Melville, *Ovid: Metamorphosis*, pp. 4–6.

3. I might note that a related tradition of multiple world ages is contained in the *Sibylline Oracles*, a proliferation of texts from the fourth century BC onwards that originated variously in Egypt, the Near East, and Europe, and even held a degree of authority for the early Christian Church. Book 1 of these oracles describes five 'generations' before the flood, and several thereafter. See Collins, 'The Sibylline Oracles' in Charlesworth, *The Old Testament Pseudepigrapha*, Volume 1, pp. 335–42.

4. Timaeus 2; see Lee, *Plato: Timaeus and Critias*, pp. 35–6.

5. Critias 2; see ibid., pp. 131–2.

6. Mackenzie, *Myths of China and Japan*, Chapter 15, p. 276.

7. Tao Teh King 18; see Legge, *Sacred Books of China*, 'Taoist Texts', Part 1 in Müller, *The Sacred Books of the East*, Volume 39, pp. 60–1.

8. These extracts are taken from the lengthy description provided in Waters, *Book of the Hopi*, Part 1, pp. 11–21.

9. Leyenda de los Soles 75:1–77:32; see Bierhorst, *History and Mythology of the Aztecs*, pp. 142–7. See also Thompson, *Maya History and Religion*, Chapter 9, pp. 331–3.

10. This idea of the gods smelling the food that the survivors first cook is found in every Near Eastern flood tradition.

11. Anales de Cuauhtitlan 2:24–49; see Bierhorst, *History and Mythology of the Aztecs*, p. 26.

12. Thompson, *Maya Hieroglyphic Writing*, Chapter 1, p. 10.

13. Severin, 'The Paris Codex: Decoding an Astronomical Ephemeris', Chapter 5, pp. 68–9, in *Transactions of the American Philosophical Society* 71 (1981), Part 5.

14. No English translation of this text is readily available, and my source is an Italian version published in 1900; see *Il Manoscritto Messicano Vaticano 3738, Detto Il Codice Rios*, Folios 4–7, pp. 24–5. Note that there appears to be some confusion about these numbers: Thompson quotes a total of 18,028 years (see *Maya Hieroglyphic Writing*, Chapter 1, p. 10), while revisionist authors Gilbert

and Cotterell quote 4081 and 5026 years for the last two ages (see *The Mayan Prophecies*, Chapter 4, pp. 71–2).

15. Ibid., Folio 4, p. 24.

16. I was unable to locate this section in the Italian translation due to my limited grasp of the Italian language, but it is cited in Spence, *History of Atlantis*, Chapter 10, p. 157 (he provides no source).

17. Alexander, 'Latin American Mythology', Chapter 7, p. 240, in Gray, *The Mythology of All Races*, Volume 11. The sources quoted are: de Molina, 'An Account of the Fables and Rights of the Yncas' translated in Markham, *Rites and Laws of the Yncas* (London, 1873). Cieza de Leon, 'Segunda parte de la cronica del Peru' (Seville, 1553), translated in Markham, *The Second Part of the Chronicle of Peru* (London, 1883), Chapter 5, pp. 5–10. Sarmiento, *History of the Incas*, translated in Markham (Cambridge, 1907), pp. 27–39. And Pietschmann, 'Some Account of the Illustrated Chronicle by the Peruvian Indian, D. Felipe Huaman Poma de Ayala', *Comptes rendus du Congres des Americanistes* 18 (London, 1913), pp. 511–12.

18. Thompson, *Maya Hieroglyphic Writing*, Chapter 1, pp. 23–6.

19. See, for example, Gilbert and Cotterell, *The Mayan Prophecies*, Chapter 2, p. 37.

20. Again, see ibid.

21. Mahabharata 3.188.22 ff; see Ray, *The Mahabharata*, Volume 2, pp. 557–8.

22. Ibid., Volume 2, pp. 558–62 and 571–81.

23. Mahabharata 12.231.11–32; see ibid., Volume 7, pp. 235–7.

24. Vishnu Purana 1.3 and 6.3; see Dutt, *Vishnu Purana*, pp. 12–3 and 434–7. See also Dimmitt and van Buitenen, *Classical Hindu Mythology*, Chapter 1, pp. 19–24 and 36–43; and Wilkins, *Hindu Mythology*, Chapter 10, pp. 353–60.

25. I do not intend to describe all of these variations, preferring to concentrate on the more original documents. However, an excellent discussion paper that provides far more detail is available at < http://users.deltanet.com/lumiere/karma/yuga.htm >.

26. Keith, 'Indian Mythology', Chapter 8, p. 221, in Gray, *The Mythology of All Races*, Volume 6.

27. For more details on the Jain cycle, see Campbell, *Oriental Mythology*, Chapter 4, pp. 220–3.

28. Baines and Pinch in Willis, *World Mythology*, p. 41. Note that this cycle is connected with the traditions surrounding the death and rebirth of the legendary phoenix; for more information see R Van Den Broek, *The Myth of the Phoenix* (E J Brill, 1972).

29. At the very least this would have occurred while the Jewish people were held in captivity in Babylon in the sixth century BC. For more information see Collins, *From the Ashes of Angels*, Chapter 7.

30. Campbell, *Oriental Mythology*, Chapter 5, p. 244.

31. Ibid., Chapter 4, p. 219.

32. Ibid., Chapter 1, pp. 7–8.

CHAPTER 7: TAKING ON THE EXPERTS

1. Campbell, *Oriental Mythology*, Chapter 3, pp. 127–8.

2. Of course, it is also clear that the time periods involved in the precessional model are based on accurate and direct observation, whereas the universal cycles model

has no similar basis. However, Campbell and others have attempted to establish mathematical and calendrical links between the two models' primary time references of 25,920 and 432,000 years respectively, and these links do appear to be in evidence in the numbers used in various versions of the Mesopotamian king lists. For more information, see the paper 'Long Live The King' on my website at <www.ianlawton.com/guindex.htm>, and also ibid., Chapter 3, pp. 116, 120 and 129 (the latter referring to an analysis by Oppert in his paper *The Dates of Genesis*). Nevertheless, even if some form of relatively late mathematical link does appear to exist it does not necessarily imply that the two models originally shared a common philosophical framework.

3. Campbell, *Oriental Mythology*, Chapter 7, p. 395.
4. Eliade, *Myth and Reality*, Chapter 4, p. 55. He goes on to discuss the various world age theories, and then the Judaeo-Christian apocalyptic traditions, in pp. 60–8, but nowhere do we receive any additional explanation for these themes. For more information see also his earlier work *The Myth of the Eternal Return*.
5. Eliade, *The Sacred and the Profane*, Chapter 3, pp. 130–1.
6. Eliade, *Myth and Reality*, Chapter 4, p. 69.

CHAPTER 8: CREATION CONFUSION

1. Jacobsen, *The Harps That Once . . .* , pp. 151–66; see especially pp. 154 and 157.
2. Atrahasis 1; see Dalley, *Myths from Mesopotamia*, pp. 15–16.
3. Waters, *Book of the Hopi*, Part 1, pp. 8–9.
4. Epic of Gilgamesh 1; see Dalley, *Myths from Mesopotamia*, pp. 52–3.
5. Epic of Creation 6; see ibid., p. 261.
6. Berossus fragments recorded by Polyhistor; see Temple, *The Sirius Mystery*, Appendix 3, pp. 553–4.
7. Genesis 1:26–27.
8. Genesis 2:7 and 2:20–2.
9. For Campbell's commentary on the *Birth of Man*, see *Oriental Mythology*, Chapter 3, pp. 108–11; on the *Epic of Creation*, see *Occidental Mythology*, Chapter 2, pp. 84–5; and on the *Epic of Gilgamesh*, see *Occidental Mythology*, Chapter 2, pp. 87–90.
10. Campbell, *Occidental Mythology*, Chapter 2, pp. 85–6.
11. Campbell, *Oriental Mythology*, Chapter 3, p. 103.
12. There are a number of similar if less detailed accounts of multiple creations or world ages in Mayan tradition; see Thompson, *Maya History and Religion*, Chapter 9, pp. 336–73.
13. Popol Vuh 1 and 4; see Tedlock, *Popol Vuh*, pp. 66–73 and 145–8.
14. Genesis 3:22.
15. Robinson, *The Nag Hammadi Library*, p. 116. However, with typical inconsistency the Gnostics also display far greater spiritual awareness when they report in the same text that Adam himself was taught about his 'descent' into manifestation, and about the 'way of ascent' back into the spiritual realm.
16. Campbell, *Oriental Mythology*, Chapter 3, p. 107, and *Occidental Mythology*, Chapter 3, pp. 106–9.
17. Despite all the distortions, this view is confirmed by a careful reading of the succeeding passages of the *Apocryphon of John*, and also of the account of the 'first fall' in the *Hypostasis of the Archons* 89–90; see Robinson, *The Nag Hammadi Library*, pp. 164–5.
18. Waters, *Book of the Hopi*, Part 1, pp. 5–9.

19. Dixon, 'Oceanic Mythology', Part 3, Chapter 1, pp. 174–6, in Gray, *The Mythology of All Races*, Volume 9.

20. Berossus fragments recorded by Polyhistor; see Temple, *The Sirius Mystery*, Appendix 3, p. 553.

21. Heidel, *The Gilgamesh Epic and Old Testament Parallels*, Chapter 2, pp. 132–3. This text does not appear to be included in the standard compendiums of either Dalley or Jacobsen. They do contain texts in which, for example, Dumuzi, Inanna, and Gilgamesh respectively visit the underworld, but none of these contains similar descriptions.

22. As an example of the former, in *The Sirius Mystery* revisionist author Robert Temple attempts to interpret these accounts of composite beings literally, comparing them with the amphibious 'Nommo' gods of the Dogon tribe of Africa and suggesting that they came from the Sirius star system. Meanwhile, Madame Blavatsky is at the forefront of those who suggest that these composite beings were at one time 'indigenous' inhabitants of the earth.

23. The only other possibility comes from Michael Newton's subjects, who sometimes report having incarnated as strange chimeric creatures; he suggests that some of these elements of ancient mythology could derive from shared memories of human souls in incarnations on other planets; see *Journey of Souls*, Chapter 10, p. 168.

CHAPTER 9: ARE WE SPECIAL?

1. The main source of this data is Richard Klein's 1999 work *The Human Career*, although the earlier dates are rounded to the nearest five million years.

2. One of the principal founders of this school is microbiologist Michael Behe, whose 1996 work *Darwin's Black Box* is a prime source for their arguments.

3. By Stephen Jay Gould in the 1980s; see the bibliography for details of his major works.

4. For more information, see for example the article by Gabrielle Walker entitled 'Snowball Earth', *New Scientist*, 6 November 1999.

5. The finest detailed defence of general evolutionary theory that I have yet come across is Daniel Dennett's 1995 work *Darwin's Dangerous Idea*, although he is of course supported by numerous scholars, including most notably Richard Dawkins. For more details see the bibliography.

6. Quoted in Cremo and Thompson, *Hidden History*, Chapter 1, p. 4.

7. Leakey, *The Origin of Humankind*, Chapter 1.

8. As an example of the prevailing Ramapithecus-inspired climate, in 1973 Bjorn Kurten, a colleague of Gould's, produced a book entitled *Not from the Apes* that argued that apes were descended from humans rather than the other way around, and that the divergence occurred thirty-five million years ago – even though he was clearly an evolutionist.

9. The discovery of the remains of 'millennium man' or *Orrorin tugenensis* in Kenya in 2000, which are six million years old, have tended to confirm this hypothesis.

10. Although the recent discovery of a complete six-million-year-old primate skull by a Franco-Chadian team in the Djourab desert in northern Chad – that is, to the *west* of the Great Rift Valley – may put the whole East Africa theory in doubt, because although it has not yet been positively identified as hominid, apparently its brain capacity suggests that it is; see the *Independent*, 1 August 2001.

11. Because I comment in some critical detail on their work in this and the next few chapters, I should indicate that I do have a copy of both. Because the intricate detail

of the original does not materially affect our consideration of the arguments, however, and because *Hidden History* is less formidable to the general reader, my references are all to the latter.

12. Cremo and Thompson, *Hidden History*, jacket text.

13. Ibid., Introduction, p. xix.

14. Cremo, *Forbidden Archaeology's Impact*, Section 3.1.2.1, pp. 198–9; he is responding to a critical review by palaeoanthropologist Colin Groves.

15. This suggestion seems to be corroborated when he suggests elsewhere that we are currently in the twenty-eighth maha yuga of the seventh manvantara (to confirm the rough arithmetic, refer back to Figure 3); see ibid., Section 1.1, p. 6.

16. For a fuller explanation of these criticisms, see the paper entitled 'Problems With Anomalous Human Remains' on my website at < www.ianlawton.com/guindex.htm >. The most complete rebuttal, which includes highly detailed case studies, is provided by archaeological researcher Michael Brass in his 2002 work *The Antiquity of Man*.

17. I would also suggest that we should not be sidetracked by the ongoing search for 'Planet X' being conducted by some highly respected astronomers; we should concentrate instead on what this planet would be like to live on, even if it is one day discovered. As for my more general criticisms of Sitchin's work, once again see the various papers on my website at < www.ianlawton.com/mesindex.htm >.

18. Sitchin, *The Twelfth Planet*, Chapter 12, and *Genesis Revisited*, Chapter 8.

19. Alford, *Gods of the New Millennium*, Chapter 2, and Baigent, *Ancient Traces*, Chapter 5.

20. It is interesting to note that some abductees report that their extraterrestrial hosts actually inform them that humankind was originally created by genetic experiment; see, for example, Colin Wilson's *Alien Dawn*, Chapter 8, p. 230. The same is true of many channelled messages from supposed extraterrestrials. I would suggest that these are either the direct result of the modern cultural influence of exposure to ufology and to Interventionist theories, whereby the recipients of these messages misinterpret their essentially spiritual nature and origin, or that the 'extraterrestrials' are playing mind games; both possibilities will be examined further in later chapters. For further explanation of how spiritual phenomena can be mistakenly interpreted as extraterrestrial see, for example, the various works by Jacques Vallée listed in the bibliography, and the paper by psychologist Kenneth Ring entitled 'Near-Death and UFO Encounters as Shamanic Initiations', *ReVision* 11, Number 3 (1989).

21. The source is an article entitled 'The Genome Project' in the *Independent*, 12 February 2001, p. 3.

CHAPTER 10: DEFINING THE WINDOW

1. Leakey, *The Origin of Humankind*, Chapter 2, pp. 29–30. Much of what follows in the next two sections is a brief summary of ibid., Chapters 2–5.

2. For more details on the various australopiths, once again see Klein's *The Human Career*.

3. The *Kenyanthropus* skull, which still has only a small australopith-type cranial capacity, was discovered in 1999 near the Lomekwi River in northern Kenya by a member of a Leakey expedition team. Because the skull is much flatter and has smaller teeth than an australopith skull, this genus is now the most likely candidate as the ancestor of the *Homo* line. See Leakey et al., 'New Hominid Genus from

Eastern Africa Shows Diverse Middle Pliocene Lineages', *Nature*, 22 March 2001, pp. 433–40.

4. A diagram of the two major versions of the early family tree (pre-Kenyanthropus) can be found in Leakey, *The Origin of Humankind*, Chapter 2, p. 44.

5. Another species that is sometimes distinguished from *Homo habilis* is *Homo rudolfensis*.

6. Because eoliths are hard to distinguish from naturally occurring flint flakes, the genuine items are more accurately referred to as Oldowan Industry tools.

7. Palaeoliths are more accurately referred to as Acheulian Industry tools. Also, a distinction is sometimes made between *Homo erectus* in Asia and *Homo ergaster* in Africa.

8. Some multi-regionalists even subsume *archaic Homo*, *Homo neandertalensis*, and *Homo erectus* into the broad category of *Homo sapiens*, and distinguish thoroughly modern humankind as *Homo sapiens sapiens*. It is because of this confusion that I tend to avoid the 'sapiens' terminology.

9. See the map in Leakey, *The Origin of Humankind*, Chapter 5, p. 115.

10. A prime modern exponent of this view is Hillary Deacon; see, for example, her 1999 work *Human Beginnings in South Africa*.

11. See Oefner et al. in the *Proceedings of the National Academy of Sciences*, June 2000.

12. See Ambrose's article 'Late Pleistocene human population bottlenecks, volcanic winter, and differentiation of modern humans', *Journal of Human Evolution* 35 (1998), pp. 115–18.

13. The orthodox anthropological view of the development of consciousness and language, to the extent that there is one in such a controversial area, can be found in Leakey, *The Origin of Humankind*, Chapters 7 and 8; much of what follows in this section is taken from this source. More details of the orthodox debates from the perspective of a staunchly atheist evolutionist is provided by Dennett in *Darwin's Dangerous Idea*, Part 3.

14. See the bibliography for details.

15. Leakey mentions the skulls of an *archaic Homo* dating to three or four hundred thousand years ago, and of a *Homo erectus* dating to nearly two million years ago. He also mentions that the flatter basicrania of Neanderthals could suggest they were a regressed species in terms of language – more so than *archaic Homo* and even *Homo erectus* – but this suggestion remains highly contentious. See *The Origin of Humankind*, Chapter 7, pp. 166–8.

16. Ibid., Chapter 7, p. 163. For an overview of these anatomical developments, see the diagram on p. 173.

17. Ibid., Chapter 5, p. 114.

18. See Richard Rudgley's 1999 work *Lost Civilisations of the Stone Age*, Chapter 16, p. 214. Prior to these recent discoveries in the Qafzeh and Skhul Caves, the earliest signs of deliberate burial were from both Neanderthal and modern human sites in Europe and the Near East dating to between eighty thousand and seventy thousand years ago.

19. Campbell, *Primitive Mythology*, Chapter 8, pp. 341–9.

20. Leakey, *The Origin of Humankind*, Chapter 6, p. 131.

21. Ibid., Chapter 6, p. 132.

22. Kuhn et al., 'Ornaments of the Earliest Upper Paleolithic: New Insights from the Levant', *Proceedings of the National Academy of Sciences*, 5 June 2001.

23. Campbell, *Primitive Mythology*, Chapter 7, pp. 287–8, and Chapter 8, pp. 313–5 and 323–30. I should note that Leakey suggests that this homogeneous view has

now been discredited by the huge variety of forms discovered; see *The Origin of Humankind*, Chapter 6, p. 132.

24. Rudgley, *Lost Civilisations of the Stone Age*, Chapter 10, pp. 151–2.

25. For more information on Upper Paleolithic cave art see Leakey, *The Origin of Humankind*, Chapter 6; Campbell, *Primitive Mythology*, Chapter 8; and Abbé H Breuil, *Four Hundred Centuries of Cave Art*.

26. The research of Jean Clottes and David Lewis-Williams is described in their 1998 work *The Shamans of Prehistory: Trance and Magic in Painted Caves*. Similar rock paintings are found not only in South Africa but also in North Africa and in the Egyptian eastern desert, and some of these may have a similar shamanic function. They all appear to be more recent, however, being at most ten thousand years old.

27. The experiments conducted by Iegor Reznikoff and Michel Dauvois in the mid-1980s are described in Leakey, *The Origin of Humankind*, Chapter 6, pp. 139–40.

28. See ibid., Chapter 6, p. 143; and Campbell, *Primitive Mythology*, Chapter 3, p. 141, Chapter 8, p. 328, and Chapter 9, p. 376.

29. Pictures of a variety of these marks are reproduced in Michael Balfour's beautifully illustrated *Megalithic Mysteries*.

30. See, for example, Rudgley, *Lost Civilisations of the Stone Age*, Chapter 5.

31. The work of Lawrence Barham in the Twin Rivers cave is described by Elizabeth J Himelfarb in 'Prehistoric Body Paint', *Archaeology* 53, Number 4 (2000).

32. See, for example, Rudgley, *Lost Civilisations of the Stone Age*, Chapter 13.

33. The discovery by Naama Goren-Inbar is described in ibid., Chapter 18, pp. 235–7. The recent work of Francesco d'Errico and April Nowall, who subjected the rock to microscopic examination and discovered flint chisel marks, a variety of abrasions in the supposed neck, arm and breast areas, and a flattened base, is described in an article in the *Independent*, 25 September 2000.

34. Fullager, Price and Head, 'Early Human Occupation of Northern Australia: Archaeology and Thermoluminescence Dating of Jinmium Rock-shelter, Northern Territory', *Antiquity* 70, Number 270 (1996).

35. These dates are mainly taken from Klein's *The Human Career*, although I have revised the start of the Neolithic back from his 10,000 years ago based on recent discoveries. Note that many commentators still refer to a 'Mesolithic' stage lasting from somewhere between 11,500 and 6000 years ago in those parts of the world such as Western Europe that were late to develop settled agriculture.

36. For more information on Catal Hoyuk and Nevali Cori, see the index references in Collins' *From the Ashes of Angels* and *Gods of Eden*. In addition a variety of information on these sites and on Gobekli Tepe is available on various websites.

37. See 'First Farmers', *Archaeology* 53, Number 6 (2000). See also <www.france.diplomatie.fr/culture/culture_scientifique/archeologie/jerf_el_ahmar/index.html> and <www.cnrs.fr/Cnrspresse/Archeo2000/html/archeo11.htm>.

38. As well as supporting the notion that a rudimentary symbolic script was used throughout the Upper Paleolithic, and that protowriting existed in a variety of forms in the Neolithic, Rudgley argues that writing proper existed in parts of Neolithic Europe several thousand years before its emergence in Sumer; see *Lost Civilisations of the Stone Age*, Chapter 4.

39. Collins suggests that even earlier evidence of protoagriculture in the Isnan or Qadan cultures of upper Egypt, about 125 miles south of modern-day Aswan, dates back to 14,500 years ago; see *Gods of Eden*, Chapter 15, p. 216 (his primary source is Fred Wendorf and Romauld Schild's 1976 work *Prehistory of the Nile Valley*).

Meanwhile agricultural researcher Edmund Marriage argues (private conversation, 8 February 2003) that there is evidence of settled farming in even more remote epochs: such as, for example, the 42,000 year-old ochre-mining site at the Vaal River in South Africa that is associated with enclosed field systems, and North African sites in which goats were being domesticated at least 18,000 years ago, as shown by the fact that males were culled for food while females were spared to produce further offspring; however, I have not been able to further corroborate these suggestions at the time of writing.

40. For more information on the excavations at Tell Hamoukar see <www-oi.uchicago.edu/OI/PROJ/HAM/Hamoukar.html>.

CHAPTER 11: ANOMALOUS ARTEFACTS

1. Many modern revisionist authors tend, as I have already indicated, to concentrate on anomalies that are indicative of supposedly advanced technology, or on attempting to redate ancient monuments of our own epoch to an earlier one. This evidence will be considered separately in a later chapter.

2. Donnelly, *Ragnarok*, Part 4, Chapter 1, pp. 345–7. His source for the boat accounts is Edward Burnet Tylor's *Early History of Humankind* (London, 1865), p. 330 (it is on pp. 322–3 in the edition I consulted), although I should note that Allan and Delair, whose work I will discuss further in a later chapter, reference Cieza de Leon's *Chronicles of Peru*, Part 1, pp. xxxii and 367, as their source for the same account – a source that should be reasonably reliable. They also briefly reference two further ancient ship reports, one in Russia in Strahlenberg, P J, *A Historico-Geographical Description of the Northern Part of North and Eastern Europe and Asia* (London, 1738), p. 405, and the other in South Africa in 'Ship Discovered in the Earth in Africa', *Quarterly Journal of Literature, Science and Arts* 5 (1818), p. 150, s.v. General Literature and Miscellaneous Communications. See *When the Earth Nearly Died*, Part 6, p. 342, Endnotes 58–61. Meanwhile, for the pottery Donnelly's source is Foster's *Prehistoric Races of the United States*, p. 56; two other contemporary sources from which he quotes regularly are Sir John Lubbock's *Prehistoric Times* and Maclean's *Manual of Antiquity of Man*.

3. Ibid., Part 4, Chapter 1, p. 353. He also notes that marble is not found locally.

4. Ibid., Part 4, Chapter 1, p. 354. The article was by David A Curtis, 'The Mississippi River Problem', *Harper's Monthly Magazine*, September 1882, p. 609.

5. Ibid., Part 4, Chapter 1, pp. 355–8. The source is Winchell's *Sparks from a Geologist's Hammer*, p. 170.

6. Wilkins, *Secret Cities of Old South America*, Chapter 9, p. 417. Researcher Ulrich Magin has confirmed that, although Wilkins himself is not the most credible of sources, both Pontano and Fulgosa were genuine figures of the times stated. The former lived in Naples and wrote a book called *De Bello Neapolitano*, which may have been the source for this account, while the latter – who has been variously referred to as Fulgosus, Fregoso, and Fregosus – compiled a book of supposed anomalies entitled *De Dictis Factisque Memoralibus Collectanea*, which was published in Milan in 1509, and includes the ship report in Book 1, Chapter 6. See Magin, 'The Petrified Ship in a Swiss Mine: An Introduction to the Mystery of Out-of-Place Ships', *Fortean Studies* 5 (1998), pp. 74–8. Note that Magin includes a number of other 'ancient ship' accounts (see pp. 78–83), but – as he admits – the primary and secondary sources for all of these are highly unreliable.

7. Ibid., Chapter 9, p. 418.

8. Ibid., Chapter 9, p. 419.

9. Steiger, *Worlds Before Our Own*, Chapter 1, pp. 1–2 and 5.

10. Ibid., Chapter 2.

11. Ibid., Chapter 3.

12. Ibid., Chapters 5 and 8–10.

13. Ibid., Chapter 9, p. 143.

14. Ibid., Chapter 9, p. 146.

15. Ibid., Chapter 2, p. 17. His source is an extract from a letter by a Mr John Lubbock that appeared in *Nature*, 27 March 1873.

16. Ibid., plates section. Note that a lengthy report of this find was provided by G F Wright in 'The Idaho Find', *American Antiquarian* 11 (1889), pp. 379–81, which is reproduced in William Corliss' 1978 work, *Ancient Man*, Chapter 3, pp. 458–60. This latter compilation contains a wealth of original articles concerning not only anomalous artefacts, but also many of the reports of anomalous human remains that are cited by Cremo and Thompson.

17. Ibid., plates section.

18. Ibid., Chapter 1, p. 6.

19. Cremo and Thompson, *Hidden History*, Chapter 5, pp. 94–101.

20. This latter possibility appears to be reduced in that often the artefacts were supposedly found many hundreds of metres along horizontal shafts.

21. Cremo and Thompson, *Hidden History*, Chapter 6, pp. 104–22. These pages include a number of the reports that I have already cited, as well as photographs or drawings of some of the artefacts. A number of other reports – of, for example, fossilised shoe prints – are omitted from my summary because they deal with supposed artefacts that are probably, in my opinion, natural occurrences rather than human-made objects.

22. Brewster's report is reproduced in Corliss, *Ancient Man*, Chapter 4, pp. 651–2.

23. For a fuller discussion of the fraudulent environment in the US at the time, see the chapter 'Archaeology and Religion' in Williams' 1991 work *Fantastic Archaeology*. For a more general perspective on frauds and hoaxes in archaeology see once again Feder's *Frauds, Myths, and Mysteries*.

24. Baigent, *Ancient Traces*, Chapter 1, pp. 3–14; see especially pp. 13–14.

25. Investigator Hubert Malthaner tracked the original object down in 1973, however, and suggests that it is quite clearly a modern cast-iron product and that there is no evidence that it was ever found *embedded* in the coal at the foundry; see 'Not the Salzburg Steel Cube, but an Iron Object from Wolfsegg', *Pursuit* 6 (1973), pp. 90–3 (reproduced in Corliss, *Ancient Man*, Chapter 4, pp. 654–6).

26. Although Baigent mentions this object, the primary source I have used is Allan and Delair, *When the Earth Nearly Died*. In general, however, their discussion of anomalous artefacts in Part 6, Chapter 4, pp. 334–8, yields few new interesting cases other than those of ancient ships that I mentioned in a previous note.

27. Baigent, *Ancient Traces*, Introduction, pp. xi–xii. The source is quoted as Belitsky, S, Goren-Inbar, N, and Werker, E, 'A Middle Pleistocene Wooden Plank with Man-Made Polish', *Journal of Human Evolution* 20 (1991), pp. 349–53. Note that Goren-Inbar also discovered the extremely early figurine that I mentioned in a previous chapter.

28. The only source for this find that I could locate is at < www.creationevidence.org/ HomePage/Museum_Tour >.

29. Cremo and Thompson, *Hidden History*, Chapter 6, p. 103. Note that in the original *Forbidden Archaeology* these reports were demoted to an appendix only.

CHAPTER 12: CATASTROPHE!

1. Taken from the title page of Donnelly's *Ragnarok*.
2. Taken from Blyth and de Freitas, *A Geology for Engineers*, Figure 2.1.9, p. 29 (after E. Antevs).
3. See, for example, Rampino, M R, and Self, S, 'Volcanic Winter and Accelerated Glaciation Following the Toba Super-Eruption', *Nature* 359 (1992), pp. 50–2.
4. See the bibliography for details of their work. Palmer is chairman of the Society for Interdisciplinary Studies, a body set up in 1974 to investigate various aspects of catastrophism, and at various times in this chapter I broadly follow various aspects of his excellent review paper 'Catastrophes: The Diluvial Evidence', presented at the SIS Silver Jubilee conference at Easthamstead Park, 19 September 1999.
5. See, for example, Blanchon, P, and Shaw, J, 'Reef Drowning During the Last Deglaciation – Evidence for Catastrophic Sea-Level Rise and Ice-Sheet Collapse', *Geology* 23 (1995), pp. 4–8.
6. See, for example, Martin and Klein's excellent 1984 reference work *Quaternary Extinctions – A Prehistoric Revolution*, pp. 358–61.
7. Velikovsky's first major work, *Worlds in Collision*, was published in 1950, but it deals with the evidence for relatively recent catastrophes in the fifteenth and eighth millennia BC – the former being supposedly the result of Venus being ejected from Jupiter as a comet, although modern opinion is that a relatively major event occurred earlier, at around 2300 BC. In any case, these events are too recent to be relevant to our current inquiry.
8. Velikovsky, *Earth in Upheaval*, Chapter 1; his main sources for the Alaskan material are Rainey, F, 'Archaeological Investigation in Central Alaska', *American Antiquity* 5 (1940), and Hibben, F C, 'Evidence of Early Man in Alaska', *American Antiquity* 8 (1943); and for the Siberian material Whitley, D G, 'The Ivory Islands in the Arctic Ocean', *Journal of the Philosophical Society of Great Britain* 12 (1910).
9. Ibid., Chapter 2; his main source is Buckland's *Reliquiae Diluvianae*.
10. Ibid., Chapter 5; his source for much of the European material is Joseph Prestwich's 1895 work *On Certain Phenomena Belonging to the Close of the Last Geological Period*. Prestwich was a professor of geology at Oxford who investigated many of the sites himself.
11. We will discuss Hapgood's other major work, *Maps of the Ancient Sea Kings*, in a later chapter.
12. Hapgood, *The Path of the Pole*, Chapter 10, pp. 259–64.
13. Ibid., Chapter 10, pp. 272–5; unfortunately Hapgood does not provide a source for this information.
14. Ibid., Chapter 10, pp. 275–7; the source is Hibben's 1946 work *The Lost Americans*, pp. 90–2 and 176–8 (I have reproduced only part of the extract).
15. I am indebted to geologist Paul Heinrich for pointing me in the direction of this recent research in a personal communication dated 13 June 2001. A selection of the references he cites regarding the Alaskan muck are as follows: Guthrie, Dale, and Guthrie, M Lee, 'Death on the Steppe: The Case of the Frozen Bison', *New Scientist* 127, Number 1727 (1990), pp. 47–51; Westgate, J A, Stemper, B A, and Pewe, T L, 'A 3 m.y. Record of Pliocene-Pleistocene

Loess in Interior Alaska', *Geology* 18, Number 9 (1990), pp. 858–61; and Preece et al., 'Tephrochronology of Late Cenozoic Loess at Fairbanks, Alaska', *Geological Society of America Bulletin* 111, Number 1 (1999), pp. 71–90. He also suggests that, while no complete and single rebuttal of the evidence collated by Velikovsky has yet been prepared, further research into the individual cases can be usefully conducted using the GEOREF database at <www.lib.berkeley.edu/ EART/georef.html>. Meanwhile, his website contains a number of relevant papers and can be found at <www.intersurf.com/~heinrich/wildside.html>.

16. Velikovsky, *Earth in Upheaval*, Chapter 4, pp. 46–7.

17. Ibid., Chapter 4, pp. 48–9.

18. Ibid., Chapter 6, and Hapgood, *The Path of the Pole*, Chapter 9, Part 1, pp. 192–219.

19. Ibid., Chapter 6, pp. 81–3.

20. See Posnansky's 1957 work *Tiahuanacu: The Cradle of American Man*, Volume 2, pp. 90–1.

21. Posnansky revised his estimate of their age to around twelve thousand years. More recently, archaeoastronomer Neil Steede has suggested an age of seven to eleven thousand years; see <www.andrewcollins.net/page/conference/ speakers/speaker_steede.html>. By contrast, conventional archaeology dates the site to the beginning of the sixth century AD.

22. Although I do not support the entirety of their conclusions from this evidence, as we will see in the next section, Allan and Delair's 1995 work *When the Earth Nearly Died* provides detailed support for the physical evidence already described (see Parts 1 and 2). Schoch, whose geological analysis of the Sphinx enclosure lies at the heart of modern attempts to redate it, also provides ample support for the catastrophe argument in his 2000 work *Voices of the Rocks*.

23. For details of the former see the press release about the work of Benny Peiser and Michael Paine entitled 'Cosmic Impacts Punctuated Human Evolution', issued by Liverpool John Moores University, 17 April 2001; for the latter, see Paine, 'Source of the Australasian Tektites?' *Meteorite*, February 2001.

24. Velikovsky, *Earth in Upheaval*, Chapter 16, p. 264.

25. Ibid., Chapter 7, pp. 105–6; his main source is Pettersson's 1953 work *Westward Ho with the Albatross*.

26. Napier, 'Cometary Catastrophes, Cosmic Dust and Ecological Disasters in Historical Times – The Astronomical Framework' in Peiser et al., *Natural Catastrophes During Bronze Age Civilisations*, pp. 21–32.

27. Allan and Delair, *When the Earth Nearly Died*, Part 4, Chapters 15–17. Some of their diagrams and figures are almost identical to those in Sitchin's *The Twelfth Planet*.

28. This information was provided by geological engineer Colin Reader in a personal communication dated 4 March 2001.

29. Velikovsky, *Earth in Upheaval*, Chapter 7, pp. 98–9.

30. Melton and Shriever, 'The Carolina Bays – Are They Meteorite Scars?' *Journal of Geology* 41 (1933), pp. 52–66. This and all the following material about the bays is taken from Andrew Collins' excellent compilation of reports in *Gateway to Atlantis*, Chapters 21–2.

31. Prouty, 'Carolina Bays and their Origin', *Bulletin of the Geological Society of America* 63 (February 1952), pp. 167–222.

32. See Carson and Hussey, 'The Oriented Lakes of Arctic Alaska', *Journal of Geology* 70 (1962), pp. 417–39; Kelly, 'The Origin of the Carolina Bays and

the Oriented Lakes of Alaska', *Popular Astronomy* 59 (1951), p. 204; and Plafker, 'Oriented Lakes and Lineaments in Northern Bolivia', *Bulletin of the Geological Society of America* 75 (1964), pp. 503–22.

33. Ingram, Robinson, and Odum, 'Clay Mineralogy of some Carolina Bay Sediments', *Southeastern Geology* 1 (1959), pp. 1–10. I should note, however, that other studies documented by Collins yielded a significantly broader range of dates, although the Duke team's dates fell within them.

34. See, for example, Velikovsky, *Earth in Upheaval*, Chapter 4, pp. 40–4.

35. Ibid., Chapter 4, pp. 44–6.

36. Ibid., Chapter 8, p. 117.

37. Ibid., Chapter 8, pp. 124–8.

38. Hapgood, *The Path of the Pole*, Chapters 4 and 7; see in particular Figure 21, pp. 94–5.

39. Ibid., Chapter 1, pp. 40–3.

40. Velikovsky, *Earth in Upheaval*, Chapter 8, p. 127.

41. It is well known that Einstein, while not totally endorsing Hapgood's theory because of concerns about the mathematics of the forces necessary to shift the crust, nevertheless wrote the foreword to the first edition of *Earth's Shifting Crust*. It is less well known that Velikovsky shared considerable communication with the great man at the same time, as revealed by his acknowledgments at the start of *Earth in Upheaval*.

42. Barbiero, 'On the Possibility of Very Rapid Shifts of the Poles', *Aeon* 4, Number 6 (1997); see also < www.unibg.it/dmsia/dynamics/poles.html >.

43. Velikovsky provides a highly readable account of all these factors, and of the effects the influence of extraterrestrial bodies *could* have, in *Earth in Upheaval*, Chapter 9. There may be aspects of his detailed analysis that do not stand up to close scrutiny from specialists in astronomy, geology and other scientific disciplines – although I suspect less so with this work than his earlier one. However, his general arguments in favour of extraterrestrial bodies initiating catastrophes that involve a degree of axial shifting strike me as reasonable. Of course, it is *possible* that an impacting extraterrestrial body, at least on land, could attempt to cause a crustal displacement rather than an axis shift, but this would appear less likely because of the resistance of the mantle attachment and the equatorial bulge.

44. Barbiero, op. cit.

45. Hapgood, *The Path of the Pole*, Chapter 1, pp. 4–17.

46. See, for example, < http://istp.gsfc.nasa.gov/earthmag/reversal.htm >. An interesting discussion of these phenomena can also be found in Allan and Delair, *When the Earth Nearly Died*, Part 4, Chapters 4–5.

47. See, for example, Jacobsen's introduction to the 'Cylinders of Gudea' in *The Harps That Once* . . ., p. 387.

48. Dalley, *Myths from Mesopotamia*, Glossary (s.v. *abubu* and *kasusu*), pp. 317 and 324.

49. Jacobsen, *The Harps That Once* . . ., Footnotes 7 and 8, p. 237. No attempt is made to translate the word *zalag*. I should also note that the entire third part of this composite text is comprised of a somewhat enigmatic description of Ninurta passing judgment on the various rocks and minerals that are found on the earth.

50. Ninurta 80–96; see Jacobsen, *The Harps That Once* . . ., pp. 240–1.

51. Ninurta 167–8; see ibid., p. 244.

52. Ninurta 174–81; see ibid., p. 245.

53. Ninurta 334–44; see ibid., pp. 251–2. Although this second part of the text then describes how Ninurta set up irrigation systems, there is no obvious contemporary explanation for the idea that the earth was icebound to the extent that the rivers contained no fresh water.

54. Of course, the Mesopotamian *Epic of Creation* has some similarities to this, and I have rejected any similar interpretation of that by Sitchin or Allan and Delair as unduly literal. Lest I be accused of double standards, I should point out that this is because there is ample evidence that the latter is an origin myth about the creation of the earth that shares much in common with the origin myths of a number of other cultures, as we will see in Part 3. By contrast, the *Ninurta Myth* is clearly attempting no such thing, and is directly comparable to other catastrophe traditions.

55. Hancock, *Fingerprints of the Gods*, Chapter 25, pp. 215–7; his sources are the Avestic texts known as the *Vendidad* and the *Bundahish*.

56. Theogony 682–707 and 820–68; see West, *Hesiod: Theogony and Works and Days*, pp. 23–4 and 27–8.

57. Metamorphosis 2:178–329; see Melville, *Ovid: Metamorphosis*, pp. 30–4.

58. Metamorphosis 1:310–449; see ibid., pp. 10–14. This is of course the story of the survivors, Deucalion and Pyrrha, and I must note that, somewhat confusingly for our purposes, it *precedes* the story of Phaethon.

59. Edda 1; see Young, *The Prose Edda*, pp. 86–92.

60. Collins, *From the Ashes of Angels*, Chapter 23, p. 338.

61. Allan and Delair provide a comprehensive review of these traditions; see *When the Earth Nearly Died*, Part 3, and in particular Table 3B, pp. 162–4.

62. A detailed discussion of ice-core samples from Greenland and elsewhere can be found in Collins, *Gateway to Atlantis*, Chapter 22, pp. 294–302. A large number of surveys of deep-sea and ice-core samples have been undertaken in the last half-century, and the results appear to show a catastrophic change around the world about 11,500 years ago. However Collins notes that this date is derived using carbon-14 dates adjusted by dendrochronology, which tends to give results in this time frame that are some one thousand years earlier than if they are not adjusted. He also notes that a charcoal-rich layer at the boundary of the Pleistocene and Holocene has recently been detected all around the world by geologists; see ibid., Chapter 22, pp. 303–4.

63. For more information see ibid., Chapter 23, pp. 315–21, and Endnotes 40–2, pp. 400–1; and also Harrison, W, 'Atlantis Undiscovered', *Nature* 230 (1971), pp. 287–9 (reproduced in Corliss, *Ancient Man*, Chapter 1, pp. 241–4).

64. Schoch, *Voices of the Rocks*, Chapter 4, pp. 106–13; see also his plates section.

65. 'Looking for Lost Riches in Cuba's Seas', Reuters press release, Havana, 14 May 2001.

66. This discovery was made by oceanographers carrying out pollution checks for India's National Institute of Ocean Technology, led by director S Kathiroli; it was first reported in an article in *The Times*, 19 January 2002. For more information see < www.grahamhancock.com >.

67. Any argument that the cities were first constructed long before in precatastrophe times would have to explain how the site came to be still occupied and only submerged much later, despite the fact that it only lies in shallow seas –

provided, of course, that the provisional carbon dating of the site, and my estimates for the date of the catastrophe, are more or less accurate.

68. See Corliss, *Ancient Man*, Chapter 1, pp. 204–8.

69. See, for example, Campbell, *Oriental Mythology*, Chapter 4, p. 152.

CHAPTER 13: THE THEOSOPHICAL PERSPECTIVE

1. See the bibliography for details.

2. 'Letters of HPB to Hartmann', *The Path*, March 1896, pp. 368–70; cited in Johnson, *The Masters Revealed*, Introduction, pp. 9–10.

3. Ibid.

4. Coleman, 'The Sources of Madame Blavatsky's Writings', in *A Modern Priestess of Isis* (London, 1895), Appendix C, p. 354; cited in McCann, Mark, and Medway, Gareth, 'Plagiarism in Occult Literature', *Fortean Studies* 5 (1998), pp. 136–7. It is relatively easy to identify the sources Blavatsky used by referring to the comprehensive indexes appended to all later publications of her work.

5. Blavatsky, *The Secret Doctrine*, Volume 1, Introductory, p. xliii.

6. All the quoted stanzas from the *Book of Dzyan* can be found in ibid., Volume 2, Part 1, pp. 17–21. The selection and numbering of the stanzas extracted from the original source is entirely Blavatsky's own. I have not reproduced stanzas 1 to 4 here, and apparently there are others that she has herself omitted.

7. Ibid., Volume 2, Part 1, p. 138.

8. Ibid., Volume 2, Part 1, pp. 249 and 434–5.

9. I have no wish to enter a lengthy debate about the extent to which Blavatsky herself may or may not have been a racist; nor do I wish to devote time to exploring how her undoubted emphasis on the Aryan race was terribly distorted by some of her successors – particularly the occult-inspired Nazi regime in Germany. She does, however, emphasise that this particular expression – *black with sin* – is merely a 'figure of speech' in the stanzas. See ibid., Volume 2, Part 1, p. 408, Footnote.

10. Ibid., Volume 2, Part 1, p. 198.

11. Ibid., Volume 1, Part 1, pp. 241–5.

12. Ibid., Volume 2, Preliminary Notes, pp. 9–10.

13. Ibid., Volume 2, Part 1, pp. 198–9.

14. Ibid., Volume 1, Introductory, p. xliii.

15. Ibid., Volume 2, Part 1, p. 300.

16. Ibid., Volume 2, Preliminary Notes, pp. 8–10.

17. Ibid., Volume 2, Part 1, pp. 274 and 350.

18. The entirety of ibid., Volume 2, Part 3, is devoted to 'scientific' matters.

19. Ibid., Volume 2, Part 1, pp. 228–30.

20. Ibid., Volume 2, Part 1, pp. 286–7.

21. Blavatsky, *The Secret Doctrine*, Volume 2, Part 3, p. 775. We should however recall from a previous note to Part 1 that the Enochian *Book of Giants* also makes the mistake of accusing the fallen angels of bestiality.

22. Ibid., Volume 1, Proem, p. 1.

23. Ibid., Volume 1, Introductory, pp. xxii–xxiii.

24. Ibid., Volume 1, Introductory, pp. xxiii–xxiv and xliv (the pertinent extracts are reproduced in Lawton and Ogilvie-Herald, *Giza: The Truth*, Chapter 5, pp. 237–42).

25. Ibid., Volume 1, Introductory, p. xliii.

26. *Blavatsky's Collected Writings*, Volume 14, p. 422; cited in an article by David Pratt entitled 'The Book of Dzyan' at <http://ourworld.compuserve.com/homepages/dp5/dzyan.htm>.

27. See Reigle, *The Books of Kiu-te* and *Blavatsky's Secret Books*.

28. Blavatsky, *The Secret Doctrine*, Volume 1, Introductory, p. xxvii, and Part 1, p. 52, Footnote.

CHAPTER 14: THE ATLANTEAN CONNECTION

1. An excellent listing of the various researchers' favoured locations from Plato's time through to 1954 is provided by Sprague de Camp in *Lost Continents*, Appendix C; most of these can be cross-referenced with his extensive bibliography.

2. The location is described in Timaeus 2, and the layout in Critias 4; see Lee, *Plato: Timaeus and Critias*, pp. 37–8 and 136–42 respectively.

3. Although Plato suggests that this metal is 'now unknown', the Romans referred to it as 'aurichalcum' and manufactured it extensively with an 80:20 copper-to-zinc mix; it was the equivalent of modern 'yellow brass'. See <http://myron.sjsu.edu/romeweb/ENGINEER/art11.htm>.

4. The Thera hypothesis is supported, for example, by Luce in *The End of Atlantis*, and by Mavor in *Voyage to Atlantis*, both published in 1969.

5. This is based on the enigmatic *Oera Linda Book*, which is alleged to be a thirteenth-century Frisian text from Denmark; see Scrutton's 1979 work *Secrets of Lost Atland*.

6. See the Flem-Ath's 1995 work *When the Sky Fell*. We will consider the faults in theirs and Hapgood's use of the Piri Re'is map to support this theory in the next chapter.

7. See Collins' 2000 work *Gateway to Atlantis*: note that his proposed date for this submergence is rather later than Plato's.

8. See, for example, Donnelly's *Atlantis: The Antediluvian World*, and Muck's 1979 work *The Secret of Atlantis*.

9. The theory of continental drift relies primarily on horizontal tectonic movement, but critics suggest that sediment cores taken from various parts of the Atlantic Ocean bed, and other anomalies, indicate that significant and rapid vertical movements of the crust have occurred. See, for example, David Pratt's 2000 article 'Sunken Continents versus Continental Drift' at <http://ourworld.compuserve.com/homepages/dp5/sunken.htm>.

10. Sprague de Camp, *Lost Continents*, Chapter 1; he also provides an excellent compilation of extracts from these original works in Appendix A.

11. Ibid., Chapter 2, pp. 28–35.

12. Ibid., Chapter 2, pp. 35–6.

13. See ibid., Chapter 2, pp. 39–43, in which Sprague de Camp provides a sensible critique of a number of detailed aspects of Donnelly's analysis.

14. Ibid., Chapter 2, pp. 43–5.

15. Ibid., Chapter 3, pp. 52–4.

16. Blavatsky, *The Secret Doctrine*, Volume 2, Preliminary Notes, pp. 6–9.

17. Ibid., Volume 2, Part 1, pp. 429 and 432.

18. Ibid., Volume 2, Part 1, pp. 317 and 430.

19. Ibid., Volume 2, Part 1, p. 426.

20. See, for example, Jacolliot, *Histoire des Vierges* (Paris, 1879). Many of the references to these works can be easily traced using the index appended to later publications

of *The Secret Doctrine*, although I have found that, at least with respect to these two authors, it is by no means exhaustive and a number of references are omitted.

21. Ibid., Volume 1, Introductory, p. xviii.

22. Scott-Elliot, *The Story of Atlantis*, p. 34.

23. Ibid., pp. 46–9. In mentioning 'personal *vril*' as the early power source he appears to be following Blavatsky's discussions of this force in connection with John Worrell Keely's experiments with 'sympathetic vibratory apparatus' in Philadelphia in the late nineteenth century; see *The Secret Doctrine*, Volume 1, Part 3, p. 563, and also Lawton and Ogilvie-Herald, *Giza: The Truth*, Chapter 4, p. 206.

24. Ibid., pp. 88–9.

25. Ibid., p. 38.

26. Ibid., Preface, p. x, and also pp. 15 and 78.

27. Ibid., Preface, p. viii–x.

28. Steiner, *Atlantis and Lemuria*, Introduction, p. 8.

29. Ibid., Chapter 1, pp. 13–14, and Chapter 3, pp. 51–3.

30. The date of its origins is discussed in Churchward, *The Lost Continent of Mu*, Chapter 7; see also Chapter 2 for the nature of its inhabitants and history, and Chapter 3, p. 36, for a map showing its supposed size and location. I might also note that Scott-Elliot's maps do show Lemuria as occupying not just the Indian Ocean but also considerable portions of the Pacific.

31. Churchward, *The Lost Continent of Mu*, Chapter 1. A page of the 'vignettes' on the Naacal tablets is reproduced on p. 7, revealing many esoteric symbols that are commonly known but with somewhat strange embellishments.

32. Ibid., addendum, preface and following pages. Note that the 1994 edition from which I quote contains the original 1926 edition, and the 1931 updates to it in the addendum.

33. Ibid., Chapter 4, pp. 51–9.

34. Ibid., Chapter 17, pp. 309–10.

35. Ibid., Chapter 4, pp. 63–79.

36. See the bibliography for details of his works on Pacific Islands.

37. Williamson, R W, *Religious and Cosmic Beliefs of Central Polynesia* (Cambridge, 1933), Volume 1, p. 8; cited in Allan and Delair, *When the Earth Nearly Died*, Part 3, Chapter 5, p. 155.

38. Ellis, W, *Polynesian Researches* (London, 1829), Volume 2, p. 57; cited in ibid., Part 3, Chapter 5, pp. 155–6.

39. Spence, *The Problem of Lemuria*, Chapter 3, p. 54; Spence reports many other similar Pacific traditions in this chapter.

40. See geologist Charles M Love's paper in *Discovering Archaeology*, 29 December 2000.

41. Spence's map of these landmasses can be found in *History of Atlantis*, opposite p. 62. Note that his emphasis on the western island being in the area of the Sargasso Sea is a clear forerunner of the theory that Atlantis lay in the vicinity of the Caribbean.

42. Ibid., Chapters 6–7.

43. Spence's map of these landmasses can be found in *The Problem of Lemuria*, opposite p. 160.

44. Spence, *The Occult Sciences in Atlantis*, Chapter 1, pp. 7–10. He is actually particularly scathing about Atlantis material that is supposedly based on 'communications from the Otherworld', and he appears to include all the theosophical works in this without mentioning them by name.

45. Ibid., Chapter 3, pp. 27–31.
46. Background information from Randall-Stevens himself comes from *Atlantis to the Latter Days*, Foreword and Part 1, Chapters 1–3.
47. Ibid., Part 1, Chapters 4–5, and Part 2, between pp. 108 and 109.
48. Ibid., Part 1, Chapter 6, p. 52.
49. Ibid., Part 1, Chapter 7, including Plates 5–7; this information is summarised in Lawton and Ogilvie-Herald, *Giza: The Truth*, Chapter 5, pp. 250–1, and also Figures 19–20.
50. Almost identical drawings appear in Lewis' 1936 work *The Symbolic Prophecy of the Great Pyramid*; see Lawton and Ogilvie-Herald, *Giza: The Truth*, Chapter 5, pp. 236–7.
51. Leslie, *Submerged Atlantis Restored* (Austin, 1911); cited in Sprague de Camp, *Lost Continents*, Chapter 3, p. 70.
52. The remainder of this section is largely a summary of what we wrote previously in *Giza: The Truth*, Chapter 5, pp. 242–9.
53. See, for example, Johnson, *Edgar Cayce in Context*, Chapter 1, p. 35.
54. Johnson provides a thorough comparison of Cayce's 'Christian theosophy' with Blavatsky's 'esoteric theosophy' in ibid., Chapter 2, pp. 43–8.
55. A number of readings consistently mention the often touted date of 10,500 BC; see *Edgar Cayce on Atlantis*, Chapter 5, pp. 142–3.
56. Johnson, *Edgar Cayce in Context*, Introduction, p. 6.
57. Sugrue, *The Story of Edgar Cayce*, Chapter 15, p. 200.
58. Ibid., Chapter 15, pp. 200–16.
59. Johnson, *Edgar Cayce in Context*, Introduction, p. 7.
60. Peniel, *The Lost Teachings of Atlantis*, Chapter 1, p. 1.
61. Ibid., Chapter 5, pp. 48–54, and Chapter 7, pp. 74–83. I might note that the description of the power plant uses language almost identical to that used by Christopher Dunn in his 1998 work *The Giza Power Plant*, which we will consider in the next chapter, and that Dunn had published his ideas in articles well before this date; moreover, Peniel suggests that multiple Halls of Records exist, including 'in the Yucatan', and that they will be discovered just prior to the 'great earth changes' – both of which ideas appear to have been lifted straight from Cayce's readings; see in particular ibid., pp. 82–3.
62. See, for example, Besant and Leadbeater, *Man: Whence, How and Whither* (Madras, 1913).
63. See, for example, the various works of Nicholas Roerich listed in the bibliography; these are cited, along with the works of explorers N M Prjevalsky and A H Franke, in Tomas, *Atlantis: From Legend to Discovery*, Chapter 3, pp. 46–9.
64. See, for example, the accounts of the travels of Henning Haslund in *Men and Gods in Mongolia*, and of Theodore Illion in *In Secret Tibet*, written in 1935 and 1937 respectively.
65. Picknett and Prince, *The Stargate Conspiracy*, Chapters 4–6. See also Jacques Vallée's important works on the topic of 'extraterrestrial' deception, *Messengers of Deception* and *Revelations*, published in 1979 and 1992 respectively.
66. The SRI was also responsible for the 'remote viewing' tests that were being conducted on behalf of the US military at the time.
67. I would suggest that the particular works to treat with caution, to the extent that they were clearly influenced by the group or the Nine, are Schlemmer's *The Only Planet of Choice* (1992), Hurtak's *The Book of Knowledge: The Keys of*

Enoch (1977), Holroyd's *Prelude to the Landing on Planet Earth* (1977), and Percy and Myers' *Two-Thirds* (1993).

68. For details of Bailey's work see the bibliography.

69. This comes from UK researcher Ray Logan's recently self-published work *The Sirius Papers*; see <www3.mistral.co.uk/raylogan> for more details. It also includes intriguing descriptions of communication with what he refers to as 'universal mind'. However, I must point out that the spiritual message of these communications was, once again, spoiled for me by the insistence that this extraterrestrial race had genetically intervened on earth many times, helped to build the Giza pyramids, and so on.

CHAPTER 15: ADVANCED TECHNOLOGY?

1. An idea of the contents of *We Are Not the First* can be gleaned from chapter headings such as 'Electricity in the remote past', 'Did the ancients master gravitation', 'Prehistoric aircraft', 'They conquered space long before we did', and 'First robots, computers, radio, television and time viewing machines'. Tomas also wrote about Atlantis and Shambhala; see the bibliography for details.

2. See James and Thorpe's essay on the subject in *Ancient Mysteries*.

3. Temple, *The Sirius Mystery*, Chapter 1, p. 32.

4. The most obvious objection is the fact that the enclosure effectively has only three sides due to the slope of the plateau, so that there is no real retaining wall at the front or east end, on which the Sphinx Temple stands. It is also beyond question that the latter structure is contemporary with the Sphinx, having been erected using blocks from the quarrying of the enclosure. Temple does not explain how water can be retained in a container that only has three sides.

5. See, for example, Gardner, *Genesis of the Grail Kings*, Chapter 7, p. 94.

6. These issues are discussed in greater detail in Lawton and Ogilvie-Herald, *Giza: The Truth*, Chapter 4, pp. 211–20, and Chapter 16, pp. 477–8, and also in correspondence with Dunn on my website at <www.ianlawton.com/gttindex.htm>. The modern experiments have been performed by Denys Stocks of Manchester University, in conjunction with the NOVA team, and a report of their achievements including impressive photographs can be found at <www.pbs.org/wgbh/nova/lostempires/obelisk/cutting.html>; see also Stocks' paper in *Popular Archaeology*, April 1986, and his 'Stone Sarcophagus Manufacture in Ancient Egypt', *Antiquity* 73, Number 282 (1999).

7. Again, see my correspondence with Dunn at <www.ianlawton.com/gttindex.htm>.

8. West, *Serpent in the Sky*, Introduction, pp. 1–2.

9. For full details of the arguments surrounding the age of the Sphinx, see Lawton and Ogilvie-Herald, *Giza: The Truth*, Chapters 7 and 16 (the latter is an epilogue that contains new material on this issue in all but the original UK hardback edition), and also the continually updated papers and correspondence on my website at <www.ianlawton.com/gttindex.htm>; for the 10,500 BC dating see ibid., Chapter 9, pp. 349–51, and Chapter 16, pp. 475–6; and for the 36,000 BC dating see the papers on West's website at <http://members.aol.com/jawsphinx/index.html>.

10. To appreciate the extent to which Sitchin distorted the evidence for this assertion, see ibid., Chapter 2, pp. 94–111. His original arguments were presented in *The Stairway to Heaven*, Chapter 13, pp. 253–82.

11. The basic premise of the so-called Orion correlation was the subject of Bauval and Gilbert's 1994 work *The Orion Mystery*. This was subsequently expanded by Bauval and Hancock in *Keeper of Genesis*, particularly with respect to the 10,500 BC dating. Apart from the fact that I disagree with the latter, I also think that the basic premise of the correlation is questionable, irrespective of its supposed date. For more information on this see Lawton and Ogilvie-Herald, *Giza: The Truth*, Chapter 9, and also my paper entitled *The Fundamental Flaws in the Orion-Giza Correlation Theory* at < www.ianlawton.com/gttindex.htm >.

12. Bauval and Hancock, *Keeper of Genesis*, Chapter 6, pp. 106–9.

13. Ibid., Chapter 3, pp. 27–33.

14. Lawton and Ogilvie-Herald, *Giza: The Truth*, Chapter 4.

15. Ibid., Chapter 1, p. 53.

16. See the papers on temple construction on my website at < www.ianlawton.com/gttindex.htm >.

17. See Frank Doernenburg's comments at < www.ramtops.demon.co.uk/baalbek.html >.

18. From an article by Hausdorf in *UFO Reality* 3, August–September 1996.

19. For example, Hancock suggests somewhere between 115,000 and 50,000 years ago; see *Fingerprints of the Gods*, Chapter 26, p. 224.

20. Dalley, *Myths from Mesopotamia*, pp. 203–27; once again this text involves the warmongering Ninurta and an array of weapons.

21. These include, for example, the 'fiery whirlwind' that took Ezekiel away (Ezekiel 1:4–28 and 3:12–4), although to anyone familiar with the Qabalah this passage is replete with esoteric symbolism; and the Lord taking Elijah up to heaven in a 'chariot of fire' (2 Kings 2:11).

22. For example, David Hatcher Childress devotes a considerable portion of his 1991 work *Vimana Aircraft of Ancient India and Atlantis* to this topic.

23. This was first 'identified' in 1969 by maverick Egyptologist Khalil Messiha; see, for example, von Däniken, *In Search of Ancient Gods*, p. 170.

24. See, for example, the photographs of various gold 'model aircraft' from Bogotá in Colombia reproduced in ibid., pp. 167, 172 and 177; most of these appear to be easily explained as stylised ornaments. The relief of the supposed helicopter was discovered by the appropriately named Ruth Hover in 1989 in a temple at Abydos after an overlying panel had fallen away – see < www.veling.nl/anne/templars/ancientaircraft_nf.html >.

25. See, for example, ibid., pp. 130–1; Welfare and Fairley, *Arthur C Clarke's Mysterious World*, Chapter 3, pp. 64–7; and De Solla Price, *Gears from the Greeks* (American Philosophical Society, 1974).

26. Welfare and Fairley, *Arthur C Clarke's Mysterious World*, Chapter 3, pp. 62–4.

27. See Paul Heinrich and Pierre Stromberg's paper 'Mystery from the Depths of Time' at < www.eskimo.com/~pierres/coso/coso.html >.

28. Welfare and Fairley, *Arthur C Clarke's Mysterious World*, Chapter 3, pp. 55–8.

29. The two skulls that were initially thought to be recent fakes were one bought from Tiffany's auction house in 1898, which is now in the British Museum, and one sent recently to the Smithsonian Institute by an anonymous donor. The two skulls on which the museum apparently refused to comment were privately owned by Carl and Jo-Ann Parks from Texas (their skull is nicknamed Max) and skull researcher Nick Nocerino from San Francisco (Sha Na Ra). See *The Mystery of the Crystal Skulls*, Chapter 16 and Plates 8–11.

30. Ibid., Chapter 5 (photographs of the Hewlett-Packard testing are included in the plate section). We might note that two separate reconstructions of the face by forensic experts suggested that the original subject was a Native American woman; see ibid., Chapter 17, pp. 259–60.

31. Ibid., Chapter 1, p. 2.

32. Ibid., Chapter 2, p. 19.

33. Ibid., Chapters 5 and 6, pp. 52–66.

34. Ibid., Chapter 7.

35. Ibid., Chapter 24.

36. For reproductions of these two maps see Hapgood, *Maps of the Ancient Sea Kings*, frontispiece and Figure 49.

37. Schoch, *Voices of the Rocks*, Chapter 4, pp. 101–6.

38. See, for example, <www.70south.com/resources/science/weather/bases/history/chapter1>. On the Oronteus Finaeus map the continent is marked as 'Terra Australis Re'.

39. Tompkins, *Secrets of the Great Pyramid*, Chapter 13, pp. 159–69.

40. See Hancock's 1998 work *Heaven's Mirror*. A number of commentators have indicated the extent to which he has to be selective with the temples at Angkor and the stars in the Draco constellation to obtain his correlation; see, for example, Alford's comments at <www.eridu.co.uk/eridu/Author/Indexed_Quotations/Angkor/angkor.html>.

41. Although I must point out that I do not necessarily agree with their assertion that the template for this 'calendar machine' was part of the wisdom imparted to Enoch by the angel Uriel, which allowed him to anticipate a cometary impact that occurred in 3150 BC.

42. See Flem-Ath and Wilson's 2000 work, *The Atlantis Blueprint*.

43. The earliest universally accepted proof of the use of *pi* by the ancient Egyptians is in the Rhind Papyrus, which dates to circa 1700 BC. Meanwhile, I am relatively open-minded about the suggestion that eight hundred years before this the architects of the Great Pyramid had *deliberately* encoded this value into its dimensions, and also that of *phi*, which lies at the heart of the 'golden mean', the Fibonacci series, and 'sacred' geometry. For more information see Lawton and Ogilvie-Herald, *Giza: The Truth*, Chapter 3, pp. 149–54.

44. Kramer, *The Sumerians*, Chapter 3, pp. 91–3.

45. For example, Mesopotamian medical practice is described in a Sumerian pharmacopoeial text dating to the end of the third millennium BC; see ibid., Chapter 3, pp. 93–9. The evidence of brain surgery comes from the recently excavated skull of a Giza construction worker, dated to circa 2500 BC; see Lawton and Ogilvie-Herald, *Giza: The Truth*, Chapter 4, p. 222. The evidence of dentistry comes from teeth with concentric grooves in small holes believed to have been drilled with a small stone-tipped bit to remove tooth decay, which were recently found in Mehrgarh in Pakistan and dated to around 6000 BC; see *New Scientist*, 11 April 2001.

46. Various examples are provided by Richard Rudgley in *Lost Civilisations of the Stone Age*.

CHAPTER 16: ORIGINS

1. Dalley, *Myths from Mesopotamia*, p. 233.

2. Baines and Pinch in Willis, *World Mythology*, p. 38.

3. Ibid., p. 128. See also West, *Hesiod: Theogony and Works and Days*, explanatory note to Theogony 116, p. 64.

4. Müller, 'Egyptian Mythology', Chapter 4, pp. 68–9, in Gray, *The Mythology of All Races*, Volume 12. This text is described as a 'papyrus copy written in the reign of Alexander II (310 BC), but which seems to go back to originals that are considerably earlier'.

5. Rig Veda 10.129; see O'Flaherty, *The Rig Veda*, pp. 25–6.

6. Morgan, *Essays from Huai Nan Tzu*, 'Beginning and Reality', pp. 31–3.

7. Ibid., 'Life and Soul', p. 58.

8. For example, this idea was expressed in Baines and Pinch's description of Egyptian origin traditions above.

9. Nihongi 1; see Aston, *Nihongi*, pp. 1–3.

10. Metamorphosis 1:6–31; see Melville, *Ovid: Metamorphosis*, pp. 1–2.

11. Dixon, 'Oceanic Mythology', Part 1, Chapter 1, p. 5, in Gray, *The Mythology of All Races*, Volume 9.

12. Ibid., Part 1, Chapter 1, p. 13.

13. Ibid., Part 1, Chapter 1, pp. 7–8. The source is Taylor, *New Zealand and Its Inhabitants* (London, 1870), p. 109.

14. Ibid., Part 1, Chapter 1, p. 11.

15. Waters, *Book of the Hopi*, Part 1, p. 3.

16. Popol Vuh 1; see Tedlock, *Popol Vuh*, pp. 64–5.

17. Willis, *World Mythology*, p.266.

18. Ibid., p. 267.

19. See ibid., p. 19.

20. See, for example, Kramer, *The Sumerians*, Chapter 4, pp. 112–13, and Roux, *Ancient Iraq*, Chapter 6, p. 93.

21. For example, the *World Mythology* compendium that I have already referenced several times, and the *Larousse Encyclopaedia of Mythology*, are both littered with examples of this emphasis on the more prosaic aspects of cosmogony traditions.

22. See, for example, the description of Oceanic cosmogony in the *Larousse Encyclopaedia of Mythology*, p. 465.

23. Campbell, *Primitive Mythology*, Chapter 2, pp. 84–8.

24. Ibid., Chapter 6, pp. 232–8.

25. Indian and Chinese mythology are discussed in Campbell, *Oriental Mythology*, Parts 2 and 3. Concerning the latter he even asserts that there are 'no stories of creation, either in these early myths of the Chou period, or in the later Confucian classics' (Chapter 7, p. 380). This may be so to the extent that none is extant, but in my opinion this situation is just as likely to reflect the losses that resulted from the 'burning of the books' as it is any original absence – and it certainly does not justify his failure to discuss the later Taoist cosmogony in any detail.

26. Ibid., Chapter 2, pp. 83–9.

27. Eliade, *Myth and Reality*, Chapter 2.

CHAPTER 17: AN ESOTERIC WORLDVIEW

1. Hall quotes *Egyptian Magic* by 'S.S.D.D.' – which turns out to be by theosophist Florence Farr and published in 1896 – in which she suggests that the Egyptians

mummified their bodies to prevent the soul from reincarnating in them, but to me this does not seem to fit the context at all; see Hall, *The Secret Teachings of All Ages*, p. 48.

2. The basic information used in this section – that is, excluding my own commentary – can be found in, for example, Budge, *The Egyptian Heaven and Hell*, Volume 3 ('The Contents of the Books of the Other World Described and Compared'), Preface and Chapters 1 and 2; and Faulkner, *The Ancient Egyptian Book of the Dead*, Introduction.

3. See Taylor's 'Dissertation on the Life and Theology of Orpheus' in his 1792 work *The Hymns of Orpheus*, pp. 90–2. For more information on Orphic works in general see West's 1983 work *The Orphic Poems*.

4. Timaeus 6–7; see Lee, *Plato: Timaeus and Critias*, pp. 46–54. Note that Plato believed that the force that continually propelled any celestial body – indeed, that lay behind the movement of any body whatsoever – was its soul. As Lee points out in his commentary, at this time the Greeks appear to have had no conception of momentum and gravity.

5. For mathematical and geometric passages see Timaeus 5, 6 and 22–4 in ibid., pp. 44, 48, and 73–81; for musical and harmonic references see Timaeus 14 in ibid., p. 65.

6. Timaeus 18; see ibid., p. 70.

7. Timaeus 10; see ibid., p. 58.

8. Timaeus 49; see ibid., pp. 122–4.

9. Timaeus 38; see ibid., pp. 97–100.

10. Timaeus 24–30; see ibid., pp. 79–87.

11. For more information on the Neoplatonic movement see Wallis' 1972 work *Neoplatonism*. The so-called *Chaldaean Oracles* also exercised a considerable influence on the Neoplatonists, and appear to have had Egyptian, Zoroastrian and Judaic roots – the latter because of the similarity of their ethereal framework with that of the Qabalah, which we will consider in a later section. For more information on these oracles see Lewy's 1978 work *Chaldaean Oracles and Theurgy*, and Aude's 1895 work 'The Chaldaean Oracles of Zoroaster' in Westcott, *Collectanea Hermetica*, Volume 6.

12. This is translated by Taylor in Part 3 of his compilation of *The Hymns of Orpheus*, pp. 22–4.

13. Ibid., pp. 41–3.

14. These are described in Copenhaver, *Hermetica*, Introduction, pp. xxxii–xl.

15. For more information on the various original compilations of source texts see ibid., Introduction, pp. xl–xlv; and on the various commentaries that were then prepared by Arabian and European Hermeticists from the seventh century onward, see pp. xlv–lix. Cophenhaver's 1992 translation is the most recent available, and given the problems of interpreting the many different versions of the original texts, and ensuring that the translation is as faithful to these originals as possible, it incorporates all the scholarship of his multitude of predecessors. By contrast, the popular translation by Walter Scott in the 1920s is regarded by most orthodox scholars as distorted and unreliable, even if his extensive commentaries are invaluable (see ibid., Introduction, p. liii) – although I should also note that his is the only modern version that includes the philosophical Stobaeus manuscripts, to which I will refer on occasion.

16. A prime example is a degree of confusion about whether or not animals, plants and even supposedly inanimate life forms have souls; in some passages they all do, in

others not. Above all, in the *Hermetica* humankind's soul is enhanced by 'mind', which no other animal possesses. See Corpus Hermeticum 1:15, 8:5, and 12:2, and Asclepius 4 and 27 in ibid., pp. 3, 26, 43, 68–9, and 83.

17. For example, most of Corpus Hermeticum 2 is devoted to the Platonic concept that all movement is caused by the soul of the thing that moves; see ibid., pp. 8–12.

18. Corpus Hermeticum 4:8; see ibid., p. 17.

19. Corpus Hermeticum 12:5; see ibid., p. 44.

20. Asclepius 11; see ibid., pp. 73–4.

21. Corpus Hermeticum 1:24–6; see ibid., pp. 5–6.

22. Corpus Hermeticum 18:14; see ibid., p. 66.

23. See, for example, Corpus Hermeticum 10:5, 13:4, and 13:7 in ibid., pp. 31 and 50.

24. Corpus Hermeticum 11:20; see ibid., p. 41. Note also that the previous passage appears to describe out-of-body experiences in which neophytes can 'command their soul to travel' to anywhere in the world instantaneously.

25. Corpus Hermeticum 1:4; see ibid., p. 1. See also 5:5, p. 19.

26. Corpus Hermeticum 13:3; see ibid., pp. 49–50. See also 10:6, 13:11 and 13:13, pp. 31 and 51–2.

27. Corpus Hermeticum 4:5; see ibid., p. 16. See also 10:8, p. 32.

28. Corpus Hermeticum 10:19–22; see ibid., pp. 34–5. See also Asclepius 28, p. 84, which in addition contains the clearly Egyptian concept of the 'merit of the soul' being 'weighed and judged' after death.

29. See, for example, Corpus Hermeticum 11:15 and 12:16 in ibid., pp. 40 and 46–7.

30. See, for example, Stobaeus Excerpt 2A in Scott, *Hermetica*, p. 150.

31. Corpus Hermeticum 4:7; see Copenhaver, *Hermetica*, p. 16.

32. Asclepius 25; see ibid., p. 82. This passage is followed up in Asclepius 26 by the suggestion that the world will be cleansed by a catastrophe of flood and fire; it is impossible to interpret whether this is a confusion of something that happened long before the texts were prepared – even though the future tense is used – or merely a version of the Judaeo-Christian apocalypse, or a genuine suggestion that the same fate could befall us in the modern epoch if we fail to learn the lessons of the past.

33. Corpus Hermeticum 1:17–19; see ibid., p. 4.

34. Corpus Hermeticum 1:14; see ibid., p. 3.

35. From the *Kore Kosmu*, the best known of the Stobaeus manuscripts also referred to as Excerpt 23; see Scott, *Hermetica*, p. 179. Meanwhile Stobaeus Excerpt 25 describes how these classes of souls inhabited four ethereal 'divisions' of four, eight, sixteen, and thirty-two subdivisions respectively, with the division nearest to the physical earth being the domain of the least advanced souls; see ibid., p. 199.

36. Corpus Hermeticum 3:1; see Copenhaver, *Hermetica*, p. 13.

37. Corpus Hermeticum 4:10; see ibid., p. 17.

38. Corpus Hermeticum 5:10; see ibid., p. 20.

39. Corpus Hermeticum 12:20–2; see ibid, pp. 47–8.

40. Stobaeus Excerpt 23; see Scott, *Hermetica*, p. 186. See also Corpus Hermeticum 10:15 in Copenhaver, *Hermetica*, p. 33. For a full discussion of the Platonic view of memory in the context of reincarnation, and of other views from around the world, see Eliade, *Myth and Reality*, Chapter 7; another fine general source is Frances Yates' 1966 work *The Art of Memory*.

41. These are *The Discourse on the Eighth and Ninth*, *The Prayer of Thanksgiving*, *Scribal Note*, and *Asclepius 21–9*. Another tractate contains an extract from Plato's Republic.

For more general background information on the Gnostic texts see Robinson, *The Nag Hammadi Library*, Introduction, pp. 1–10.

42. It is interesting to compare this with a passage in the Hermetic *Kore Kosmu*, which suggests that the first incarnations into human form were a karmic punishment for souls that had already erred by 'overstepping the bounds of their own divisions of the atmosphere', and claiming 'nobility equal to the gods in heaven'; the fact that this is so at odds with other Hermetic passages shows how self-contradictory these texts can become after centuries of editing and translation; see Stobaeus Excerpt 23 in Scott, *Hermetica*, p. 184. However, for completeness we should also note the similarity between the Gnostic view of the initial fall and that of Islam, in which a 'lesser god' is condemned to incarnation on earth because he 'refused to bow before Adam', and he in turn pledges to act as a negative influence on humankind's development – which he achieves by making Adam partake of the 'forbidden tree'; see Koran 7:11–25.

43. The main Gnostic texts that all contain these same basic messages are the *Apocryphon of John*, the *Hypostatis of the Archons*, *On the Origin of the World*, and the *Tripartite Tractate*. To a large extent they pick up on and elaborate the themes in Genesis.

44. Robinson, *The Nag Hammadi Library*, p. 403.

45. Ibid., pp. 324–5. For confirmation of the idea of the seven lower spheres see *On the Origin of the World* in ibid., p. 174.

46. Ibid., pp. 171–3.

47. Ibid, pp. 61 and 64. Further descriptions of the ultimate deity can be found, for example, in the *Apocryphon of John*; see ibid, pp. 106–7.

48. Ibid., pp. 182–3.

49. This work is included in a compilation of Renaissance alchemical tracts that was first published in Latin in 1678 and entitled *The Hermetic Museum*; see Volume 1, pp. 141–7.

50. The anonymous tract is in ibid., Volume 1; note, however, that it also contains a highly literal interpretation of the creation of Adam in Genesis, including an apparent acceptance of the longer life spans of the biblical patriarchs that is supposedly related to them having possessed the 'stone'. As for Paracelsus, his *Complete Writings* was first published in Latin in 1616.

51. For more information on the history of alchemy and its leading figures see Yates' 1979 work *The Occult Philosophy in the Elizabethan Age*, and on its practices see Hall, *The Secret Teachings of All Ages*, pp. 149–60.

52. Dee's major work is *The Hieroglyphic Monad*, first published in Latin in 1564; it contains a number of theorems based on numbers and planetary significance that clearly have a Qabalistic origin but are difficult to put into any real context. Levi wrote a number of books, one of the most important being *The Key of the Mysteries*, first published in French in 1861.

53. For example, Chapter 13 of Fortune's *Principles of Hermetic Philosophy* – recently published in book form with additional commentary by Knight – is devoted to a discussion of reincarnation in the context of astrology.

54. The *Fama Fraternitatis* and contemporary *Confession Fraternitatis* are both reproduced in Yates' 1972 work *The Rosicrucian Enlightenment*, Appendix, pp. 238–60; on the face of it neither reveals much in the way of real details about the Rosicrucian worldview. R Swinburne Clymer's 1965 work *The Rosy Cross: Its*

Teachings incorporates twelve Rosicrucian manifestos from various periods, but again they do not appear to be particularly revealing.

55. For example, H Spencer Lewis' 1932 work *Rosicrucian Questions and Answers* discusses issues such as reincarnation at some length, while his 1938 work *Rosicrucian Manual* also provides interesting insights. Meanwhile Hall's *The Secret Teachings of All Ages* contains considerable further background on the history of the movement and its esoteric worldview; see pp. 137–48.

56. Some of the finest works in this area, which describe the authors' journeys into spiritual enlightenment in autobiographical format, are by Paramahansa Yogananda and his pupil Norman Paulsen; see the bibliography for details.

57. See the bibliography for details of their major works.

58. This is the view expressed in conversation by my colleague Michael Carmichael, who as a dedicated alchemical researcher has 'been there, done that' on both fronts.

59. See Harner's 1980 work, *The Way of the Shaman*, pp. 1–10; cited in Narby, *The Cosmic Serpent*, Chapter 5, pp. 52–6.

60. For a highly useful further discussion of these links, and of the work of Michael Carmichael in investigating the ancient Egyptians' use of psychoactive plants, see Picknett and Prince, *The Stargate Conspiracy*, Epilogue, pp. 348–56. For more general information see also Rudgley's 1993 work *The Alchemy of Culture*.

61. I might note, however, that Harner also describes seeing 'giant reptilian creatures' that showed him by telepathy how they had originally come to earth to escape from their home planet, and had as a result created all life here – a refrain that we have met before in different guises in channelled material; nevertheless, it is interesting that Harner himself felt that these creatures had something to do with DNA, which is of course the theme that Narby expanded; see Narby, *The Cosmic Serpent*, Chapter 5, p. 55. To the extent that we accepted in Part 2 that all life on earth may have been seeded by microscopic organisms from elsewhere in the cosmos, this is an interesting angle of investigation, and it just may be that DNA somehow holds a clue to a number of mysteries; however, I still have reservations about the idea that intelligent extraterrestrials deliberately kick-started physical life on this planet, and remain more inclined to see all this as a distortion of a more spiritual message concerning ethereal entities that I will further elucidate in the next chapter.

62. See Clottes and Lewis-Williams, *The Shamans of Prehistory: Trance and Magic in Painted Caves*. The latter's work is also described in Leakey, *The Origin of Humankind*, Chapter 6, pp. 145–9.

63. Waters, *Book of the Hopi*, Part 1, pp. 9–11 (including Footnote).

64. See, for example, Campbell, *Primitive Mythology*, Chapter 6, p. 265. This entire chapter is devoted to shamanism. Another fine source of general information is Eliade's 1964 work, *Shamanism: Archaic Techniques of Ecstasy*.

65. For further discussion of the dream time see, for example, Campbell, *Primitive Mythology*, Chapter 7, pp. 289–90.

CHAPTER 18: THE COSMIC DOCTRINE

1. Fortune, *The Cosmic Doctrine*, Introduction, pp. 1–2.
2. Ibid., Introduction, p. 12.
3. Ibid., Introduction 2, p. 17.
4. Ibid., Introduction, pp. 1 and 8.
5. Ibid., Introduction, p. 2.

6. Ibid., Introduction 2. It is also interesting to note that Newton's subjects describe how the most advanced guides teach by flashing 'metaphoric picture puzzles' into their minds, which seems remarkably reminiscent of using patterned thought-forms; see *Journey of Souls*, Chapter 11, p. 172.

7. The exception being that I use the words *cosmos* and *universe* interchangeably, whereas somewhat confusingly Fortune tends to use the latter word to describe a solar system.

8. Fortune, *The Cosmic Doctrine*, Section 1.

9. Ibid., Section 2.

10. Ibid., Section 3.

11. Nevertheless, I might note that the communications assert that sidereal astrology is related to the phenomenon of precession. Given that sidereal astrology is supposed to derive its influences from the twelve *cosmic* rays – in other words, from the periods denoted by our entire solar system passing through the various cosmic ray segments as it orbits around in the outer plane of the cosmos as a whole – rather than the highly localised periods of stellar procession as observed from earth that derive from its own axial wobble, then either this assertion is false or there is something in the phenomenon of precession that we have not yet grasped. See ibid, Chapter 20, pp. 116–17.

12. Ibid., Afterthoughts, p. 190, Footnote.

13. Ibid., Afterthoughts, pp. 193, 200 and 210.

14. Ibid., Figures 1–16, pp. 213–18.

15. Ibid., Chapter 21, pp. 122–3.

16. Newton, *Journey of Souls*, Chapter 11, pp. 195–7.

17. Ibid., Chapter 10. pp. 159–60.

18. Ibid., Conclusion, p. 275.

CHAPTER 19: ESOTERIC SCIENCE

1. A fuller discussion of the scientific concepts and history outlined in this section and the previous one can be found in Fritjof Capra's groundbreaking 1976 work *The Tao of Physics*, Chapter 4, pp. 61–93, Chapter 13, pp. 222–6, and Chapter 14, pp. 229–47. He also reconfirms the extent to which the Eastern worldviews of Hinduism, Buddhism and Taoism regard the physical world as a mere illusion; see ibid., Chapters 5–9.

2. See ibid., Chapter 10, pp. 152–4, and Chapter 11, pp. 168–73.

3. See ibid., Chapter 18, pp. 331–3.

4. See ibid., 'Afterword to the Second Edition', pp. 341–6.

5. See ibid., 'Afterword to the Second Edition', pp. 352–3. For more details see Michael Talbot's 1991 work *The Holographic Universe*, Chapter 2; and for the full explanation see Bohm's 1980 work *Wholeness and the Implicate Order*, in particular Chapter 7.

6. See Capra, *The Tao of Physics*, Chapter 4, pp. 71–4, and Chapter 12, pp. 177–207.

7. Stobaeus Excerpt 16; see Scott, *Hermetica*, p. 173.

8. Timaeus 7; see Lee, *Plato: Timaeus and Critias*, p. 52. In the preceding passage he notes that time is not a relevant concept in the higher ethereal realms.

9. For more information on string theory see, for example, Brian Greene's 1999 work *The Elegant Universe*.

10. It is interesting to note that in his 1994 work *The Infinite Harmony*, Michael Hayes attempts to show that octave structures are inherent to the functioning of DNA,

compares the latter with the Chinese I Ching, and suggests that Hermetic knowledge is encoded within it. This approach has certain basic similarities with that adopted by Jeremy Narby, which I discussed in a previous chapter. Meanwhile, although it has less direct relevance to our discussion of vibration and harmonics, Katya Walter's 1996 work *The Tao of Chaos* again explores the similarities between the Chinese I Ching and the genetic code, and suggests this is evidence of a master plan in which the divine is the all-encompassing pattern present in all life.

11. For one of the finest analyses of these phenomena, undertaken predominantly in the context of Bohm's theories of implicate order, see Talbot's *The Holographic Universe*, Parts 2 and 3. Among the many additional sources for material on the paranormal, I would in particular recommend Lyall Watson's *Supernature* and Dean Radin's *The Conscious Universe*, first published in 1973 and 1998 respectively.

12. A prime example of the fact that this attitude is already changing is provided by Brian Josephson, a Nobel Laureate and professor of physics at Cambridge University who heads the Mind-Matter Unification Project. For some time he has been exploring how statistically-validated but supposedly paranormal phenomena such as telepathy might be explained by a different approach to quantum theory and nonlocal connections that, instead of relying on the form-oriented methods of traditional science, recognises the meaning-oriented context in which all biosystems operate. For example, see his paper 'Biological Utilisation of Quantum NonLocality', *Foundations of Physics* 21 (1991), pp. 197–207.

EPILOGUE

1. See, for example, Campbell, *Primitive Mythology*, Chapter 5, pp. 202–3.
2. Newton, *Journey of Souls*, Chapter 11, pp. 174–6.
3. Ibid., Chapter 11, p. 171.
4. Ibid., Chapter 10, pp. 161–8 and Chapter 11, pp. 186–8.
5. This does not alter my conviction that after one hundred thousand years ago the angelic souls that assisted modern humankind's cultural evolution *would* have physically incarnated, rather than just materialised at will, because such work required significant human interaction.
6. For a fine overview of the extent to which evidence is mounting see Rudgley, *Lost Civilisations of the Stone Age*, Afterword, pp. 261–3.
7. Newton, *Journey of Souls*, Conclusion, p. 276.

BIBLIOGRAPHY

BY THE AUTHOR

Lawton, Ian, and Ogilvie-Herald, Chris, *Giza: The Truth*, Virgin, 1999 (published in the US by Invisible Cities Press, 2001).

ANCIENT HISTORY, TEXTS, AND MYTHOLOGY

Aston, W G (trans.), *Nihongi*, Kegan Paul, 1896.

Augustine, Saint, *The City of God* (7 volumes), Heinemann Young, 1958–98 (see also www.ccel.org).

Baines, John, and Malek, Jaromir, *Atlas of Ancient Egypt*, Oxford, 1980.

Best, Robert M, *Noah's Ark and the Ziusudra Epic: Sumerian Origins of the Flood Myth*, Enlil Press, 1999.

Bierhorst, John (trans.), *History and Mythology of the Aztecs: The Codex Chimalpopoca*, University of Arizona Press, 1992.

Budge, E A Wallis (trans.), *The Egyptian Heaven and Hell* (3 volumes in 1), Dover, 1996.

Budge, E A Wallis, *Osiris and the Egyptian Resurrection* (2 volumes), Philip Lee Warner, 1911.

Campbell, Joseph, *The Masks of God* (4 volumes: *Primitive Mythology, Oriental Mythology, Occidental Mythology*, and *Creative Mythology*), Arkana, 1991 (first published 1959–68).

Campbell, Joseph, and Musès, Charles, *In All Her Names*, Harper, 1991.

Charlesworth, James H (ed.), *The Old Testament Pseudepigrapha* (2 volumes), Darton, Longman and Todd, 1983.

Coomaraswamy, Ananda K, and Sister Nivedita, *Myths of the Hindus and Buddhists*, Dover Publications, 1967 (first published 1916).

Copenhaver, Brian (trans.), *Hermetica: The Greek Corpus Hermeticum and the Latin Asclepius*, Cambridge University Press, 1998.

Cory, I C, *Ancient Fragments*, Wizards Bookshelf, 1975 (first published 1832).

Cotterell, Arthur (ed.), *The Penguin Encyclopaedia of Ancient Civilisations*, Penguin, 1988.

Dalley, Stephanie (trans.), *Myths from Mesopotamia: Creation, The Flood, Gilgamesh and Others*, Oxford World's Classics, 1991.

Dimmitt, Cornelia, and van Buitenen, J A B, *Classical Hindu Mythology: A Reader in the Sanskrit Puranas*, Temple University Press, 1978.

Dutt, Manmatha Nath (trans.), *Vishnu Purana*, Calcutta, 1894.

Dutt, Romesh C (trans.), [Extracts from] *The Ramayana and The Mahabharata*, Everyman, 1944 (first published 1910).

Eisenman, Robert, and Wise, Michael (trans.), *The Dead Sea Scrolls Uncovered*, Penguin, 1993.

Eliade, Mircea, *The Myth of the Eternal Return*, New York, 1954.

Eliade, Mircea, *The Sacred and the Profane: The Nature of Religion*, Harcourt, 1959.

Eliade, Mircea, *Myth and Reality*, Waveland Press, 1998 (first published 1963).

Eliade, Mircea, *Shamanism: Archaic Techniques of Ecstasy*, Arkana, 1989 (first published 1964).

Faulkner, Raymond (trans.), *The Ancient Egyptian Pyramid Texts*, Oxford University Press, 1969.

Faulkner, Raymond (trans.), *The Ancient Egyptian Coffin Texts*, Aris and Phillips, 1978.

Faulkner, Raymond (trans.), *The Ancient Egyptian Book of the Dead*, British Museum Press, 1996.

Feuerstein, Georg, Kak, Subhash, and Frawley, David, *In Search of the Cradle of Civilisation*, Quest, 1995.

Fowden, Garth, *The Egyptian Hermes*, Cambridge University Press, 1986.

Frazer, James George, *The Golden Bough: A Study in Magic and Religion*, Penguin, 1996 (12 volumes, first published 1890–1915).

Graves, Robert, *The White Goddess*, Faber and Faber, 1999 (first published 1948).

Gray, Louis Herbert (ed.), *The Mythology of All Races* (13 volumes), Marshall Jones Co., Boston, 1916–64.

Guirand, Felix (ed.), *The Larousse Encyclopaedia of Mythology*, Paul Hamlyn, 1965.

Heidel, Alexander, *The Gilgamesh Epic and Old Testament Parallels*, University of Chicago Press, 1949.

Heidel, Alexander (trans.), *The Babylonian Genesis*, University of Chicago Press, 1951.

Hodge, Stephen, *The Dead Sea Scrolls*, Piatkus, 2001.

Il Manoscritto Messicano Vaticano 3738, Detto Il Codice Rios, Rome, 1900.

Jacobsen, Thorkild, *The Sumerian King List*, Chicago, 1939.

Jacobsen, Thorkild (trans.), *The Harps That Once . . . Sumerian Poetry in Translation*, Yale University Press, 1987.

Jung, Carl, *Psychology and Alchemy*, Routledge, 1993 (first published 1953).

Kramer, Samuel N, *Sumerian Mythology*, Harper and Bros., 1961.

Kramer, Samuel N, *Mythologies of the Ancient World*, Anchor, 1961.

Kramer, Samuel N, *The Sumerians, Their History, Culture and Character*, University of Chicago Press, 1971 (first published 1963).

Laurence, Richard (trans.), *The Book of Enoch the Prophet*, Wizards Bookshelf, 1995 (first published 1883).

Lee, Desmond (trans.), *Plato: Timaeus and Critias*, Penguin Classics, 1977.

Lenormant, François, and Chevallier, E, *The Ancient History of the East* (3 volumes), Asher and Co., 1870.

Levi-Strauss, Claude, *Myth and Meaning*, Routledge, 1978.

Lewy, Hans, *Chaldaean Oracles and Theurgy*, Études Augustiniennes, 1978.

Mackenzie, Donald A, *Myths of China and Japan*, Gresham, 1923.

Melville, A D (trans.), *Ovid: Metamorphosis*, Oxford World Classics, 1998.

Meyer, Eduard, *Chronologie Egyptienne* (trans. from German by Alexandre Moret in *Annales du Musée Guimet, Bibliotheque D'Études*, 24), Paris, 1912.

Milik, J T, *The Books of Enoch – Aramaic Fragments of Qumran Cave 4*, Oxford University Press, 1976.

Morfill, W R (trans.), and Charles, R H, *The Book of the Secrets of Enoch*, Oxford, 1896.

Morgan, Evan, *Tao, The Great Luminant: Essays from Huai Nan Tzu*, Kegan Paul, 1933.

Müller, Max (ed.), *The Sacred Books of the East* (50 volumes), Oxford, 1879–91 (see also www.sacred-texts.com/sbe/index.htm).

Murray, Alex (ed.), *History of the Jews* (2 volumes), London, 1874.

O'Flaherty, Wendy Doniger (trans.), *The Rig Veda*, Penguin Classics, 1981.

Philippi, Donald L (trans.), *Kojiki*, Princetown University Press, 1969.

Prasad, Ganga, *The Fountain-Head of Religion*, Book Tree, 2000 (first published 1927).

Rackham, H, Jones, W H S, and Eichholz, D E, *Pliny: Natural History* (10 volumes), William Heinemann, 1938–57.

Ray, Pratapa Chandra (trans.), *The Mahabharata* (9 volumes), Calcutta, 1884–94.

Reymond, E A E, *The Mythical Origin of the Egyptian Temple*, Barnes and Noble, 1969.

Robinson, James M, *The Nag Hammadi Library*, HarperCollins, 1990.

Roux, Georges, *Ancient Iraq*, Penguin, 1992 (first published 1964).

Rundle Clark, R T, *Myth and Symbol in Ancient Egypt*, Thames and Hudson, 1959.

Scott, Walter, *Hermetica*, Solos Press, 1992 (first published in 4 volumes 1924–36).

Smith, George, *The Chaldean Account of Genesis*, London, 1876.

Taylor, Thomas (trans.), *The Hymns of Orpheus*, Philosophical Research Society, 1981 (first published 1792).

Tedlock, Dennis (trans.), *Popol Vuh: The Mayan Book of the Dawn of Life*, Touchstone, 1996.

Thompson, J Eric S, *Maya Hieroglyphic Writing*, University of Oklahoma Press, 1960.

Thompson, J Eric S, *Maya History and Religion*, University of Oklahoma Press, 1970.

Thompson, J Eric S, 'The Dresden Codex: A Maya Hieroglyphic Book', *Memoirs of the American Philosophical Society* 93 (1972).

Vermes, Geza, *The Dead Sea Scrolls in English*, Penguin, 1962.

Waddell, Laurence A, *Egyptian Civilisation: Its Sumerian Origin and Real Chronology*, Lucas and Co., 1930.

Waddell, Laurence A, *Makers of Civilisation in Race and History*, Angriff Press, 1970 (first published 1930s).

Waddell, W G (trans.), *Manetho*, Harvard University Press, 1997 (first published 1940).

Wallis, R T, *Neoplatonism*, Duckworth, 1972.

Waterfield, Robin (trans.), *Herodotus: The Histories*, Oxford World Classics, 1998.

Waters, Frank, *Book of the Hopi*, Penguin, 1977.

Werner, Edward T C, *Myths and Legends of China*, Sinclair Browne, 1984 (first published 1922).

Werner, Edward T C, *A Dictionary of Chinese Mythology*, Kelly and Walsh, 1932.

West, M L (trans.), *Hesiod: Theogony and Works and Days*, Oxford World Classics, 1999.

West, M L, *The Orphic Poems*, Oxford University Press, 1983.

Westcott, W Wynn, *Collectanea Hermetica* (6 volumes), Theosophical Publishing Society, 1895.

Willis, Roy (ed.), *World Mythology*, Duncan Baird, 1993.

Wilkins, W J, *Hindu Mythology*, Curzon Press, 1900.

Wise, Michael, Abegg, Martin, and Cook, Edward, *The Dead Sea Scrolls: A New Translation*, HarperCollins, 1996.

Woolley, Leonard, *The Sumerians*, Oxford, 1929.

Young, Jean I (trans.), *Snorri Sturluson: The Prose Edda*, University of California Press, 1964.

ARCHAEOLOGY AND EVOLUTION

Balfour, Michael, *Megalithic Mysteries*, Parkgate Books, 1997.

Behe, Michael, *Darwin's Black Box: The Biochemical Challenge to Evolution*, Free Press, 1996.

Brass, Michael, *The Antiquity of Man: Artefactual, Fossil and Gene Records Explored*, PublishAmerica, 2002.

Breuil, Abbe H, *Four Hundred Centuries of Cave Art*, Centre d'Études et de Documentation Prehistorique, undated.

Chomsky, Noam, *Language and Mind*, Harcourt Brace Jovanovich, 1972.

Chomsky, Noam, *Language and Problems of Knowledge*, MIT Press, 1988.

Clottes, Jean, and Lewis-Williams, David, *The Shamans of Prehistory: Trance and Magic in Painted Caves*, Harry N Abrams, 1998.

Crick, Francis H C, *Life Itself: Its Origin and Nature*, Simon and Schuster, 1981.

Darwin, Charles, *On the Origin of Species*, Penguin, 1985 (first published 1859).

Darwin, Charles, *The Descent of Man*, John Murray, 1871.

Dawkins, Richard, *The Selfish Gene*, Oxford University Press, 1989 (first published 1976).

Dawkins, Richard, *The Blind Watchmaker*, Longmans, 1986.

Dawkins, Richard, *River Out of Eden*, Phoenix, 1996.

Deacon, Hillary, *Human Beginnings in South Africa: Uncovering the Secrets of the Stone Age*, David Philip, 1999.

Dennett, Daniel, *Consciousness Explained*, Little Brown, 1991.

Dennett, Daniel, *Darwin's Dangerous Idea*, Penguin, 1995.

Denton, Michael, *Evolution: A Theory in Crisis*, Burnett, 1985.

Feder, Kenneth L, *Frauds, Myths, and Mysteries: Science and Pseudoscience in Archaeology*, Mayfield, 1999.

Gould, Stephen Jay, *The Panda's Thumb*, Norton, 1980.

Gould, Stephen Jay, *The Flamingo's Smile*, Norton, 1985.

Gould, Stephen Jay, *Bully for Brontosaurus*, Norton, 1991.

Gould, Stephen Jay, *The Book of Life*, Norton, 1993.

Klein, Richard, *The Human Career*, University of Chicago Press, 1999.

Kurten, Bjorn, *Not from the Apes*, Readers Union, 1973.

Leakey, Richard, *The Making of Humankind*, E P Dutton, 1981.

Leakey, Richard, *The Origin of Humankind*, Phoenix, 1995.

Leakey, Richard, and Lewin, Roger, *Origins Reconsidered*, Doubleday, 1992.

Lewin, Roger, *Complexity: Life at the Edge of Chaos*, Macmillan, 1992.

Lewin, Roger, *The Origin of Modern Humans*, W H Freeman, 1993.

Maynard Smith, John, *The Theory of Evolution*, Cambridge University Press, 1993.

Milton, Richard, *Shattering the Myths of Darwinism*, Park Street Press, 2000.

Morell, Virginia, *Ancestral Passions: The Leakey Family and the Quest for Humankind's Beginnings*, Touchstone, 1996.

Pinker, Steven, *The Language Instinct: The New Science of Language and Mind*, William Morrow, 1994.

Popper, Karl, and Eccles, John, *The Self and its Brain*, Springer-Verlag, 1977.

Wendorf, Fred, and Schild, Romauld, *Prehistory of the Nile Valley*, Academic Press, 1976.

Wesson, Robert, *Beyond Natural Selection*, MIT Press, 1991.

Williams, Stephen, *Fantastic Archaeology: The Wild Side of North American Prehistory*, University of Pennsylvania Press, 1991.

GEOLOGY AND CATASTROPHE

Allan, Derek, and Delair, Bernard, *When the Earth Nearly Died*, Gateway, 1995 (republished in the US under the title *Cataclysm*).

Clube, Victor, and Napier, Bill, *The Cosmic Winter*, Basil Blackwell, 1990.

Filby, Frederick A, *The Flood Reconsidered: A Review of the Evidences of Geology, Archaeology, Ancient Literature and the Bible*, Pickering and Inglis, 1970.

Goodman, Jeffrey, *The Earthquake Generation*, Turnstone, 1979.

Hapgood, Charles, *The Path of the Pole*, Souvenir, 2001 (first published 1958 under the title *Earth's Shifting Crust*).

Hibben, Frank C, *The Lost Americans*, Thomas Y Crowell, 1946.

Hugget, Richard, *Cataclysms and Earth History: The Development of Diluvialism*, Clarendon Press, 1989.

Martin, Paul S, and Klein, Richard (eds.), *Quaternary Extinctions – A Prehistoric Revolution*, University of Arizona Press, 1984.

Palmer, Trevor, *Controversy – Catastrophism and Evolution: The Ongoing Debate*, Plenum Press, 1999.

Peiser, Benny, Palmer, Trevor, and Bailey, Mark (eds.), *Natural Catastrophes During Bronze Age Civilisations*, Archaeopress, 1998.

Schoch, Robert M, *Voices of the Rocks*, Harmony, 1999.

Spedicato, Emilio, *Apollo Objects, Atlantis and the Deluge: A Catastrophist Scenario for the End of the Last Glaciation*, Instituto Universitario di Bergamo, 1990.

Velikovsky, Immanuel, *Worlds in Collision*, Abacus, 1972 (first published 1950).

Velikovsky, Immanuel, *Earth in Upheaval*, Buccaneer, 1955.

Walworth, Ralph Franklin, and Sjostrom, Geoffrey, *Subdue the Earth*, Panther, 1980.

White, John, *Pole Shift*, ARE Press, 1997 (first published 1980).

THEOSOPHY

Bailey, Alice A, *Initiation, Human and Solar*, Lucis Publishing, 1922.

Bailey, Alice A, *A Treatise on Cosmic Fire*, Lucis Publishing, 1973 (first published 1925).

Bailey, Alice A, *A Treatise on the Seven Rays* (5 volumes), Lucis Publishing, 1936.

Blavatsky, Helena, *Isis Unveiled* (2 volumes), Theosophical Publishing House, 1972 (first published 1877).

Blavatsky, Helena, *The Secret Doctrine* (2 volumes), Theosophical University Press, 1988 (first published 1888).

Blavatsky, Helena, *The Voice of the Silence*, Quest Books, 1996 (first published 1889).

Blavatsky, Helena, *Collected Writings* (15 volumes), Quest Books, 1960–80.

Cranston, Sylvia, *HPB: The Extraordinary Life and Influence of Helena Blavatsky*, Putnam, 1993.

Johnson, K Paul, *The Masters Revealed: Madame Blavatsky and the Myth of the Great White Lodge*, State University of New York Press, 1994.

Reigle, David, *The Books of Kiu-te*, Wizards Bookshelf, 1983.

Reigle, David, and Reigle, Nancy, *Blavatsky's Secret Books*, Wizards Bookshelf, 1999.

Sinnett, Arnold P, *Esoteric Buddhism*, Houghton Mifflin, 1884.

ATLANTIS AND LOST CONTINENTS

Bramwell, James, *Lost Atlantis*, Harper, 1938.

Cayce, Edgar Evans, *Edgar Cayce on Atlantis*, Howard Baker, 1969.

Childress, David Hatcher, *Ancient Tonga and the Lost City of Mu'a*, Adventures Unlimited Press, 1996.

Childress, David Hatcher, *Lost Cities of Ancient Lemuria and the Pacific*, Adventures Unlimited Press, 1998.

Childress, David Hatcher, *Ancient Micronesia and the Lost City of Nan Madol*, Adventures Unlimited Press, 1997.

Churchward, James, *The Lost Continent of Mu*, BE Books, 1994 (first published 1926).

Churchward, James, *The Sacred Symbols of Mu*, BE Books, 1988 (first published 1933).

Collins, Andrew, *Gateway to Atlantis*, Headline, 2000.

Donnelly, Ignatius, *Atlantis, the Antediluvian World*, Sampson Low and Co., 1882.

Flem-Ath, Rand, and Flem-Ath, Rose, *When the Sky Fell*, Wiedenfeld and Nicolson, 1995.

Haslund, Henning, *Men and Gods in Mongolia*, Adventures Unlimited Press, 1992 (first published 1935).

Illion, Theodore, *In Secret Tibet*, Adventures Unlimited Press, 1991 (first published 1937).

Johnson, K Paul, *Edgar Cayce in Context*, State University of New York Press, 1998.

Luce, J V, *The End of Atlantis*, Thames and Hudson, 1969.

Mavor, James W, *Voyage to Atlantis*, Souvenir Press, 1969.

Muck, Otto, *The Secret of Atlantis*, Fontana, 1979.

Peniel, Jon, *The Children of the Law of One and the Lost Teachings of Atlantis*, Network, 1998.

Randall-Stevens, H C, *From Atlantis to the Latter Days*, Knights Templars, 1981 (first published 1954).

Roerich, Nicholas, *Heart of Asia*, New York, 1929.

Roerich, Nicholas, *Gates into the Future*, Riga, 1936.

Roerich, Nicholas, *Himalayas, Abode of Light*, Bombay, 1947.

Scott-Elliot, W, *The Story of Atlantis and the Lost Lemuria*, Theosophical Publishing House, 1968 (first published 1896).

Scrutton, Robert, *Secrets of Lost Atland*, Sphere Books, 1979.

Smith, A Robert, *The Lost Memoirs of Edgar Cayce*, ARE Press, 1997.

Spence, Lewis, *History of Atlantis*, Senate, 1995 (first published 1926).

Spence, Lewis, *The Problem of Lemuria, the Sunken Continent of the Pacific*, Rider and Co., 1932.

Spence, Lewis, *The Occult Sciences in Atlantis*, Aquarian Press, 1978 (first published 1943).

Sprague de Camp, Lyon, *Lost Continents: The Atlantis Theme in History, Science, and Literature*, Dover, 1970 (first published 1954).

Steiner, Rudolf, *Atlantis and Lemuria*, Anthroposophical Publishing Company, 1923 (first published 1911).

Sugrue, Thomas, *The Story of Edgar Cayce: There Is a River*, ARE Press, 1997 (first published 1942).

REVISIONIST HISTORY

Alford, Alan, *Gods of the New Millennium*, Hodder and Stoughton, 1997.

Baigent, Michael, *Ancient Traces*, Penguin, 1999.

Bauval, Robert, and Gilbert, Adrian, *The Orion Mystery*, Mandarin, 1995.

Bauval, Robert, and Hancock, Graham, *Keeper of Genesis*, Mandarin, 1997 (republished in the US under the title *The Message of the Sphinx*).

Childress, David Hatcher, *Vimana Aircraft of Ancient India and Atlantis*, Adventures Unlimited Press, 1991.

Collins, Andrew, *From the Ashes of Angels*, Signet, 1997.

Collins, Andrew, *Gods of Eden*, Headline, 1998.

Corliss, William R, *Ancient Man: A Handbook of Puzzling Artefacts*, Sourcebook Project, 1978.

Cremo, Michael, *Forbidden Archaeology's Impact*, Bhaktivedanta Book Publishing, 1998.

Cremo, Michael A, and Thompson, Richard L, *Forbidden Archaeology*, Bhaktivedanta Institute, 1993.

Cremo, Michael A, and Thompson, Richard L, *The Hidden History of the Human Race*, Govardhan Hill, 1994.

Donnelly, Ignatius, *Ragnarok, the Age of Fire and Gravel*, Sampson Low and Co., 1883.

Drake, W Raymond, *Gods and Spacemen in the Ancient East*, Sphere, 1973 (first published 1968).

Dunn, Christopher, *The Giza Power Plant*, Bear and Co., 1998.

Elkington, David, and Ellson, Paul Howard, *In the Name of the Gods: The Mystery of Resonance and the Prehistoric Messiah*, Green Man Press, 2001.

Flem-Ath, Rand, and Wilson, Colin, *The Atlantis Blueprint*, Little Brown, 2000.

Gardner, Laurence, *Genesis of the Grail Kings*, Bantam, 2000.

Gilbert, Adrian, *Signs in the Sky*, Bantam, 2000.

Gilbert, Adrian, and Cotterell, Maurice, *The Mayan Prophecies*, Element, 1995.

Gooch, Stan, *Cities of Dreams: When Women Ruled the World*, Aulis Books, 1995 (second edition).

Hancock, Graham, *Fingerprints of the Gods*, Mandarin, 1996.

Hancock, Graham, and Faiia, Santha, *Heaven's Mirror: Quest for the Lost Civilisation*, Michael Joseph, 1998.

Hapgood, Charles, *Maps of the Ancient Sea Kings*, Adventures Unlimited Press, 1996 (first published 1966).

James, Peter, and Thorpe, Nick, *Ancient Inventions*, Ballantine, 1994.

Knight, Christopher, and Lomas, Robert, *Uriel's Machine*, Century, 1999.

Kolosimo, Peter, *Not of this World*, Sphere, 1971.

Kolosimo, Peter, *Timeless Earth*, Sphere, 1974.

Lockyer, Norman, *The Dawn of Astronomy*, Macmillan, 1894.

Miller, Crichton, *The Golden Thread of Time*, Pendulum Publishing, 2001.

Morton, Chris, and Thomas, Ceri Louise, *The Mystery of the Crystal Skulls*, Thorsons, 1998.

O'Brien, Christian, and O'Brien, Joy, *The Genius of the Few*, Dianthus Publishing, 1999 (first published 1985).

O'Brien, Christian, and O'Brien, Joy, *The Shining Ones*, Dianthus Publishing, 1997.

Picknett, Lynn, and Prince, Clive, *The Stargate Conspiracy*, Little Brown, 1999.

Rudgley, Richard, *Lost Civilisations of the Stone Age*, Arrow, 1999.

Rudgley, Richard, *Secrets of the Stone Age*, Century, 2000.

de Santillana, Giorgio, and von Dechend, Hertha, *Hamlet's Mill*, Godine, 1977 (first published 1969).

Schwaller de Lubicz, René, *Sacred Science*, Inner Traditions, 1988 (first published 1961).

Sitchin, Zecharia, *The Twelfth Planet*, Bear and Co., 1991 (first published 1976).

Sitchin, Zecharia, *The Stairway to Heaven*, Avon, 1980.

Sitchin, Zecharia, *The Wars of Gods and Men*, Avon, 1985.

Sitchin, Zecharia, *Genesis Revisited*, Avon, 1990.

Sitchin, Zecharia, *The Lost Realms*, Avon, 1990.

Sitchin, Zecharia, *When Time Began*, Avon, 1993.

Steiger, Brad, *Worlds Before Our Own*, Berkley, 1979.

Temple, Robert, *The Sirius Mystery*, Arrow, 1999 (first published 1976).

Temple, Robert, *The Crystal Sun*, Century, 2000.

Tomas, Andrew, *We Are Not the First*, Souvenir, 1971.

Tomas, Andrew, *Shambhala: Oasis of Light*, Sphere, 1972.

Tomas, Andrew, *Atlantis: From Legend to Discovery*, Sphere, 1973.

Tomas, Andrew, *On the Shores of Ancient Worlds*, Souvenir, 1974.

Tompkins, Peter, *Secrets of the Great Pyramid*, Galahad, 1997 (first published 1971).

Vallée, Jacques, *Messengers of Deception: UFO Contacts and Cults*, And/Or Press, 1979.

Vallée, Jacques, *Revelations: Alien Contact and Human Deception*, Souvenir Press, 1992.

von Däniken, Erich, *Chariots of the Gods*, Souvenir Press, 1969.

von Däniken, Erich, *In Search of Ancient Gods*, Souvenir Press, 1975.

Welfare, Simon, and Fairley, John, *Arthur C Clarke's Mysterious World*, Collins, 1980.

West, John Anthony, *Serpent in the Sky*, Quest, 1993 (first published 1979).

Wilkins, Harold T, *Mysteries of Ancient South America*, Rider and Co., 1946.

Wilkins, Harold T, *Secret Cities of Old South America: Atlantis Unveiled*, Rider and Co., 1950.

Wilson, Colin, *From Atlantis to the Sphinx*, Virgin, 1997.

Wilson, Colin, *Alien Dawn*, Virgin, 1998.

ESOTERIC AND MYSTICAL

Baines, John, *The Secret Science*, John Baines Institute, 1994 (first published 1980).

Carpenter, Sue, *Past Lives: True Stories of Reincarnation*, Virgin, 1995.

Castaneda, Carlos, *The Teachings of Don Juan: A Yaqui Way of Knowledge*, University of California Press, 1968.

Castaneda, Carlos, *A Separate Reality: Further Conversations with Don Juan*, Simon and Schuster, 1971.

Castaneda, Carlos, *Journey to Ixtlan: The Lesson of Don Juan*, Simon and Schuster, 1972.

Castaneda, Carlos, *The Art of Dreaming*, HarperCollins, 1993

Clymer, R Swinburne, *The Rosy Cross: Its Teachings*, Beverly Hall Corporation, 1965 (sixth edition).

Cranston, Sylvia, and Williams, Carey, *Reincarnation: A New Horizon in Science, Religion and Society*, Theosophical University Press, 1993.

Crowley, Aleister, *777, and Other Qabalistic Writings*, Samuel Weiser, 1999 (first published 1912 and 1955).

Crowley, Aleister, *The Book of the Law*, Samuel Weiser, 1976 (first published 1938).

Dee, John, *The Hieroglyphic Monad*, John M Watkins, 1947 (first published 1564).

Fiore, Edith, *You Have Been Here Before*, Ballantine Books, 1978.

Fortune, Dion, *The Cosmic Doctrine*, Samuel Weiser, 2000 (first published 1949).

Fortune, Dion, *The Mystical Qabalah*, Samuel Weiser, 2000 (first published 1935).

Fortune, Dion, and Knight, Gareth, *Principles of Hermetic Philosophy*, Thoth Publications, 1999.

Fulcanelli, *Dwellings of the Philosophers*, Archive Press and Communications, 1999.

Grof, Stanislav, *Realms of the Human Unconscious: Observations from LSD Research*, Viking Press, 1975.

Gurdjieff, George, *Beelzebub's Tales to His Grandson* (Part 1 of the *All and Everything* series), Arkana, 1999 (first published 1950).

Gurdjieff, George, *Meetings with Remarkable Men*, E P Dutton, 1991 (first published 1959).

Hall, Manley P, *The Secret Teachings of All Ages: An Encyclopedic Outline of Masonic, Hermetic, Qabbalistic and Rosicrucian Symbolic Philosophy*, Philosophical Research Society, 1988 (first published 1928).

Harner, Michael, *The Way of the Shaman*, Harper and Row, 1980.

Holzer, Hans, *Life Beyond: Compelling Evidence for Past Lives and Existence After Death*, Contemporary Books, 1994.

Huxley, Aldous, *The Doors of Perception*, Chatto and Windus, 1954.

Iverson, Jeffrey, *More Lives Than One?*, Pan Books, 1976.

Iverson, Jeffrey, *In Search of the Dead*, BBC Books, 1992.

Kastenbaum, Robert, *Is There Life After Death*, Rider and Co., 1984.

Knight, Gareth, *A Practical Guide to Qabalistic Symbolism* (2 volumes), Kahn and Averill, 1998 (first published 1965).

Leary, Timothy, *Turn On, Tune In, Drop Out*, Ronin Publishing, 1999 (first published 1965).

Levi, Eliphas, *The Key of the Mysteries*, Rider and Co., 1959 (first published 1861).

Lewis, H Spencer, *Rosicrucian Questions and Answers*, AMORC, 1932.

Lewis, H Spencer, *Rosicrucian Manual*, Rosicrucian Press, 1938 (seventh edition).

McKenna, Terence, *The Archaic Revival: Speculations on Psychedelic Mushrooms . . .*, HarperCollins, 1991.

McKenna, Terence, *True Hallucinations*, HarperCollins, 1993.

Moody, Raymond, *Life After Life*, Bantam, 1976.

Narby, Jeremy, *The Cosmic Serpent*, Phoenix, 1999.

Newton, Michael, *Journey of Souls: Case Studies of Life Between Lives*, Llewellyn, 2002 (first published 1994).

Newton, Michael, *Destiny of Souls*, Llewellyn, 2001.

Paulsen, Norman, *The Christ Consciousness*, Solar Logos Foundation, 2002 (first published 1985)

Paulsen, Norman, *Sacred Science: Meditation, Transformation, Illumination*, Solar Logos Foundation, 2000.

Regardie, Israel, *A Garden of Pomegranates*, Llewellyn Publications, 1999 (first published 1932).

Regardie, Israel, *The Tree of Life*, Llewellyn Publications, 2001 (first published 1932).

Rudgley, Richard, *The Alchemy of Culture: Intoxicants in Society*, British Museum Press, 1993.

Scott, Ernest, *The People of the Secret*, Octagon, 1983.

Shah, Idries, *The Sufis*, Jonathan Cape, 1969.

Shroder, Tom, *Old Souls: Compelling Evidence from Children Who Remember Past Lives*, Touchstone, 2001.

Shulgin, Alexander, *Pihkal: A Chemical Love Story*, Transform Press, 1991.

Shulgin, Alexander, *Tihkal: The Continuation*, Transform Press, 1997.

Steiner, Rudolf, *Theosophy*, Steiner Press, 1989 (first published 1922).

Stemman, Roy, *Reincarnation: True Stories of Past Lives*, Piatkus, 1999.

Stevenson, Ian, *Twenty Cases Suggestive of Reincarnation*, University Press of Virginia, 1980 (first published 1966).

Stevenson, Ian, *Children Who Remember Past Lives*, University Press of Virginia, 1987.

Stevenson, Ian, *Where Religion and Biology Intersect*, Praeger, 1997.

Various, *The Hermetic Museum* (2 volumes), James Elliot and Co., 1893 (first published 1678).

Waite, A E, *The Complete Writings of Paracelsus of Hohenheim*, London, 1894 (first published 1616).

Whitton, Joel, and Fisher, Joe, *Life Between Life*, Grafton Books, 1986.

Wilson, Robert Anton, *Cosmic Trigger: Final Secret of the Illuminati*, New Falcon Publications, 2000 (first published 1977).

Yates, Frances A, *Giordano Bruno and the Hermetic Tradition*, Routledge and Kegan Paul, 1978 (first published 1964).

Yates, Frances A, *The Art of Memory*, ARK, 1984 (first published 1966).

Yates, Frances A, *The Rosicrucian Enlightenment*, ARK, 1986 (first published 1972).

Yates, Frances A, *The Occult Philosophy in the Elizabethan Age*, Routledge and Kegan Paul, 1979.

Yogananda, Paramahansa, *The Autobiography of a Yogi*, Self Realisation Fellowship, 1994 (first published 1952).

ESOTERIC SCIENCE

Barbour, Julian, *The End of Time*, Weidenfeld, 1999.

Bohm, David, *Wholeness and the Implicate Order*, Routledge, 1995 (first published 1980).

Capra, Fritjof, *The Tao of Physics*, Flamingo, 1992 (first published 1975).

Greene, Brian, *The Elegant Universe*, Jonathan Cape, 1999.

Hawking, Stephen, and Penrose, Roger, *The Nature of Space and Time*, Princetown University Press, 1996.

Hayes, Michael, *The Infinite Harmony: Musical Structures in Science and Theology*, Weidenfeld and Nicolson, 1994.

Hunt, Valerie, *Infinite Mind: Science of Human Vibrations of Consciousness*, Malibu Publishing, 2000.

Radin, Dean, *The Conscious Universe*, Harper, 1998.

Smolin, Lee, *Three Roads to Quantum Gravity*, Basic Books, 2001.

Talbot, Michael, *The Holographic Universe*, HarperCollins, 1996.

Walter, Katya, *The Tao of Chaos*, Element, 1996.

Watson, Lyall, *Supernature: The Natural History of the Supernatural*, Hodder and Stoughton, 1973.

Zee, Anthony, *Fearful Symmetry: The Search for Beauty in Modern Physics*, Princeton University Press, 2000.

INDEX